D0906475

Rethinking Eastern African Literary
and Intellectual Landscapes

# Rethinking
# EASTERN AFRICAN
## LITERARY AND
## INTELLECTUAL LANDSCAPES

Edited by
James Ogude, Grace A. Musila and Dina Ligaga

AFRICA WORLD PRESS
TRENTON | LONDON | CAPE TOWN | NAIROBI | ADDIS ABABA | ASMARA | IBADAN | NEW DELHI

## AFRICA WORLD PRESS

541 West Ingham Avenue | Suite B
Trenton, New Jersey 08638

Book and cover design: Saverance Publishing Services

Library of Congress Cataloging-in-Publication Data

Rethinking eastern African literary and intellectual landscapes / eds. James Ogude, Grace A. Musila and Dina Ligaga.
    p. cm.
Includes bibliographical references and index.
 ISBN 978-1-59221-886-8 (softcover-13 : alk. paper) -- ISBN 1-59221-886-5 (softcover-10 : alk. paper) -- ISBN 978-1-59221-885-1 (hardcover-13 : alk. paper) -- ISBN 1-59221-885-7 (hardcover-10 : alk. paper)
 1. East African literature (English)--History and criticism. 2. East African literature--History and criticism. 3. Africa, East--Intellectual life. I. Ogude, James. II. Musila, Grace A. III. Ligaga, Dina.
 PR9340.5.R48 2011
 820.9'9676--dc23

                    2011044069

# Contents

# Introduction

This book brings together like-minded scholars of Eastern African literatures and cultures whose interest in scholarship swivels around past and contemporary intellectual traditions in Eastern Africa. By referring to Eastern Africa, we seek to move beyond the traditional East African countries of Kenya, Uganda and Tanzania to include Somalia, Ethiopia and the Indian Ocean world, among others. The book is at one level archival and at another, a critical reflection on the state of production and consumption of Eastern African cultures. It does not necessarily take a distinct thematic approach, but rather attempts to bring together a range of voices from the region using a series of diverse genres, narratives and intellectual traditions, past and present, that continue to define what are now called contemporary Eastern African cultures. The essays in the volume point to how Eastern Africa has always constructed, imagined and mapped out its cultural destiny – sometimes through sheer ingenuity and deliberately engineered artistic projects or simply through a rich cultural resourcefulness that has always been in the character of the region. The book includes a reading of canonical texts as well as those not always easily glimpsed through such canonical lenses. As such, the book brings attention to other literary and popular forms such as poetry, music, dramas and other forms of media that have defined and continue to define what presently constitutes Eastern African literary and intellectual forms.

One of the key postulations of this book is that Eastern Africa has always defined itself through its literatures. As Simon Gikandi has reminded us, "the primary medium through which the nationalist project was imagined and witnessed" in East Africa after the World War II, was through its literatures (2007: 1). Gikandi is of course referring to Eastern Africa's engagement with colonial modernity, arrested decolonization and the legacy of colonialism that leading East African writers like Ngugi wa Thiong'o and Nuruddin Farah - covered in some of the chapters in this book— grapple with. The legacy of colonialism in particular, whether in the form of the lingering presence of the colonial archive and its tyranny on the social imaginary or in the pervasive discourses of whiteness prevalent in the postcolonial state, continues to be a major pre-occupation of many artists in the region.

The book also signals the important fact that the sources of Eastern African cultures are multifaceted and have always been negotiated through a complex trafficking of ideas between its peoples, both at home and in the Diasporas, but also through its historical contacts with the rest of the world – a phenomenon that predates European colonialism in the region. Some of the papers in the collection gesture towards those currents closely associated with Eastern Africa's encounter with the Far East through trade across the Indian Ocean and the Swahili civilization of the East African Coast which as Simon Gikandi writes, "is clearly one of the most important examples of cultural hybridity in the premodern period" (2007, 2). The Swahili tradition with its complex *mashairi* poetics and *taarab* music is one such enduring influence in the region. There is also the `Indian Ocean' literature stream written by the Arab, Asian and Indian Diasporas that calls for greater attention and recognition in the region's literatures.

The significance of this volume is that it traverses a range of cultural landscapes and intellectual contours. And although some chapters do pay attention to the canon, several others focus on the popular arts, a category that is increasingly receiving some compelling intellectual attention from scholars (Ogude and Nyairo, 2007; Njogu and Oluoch-Olunya, 2007; Askew, 2002). We have therefore avoided the tendency to privilege canonical texts as the only legitimate sources of cultural insights by extending the debates to include popular arts and performance, especially in the area of music, radio drama and ritual, pointing clearly to the fact that popular art has become one of the most powerful windows on the daily struggles of the people of Eastern Africa and one of the very few vehicles open to them to negotiate complex issues of power away from the watchful eyes of the state. Although popular cultural forms like music, drama or documentary cinema, are still some of the most common avenues through which people perform and negotiate their identities, one of chapters in the volume by George Ogola, introduces an increasing influence of new media, specifically the cyber space, as one of the central tools of shaping modern identities.

There is therefore a subtle acknowledgement in the book that the instruments of recovery and representation in the East African cultural landscape continue to be diverse and complex. They continue to mutate with time. Whether through the new media now in vogue, the old genres of music or simply narratives in popular periodicals, what is clear is that Eastern Africa's entanglements with modernity and the postmodern moment, continue to be mediated through a range of local and borrowed metaphors and tropes as well as rigorous translations of both traditional and foreign forms – thus gesturing towards what is evidently a complex transcultural aesthetics.

The book therefore seeks to 'imagine' the Eastern African region in ways that would crystallize its uniqueness – i.e. what sets it apart from the other regional blocks – while still capturing the region's multifariousness – its heterogeneity and the tensions that come with this multiplicity. How can we, for example, think creatively about Eastern Africa, both within the regional/nation/state geographies of Ethiopia, Kenya, Uganda, Tanzania, Zanzibar, Pemba, Somalia etc – but also outside of those boundaries, in more fluid ways? What are the contemporary debates in literary and cultural studies, and how do the writings and cultural productions emerging from the Eastern African region inflect or uniquely comment on these debates? What are the trans/national movements, spaces and intersections of subjectivity in the region? What are some of the region's distinctive contributions to continental and global intellectual traditions over the years?

Although the papers in this volume do not give direct answers to all these questions, they nevertheless draw attention to some of these concerns. The volume provides diverse papers, which speak to Eastern Africa's connectedness to the rest of the world through colonial modernity, but more recently how the region has sought to transform local and received institutions to grapple with local experiences. The book has been divided broadly into four sections: Literary and Intellectual traditions, the Eastern African Canon and the Post-colonial Imaginary, Diasporic Literatures and finally Performance and Media.

## LITERARY AND INTELLECTUAL TRADITIONS

In the first two decades of independence, Eastern African intellectuals especially in the area of cultural production played an important role in shaping the debates around the decolonization project. The Eastern African academies and intellectuals were pivotal in setting the tone of a number of intellectual debates that emerged in the immediate aftermath of independence on the continent, especially around black aesthetics and the relevance of the English language syllabus in institutions of learning, and yet these remarkable contributions are often only grudgingly acknowledged if not simply dismissed as nativist in certain academic circles. At a theoretical level, we need to determine whether we have paid sufficient attention to how local patronages, past and present, impact on the production and consumption of culture and how they interface with global or external patronages.

The chapters in this section variously examine aspects of these rich literary and intellectual traditions in the region. The section maps out the institutional structures that have shaped knowledge formation and production in Eastern Africa and deal variously with the development of Eastern African literature. The papers sometimes engage with, but largely challenge dominant institutional politics and structures by revisiting the very debates that structured them.

James Ogude's chapter draws attention to how East Africa was home to a range of intellectual interventions that shaped the emerging literary traditions not just in the region, but also on the continent. The chapter offers an alternative reading to the emergence of the black aesthetics debate and indeed, the curriculum revolution in East African Universities in the late 1960s and early 1970s. Ogude's argument is that the black aesthetics debate in the region and the abolition of the English department at Nairobi University marked an important turning point in literary and cultural traditions of the region and the ramification of the debates and institutional re-arrangement of erstwhile colonial structures would be felt way beyond the region. The intellectual currents formed an important trajectory in the development of literary and cultural traditions in the region and deserve a re-reading, to draw out their salient features, but also to bring to surface their true intellectual import. The thrust of the chapter revolves around the argument that the emergence of these radical interventions, nurtured in institutions of higher learning, should be read correctly as forming part of those early critiques of difference and universalism, the twin theoretical tenets that underpinned the English Language syllabus and the idea of aesthetic value in former British colonies. The fundamental contradiction inherent in theories of difference, especially in regard to Africa, is that it sought to invent Africa as the site of radical difference – the marginal Other. The black aesthetics debate and the radical curriculum change that was witnessed in the region were therefore a radical challenge, and not a nativist response, to these systems of dominance. By speaking to specific examples, the chapter concludes that the emergence of these intellectual traditions inaugurated significant changes in the literary landscape of the region which persist to this day. In striking ways the paper also sets the tone to some of the issues discussed elsewhere in this book, particularly, Grace A. Musila's argument on discourses of whiteness which continue to inform a range of metropolitan imaginaries about Africa, especially a nagging specter of colonial archives on the postcolonial imagination of Africa.

Tom Odhiambo and Garnett Oluoch-Olunya each deal with a very specific genre of literature that has remained elusive in terms of scholarship of mainstream literature. Yet the literary magazine has acted as a voice from which various literary voices have emerged, and against which new debates on literature and culture have sprung. Tom Odhiambo's paper looks at the politics of production of the Eastern African literary magazine, *Kwani?*; and provides an important link to the first two decades of post-independence optimism that gave birth to the intellectual currents that Ogude's chapter touches on. If Ogude's paper is about those initial intellectual traditions that helped to map out what is now loosely called the East African literary history, a period born out of the nationalist triumph and hope that followed flag independence, Odhiambo's chapter speaks to a contemporary intellectual tradition, born in what has come to be called the second liberation in Kenya. Odhiambo's paper traces the emergence of *Kwani?* and its sister series, *Kwanini?*; literary journals and booklets born in the post-Moi dictatorship. They were born in a context of freedom and political transition. This new literary tradition signaled a remarkable re-emergence of artistic and cultural re-invention that echoed back to the traditions of the 1960s and 1970s. But as Odhiambo argues, the grammar of radical change that had defined its inauguration as a novel tradition would prove to be its undoing. Issue after issue of *Kwani?* was bound by specific macro-themes driven largely by topical issues of the day. The novelty though resided in the fact that *Kwani?* was seeking to collapse genre boundaries and equally striving to reach out for a transnational audience. This, however, became a major contradiction for a literary voice that had signaled a singular intention to nurture and grow local talent. Caught between the desire to remain relevant through local agenda and retain an international appeal, *Kwani?* would appear to have painted itself into a corner through mechanically driven narratives workshopped and artificially engineered to meet the agenda set by its sponsors and the political climate of the day. Odhiambo questions *Kwani?*'s drifts towards a naked relationship between the arts and politics. What perhaps Odhiambo intimates here but does not fully explore is the fact that *Kwani?* editors seem to understand power and its workings in very stark hierarchical and simple binary terms: the people versus *serikali* (the government). The chapter seems to suggest that layered and complex manifestations of the mechanics of power in the daily lives of people or simply how institutionalized authority works to perform power in processes where the people themselves may be implicated in their own oppression, is something that *Kwani?* editors have totally deleted in their vision of the journal. For example, as the hopes of the second liberation withered and gave way to national despair, especially after the 2007 post-election violence, *Kwani?'s* response to the politics of the day became predictable and its claims to new literary and cultural revival suspect. There were obviously no new talents emerging and unlike the intellectual community of the 1960s and 1970s, Odhiambo avers, *Kwani?* is failing to develop a corporate identity with the bulk of its editorial board members residing outside the region. Odhiambo's argument is that the stated intention of *Kwani?* to produce local material for local readers is in tension with its reading publics and its real creative drivers who are both transnational and cosmopolitan. *Kwani?* as a Ford Foundation-sponsored project also suffers from the problems of patronage and pre-determined agenda set by the donors that both Garnett Oluoch-Olunya and Christopher J. Odhiambo write about in great depth in the book. Whatever the limitations of *Kwani?*, Odhiambo concedes that the journal's lasting value so far has been in its dogged strive to challenge literary orthodoxy and any categorization that is purely literary. The five volumes released so far have sought to broaden the boundaries of creativity.

Garnett Oluoch-Olunya's paper draws attention to the development of the literary magazine genre in Eastern Africa more generally. It takes up the issue of the new creative impulse in the region by drawing attention to another recently founded outlet for the arts, *Jahazi*, a journal of the arts, culture and performance. The core of Oluoch-Olunya's paper is really that, *Jahazi*, is part of a longstanding tradition of the creative arts in Africa in which journals have always provided the nurturing ground for new creativity in the arts. In a broad historical overview, Oluoch-Olunya draws compelling attention to what she calls an 'entangled literary heritage' dating back to Rajat Neogy's *Transition* and its literary precursor, *Presence Africaine*. The entanglement that Oluoch-Olunya writes is about the post-colonial world in which the sheer intimacy of survival within one space necessitates the crossing of paths and the collapsing of boundaries that all literatures attempt to promote, even under very difficult conditions. In a context haunted by a colonial legacy and a conflicted post-colonial presence, the challenges to creative discursive platforms where the arts are likely to flower are often daunting. If Neogy's *Transition* was compelled by the historical imperatives of its emergence to pursue a robust engagement with the politics of the day and was decidedly framed by an elite audience it sought to hail, *Jahazi*, according to Oluoch-Olunya, locates itself between the academy and the world of Art; between mainstream cultural production and the micro-narratives of the ordinary people. As its name— Swahili for 'dhow'— suggests, it is a metaphor for movement, transnational transactions and networks rooted in the history of a region whose early contacts with the rest of the world, remains deeply understudied. *Jahazi* therefore signals memories of fractured history crying out for order, cross-cultural dialogue and a reimagining of a cultural cartography that would allow it to embrace its many histories. In this desire for cross-cultural dialogue and a persistent search for cultural renewal, *Jahazi*, like *Transition* and *Presence Africaine* before it, are similar. They are also similar in the sense that they point to the politics of cultural production as a constant project of negotiation, quite often between vulnerable cultural practioners such as Neogy and Bantu Mwaura and their local and international patrons; between the desire for intellectual agency and the instrumentality of sponsors, and the constraints of a cultural space that is constantly under siege. In a postcolonial context within which 'pirates' make their demands in dollars, the question is, will *Jahazi* survive what Oluoch-Olunya describes as 'a jagged terrain'?

Christopher J. Odhiambo's chapter extends the debates on the problematic of patronage and its pervasive influence on the arts, specifically on intervention theatre in post-colonial East Africa where art sponsors are either part of the official institutions of governance or simply non-governmental organizations driven by pre-determined agenda that may end up deleting the voices and agency of the artists. Odhiambo argues that patronage and arts have traditionally enjoyed a healthy and symbiotic relationship in which the artists and their patrons retained a degree of independence from each other while avoiding the temptation to police the boundaries between them. It is this concomitant and yet fluid and equally porous relationship that ensured that the artist retained his voice. To be sure there were instances when artists such as the court griot that advised the royal families in traditional set ups were seen as the voices of those in authority rather than the ordinary people, but even then they were more of the repositories of knowledge and the custodians of a community's memory. Except in a few instances, they were thus accountable to the community and a whole generation of lineage running deep into history. Artists in this sense were respected counselors, seers and moderators of the excesses of authority. Odhiambo traces the disjuncture between patronage and art with the advent of commodity production which instantly turned art into a commodity for sale. The advent of commodity relations brought a range of institutional interests that with time eroded the independence of the artists. In the context of East Africa as in many other developing countries, the compromise has been driven largely by donor funding and an instrumental approach to creativity. Artists are often compelled to craft their art around set agenda, effectively allowing the sponsor to circulate its source ideology and cultural aesthetics. In such a context, theatre, instead of being disruptive of authoritarian ideologies, ends up reinforcing hegemonic and repressive ideologies of donor agencies or the state. Odhiambo's argument is that the influence of patrons in the form of donors has often forced artists to tailor their works to suit the demands of their sponsors – ultimately compromising the integrity of their art. This is a chapter that is likely to generate interesting debate on contemporary problems facing the arts in a continent in which funded theater remains the dominant vehicle of communication among marginalized communities in areas of health, education and civic responsibilities.

Yet another chapter that challenges our understanding of Eastern African literatures is Susan Kiguli's paper, which draws attention to the articulation between critical and creative practice in African literary scholarship and in particular East Africa. And although it is now taken for granted that a number of African writers do theorize their crafts through critical reflections in essays, very little has been done to document this systematically in East Africa, with a few exceptions to Ngugi's work. Susan Kiguli's chapter turns the focus on two leading East African writers, Okot p'Bitek and Ngugi wa Thiong'o, pointing to a complex duality that exists between their fiction and critical essays. And although it is often difficult to determine which one comes first, what is not in doubt is the fact that for these two writers, a dialogic engagement between theory and practice is a necessary concomitant for a healthy literary tradition. After all, both Okot and Ngugi emerged as leading voices in East Africa at a critical moment in the region's history and that is the immediate aftermath of *Uhuru*. As writers, they struggled to find a distinctive voice that would fully capture the challenges of the moment, particularly in a context that had no clear literary models and a written literary tradition to emulate. They were pioneers. As pathfinders, they had to `make statements' and to invent traditions that would become the touchstone for those who followed them. If they were deeply influenced by the intellectual climate and the political currents of the time as Susan Kiguli's chapter suggests, it is because they were dealing with events that they were deeply implicated in; a tumultuous historical process that was unfolding before their eyes. They were witnesses and chroniclers of this history. As witnesses they turned to fiction and song as instruments of representation, but as chroniclers, they had to be more contemplative, make value judgment and provide philosophical reflections on a historical legacy that had shaped their youth and the destiny of their people in many ways. Brought up in a context that had been ravaged by cultural imperialism, Okot p'Bitek was driven to embrace a form of poetics that took him back to the cultural roots of his people, albeit mediated by his Western schooling. Indeed, the `nativist' impulse in p'Bitek's works that Kiguli draws our attention to in her chapter came to him naturally – at the feet of his mother, a traditional singer and poet in her own right. Similarly, Ngugi's radical poetics is also rooted in his tormented childhood, growing under the shadow of colonial violence and as a son of an *ahoi* (a squatter), Ngugi did not have a normal childhood. If the Marxist assertion that being determines consciousness has any veracity, it is certainly true in Ngugi's experience. And one is not talking here of crude social determinism, but rather what E'skia Mphahlele has called the tyranny of place and time – the way context in its broadest sense (geography, history, location, intellectual climate and social events), exert themselves on a writer's imagination. Kiguli's argument is that the two East African writers were located at a critical juncture of the region's history; they seized the initiative and groped for a grammar and philosophical insights with which to shape its future. The complex dialogue through theory and practice, creative writing and contemplation that have come to define the works of these two giants of East African culture are very much part and parcel of the region's intellectual and cultural re-awakening whose waves continue to be felt today. One such wave as Kiguli argues, is the assumption that art has to be about and for the people, meaning the peasantry and the urban underclass. This is an ideal that continues to be pursued and animatedly debated in the institutions of cultural production in the region that you would not find elsewhere on the continent. Whether or not we agree with them, East Africans continue to see art as an important agent of change and creative imagination as an important aspect of a people's social activity.

The last chapter in this section examines women's writing in Uganda under the auspices of FEMRITE Publications Ltd. For Lynda Spencer, FEMRITE – a publishing house which grew out of the Ugandan Women Writers' Association – has contributed significantly to the expansion of the Ugandan women's literary corpus. FEMRITE is a Ugandan-based non- profit making association which was born out of the need to organize literary women writers nationally and internationally, collect and disseminate information on gender related issues, advocate for increased women's literacy programs by incorporating literature generated from local communities, while simultaneously encouraging a positive portrayal of women by promoting gender sensitive literature in society. Spencer reads the emergence of FEMRITE as a site for the articulation of a feminist critique and comments on the various forms of cultural and political marginalization of women located at the intersection of modernity and tradition. Spencer reads a selection of short stories published by FEMRITE as offering critical commentary on the ways in which romance, sex and marriage represent contradictory demands and conflicting desires, by on the one hand, projecting a traditional view of marriage, and on the other hand, challenging traditional patriarchal power by constructing alternative forms of female subjectivity.

## THE EASTERN AFRICAN CANON AND POSTCOLONIAL IMAGINARIES

This section re-reads the Eastern African canon by engaging with well-known canonical writers as well as staple genres such as Swahili poetry. While it offers critical reflections on key debates which have engaged canonical East African Anglophone writers, it further seeks to spark new debate around the rich archive of Swahili literary traditions. Where Fiona Moolla and Isaac Ndlovu examine the contributions of two canonical writers from the region – Somalia's Nurrudin Farah and Kenya's Ngugi wa Thiong'o —, Edwin Mosoti and Tom Olali's chapters engage with the canonical, yet under-explored genre of poetry from Tanzania and Kenya, with interesting insights. This poetry can be described as canonical not only because the particular manifestations of the genre, as discussed by Mosoti and Olali – the Swahili *Mashairi* and *Hamziyyah* respectively — but also because the two sets of texts occupy a canonical position in Swahili literary archives in the region. Indeed, it is partly owing to this canonical status that *Mashairi* for instance, has been able to have powerful influences on contemporary Tanzanian and Kenyan poetry in English, as Mosoti illustrates here. This section therefore weaves together an array of texts whose connections are not always apparent but which, it seems, constantly reference each other both in terms of themes and ideas.

For Fiona Moolla, an interrogation of the tensions between the "individual as acted upon by power" and the individual as an agent "of social transformation," has been an enduring concern across Nurrudin Farah's *oeuvre*. Moolla suggests that it is this interest in the individual as a vehicle of social change which draws Farah to the novel genre, even as it remains a genre with limited potential to articulate Farah's vision of social change; paradoxically articulating individual freedom, yet "preclude[ing] the utopian social horizon crucial to [Farah's] vision." Moolla reads Farah's *oeuvre* as resolving these contradictions of the novel by mirroring the developments of the genre from the realist mode in his early novels to the postmodernism of his later work. As she notes, the realist novel "generates irony to resolve the contradiction at the heart of individualist subject formation, [yet] the modernism of some of Farah's subsequent novels allow irony to reflect on itself, [a development which] also registers as a critique of the sovereign, rational, Cartesian subject, but it is a reaction which proceeds from the model of the subject as individual which effaces itself."

On his part, Isaac Ndlovu reads Ngugi wa Thiong'o's *Detained: A Writer's Prison Diary* (1981), as a reflection on the continuities between colonial and post-colonial violence, as embodied in the prison institution. Ngugi's observations about these continuities reiterate both Frantz Fanon's (1967) prophetic warning about the poisoned gift of the colonial state and independence and the postcolonial leadership's culpability in re-convening oppressive colonial legacies; and Achille Mbembe's (2002) observations about the spectacle of power and its performance in the postcolonial state. The dramatization of power through violence and brutality – which lies at the core of Ngugi's critique — has been an important cross-disciplinary concern in much scholarship on the Kenyan state; and continues to invite further engagement. Indeed, what Ndlovu identifies as the paradoxical hyper-visibility and invisibility of Ngugi's arrest, in the way it was "simultaneously a spectacle [yet mediated by] an attempt at concealing it from the public" is consistent with the historian Atieno Odhiambo's (1987) description of detention without trial as one of the core instruments in the reinforcement of what he terms "the ideology of order." For Ndlovu though, while Ngugi's *Detained* offers interesting re-scriptings of both the diary form and the prison narrative— in so far as it avoids the personal confessional narrative in favour of a broader reflection on the workings of violent repression and as a weapon of post/colonial 'psychological warfare'—; it occasionally betrays faultlines that fracture Ngugi's Marxist-oriented vision of ordinary people's revolutionary potential.

As remains the case in many other regions on the continent, there has been a dearth of critical attention paid to poetry in East Africa. This despite the rich indigenous poetic traditions in the region, not only in the form of oral poetry, which has historically occupied pride of place in pre-colonial African textualities; but even more strikingly, in light of the rich Swahili poetic traditions of the East African coastline. In similar vein, recent work on Indian Ocean Studies has continued this neglect, largely overlooking a rich archive of insights that Swahili poetic traditions stand to yield into our understanding of the Indian Ocean Worlds. Here though, Edwin Mosoti and Tom Olali read Swahili poetry with keen interest in the intellectual traditions underpinning two genres of Swahili poetry: *Mashairi* and *Hamziyyah*. Mosoti's reflection on the imprint of *Mashairi* on contemporary Kenyan and Tanzanian poetry of English expression offers a fascinating reframing of the vexed language question in the region; inviting us to think about the relationship between Swahili and English in the region, as an intellectual symbiosis. Mosoti excavates the formal, structural and content influences of classical Swahili poetry (*Mashairi*) on contemporary poetry of English expression from Kenya and Tanzania. For him, contemporary Swahili poetry "appropriates proclivity for storytelling and didacticism, its worldview, in particular, perception of the role of poets and language of poetry, its special choric devices and finally, its rigid prosodic patterns" resulting in an anticipatory gesture towards what he describes as "a third poetics or tradition that is neither wholly Swahili nor identifiably English in orientation."

Tom Olali's paper revisits what he describes as the oldest known Swahili poem in Islamic tradition: the *Kasida ya Hamziyyah*. Olali reflects on the role of this Swahili panegyric which remains canonical both in sections of Swahili Islamic culture and broadly, the celebration of the birth of Prophet Muhammad. Beyond a close reading of the *Hamziyyah*, Olali is interested in tracing the role of the *Hamziyyah* in Swahili moral-religious cosmologies. For him, it is precisely in its celebration of Prophet Muhammad's greatness that the *Hamziyyah* has historically been central to Swahili Islamic spirituality; while at the same time, embodying elements of classical Swahili poetics, and a rich vocabulary drawn from the kiNgozi dialect.

## EASTERN AFRICAN DIASPORAS

In light of the ubiquity of global currents of movement and exchange, it is difficult for any region in the world to lay claim to particular manifestations of Diasporic presences. Yet, we would like to argue, this claim to unique configurations of Diasporas is possible, and indeed persuasive, in the Eastern African context; primarily in light of the region's unique multi-layered histories. As ongoing work on Indian Ocean Worlds indicates, the Eastern African coastline was a cosmopolitan site long before the arrival of the key colonial powers in the region; primarily fueled by Islam, international trade and the accompanying interactions with the Indian Ocean communities. Scholars further point to the Swahili as one of the classical examples of what can be termed indigenous modernities in Africa. Alongside these cosmopolitanisms, Eastern Africa's subsequent colonial experience – primarily British colonialism— added a further layer to the region's history, not only in the terms of the colonial state, but ultimately, in the particular manifestation of British settler colonialism in Kenya, and administrative colonialism in Uganda. Related to this was the economic project in the region, which necessitated the building of the Kenya – Uganda Railway; ultimately resulting in the one of the first flows of indentured Indian labour in the region. The chapters in this section engage with the cultural interactions and influences of texts in both the local and the global contexts, and their impact on the larger body of Eastern African literatures and cultures. Specifically, the chapters examine textual commentaries on a number of discourses relating to the Indian Ocean Worlds, constructions of postcolonial Whiteness in the region and the Eastern African Asian community.

In her reading of the prolific Zanzibari novelist, Abdulrazak Gurnah's *Paradise* (1994) and *Desertion* (2005), Maria Olaussen examines the depiction of migration, dislocation and the consequences of a paradigmatic shift from a world informed by Indian Ocean trade relations to a Euro-centric understanding of modernity dominated by the Black Atlantic. For Olaussen, "whereas the Indian Ocean paradigm allows for a multifaceted and complex interaction between different communities and, above all, remains open to the possibilities for individuals to move between different positions, from slave to merchant to settler, the Atlantic Ocean imposes a more rigid and racialised dichotomy." While the Indian Ocean World is often celebrated as a site that signals alternative modernities, Olaussen reads Gurnah's writing as problematising this interpretation, in so far as it signals the inherent problems in both "the representation of modernity as a European phenomenon [and efforts] at reconceptualizing this through ideas of alternative modernities."

Grace A. Musila turns to a fairly underexplored field in Eastern African Studies: postcolonial whiteness in the region. Concerned with discursive constructions of whiteness in postcolonial Eastern Africa, Musila brings together three seemingly unrelated case studies – the 2005 and 2006 cases of two Kenyans allegedly shot dead by pioneer settler Lord Delamere's great-grandson, Tom Cholmondeley; *Ivory Hunters*, a

1989 feature film on poaching set in Kenya; and the narration of the 1988 Julie Ward murder case in her father's book, *The Animals are Innocent* – in a reflection on wildlife tourism and conservation as important registers in the performance of whiteness in postcolonial Kenya. For Musila, these three sets of texts illuminate questions of control and ownership of land and wildlife as important co-ordinates of whiteness which, though having their genesis in colonial Kenya, have calcified into a distinct economy of ideas on white identity in postcolonial Kenya. At the same time, Musila suggests, the predominance of the figure of white male authority across the three cases signals the desire for re-insertion of white male authority as an underlying preoccupation of postcolonial whiteness in Kenya. In some ways, she argues, "postcolonial whiteness in Kenya remains a highly gendered one, at the heart of which lies a nostalgic struggle to affirm and restore a white male authority reminiscent of that of the settler colony."

Finally, through a reading of Neera Kapur-Dromson's autobiography, *From Jhelum to Tana* (2007) Godwin Siundu examines the ways in which women writers in the East African Asian community engage with the region's histories within the matrices of gender and racial politics. For Siundu, such women writers can be seen as filling the lacunae of social histories created by a predominantly male library of writings in the community, which privilege fairly narrow conceptions of 'the political,' often at the expense of a rich multi-textured body of social histories. At the same time, Siundu argues, Kapur-Dromson reworks the autobiography to accommodate a wider array of communal narratives, and various generations' experiences with their diasporic location in the region; albeit not without the challenge of privileging racial and communal concerns, over other identity locations. Siundu here reads Kapur-Dromson's autobiography as broadening the frontiers of debate on East African immigrant communities and urging us to rethink strands of herstories that are often taken for granted as 'the known.' By insisting on the inadvertently limiting boundaries of feminist interpretative lenses which often 'ghettoize' women's narratives, Siundu proposes the interrogation of women writers' "engagement with scholarly and experiential aspects of history, particularly its less written-about variants of the personal and social narratives as history." In his discussion, Siundu takes his cue from Kapur-Dromson's auto/biography, to excavate muted strands of personal and social histories of the East African Asian community which, he argues have hitherto been muffled by the broad strokes of the community's grand nationalist narratives that occupy a hegemonic position in the East African Asian community's archives. At the same time, in reflecting on *From Jhelum to Tana*, Siundu simultane-ously sheds some light on what he identifies as a critical blindspot that continues to haunt the work of women auto/biographers in the region. Following Susan Friedman's persuasive observation that "a woman's autobiographical self often does not oppose herself to all others, does not feel herself to exist outside of others, and still less against others, but very much with others in an interdependent existence that asserts its rhythms everywhere in the community" (cited in Mason 1979, 79); Siundu reads Kapur-Dromson's auto/biography as offering nuanced revelations on aspects such as "social history, the communal dynamics within the domestic spaces and, generally, the immigrant communities' management of aspects of the "everyday life."

## PERFORMANCE AND MEDIA

The last section of the book draws attention to popular culture, performance and the media; and emphasizes the connectedness of such cultures to the Eastern African intellectual and cultural traditions. Drawing attention to the importance of everyday life and cultures in Eastern Africa, the section presents an array of forms that are produced, circulated and consumed within spaces not necessarily constrained by institutional politics and often marginalized in scholarship. It draws attention to a rich yet seemingly amorphous body of work that draws from the everyday cultures of Eastern Africans, from music and ritual to television and radio dramas.

Two papers in this section engage with the role of popular music in shaping political and social identities, but also in offering alterna-tive ways of reading society. Tom Mboya's paper, a reading of a leading Kenyan *Benga* musician, Okatch Biggy, draws attention to an important aspect of culture in East Africa which is popular music. We use the term popular music here to mean a hybrid of musical traditions and styles – a musical genre driven by mass consumption and consumers who invest it with a great deal of cultural and ideological capital. It is an area that has increasingly received marked attention in cultural studies from the region, partly because of its enormous importance in daily life as one of the most popular sources of entertainment, but equally because many still consider music as an important aspect of their social identities. In East Africa, it remains one of the few viable cultural industries in spite of the challenges that confront artists on a daily basis because it remains largely confined to the informal market. It is, nevertheless, an important industry in the region and one whose influence continue to cut across class, gender and quite often ethnic divide. And although scholarship on popular music in East Africa point to a range of competing approaches, most of them are historically driven and are often in tension with one another. Central to this tension has been the amount of premium that should be attached to the musical text in relation to other musical elements such as its authorship, production, and the demands of a particular musical genre. In cultural and media studies, the tendency has been to privilege the musical text, its production and mediation, or its reception. In these studies, what have been privileged are the thematic concerns of the musical text and indeed their social import and relevance either as instruments of identity formation of the imagined audience or the quality of their social critique as art. Thus studies of popular music in East Africa have tended to construct it as both an aesthetic discourse, but also as a sociologically grounded study on the politics of production and consumption. As an aesthetic discourse, studies tend to see musical texts as poetic representations of social realities and whose meanings are mediated through the demands of specific musical genres and the aesthetic vision of the musician. And as sociologically grounded texts, they are driven by the interests of the audiences they seek to hail and the politics of production and consumption – meaning the relation between the creation of cultural products and the economic contexts of that creation. This process involves creating audiences, and an active engagement between texts and their consumers.

Tom Mboya's approach straddles the thin line between popular music as an aesthetic discourse and popular music as sociologically grounded. The late Okatch Biggy – easily one of Kenya's most successful *Benga* musicians – had created a culture of stardom around his performance and with it a mass following, especially among the Luo of Kenya, a community that had become his target audience. Mboya's paper directs attention to how leisure and sociological concerns of music interface. Mboya's argument is that Biggy had astutely latched onto a stereotype about the Luo as a people of bacchanalian lifestyle, *raha*, and turned the stereotype on its head. Instead of deriding it, the performance and consumption of leisure is celebrated as a life richly lived and indeed a marker of economic agency among the Luos. Without politicizing his music or engaging with the stereotype in an overt manner, Biggy works through an aesthetically driven musical performance to underscore his point: leisure is aesthetically pleasing; it is good and worthy of celebration. Biggy posits leisure as a fundamental human activity worthy of affirmation, and in doing so frees his target audience – the Luos – of a stigma rooted in negative ethnicity whose perverted logic reduces all consumers of leisure as economically wasteful and unproductive and as a natural corollary, a people that cannot be trusted with political power and leadership. Mboya's point is that Biggy engages in a deconstructive discourse in order to undermine a negative ethnic stereotype, but does so by drawing attention to music as an aesthetic discourse with major sociological implications.

Maria Suriano's chapter, based on an ethnographic research, examines how the forms and functions of popular music have transformed in line with the major political shifts in Tanzania between the mid-1950s and the mid-2000s. The chapter chronicles the major changes over time in the relationship between musicians and power in colonial and postcolonial Tanzania. It takes a historical approach, highlighting links between musicians and colonial rule, before tracing the post-independence relationship between these musicians and Tanzanian politicians. Arguing that the new genre of *Bongo Flava* departs from the instrumental uses of music in the previous era, Suriano draws attention to the myriad way in which this genre of music allows for a more democratic engagement between politicians and citizens.

Dominic Dipio's chapter focuses on the male ritual of circumcision called *imbalu*, among the Bagisu of Uganda. The chapter introduces an important dimension to performance in East Africa because it is about a traditional ritual, regarded as the source of drama in Africa. Ritual provides a critical lens through which social tensions in society are negotiated or resolved. By its very nature, ritual is steeped in myth and quite often regulated by social taboos and norms that define society. In its dramatic enactment, it works to surface basic contradictions and power structures in society. Dipio's chapter, for example, sets out to show how the *imbalu* ritual serves to draw attention to the gendered nature of the Bagisu and more importantly how the ritual is a dramatization of how masculine identities are constructed and promoted in this society. The chapter significantly highlights the irony surrounding this practice, especially in relation to its origins. The ritual was introduced to this society by a woman, twice removed from the male circumcision rite. Nabarwa, the woman who according to myth introduced circumcision among the Bagisu, was an outsider from a neighboring community of the Pokot and got married to a Bagisu man, Masaba, who she compelled to undertake the ritual before any union between them could take place. But she is also an outsider because the ritual that she introduces to this non-circumcising community valorizes masculine values and encourages female subordination. The women, as the chapter demonstrates, remain outside the inner ring where the ritual takes place, and the ritual is constructed in a manner that creates the divide between the private and the public spheres, which the female and the male occupy respectively. For a ritual that started with a female figure at its centre, the reversal of roles here for women is indicative of how societies structured through male domination work to perpetuate female subordination. It is nevertheless an interesting example of cross-border movement of cultures and traditions – an indication of the porous nature of cultural boundaries within the region. It is a ritual at cross-roads and as Dipio demonstrates, which is gradually being transformed from within and from without, pointing to the fluidity of these cultural modes and their disarticulation from their original practices.

Apart from a preoccupation with popular cultural practices, this book signals the role that technologies play in shaping culture. Two chapters in this section focus on one of the most enduring cultural influences in Africa: the broadcasting institution. They offer readings of both the radio and television broadcasting cultures, both selecting programmes that have been running for a considerable period of time.

Dina Ligaga's chapter, for instance, looks at one of Kenya's longest running radio drama programmes, *Radio Theatre*. Significantly locating the programme within its production for a state braodcaster, the paper draws attention to the tensions that exist and impact on a programme that is produced for a state institution, but that lends itself to be read as representative of everyday realities. The over-arching question signals the role of the state in influencing cultural productions in such a way that it is able to locate itself within the realm of the everyday. Thus Ligaga's paper offers a critical reading of one radio drama that was produced during Kenya's Independence Day in order to look at the manner in which it reproduced national narratives within the realm of the everyday. Arguing that such reproductions reveal particular notions of nationalism reflective of wider political and social constructions of Kenyan nationalism, the chapter looks at the play's representation of such ideas of nation and nationhood as 'accepted' versions of Kenyan nationalism. The chapter contests the radio play's easy representations of Kenya's historical narratives, arguing that it has become part of institutional circulation of versions of nationalism in Kenya and shows that narratives such as those adopted by the play, circulated every year, legitimize specific notions of nationalism, while deleting competing narratives from Kenyan history.

Re-emphasizing the role of state broadcasting in mediating culture, Fred Mbogo's chapter focuses on *Vioja Mahakamani*, Kenya's longest running television programmes. Mbogo's chapter looks at this programme as a site of performance between the state and the ordinary 'mwananchi'. *Vioja Mahakamani*, quite literally means 'chaos' or 'drama' in the courtroom, offering the possibility of a Bakhtinian carnivalesque reading of how the ordinary man engages with structures of the state. Indeed, Mbogo reads *Vioja Mahakamani* as a parody of the judicial system, analyzing what Linda Hutcheon, citing Bakhtin calls "authorized transgression" (2000, xii). Mbogo uses characterization and language as major tropes through which parody occurs. He, for instance, draws attention to the manner in which characters representative of the law (the prosecutor, the judge and the police), constantly attempt to place themselves above the 'rest', through their uses of standardized language, and their conservative mannerism. Characters that either appear as witnesses or criminals however, bring in drama and often do not care for the courtroom rules. Their 'chaos' is evident in the kinds of transgressive yet humorous language and behaviour they adopt.

George Ogola's chapter makes an important link between the traditional forms of media and the so called new media. Focussing on Kenya's diaporic community, Ogola examines how they use cyber space to negotiate their identities, especially in relation to their `motherland' – Kenya. Ogola reads the Kenyan blogosphere as a symbolic discursive space in which traditional notions of migrancy are interrogated and disrupted. Far from being definitive and representative of the Kenyan blogosphere, Ogola's selected sites of study are seen as important pointers to the disjunctures and conjunctures that we have come to associate with the Diasporic communities the world all over. Ogola argues that although the Kenyan blogsphere had existed for sometime now, it only emerged into prominence in the aftermath of 2007 post-election violence that engulfed the country. Following the banning of of live broadcasts and reporting of the violence in the print media, the Kenyan blog emerged as an important platform on which Kenyans could express their fears and anxieties outside the watchful eyes of the state. Ogola's central argument though is that, far from the conventional wisdom that diasporic displacement would lead bloggers to question accepted notions of national identity, ethnic solidarity and territorialized identities, studies of the narratives posted on the blogs dealing with post-election violence by the Kenyan Diasporic community point to a very complex picture. To the contrary, Ogola's chapter questions the tendency to see `Diasporas as homogeneous groups, collectively aggrieved, uniformly alienated and sharing common values'. As Ogola further argues, "... while de-territorialization takes place among Diasporas, a corresponding re-territorialization also occurs hence the existence and indeed vibrancy of 'ethnic enclaves' in the Western Metropoles", typified by the examples of the blogs cited in the chapter that were bluntly rooted in specific ethnic nationalisms and class interests. Thus the tendency to see the new media and specifically blogs as representative of a generation that is post-ethnic is suspect. The chapter also points to the fact that the blog space is not as neutral as many are wont to argue and it is indeed, a site controlled by what Ogola calls 'techno-elites' whose influence on the tone of the debates and blog narratives was evident. For example, ethnically driven blogs, tended to validate specific narratives on violence at the exclusion of alternative or oppositional voices, while equally displaying an ambivalent relationship with the nation state. Alternatively, the bloggers that privileged the economic agenda and the stability of the nation state almost always bought into the neo liberal idea of democracy, and quite often displayed clear class anxieties over the possible collapse of the nation state. Ogola's point is that "diasporic identities are in fact shaped by shifting variables, often temporal, spatial and experiential".

It is our hope that the layered debates reflected in the following chapters, diverse as they are, will give our readers a glimpse into the intellectual cartographies and cultural impulses from the Eastern African region. Some of the issues tackled here continue to mutate and are likely to develop beyond our imagination, but what is certain is that Eastern African intellectual landscape is growing in complexity and its multiple cultural trajectories reflected in these chapters point to a constant need for a re-reading and a re-mapping of our cultural contours - indeed a constant challenge to our cultural certainties and entrenched notions of cultural production and consumption.

# SECTION I:
## Literary and Intellectual Traditions

## Chapter 1

# THE EMERGENCE OF LOCAL PATRONAGES AND INTELLECTUAL TRADITIONS IN POST-INDEPENDENCE EAST AFRICA: NATIVISM OR A CRITIQUE OF DIFFERENCE AND UNIVERSALISM?

*James Ogude*
Department of African Literature,
University of the Witwatersrand

## INTRODUCTION

Three decades ago, David Maughan Brown (1979) observed that before the Black Consciousness movement was in vogue in South Africa, some of the issues embedded in the black consciousness philosophy and theory were already widely discussed in East Africa. Maughan-Brown was referring specifically to the debates in the early sixties about black aesthetics and its place in the project of cultural re-engineering that was beginning to take place in East Africa. The re-engineering I am referring to was mooted in the rhetoric of the nationalist politicians namely: Julius Nyerere's *Ujamaa*, Milton Obote's *The Common Man's Charter* and indeed, Tom Mboya's and by extension Kenyatta's, the Sessional Paper no 10. Common to all these was the rhetoric of nation-building. However, away from the political theatrics that were being staged everywhere, there was yet another significant debate, being robustly carried out in the corridors in East Africa – specifically in the erstwhile English departments that were seen correctly or incorrectly as the custodians of cultural renewal and practices. This debate related to English School Culture which aimed to produce men and women of culture modeled after the elite British middle class.

What this robust, yet curiously regional, debate signaled was an emergence of an intellectual tradition which was partly spurred on by the new cultural space that had been created by political independence. It was also driven by a seething desire to break loose and grope for a new cultural horizon that would move away from the cultural strangle-hold of the English School culture and a Eurocentric idea of universal-ism and difference. At the heart of the drive for black aesthetics was the argument that colonial discourse had created the idea of an irrational Africa as the validating exception to the rational order of the modern Western world, and as such African literary and cultural texts should be engaged in creating an imaginary universe in which the rationality of pre-colonial Africa, and thereby that of postcolonial Africa, is affirmed. This affirmation would also look to Africa's oral sources as a means of imbuing this transformative process with a new cultural ethos rooted in the continent.

The motivation for my return to these debates is twofold. Firstly, I am interested in the emergence of local literary patronages and intel-lectual traditions in East Africa which in my view have never been suffi-ciently theorized as marking important moments in the region's literary scholarship. By patronages I mean those institutional frameworks that shape the way forms of knowledge, cultural or otherwise, are produced and consumed, and by intellectual traditions I refer to the institutional-ization of specific discursive practices that set the norms and grammar with which we speak or what Foucault would refer to as the rules that make "it possible to delimit the group of concepts, disparate as they may be" (1972, 59). Secondly, I am interested in making a new and important argument; that a number of intellectual interventions that were made in the late sixties and seventies in East Africa, far from being nativist[1] as they have been labeled, were in fact offering an invaluable and relevant critique of a European idea of difference and by extension universal-ism which had been at the centre of modern philosophy in Europe for decades and found its way into Africa through colonialism.[2] I argue that because black aesthetics and the movement to establish the depart-ment of African literature and languages had been closely associated with a certain ideology of authenticity or Africanism, the real value of these two important interventions and their positive contribution to the development of East African literary and intellectual landscape has never been fully appreciated in scholarship. The response has been so negative that the black aesthetics debate would continue to haunt Ngugi and his colleagues at Nairobi University for decades. Like the initiators of black aesthetics before them, they were dismissed as pursuing a nativist agenda, defined purely on racial lines. Apollo Amoko, perhaps one the most eloquent critic of this new regime of aesthetics that was inaugurated by the East African scholars writes: "The thrust of my biographical critique of the Nairobi Revolution is that an indefensible form of literary nativism undergirded and undermined the movement" (2001, 34).

But we need to pause here and reflect briefly on the specific issues that form the basis of Amoko's (2001) article because they are critical to my intervention. Although the article sets out to critique the so-called traditional English literature canon, especially its rootedness in what Amoko refers to as "a pervasive reality of university pedagogies within which literature is understood as an exemplary representation of national culture" (2001, 25), Amoko actually uses it to offer a scathing critique of a memo penned by James Ngugi, Henry Owuor-Anyumba and Taban Lo Liyong, 'On the Abolition of the English Department' at Nairobi University (Ngugi 1972, 145-50). The content and substance of this memo is now so widely known and acknowledged that it does not merit any repeating here, suffice to say as Carol Sicherman does, that the memo should be seen within the broader movement of "the canon revision endemic in international academia in the later twentieth century" (1998, 129).

## THE INVENTION OF AFRICA THESIS
## AND ITS FAULTLINES

It is significant that Amoko's critique takes as its point of departure the now widely circulated argument of Vincent Mudimbe that Africa was an invention of Europe, and by extension, modern African literature was also tied to the colonial library and as such any attempts to assess its aesthetic value must begin there. At the heart of Mudimbe's argument is that the colonial library provided the conditions for existence of African literature. In other words, African literature is implicated in that endless repudiation of the Western world's representation of Africa as the irrational 'Other'. The guts of Amoko's argument is the idea that modern African literature was "imprisoned in the very economy of practice it sought to transcend," as Gikandi ( , 3) would have it. Or as Amoko muses, "These literary texts depended, for their revisionary power, on the grammar and conceptual infrastructure of colonial social science and, in effect, normalized an anthropological *episteme* for Africa" (2001, 22).

This is a self-validating argument that now calls for greater scrutiny and one that has now become less persuasive than when it landed on our shores. The argument that Europe invented Africa and because Europe invented Africa, African agency would forever be tied-in-with Europe; indeed, the argument that the grammar and the conceptual grasp of the continent must of necessity begin with the colonial library, needs to be interrogated. Mudimbe's thesis is of course in response to a wave of movements among African politicians and historians, who after Africa's independence, moved to find a domain that could be defined as both unambiguously African and resistant to imperialism. And yet both Mudimbe's notion of Africa as a Western invention and Africa's foundational historian's search for Africa's survivals beneath the surface of colonialism seem to me problematic for a number of reasons. Although Mudimbe and like-minded scholars concede that the making of black culture and identity in general was as much a product of the West as it was indigenous to Africa, and that the process that created the current Africa and the Diaspora in the first place, could not shape African culture(s) without Western culture itself being transformed, there is almost always the assumption that Africa had very little agency, if any, outside that created by colonialism and by extension the colonial library. The implication here is that Africa's influence was on the terms and conditions set and imposed by colonialism/modernity. This has created the dilemma in which we express the desire to have a colonial subject or a former colonial subject that has a rich and complex consciousness and also freedom to exercise autonomy and yet there is a very real danger of remaining in the category of victim, and for colonialism to remain resolutely hegemonic, despite the contradictions of its modernizing projects and its insistence on maintaining boundaries.

This view of colonialism as an all-consuming phenomenon that destroys everything in its wake is the view of colonial discourse that could contain its challenges and tensions, which must now be questioned. And yet, this is the argument at the heart of Amoko's article. He writes:

> .... to the extent that the movement sought hurriedly to substitute a discourse of authentic "African-ness" for a discourse of alien 'Englishness' as the condition for existence for appropriate literary education in African universities, it represented a reactionary instrumentalization of the aesthetic

and an ironic affirmation of the idea of Africa invented by the
colonial library. (2001, 22)

A closer reading of the famous memo that Amoko refers to, does not
point to a single reference to an "authentic African-ness," that he reads
at the heart of this memo. Instead one comes across a curriculum that is
rooted in a concentric understanding of identity formation. This is what
Carol Sicherman has in mind when she writes in response to the memo
that the: "Concentric curricular circles placed East African literature
and orature in the center of the first year, with other Third World and
then European literatures introduced in the following years. The shift
from "English" to "Literature" had nationalistic ramifications: by making
regional literature the curricular core, the abolitionists redefined the
nation" (1998, 129). Although I may not go as far as suggesting that
the abolitionists have re-defined the nation as Sicherman argues, what
was certain, as the Nairobi troika point out in the memo, is that they
were "clearly mapping out the directions and perspectives the study of
culture and literature [would] inevitably take in an African university"
(1998, 146).

## THE MEMO AND ITS COSMOPOLITAN VISION

I want to linger on the concentric idea which was at the heart of
the new curriculum because in terms of identity formation, concen-
tricity often signals tension and dialogue between various layers that
constitute the concentric whole. I want to imagine that in suggesting
this concentric curriculum, Ngugi and his colleagues in Nairobi were
in fact pointing to the complexity of the cultural renewal that they were
seeking to create. Far from legitimizing itself through ethnic and racial
identities as Amoko argues, the Nairobi *troika* was calling for a curriculum that would allow the students to grapple with the flow of cultural
streams that did not seek to centre English-ness as the original source of
culture. It was, in my view, seeking to show how knowledge of local cultural formations can allow for a sharper engagement with other related
and divergent cultural streams. They were speaking to specific cultural
sources that have shaped and continue to constitute what is now widely
referred to as modern African literature. It is to these rich sources of
modern African literature that item 9 in the memo speak:

We know that European literatures constitute one source of influence on modern African literatures in English, French, and Portuguese;
Swahili, Arabic, and Asian literatures constitute another, an important

source, especially here in East Africa; and the African tradition, a tradition as active and alive as ever, constitutes the third and the most significant. This is the stuff on which we grew up, and it is the base from which we made our cultural take-off into the world (1998, 146-7).

Apparently, the Nairobi *troika* did not want to see literature and culture in general as "antiseptically quarantined from its worldly affiliations, but as an extraordinarily varied field of endeavor" as Edward Said (1994, xv), in a different context, has elegantly put it. Instead, they were giving effect to what Said has described in one of his most influential texts as "overlapping territories, intertwined histories" of the empire and of the world, which he argues, global culture is indebted to (1994, 1-72). At one point in his paper, Amoko's ambivalent dis-enchantment with the Ngugi revolution is evident and he accedes to the global and cosmopolitan nature of the curriculum. He writes: "On the one hand, I continue to admire its commitment to a truly global conception of literature, a cosmopolitan commitment not generally characteristic of Western English programs. On the other hand, I find myself opposed to the Africanist discourse at the heart of my undergraduate education" (Amoko 2001, 30).

Amoko's apprehensions about this radical intellectual break are of course underpinned by a glaring fear of anything defined on ethnic or racial lines. This is amplified further down in the article when he observes: The Nairobi troika's literary nationalism is driven, ultimately, by a racialist black aesthetic; hence they contend thatalready African writing, with sister connections in the Caribbean and Afro-American literatures, has played an important role in the African renaissance" (2001, 37). But why, one may venture to ask, should Africa's connections with the Caribbean and Afro-American literatures be dubbed racialist and nativist? To ask this question is also to ask whether one can speak of an African Diaspora in Europe and the Americas without some concrete intellectual encounter with Africa. Why therefore, should the search for these historical and intellectual connections be dubbed nativist? Indeed, if Stuart Hall is right in arguing that "The African diasporas of the New World have been in one way or another incapable of finding a place in modern history without the symbolic return to Africa" (1995, 9), then Amoko's nativist and racialist claims are suspect if not altogether unfounded. Ntongela Masilela has, for example, written that: "[T]he placement of the intellectual bridge of trans-Atlanticism across the vast ocean between Africa and the African diaspora was not because of racial ontologies or myth of the search for origins, but rather because of political solidarity, intellectual affiliations, cultural retainments, and historical appropriations" (1996, 90).

## NATIVISM OR ANXIETIES OF THE POSTCOLONIAL INTELLECTUALS?

The claims of nativism and racialist black identity only find force when we seek either to diminish or delete altogether the shared historical experience of slavery and a special form of colonialism whose social basis was rooted in a certain form of European discourse; a discourse dependant on difference and by extension, universalism, since as Simon Gikandi has observed in a different context, "all theories of modernity, even theories of difference, seem to derive their authority from a certain claim to universality" (2001, 6). In the history of Africa and its diasporas, the notion of African difference is deeply embedded in the discursive practices of the West that it is difficult to offer a sustained critique of those practices without pointing to the foundation which is rooted in a certain form of ethical and moral difference, which is the flipside of Eurocentrism.

And yet, beyond the gestures towards the black Diaspora, the curriculum also signaled a comparative approach to literature – now in vogue in North America – in which "knowledge of Swahili, English and French should be compulsory" (Ngugi, 147). Thus, at the level of language, provincialism was being discredited and the diversity in modern African literature was being acknowledged and credited. Indeed, the Nairobi troika, moved to re-define oral literature as 'a living tradition' as opposed to some ossified cultural resource to be excavated (ibid., 148). And yet the detractors, Amoko included, wished to diminish the value of oral literature research at Nairobi University and the other public universities in East Africa as ethnic and fundamentally aimed at interpellating the student researchers "as the natural subjects of various ethnic nationalities" (Amoko 2001, 32). On the contrary, and in my personal experience at Nairobi University from 1976 to 1982, the study and research in oral literature was never aimed at hailing students into their ethnicities.

Under Henry Owuor Anyumba, oral literature research stood out as one of the best forms of ethnographical research practices and it would benefit a number of us many years later.[3] I can recall vividly that second year students often joined MA students to undertake some research in an aspect of one or two ethnic communities to capture a range of rituals, dance, music and a number of oral performances in their natural contexts. In 1978, the research trip took us to Mbere, a sub-ethnic community of the Embu of Kenya to study their circumcision rituals and related oral performances that accompanied this important rite of passage among the Mbere. The second research trip took us to the coastal region of Kenya. I was doing my MA studies and led a group of second year students to Malindi to study a religious ritual known as *Maulidi* – largely practiced by the Islamic community during the month of December, when the new moon is sighted. In both instances, the research focused on performances of rituals accompanied with a whole range of cultural repertoires in their contexts. The rituals were rooted in contemporary culture, even though their roots run deep into history. At no point did I feel that I was being hailed as the natural subject of an ethnic community because of the research. At any rate, most of the students in these two trips did not come from these communities and out of eight five of the postgraduate students came from Southern Africa: Lesotho and Swaziland. All of us went out there not to prove our own cultural rootedness or nativist affinity to any of the communities, but as seekers of knowledge to understand, record and archive vibrant cultural experiences as these were performed before our eyes. We probed into the history of these rituals, interviewed a range of expert artists central to these rituals, explored the symbolic and social dimensions of these performances and grappled to understand the metaphors and images that the local communities used to colonise meaning and their spaces – to understand their world. Thus, Amoko's assertion that: "During these courses one would ideally be required to record, transcribe, translate, classify, and critique the oral literature of one's ethnic community; one would, in short, be pedagogically interpellated as an ethnic national subject," is not entirely true.[4] My experience at Nairobi University was that one took recourse to one's ethnic community as a site of oral literature research due to language constraints, although I see no intellectual or ideological rationale for this uneasiness with conducting research that is situated within one's ethnic community. The tendency to want to run away from ethnographical research among African scholars in the West who style themselves as transnationalists and multiculturalists, has now lost its academic capital and has become, as Anthony Appiah reminds us, sterile and very much a reflection of the anxiety of the post-colonial intellectuals residing there. He writes:

> Postcoloniality is the condition of what we might ungenerously call a comprador intelligentsia: a relatively small, Western style, Western-trained group of writers and thinkers, who mediate the trade in cultural commodities of world capitalism at the periphery. In the west they are known through the Africa they offer; their compatriots know them through an Africa they have invented for the world, for each other, and for Africa. (1991, 348)

In support of Appiah, my argument is that such scholars have positioned themselves as intermediaries and have sought to simplify African realities for Western consumption, but in ways that generally conform to a pre-existing stereotypical image of African pathology – whether such a pathology lies in what is seen as 'anachronistic' nationalism or a crude resort to racialism – is a mute point. The problem is that these representations of Africa persist even in instances where the continent and its people have moved on. My concern here is that a certain form of cosmopolitanism which seeks to delete micro-narratives rooted in local knowledge and as such dismissing them as ethnic is not only a re-emergence of European idea of universalism and difference, but equally an over-simplified definition of cosmopolitanism as anti-local. A study of African oral cultures in their local contexts is often reduced to a curious elevation of the autochthon to levels of respectability, although these scholars will grudgingly acknowledge the excellent pioneering work done, mainly by white scholars, in areas such as anthropology, history, sociology and more recently in popular culture studies.[5] It is noteworthy that these excellent studies have been rooted in popular oral sources and have served to place greater premium on locally fuelled, literary and cultural studies in the continent. They have been part of that broader project in the continent to re-assess the issue of aesthetic value which hitherto had been unquestioningly predicated on the English tradition and its legitimacy as a universal form. Both the purveyors of black aesthetics and curriculum changes in literature were calling for a re-imagination of aesthetics that would allow African literature and criticism to develop its own aesthetic standards and value within a complex cultural synthesis that had become part of a cultural re-awakening in the region. Pio Zirimu, one of the organizers of a colloquium on Black Aesthetics held at Nairobi University in June 1971, stressed the impact of specific cultural formations in shaping aesthetics by observing that: "Aesthetics being the perception or even philosophy of beauty principally in art, but also in nature, is derived from people, from a people's way of life." He adds:

> The authentic critical standards must be born from the works of specific societies and their representative creators. That is where it all begins, criticism. Not in Aristotle's *Poetics*. The *Poetics* was written from Greek dramatic performance and experience, it was a distillation and a summation of what appeared to be operating principles from observed plays; it did not predate, precede the actual plays, the performance and the dramatic spectacle and audience "viewance." Our

> plague has been to think that Greece was the universe and
> Aristotle was the world's oracle. (1973, 58-9)

What I understand Zirimu to be saying is that the making of an aesthetic value is something born out of artistic and critical praxis, a process through which a given art is forced to reflect on itself against societal norms of what is 'ugly' and 'beautiful'; against societal ideal of what is beautiful. The idea of the beautiful may be borrowed or transformed, but in the final analysis it is mediated and shaped into form through a rigorous inter-penetration between the local and the global; through the interface between the traveler and the stay-at-home, as Walter Benjamin (1968) would have it. In this sense, it is possible to argue that Zirimu is not necessarily against borrowing from Aristotle's poetics, but rather its wholesale and uncritical adoption into new contexts.[6] Zirimu is also saying that through this kind of dialogic critical reflection, every society and culture will of necessity seek to define and re-define its own sense of what is beautiful. Ali Mazrui, in "Aesthetic Dualism and Creative Literature in East Africa" puts an interesting inflection on the debate at the same conference:

> Aesthetic values are often the most conservative of all values in response to foreign influence. It is often far easier to convert to the ethics of a conquering power, than the aesthetics. An African is often more easily converted to Western Christianity than to Western classical music.... As between societies which are otherwise very different, agreement between right and wrong, good and bad, is often easier to achieve than agreement on what is beautiful and what is ugly. (1973, 33)

If it is true, as Mazrui suggests, that aesthetics evolve a lot more slowly than other aspects of human culture, then the proposition that colonialism meant the death of African aesthetics thereby leading to its radical permutation into something hitherto unknown to the Africans needs to be challenged. It is true, as the Nairobi troika argue in their memo, that modern African literature was shaped by a range of competing aesthetic values across the globe, but the change was not as complete and final as many have tended to suggest. The so-called 'English School' syllabus, for example, had a significant impact on its products here in Africa, but it is /equally true that the impact was never as overwhelming to the extent that it supplanted local aesthetic values. There is no place where this is more evident than in the foundational narratives written by pioneer African writers like Chinua Achebe in

West Africa, Sol Plaatje in South Africa, Ngugi wa Thiong'o and Okot p'Bitek in East Africa. The fact that their narratives were saturated by vernacular idioms and local syntactic structures, that made themselves felt through English expressions, was not just a deliberate attempt to salvage fast-fading oral traditions that were threatened by a new order, it was also testimony to their close affinity to these values and a certain form of aesthetics whose tyranny and power would continue to shape modern African writing for generations to come. There was a discernible cultural unconscious, to borrow Jameson's phrase that no attempts by European modernity could have succeeded in erasing, even several decades after the end of colonialism in Africa. A great deal has been made of the hybrid nature of modern African literature, and yet little attention has been paid to the fact that an aesthetic format that is far more closely aligned to modern African cultures, in their multiple streams was emerging, and which provides a distinctly African voice that was divorced from the European mainstream culture. And yet, the debate has always proceeded as if the hybrid nature of modern African literature is nothing but another piece of evidence that this new cultural phenomenon is only 'the bastard child' of Western colonialism and therefore its variant, albeit a weak one, in need of shoring up to realize its full aesthetic potential.

It must now be obvious that the idea of black aesthetics in the mind of its proponents in East Africa was driven by the desire to return aesthetics to its true owners; the people, from whom it derives its inner values. Black aesthetics was aimed at turning received European aesthetics, with its moral and ethical economies of difference and universalism, on its head. Black aesthetics emerged therefore as a vehicle for reclaiming and appropriating new voices from sites of repression or what Foucault would call subjugated knowledges – it was an instrument of legitimation and affirmation of the 'other'. In this connection, Simon Gikandi makes a pertinent observation that "modern criticism may have sought to suppress difference within imagined Europe, but it anchored itself on the existence of the Other. While modernity was premised on its invocation of universal reason, this rationality was structured by counterpoints located elsewhere" (2001, 11). My point is that, although modernity instituted its authority through the elision of difference, it nevertheless consigned difference to invented margins or what it considered as zones of irrationality.[7] This is why it has been forcefully argued by a number of post-colonial scholars, that when it comes to the history of colonialism in Africa, post-modernist discourse of difference remain ambivalent and need to be modified because modernity, and by extension modernist criticism, did not lead to elision of difference on the continent; instead, it foregrounded difference as the defining feature of Africa. It is on this basis that black aesthetics could only have emerged as a critique of this difference and the universal logic of modernity, while reaching out for a trans-national cultural enterprise, premised on a shared historical experience and/or overlapping territories and histories. In writing about the rise of the notion of a black aesthetic in the USA, Clyde Taylor has observed that:

> What gave the formulation "Black Aesthetic" its force was that, like its parallel concept, "Black Power," it had the effect of a profanity screamed in a chapel, a disruptive challenge to orthodoxy and tradition. Like the "Black power," it was "unspeakable." To base an aesthetic on Blackness was to situate the classically unaesthetic in the place of "the best that has been thought and said in the world." As Black aestheticians never tired of pointing out, the associations of Blackness had always been placed at the opposite end of civilizing light .... The most ruptive intervention of the Black Aesthetic was an argument validating its existence as an ethnic discourse, since the dominant tradition had all along been "a White Aesthetic": "The acceptance of the phrase 'Black is Beautiful' is the first step in the destruction of the old table of the laws and the construction of new ones, for the phrase flies in the face of the whole ethos of the white aesthetic." (1998, 4)

In the East African experience, as with the African Americans, this radical reversal and restitution of values was at the heart of the black aesthetics movement. In the first instance, it was a project of restoration, the struggle to wrest the space upon which black aesthetics could be celebrated, unfettered. In doing this, the black aestheticians started by interrogating the so-called 'universal value of art' which was at the heart of the English School syllabus and with it the autonomy of art would soon be put under scrutiny. After all, the essence of modernist 'white aesthetic' had rested upon the idea of art's autonomy and its capacity to move towards the sublime, thereby transcending base human morality to encapsulate the beautiful, free from all fetters of society. And yet what was never fully questioned was the basis for the universality of the aesthetic, which as Clyde Taylor has argued, had tended to collapse the hierarchies of values in diverse and different societies far too easily. The quest for the universality of the aesthetic would ignore the fact that even what may appear to be close value hierarchies in different cultures, are often contingent upon specific "cultural cosmologies and ideological configurations" (1998, 19) within those cultures. He writes: "Two societies often venerate the same object, but for entirely different reasons, as we are reminded when a museum piece is reclaimed by its originating cultural community for its ritual or other value. Or the intensity of veneration in two societies may appear similar but very differently motivated" (ibid.).

Taylor's argument echoes Mazrui's argument earlier on, that aesthetic taste and divide among various communities may perhaps be more pronounced and often sharper than we are willing to admit. A good example in the context of East Africa is the sharp tension generated around female circumcision in Ngugi's *The River Between*. Here the cultural battle is fought over the female body, and yet it's symbolic significance and by extension its aesthetic value is read very differently by the two antagonistic groups: the Gikuyu and the colonizer. For the colonizer, it signifies ugliness and darkness at the heart of this 'primitive' African community. The grammar deployed in naming the ritual is straight out of the colonial library; it is the tension between 'civilization' and by extension universal values on the one hand, and 'backwardness' and regressive values of an insular society, on the other. But for the Gikuyu, the ritual embodies beauty – the kind of aesthetic premium that Muthoni places on it: "want to be a woman made beautiful in the tribe" (Ngugi 1965, 44). Failure to pass through this rite of passage, leads to a curse – *thahu* – among the Gikuyu. So what the white missionaries see as the ultimate expression of ugliness in this community is at the core of what is beautiful. This tension is born out of different cultural cosmologies and ideological configurations even if one seeks to hide its naked bias by evoking some universal values of 'civilization'. It is for this reason, that the protagonist of the novel, Waiyaki, regards "Livingstone, for all his learning and holiness, a little dense in attacking a custom whose real significance in the tribe he did not understand and probably never would understand" (ibid.).

## THE GAINS OF THE TWO INTELLECTUAL TRADITIONS

And yet the debate around black aesthetics did not remain locked in some endless binary opposition. In East Africa, the new debates were increasingly redefining symbolic and cultural expression in ways that sought to complicate the idea and function of the aesthetic. With the re-emergence of de-colonization politics in the immediate aftermath of independence, and the restlessness that followed in the early phase of independence, black aesthetics came to be viewed as an ideal devoid of a clear purpose to transform the lives of ordinary people. By the time the Nairobi troika called for the abolition of the English department, a quiet revolution was also beginning to take place – a revolution that would force cultural practitioners to push the debate around black aesthetics to its logical extreme and among artists and critics issues raged in public and private forum: How does one put art to the service of the people? Indeed, how does one link art to social issues that affect ordinary people way beyond aesthetics?

Of course, these questions were only possible because by the mid-1970s, when the black aesthetics debate was on the wane in East Africa, it had in fact established its arguments that a community's cultural productions are rooted in its political, social, and historical contexts. As early as 1972, Ngugi wa Thiong'o was already writing: "Literature does not grow or develop in a vacuum; it is given impetus, shape, direction and even area of concern by social, political and economic forces in a particular society" (1972, xv). Black aestheticians in East Africa were struggling to circumvent what had stifled black aesthetics among African Americans, namely, the disconnection between them and the ordinary black man and woman. An important clarion call for committed literature that engaged with representations of social issues from below, but ultimately devolving literary and cultural consumption of art to the people would be the intervention that made all the difference. Two important developments took place. The first one had to do with a shift that would see aesthetics and/or literature gradually move to its social and historical role as the centre for popular ideology that it had assumed in Europe in the last two centuries, but with one vital exception. Whereas in Europe aesthetics had come to symbolize what Taylor has described as "a middle-class parlor game" (1998, 10), in East Africa, aesthetics occupied a revolutionary space – an avant-garde art whose overriding motivation was a positive representation of the plight of ordinary workers and peasants. The second development not only saw aesthetics as ethnically rooted, but more significantly as class-bound. Again, if in Europe aesthetics had been used as an instrument of legitimating middle-class values and taste, in East Africa it was seen as the instrument of class war in which the values of the repressed and silenced would find expression. The emergence of Free Travelling Theatres, for example, in the three East African universities in the 70s was aimed at the divide between the elite located at institutions of higher learning and ordinary people located away from the 'ivory towers' of scholarship. Concerned about this divide, Ngugi wa Thiong'o went a step further and founded a radical theatre practice in which the academics would be forced to work with the peasants in Ngugi's home village and established the Kamiriithu theatre. It was this kind of radical intervention that forced the Kenyatta regime to send Ngugi into solitary confinement. Ngugi had engineered a theatre practice that grew organically out from ordinary peasant's issues. This theater practice enabled ordinary peasants to act out their problems, thereby sharpening their political agency. In Uganda, the impact of Black Aesthetics would soon be felt through the remarkable response and general outpour of texts challenging Idi Amin's military dictatorship in Uganda. Although the rebellion against the Makerere tradition, rooted in the English School syllabus, had begun during the first republic in Uganda under Obote, politically charged art would emerge in earnest during Amin's decade of tyranny and violence. These themes are vividly captured in the works of John Ruganda's, *The Floods* and Robert Serumaga's *The Elephants*, which worked through mime, song and dance to avoid Amin's censure. The radicalism led to Serumaga's arrest in 1977 for allegedly plotting to overthrow Amin. The East African Cultural Revolution led to a number of developments which, in my view, marks it out as an important intellectual trajectory in East Africa. It led to an important development in literary scholarship, namely; a critical re-assessment of the relationship between African writing in English and oral and written texts in the indigenous languages. In East Africa, the translation of Okot p'Bitek's *Song of Lawino* from Acoli signaled this moment that would eventually draw attention to the fact that most of the East African writers, although writing in different periods and in very different genres, are directly or indirectly influenced by the body of indigenous oral and written material. The focus on orality, as Ato Quayson (1997) has shown in the case of West Africa, established contexts for constructing and expressing opposition to domination throughout and beyond the colonial period. However, Quayson's work also acknowledges that these indigenous language cultures themselves were constructed, in their present form, within a complex dialogic relationship with external influences. Quayson writes: "the noting of indigenous influences on African literature was part of the project of defining the national status of the emerging literatures, especially after decolonization" (1997, 3).

The second thing that would mark black aesthetics as a significant watershed in the literary history of East Africa was the emergence and tolerance towards aesthetic pluralism. This is an important offshoot of the revolution of the Nairobi Troika. Very few have acknowledged it as a direct response to the black aesthetics debate that was challenging the hegemony of English aesthetics. This transformative view of aesthetics would find its fertile ground in the former English departments of East Africa's institutions of higher learning and the high school curriculum across the region. For the first time, texts from the region and the rest of the continent could be taught alongside texts from the black Diaspora in high schools. Okot p'Bitek's *Song of Lawino*, Ngugi's and Achebe's novels and Soyinka's *Kongi's Harvest* and *The Lion and the Jewel*, would be read alongside Dickens, Shakespeare and Thomas Hardy. And although under Daniel arap Moi's regime in Kenya, for example, Ngugi's texts were outlawed in schools and Soyinka's *Kongi's Harvest* was banned allegedly because it contained violent scenes, and Achebe's *A Man of the People*, condemned by the Kenyan Catholics for having some sex scenes, the path of change set by the cultural revolution could never be reversed by the politicians (see appendix 1 for an excerpt from the Kenyan Advanced Certificate of Education syllabus). The syllabus, two decades after the Nairobi revolution, still speaks of the cosmopolitan and concentric nature of literary studies in Kenyan high schools.

Finally, the debate also created the space within which new and local African writers could express themselves without feeling that they were writing under the shadow of colonial tutelage. And although Heinemann AfricanWriters Series has done a commendable work in giving African writers a voice, in East Africa, their influence was slow and gradual. It would take two local publishing initiatives to reach the levels of the good work started by Heinemann, and later East African Literature Bureau, by Charles Richards, a former publisher with the Church Missionary Society in the 1930s and founder of a local publishing enterprise in the 1940s called Ndia Kuu Press (Chakava 1996, 1-9). It also took a local initiative led by a group of local academics to create the space for bolder and more experimental writing to emerge from East Africa. Henry Chakava has described 1965 as a watershed year for publishing in the region and singled out the emergence of East African Publishing House (EAPH), as the most important initiative. The significance though of this new publishing outfit resides in the fact that "it was started by a group of academics from Eastern Africa who constituted the East African Institute of Social and Cultural Affairs, in association with the British publisher Andre Deutsch" (1996, 9). As Chakava notes: "[T]he new publisher was expected to cater more satisfactorily to the academic and general education needs of the local communities and to reflect a more positive image of the African heritage, which, it was felt, the existing foreign publishers had failed to do" (ibid.). Although the short partnership with Andre Deutsch failed, it is significant that by 1966, EAPH published Okot p'Bitek's *Song of Lawino*, which rapidly became one of the landmark texts of African literature. It is also worth mentioning that the emergence of popular literature series was also closely associated with EAPH. A good example is that of Charles Mangua, whose novel, *Son of Woman* (1971), published by East African Publishing House, and was one of the earliest texts to be associated with the new popular' writing series in Africa. "The emergence of a large body of popular writing in many parts of East and West Africa," Gareth Griffiths has written, "announces the latest in series of ongoing appropriations Africans have made of the publishing practices, as well as languages and literary forms of the ex-colonial cultures" (2000, 103).

In conclusion, I wish to argue that although not all of these developments may be linked to the emergence of black aesthetics and the changes in the debates about the Literature syllabus in East Africa, these radical interventions were nevertheless pivotal in opening up spaces for local voices and local initiatives, that hitherto had been constrained by external patronage in the production of African English writing. And that, although the development of modern African literature in East Africa has to be understood in the light of the wider t ensions and struggles between outside and local appropriations, these interventions fueled by debates around black aesthetics and an African-centered Literature syllabus in the 1960s, were critical in mapping out a new trajectory of literary production and scholarship in the region. In engaging with the specific ideological and political constraints imposed by English colonial culture and its moral warheads of difference and universality, these interventions became some of the sharpest critiques of Eurocentric aesthetic values and taste. It is against this backdrop that the emergence of black aesthetics should be seen as a historical phenomenon born from the cultural context within which Africa's difference had been assumed or even taken for granted.

## Notes

1. By nativism, I am making reference to those forms of knowledges that are rooted in essentialized identities – they remain insular and averse to any competing versions of identity or external influences.

2. I am using universalism to refer to those theories that are critical of ideology and were constructed in Western Europe and by extension were rooted in the concept of instrumental reason developed since enlightenment. Instrumental reason was the opposite of the religious and the metaphysical. But as Larrain argues in *ideology and Cultural Identity*, 'it was

contrasted with what was simultaneously happening in other parts of the world. Most of these theories held conceptions of the non-European, of the 'other', which emphasized the contrast between the chaotic and irrational ways of the 'other' and a rather triumphalistic and optimistic notion of their own rational European cultural identity.' And of significance to me is Larraine's argument that, 'This identity conceived of itself as the centre where history was being made and it was able to place and recognize everybody else as peripheral', 142. It is within this context that most theories of development, rooted in their critique of ideology, constructed the 'other' that had to be saved from the so called traditional patterns of backwardness and stagnation. These notwithstanding, modernity and its universalistic and totalizing theories have been criticized by those historical accounts which emphasized difference over uniformity, cultural relativism as opposed to objective truth and historical discontinuity as against unilineal and teleological conceptions of history. Yet my point is that these positions did not necessarily cease to construct Europe as the centre and non-European 'other' as peripheral and inferior – hence my argument that all theories of modernity will always make some claim to universalism. This is an issue that Ngugi discusses at length in his widely acknowledged collection of essays, *Moving the Centre*. The contradiction in European thoughts that swivels around universalistic and historicist theories is that, 'While the universalistic theories of modernity looked at the 'other' from the perspective of the European rational subject, thus reducing all cultural difference to its own unity, historicist theories looked at the 'other' from the perspective of its unique and specific cultural set-up, thus emphasizing difference and segmentation. If the former may neglect the other's specificity, the latter may lead to the construction of the 'other' as so different as to be inferior and less than human', asserts Larraine, 142.

3. In recognition of the impact and influence of oral literature studies in the Literature Department at Nairobi University, Simon Gikandi, now a Professor of English at Princeton University and a contemporary at Nairobi from 1976 to 79 has dedicated his book, *Ngugi wa Thiong'o*, to Anyumba and Okot p'Bitek, the two leading scholars of oral literature at the time.

4. Amoko, Ibid., 32. It is, however true, that curriculum developers in Kenya at Secondary School level encouraged a deliberate ethnicization of the study of Oral Literature, often giving a distorted understanding of Oral Literature as residing in rural areas. David A. Samper (1997), in a paper titled 'Love, Peace, and Unity': Romantic Nationalism and the Role of Oral Literature in Kenya's Secondary Schools'. *Folklore Forum* 28:1, draws attention to the link between Moi's manufactured and politicized nationalism to the rise of this 'tribalised' study of oral literature, a major deviation from what the authors of the literature revolution at Nairobi University had envisaged.

5. I have in mind the works of Scholars such as, Fabian, Johannes, *Power and Performance: Ethnographic Explorations through Proverbial Wisdom*

*and Theatre in Shaba, Zaire.* Madison: University of Wisconsin Press, 1990; Barber, K. with John Collins and Alain Ricard. *West African Popular Theatre.* Oxford: James Currey (The work focuses on the performative elements in contemporary indigenous oral popular culture); Barber, K. and P. F. de Moraes Farias. *Discourse and its Disguises.* See also a foundational study of Hofmeyr, I. *We spend Our Years as a Tale That Is Told: Oral Historical Historical Narrative in a South African Chiefdom.* London: James Currey.

6. See Edward Said's critique of uncritical use of imported theories in his book, *The World, the Text and the Critic.* Cambridge: Harvard University Press, 1983.

7. Said's *Orientalism,* gives a sharp reading of what I am referring to here – especially how the West constructed the marginal Other in the history of the Empire.

# Chapter 2

# *Kwani?* and the Imaginations around Re-invention of Art and Culture in Kenya

*Tom Odhiambo*
University of Nairobi

## INTRODUCTION

Some years back Taban lo Liyong popularized and bequeathed to the East African cultural and literary community a tag that has odiously hung around its neck for a long time. Taban asserted that East Africa had become a 'literary desert.' This phrase has been one of the most [ab]used propositions about the state of literary and intellectual life in East Africa. It has been used in arguments concerning the quality and quantity of literature produced in the East African countries of Kenya, Uganda and Tanzania but it has been a most convenient tool for individuals who are nostalgic about the 1960s to the early 1970s as the 'golden years' of East African literary and intellectual life,

Those so-called golden years were marked by robust literary output and intellectual debates thanks to the anti-colonial struggles in the region, and the rest of the colonized world, which had found eager followers in the universities and school systems all over the region. The close relationship between political and cultural nationalism had given birth to a mutually beneficial relationship between the political and intellectual classes. In particular, poetry, drama and fiction drew its inspiration from the political struggles and in turn encouraged/

inspired those struggles in the region. One only needs to read Ngugi wa Thiong'o's fiction and essays – including the latest *Wizard of the Crow* and *Re-Membering Africa* – to appreciate the marriage between politics and intellectual/literary life in East Africa. Most of the early writing dramatized the cultural anxieties of the new nations as well as proposing new agendas on nation-formation and national development. To a large degree this early writing was the cultural tool through which a new, liberated but also self-re-defining community could be imagined, to borrow from Benedict Anderson (1991).

However, this cozy relationship between the state and the academia as well as artists did not last long as the 1970s saw an increase in state intolerance of artists and scholars who criticized the new rulers. Artists were jailed, hounded into exile or killed. For some, association with the art easily became a badge of dishonour when relating to the state. Ngugi's *Detained: a Writer's Prison Diary* is testimony to the condition that was unraveling in the 1970s. Yet the state continued to claim a role in the production, dissemination and conservation of art and culture as attested to in the many institutions of art and culture that the government managed including ministries of culture, national museums and theatres. One could therefore argue that Taban's speculation of a literary desert in East Africa was both a critique of the decline in the quality and quantity of literary work from the region at the time as well as a cry about the deterioration in the status of artists and intellectuals as important actors in the production of art and literature.[1] In a sense, this statement was also an argument about *who* was expected to be in the forefront of literary production. Therefore, for me, it is important to show how Taban's statement has been re-echoed over time in the region. That statement was repeated in the 21st century when the periodical *Kwani?* was founded. This essay is a preliminary commentary on what *Kwani?* purports to be and has been as evidenced in its publications. I seek to demonstrate, briefly, by sketching *Kwani?*'s profile and claims, that the evidence so far suggests that the magazine has achieved little of its initial objectives, and that its stated intentions are undermined by its reliance on donor funding, its transnational and global tendencies, and its editorial practices which have probably encouraged the production of what it calls 'non-creative fiction' more than fiction.

## THE ORIGINS OF SOME 'WIND OF CHANGE'

*Kwani?* arrived on the literary scene in Kenya in style, so to speak, when its first issue was launched in 2003. It was an idea that was born in the backyard of a journalist's house, with the enthusiastic support of several young Kenyan journalists, aspiring writers and others who were 'concerned' about the state of Kenyan literature. The idea was given life by Binyavanga Wainaina, a Kenyan writer who had been living in Cape Town before he won the Caine Prize for African Writing in 2002 for his story 'Discovering Home' after which he relocated back to Kenya and became the founding editor and driving force behind *Kwani?* Subsequently, *Kwani?* published works by distinguished writers such as Yvonne Owuor and Pareselelo Kantai who went on to be shortlisted for the Caine Prize, with the former winning the prize in 2004 for the story '*The Weight of Whispers*'.

There are two important questions which should invite critical debate on the role and, so far, the performance of the magazine. Firstly, what motivated this group of young Kenyans who founded *Kwani?* And what was it that the *Kwani?* generation sought to do that was different from previous such literary and cultural projects?

Writing in the first editorial of *Kwani?* in 2003 Binyavanga offers these remarks to contextualize the rise of the publication:

> Lately I seem to meet all kinds of interesting people. Mostly young, self-motivated people, who have created a space for themselves in an adverse economy by being innovative. I have met a guy who engraves glass with exquisite skills; another guy who designs clothes, bags and other products for factories. I have met people who have never studied music, but who have created a style of Hip-Hop that is completely Kenyan; writers who have never studied literature who are writing at a level I did not know existed in this country. I have met a film director who managed to make a film in three weeks, with virtually no budget, who made another film in Sheng, using unknown actors. I have met an artist who is twenty years old, and who must have Kenya's largest art exhibition – all around the streets and alleyways of Eastleigh and Mathare. His name is Joga. I have met a writer, who has the power of words to evoke place like no Kenyan I know. He works as a gardener in Nairobi. His name is Stanley Gazemba. (*Kwani?* 1, 6)

This is the context in which *Kwani?* was founded; a context that was fertile with imagination and creativity, a world in which Kenyans artists and writers could be defined by their 'innovation' as Binyavanga suggests. And it is this seeming 'independence' that Binyavanga highlights in declaring and claiming *Kwani?* as their own (eagerly anticipated) place in the larger space of culture and literature in Kenya. He wrote further, in explaining his sketch of the Kenyan art scene that he evokes in the quotation above:

> To me this says we are finally becoming a country. When art as expression starts to appear, without prompting, all over the suburbs and villages of this country, what we are saying is: we are confident enough to create our own living, our own entertainment, our own aesthetic. Such an aesthetic will not be donated to us from the corridors of a university; or from the ministry of culture, or by The French Cultural Centre. It will come from the individual creations of thousands of creative people. (Kwani? 1, 6)

Binyavanga could not have been more explicit about what *Kwani?* sought to achieve on the literary and art scene in Kenya. But his comments should be contextualized into the political/ landscape of post-colonial Kenya at that time. *Kwani?* was launched at a time when the then president, Moi's, two and a half decades in power had come to an end. The country was bubbling with 'newness'; which is the spirit which the first issue of *Kwani?* indeed celebrates and undoubtedly promotes. The public space in Kenya was being recalibrated and readied for innovative and often revolutionary ideas and practices of transformation. For instance, the Frequency Modulation (FM) radio stations were just about to become a major factor and agency for Kenyans to debate on issues of public interests: politics, the economy, race, ethnicity, the workplace, the family, and even what would have been considered no-go areas such as sex, the private lives of politicians, corruption within the government, a few years before became common on the FM stations.

A 'poem by Muthoni wa Gatumu' on the blurb of *Kwani?* 1 captures the 'daring mood' of the time:

what I would like to do – what I really want
is to once again take between forefinger and thumb
2 pinches of freshly ground highlands' snuff,
inhale it slowly through each eager nostril
then await in anticipated bliss
for that heady buzz and building rush
which steadily multiplies
into heavenly
explosive
sneeze,
in public.

*Kwani?* could therefore be partly read as some kind of 'head-clearing' effort by a group of young Kenyan writers, some born and bred in Kenya but having lived outside the country for a better part of their youth. These writers, like the character in the poem above who seeks 'high-lands' snuff, have their heads clogged with competing identities – are you a Kenyan; are you a foreigner; are you half-Kenyan, half-foreigner; are you too Westernised to be Kenyan? In addition to the question of nationality, these writers were/are confronted with the subject of ethnic identity. Yet for most of them their urban and cosmopolitan childhoods had largely shielded them from the everyday politics of ethnicity and belonging in Kenya. A stay in Europe, America, Asia or other places had marked them as 'Africans' and nothing more. But a 'return' to Kenya had either revived in or presented to them the conundrum of belonging in which the most significant index of belonging is ethnicity. Thus one had to figuratively 'explosive[ly] sneeze, in public' as a way of freeing oneself of the tension in one's head. Consequently, *Kwani?* was able to frame its project, often, in controversial but as well as revolutionarily and exciting style.

## THE ISSUES

The first issue of *Kwani?* was published in 2003 with Binyavanga Wainaina as the editor. As the inaugural issue it was a milestone because it had some of the most innovative creative writing from the East African region headlined by Yvonne Owuor's story: 'Weight of Whispers' which had won the Caine Prize for African Writing in 2003; and it had an essay by Mahmood Mamdani: 'A Brief History of Genocide', and reflections from his visit to Rwanda after the genocide; historical pictorial snapshots of postcolonial Africa called: *Scenes from the Past* by Marion Kaplan; interview with a Kenyan Hip-Hop group *Kalamashaka*, among other pieces of writing, reportage, picture-story, poetry, biography and others. The first issue of *Kwani?* was irreverent, flamboyant, it breached artistic and genre boundaries and indeed seemed to suggest a literary revolution.

*Kwani?* 2 (2004) seems to be a victim of the success of *Kwani?* 1. Reader expectations had been heightened by the innovativeness one encounters in the first issue. Indeed, following in the tradition it had set, Pareselelo Kantai's short story: 'Comrade Lemma & the Black Jerusalem Boys Band' which was published in this issue was shortlisted for the Caine Prize for African Writing in 2004. It also had its share of creative and non-creative writing. This is the issue that one would describe as in

27

'search of its identity' because it was grappling with whether to continue the claim made in the first issue by Binyavanga about *Kwani?* being about Kenya, or to continue making overtures to narratives from the rest of the continent and the world. But having been founded within a global matrix of cultural transactions and partially having to rely on the network of transnational contributors and readers, *Kwani?* 2 seemed to have been unwilling to 'localize' itself too much, hence the reference to 'Kenyans at home and abroad' in this issue. The editors seem to have wanted to retain the tradition of 'revolution' which is partly communicated through the choice of the cover photograph of a 'dreadlocked' person – thus possibly signal and the Bob Marley youth and freedom loving generation both the renewal of the Mau Mau discourse in the post-Moi era as well as subtly invite its youthful readers to see themselves as the new revolutionaries – as well as remain loyal to the magazines global readership.

*Kwani?* 3 (2003) is what can be described as the 'Sheng' edition. It reads like an experiment at broadening the range of audiences for the publication. Like many in some of the previous issues of *Kwani?* the writers in this edition were 'workshopped.' Billy Kahora, the assistant editor of the issue notes that the writers were engaged in looking at 'Some Questions That Face Kenyan Writers Today.' The writers "... discussed how to make what they were writing reflect the Kenyan street, the Kenyan shamba, the Kenyan bar, and of course the language of the Kenyan family, especially dialogue with.... How to scratch beyond the surface and micro-narrate beyond the grand Kenyan themes affecting us all today. In Meja Mwangi's words – to strive for the wind" (*Kwani?* 3, 6). The idea behind this writing about the street and its lingo seems to be the direct result of fear that the magazine was writing for a 'particular' audience instead of the general Kenyan public that Binyavanga so lavishly claimed as the producers of their own culture, art and entertainment.

Yet even as it sought to project newness in its experimentation with Sheng, this issue looks back to the 1970s for inspiration. Its retro cover page illustration of Nairobi and afro-wearing women and bellbottomed trouser-wearing men seeks to hint at the energetic and revolutionary impulses of the 1970s as shared with the yearning for something new in the 21st century. *Kwani?* 4 (2007) was the post-referendum edition. The referendum was held after the post-Moi dream of a corruption-free and inclusive Kenya had spectacularly collapsed in 2003 when the then NARC government was split in the middle with one side accusing the other of reneging on a 'gentlemen's agreement' to rewrite the constitution and curb some of the powers of the president. The proposed new constitution presented to the people by the government was defeated. The ensuing political realignments caused feelings of exclusion from the government among other ethnic groups in Kenya. The Kikuyu, who made up the largest number of the population as an ethnic group, had more than their/a fair share of the government, felt isolated from the rest of Kenyans. This sense of 'Kikuyu isolation' informs *Kwani?* 4. Binyavanga wrote in the editorial that:

> Over the last two years a kind of insanity has overtaken many Gikuyus. Messiahs have come to 'save us' from the 'beats of the west' – and these 'beasts of the west' are of course, the problem with Kenya. The same people who had vowed in 2002 to allow a Kenya for Kenyans are now selling Kenya – with their massive vote – to a bunch of people who do not know the price of a pint of milk, or care – except when they own the milk manufacturing plant that stole machinery from a KCC which we built with our money. (*Kwani?* 4, vi)

The theme of politics is developed further in *Kwani?* issue 5 parts 1 and 2 which were issues arising out of the post-election crisis in Kenya after the December 2007 general elections. In response to this, *Kwani?* 5 posted a number of 'witness and victim' accounts from Kenyans who were directly and indirectly affected by the violence. Part 1 is called *Beyond the Vote: Maps and Journeys* whilst the title of Part 2 is: *Beyond the Vote: Revelations and Conversations*. Both issues were the most detailed and amongst the first published accounts of the nature and consequences of this post-election crisis.

## *KWANINI?* SERIES AND OTHER PUBLICATIONS

These texts are part of Kwani Trust's venture into publishing beyond the magazine. They are pocketsize texts that are meant to be easy to carry around, supposedly motivated and founded on the claim that Kenyans do not generally read. Some of the titles that have been published under the *Kwanini?* series include: *The Life and Times of Richard Onyango* by Richard Onyango, which is about the love-life between a visual artist and a white woman on the Kenyan Coast; *The Life of Mzee Ondego* by Enock Ondego, which tells the story of the first Kenyan to compose songs for the entertainment of the first president of the republic, Jomo Kenyatta; *How to Write About Africa* by Binyavanga Wainaina, who tongue-in-cheek offers advice on how to produce writing on Africa that will sell to a non-African audience; *You in America* by Chimamanda Adichie, a travelogue tracing the journeys of African migrants into America; *Weight of Whispers* by Yvonne Adhiambo Owuor, a story that details the cost of violence; *Discovering Home* by Binyavanga Wainaina, a journey of root-tracing; *Internally Misplaced* by Wambui Mwangi that narrates of the tensions and traumas arising from the December 2007-February 2008 post-election crisis in Kenya; *The True Story of David Munyakei: the Goldenberg Whistleblower* by Billy Kahora, which dramatizes the ups and downs of the man who revealed the scheme to steal public funds. As of 2011 *Kwani?* is yet to release a novel by any Kenyan writers, although it has (re)issued books such as *Half of a Yellow Sun* and *Purple Hibiscus* by Chimamanda Adichie, *The Stonehills of Maragoli* by Stanely Gazemba and *Kizuizini* (Kiswahili for 'In Detention') by Joseph Muthee, *The Tales of Kasaya* (Eva Kasaya), among others.

## CAN *KWANI?*'S CLAIMS OF LITERARY AND CULTURAL REVIVAL STAND SCRUTINY?

The founding claims of *Kwani?* are not different from those of other earlier journals that promoted literature, art and culture in the post-colonial period. Peter Benson quotes a reviewer of *Okyeame* (who he speculates might have been Gerald Moore), a literary journal of the Ghanaian Writers Association in *Black Orpheus* no. 10, who underlines what such journals stood for at the time:

> The function of periodicals in nurturing the new literatures in Africa and the Caribbean cannot be overstated. They represent necessary documentary proof of fashion and growth. Their function is not so much to preserve as to link. Often they stand at the very beginning of the development of local literature, setting up standards and providing a literary market for buyer and seller – the indigenous reading public and its artist. (1986, 19)

To a large degree, such new periodicals would have to seek a motivation, which Benson, quoting Uli Beier, the founding editor of *Black Orpheus* characterises as 'inspiration' and 'discovery'. It is not by chance that Binyavanga Wainaina's short story that won him the Caine Prize for African Writing was titled *Discovering Home*. Indeed, it is this journey of discovery that uproots him from Cape Town and lands him back in Nairobi. Back in Nairobi, Binyavanga seems to 'discover' that local writing is 'not inspirational'; at least not to the extent that such writing could truly reflect Africa as well as compete for global recognition. Therefore, a journey of self-discovery becomes a journey of both a cultural literary and re-discovery and recovery.

But the adopted position of the need for recovery, the desire to (re)-imagine one's identity and that of his community is conditioned by the colonial and postcolonial histories, as Simatei, in discussing the contexts of literature in East Africa, highlights (2001, 9). Thus, the two texts that preface *Kwani?* 1 are both connected to the Rwandan genocide; quite clearly demonstrating how the burden of history could easily undermine or over-determine the project from creating something new and revolutionary as intended by the *Kwani?* founders. Yvonne Adhiambo Owuor's 'Weight of Whispers' and Mahmood Mamdani's 'A Brief History of Genocide', the pictorial 'Scenes from the Past', *Kalamashaka*'s (a ghetto hip-hop group) interview with Binyavanga Wainaina and Andia Kisia's 'A Likely Story', are all bound by history and in turn attempt to interrogate it...

Of the first five texts in the first issue of *Kwani?*, only *Weight of Whispers* is a creative story. Yet even Owuor's story has its foundations within a complex historical reality and discourse of Africa's troubled postcolonial politics and its consequences. The other texts are either academic commentaries or what *Kwani?* seems to have adopted as its distinguishing mark: creative non-fiction. This is writing that combines social commentary or reporting with elements of fiction-writing. The writer for *Kwani?* is therefore under no obligation to write pure fiction but is expected to at least produce a text that reflects (on) the society Beyond the creative non-fiction genre, the periodical's major innovation is the mixing of genres in its issues. All *Kwani?* issues are one challenge to literary orthodoxy. An issue of *Kwani?* is likely to have creative fiction, poetry, interviews, academic essays, photography, pictorial narratives, cartoons, extracts from blogs, auto/biographies, or investigative stories. The language could be formal English, Sheng or Swahili. The texts could be newly written or extracted from material recently published or from the archive. The journal defies, or projects itself as defying, any categorization as strictly literary. Primarily the magazine's editorial leave no doubt that the magazine is a literary publication focused on promoting a reading and writing culture. But it seems that its editors are also aware of how even what was previously a well-defined terrain such as literature is no longer clearly knowable or navigable; that scientific and technological innovations, travel of people, goods and ideas, or encounters between cultures have all significantly stretched the frames by which literature is produced and consumed. The editors, then, appear to be deliberately offering writers in *Kwani?* to exploit such possibilities to constantly destabilize the nature and meaning of literature

Based on a reading of its 'hydra-like character', one can speculate that it provides a wide range of possibilities for modern artists and cultural producers who seek to work in a mult-imedia environment. Thus *Kwani?* itself, like many other contemporary literary and art journals (such as *Granta, The St. Petersburg Review* or *Chimuranga*) presents itself as always pushing the limits of literary and artistic creativity with the intention to breach and broaden the boundaries of creativity. This approach may serve some of its interests well to appear as a member of a global family of artists but there is also the danger that it may also undermine its image as a quality literary artifact.

## POLITICS OF CULTURAL PRODUCTION AND DONOR-FUNDING AND THE QUESTION OF WHO CAN SPEAK FOR WHOM, ABOUT WHAT AND IN WHAT FORUM

A major claim of *Kwani?* is that it is an agent for literary and cultural change and transformation. Billy Kahora, the current editor, explains this position in the editorial to *Kwani?* 5 Parts 1 and 2:

> *Kwani?* has long been interested in politics rather than politicians; in human affairs not demagoguery. We are in this business to tell the individual's story as a citizen in the space called Kenya, his or her relationship to *serikali* or state or whatchamacallit (in Pokot, Kenya is the Other) rather than to build one-dimensional narratives from sound bites by Big Men. What is the relationship between Kenyans and government? That is a question we perpetually ask ourselves, especially in an election year. The last election was in 2002, when *Kwani?* was in its infancy. Another five years would be too long a wait. So I continued to wax lyrical in the workshops on the relationship between citizens and manifestations of power. How Kenyan men and women can relate to parliament, government and their MPs. And we were like almost everybody else, naïve and hopeful. (2008a, 9)

This claim to be more interested in 'politics rather than politicians' *Kwani?* is interested in has to do with power and authority. Somehow the revelatory nature of *Kwani?* undermines its earlier claim to be a forum for literary and cultural revolution. This is not to suggest that art and culture should be disinterested in politics but rather to emphasise the point that *Kwani?*'s earlier claim to a purely literary identity may have been weakened by the direction it took in some of its issues.

In the editorial cited above a lot is revealed about how art and cultural commodities may be adversely affected by the agenda of funding agencies. The last issue of *Kwani?*, and probably some earlier issues, was a 'workshopped' publication. The writers of many of the texts in the two issues had been sent out into the country to capture the political spectacle of the 2007 general elections. But the events following those elections forced a change of expectations from the *Kwani?* editorial team. The writers were therefore instructed again to draw upon the post-election conflict for their stories (2008a, 11).

The 'instruction' of and to writers is made possible through the mechanics of producing articles – a workshop structure in which writers are literally taught how to describe and the availability of resources to reward those who write. The fact that Kwani Trust is a Ford Foundation Grantee implies the possibility of some of its creative writing and publishing projects being driven by these particular ideological regimes. In other words, funds may be made available or withheld depending on particular donor funding priorities and demands. The obvious question that this donor-trustee relationship invites is: how independent or even creative can one claim to be if the benefactor is always likely to be instrumental in influencing the end products from the trustee? Is it possible that this control of such an initiative could result in more of an advertorial kind of writing that is generically agenda-setting than encouraging truly creative independence?

Of course, *Kwani?* is not the only literary/cultural/art project that is 'pre-determined ' by the donors. Given the paucity of government funding to sustain the arts and culture, consequently, this sector heavily relies on donor funding. The German cultural organization, Goethe-Institut, the Alliance Francaise, the Italian Cultural Centre, and other various European donors in Nairobi have a significant influence on the production and consumption of art and cultural products in the country. This reliance on external funding combined with the 'management' of the funded projects by donors raise doubts about the long-term viability of these projects as well as limit their creativity.

## CONCLUSION

The claim to breaking new grounds by being 'Africa's BEST Creative Writing' (on the cover page of issue 5 part 1) made by *Kwani?* will remain just a self-promoting advertorial for some foreseeable future for a number of reasons. Firstly, *Kwani?* is a young journal with just five volumes since its inception in 2003. As I have demonstrated in part, much of the content of the issues in circulation is a mix of different types of texts with little sustained creative writing, especially of fiction, for it to be judged by its readership or the broader literary and cultural community as a successful literary magazine.

Secondly, the regular contributors to *Kwani?* or the circle of writers whose work has been associated with *Kwani?* may yet be able to claim the same kind of corporate identity of the writers of the 1960s and 1970s. The literary creativity of those early post-colonial years was nurtured in the communal environments of the high school, college or university and thrived mainly in urban centres through the maintenance of the networks and an emergent protest fiction reading culture. However, most of the young writers in *Kwani?* who have been called "Generation X, were born between 1968 and 1982 and came of age as Kenya went through its single party shenanigans in the late 1980s, and in the 1990s with all the politico-economical and socio-cultural upheavals of the time" (2008a, 10) are fairly mobile, in many ways. For example, Binyavanga now lives in the United States of America. Parselelo Kantai whose work has appeared in some issues of *Kwani?* is an investigative journalist who now writes for foreign publications such as the *Africa Report*. Yvonne Owuor now works at the Agha Khan University in Nairobi. Many local contributors to *Kwani?* are not full-time writers with a number of them relying on other sources of income.

The seeming state of mobility that partially characterises the 'Kwani?' generation raises a third question: can this group of writers convincingly claim to be producing a new cultural economy as well as intellectual tradition? Is it possible that individuals whose writing is often more 'transnational' than national argue that they represent the local? Is it not that the globalised identities and belongingness of some of such individuals as Binyavanga, Doreen Baingana, Shailja Patel, Billy Kahora, Mukoma wa Ngugi, Steve Partington, among other many contributors suggest a complex dynamics that defies the logic of naming *Kwani?* as typically Kenyan? Is the desire to 'localize' *Kwani?* not likely to run counter to the expectations to reach and be read beyond the borders of Kenya, especially considering that the reception of *Kwani?* outside the country probably matters more than what local readers think of it. In a globalised world, a cosmopolitan identity is the core identity that defines many of the individuals who write for and in *Kwani?*, will, for sure, sit uncomfortably with the tendency to localize their identity. What these writers produce may be described as residing within the domain of 'the literary transnation' (Wilson et al, 2010, 5), which is made up of texts that defy borders, is both generic and geographical, rather than as merely localized Kenyan/African literature. To some degree *Kwani?* added a significant impetus to creative writing and publishing in Kenya. It probably revived the spirit of cross-border literary interaction and sharing that those earlier periodicals such as *Transition, Black Orpheus, Zuka, Drum*, or *Presence Africaine* inaugurated. The publication of works by local, regional, continental and even those in the diaspora suggested that the journal could re-inscribe Kenya onto the global literary and cultural scene by its enduring presence. The *Kwani?* public poetry performances, otherwise known as 'open-mic' sessions have added variety to the literary/cultural menu available in Nairobi, even though some sessions are held in restaurants – such the Kengeles in Lavington, one of the wealthy suburbs of Nairobi – beyond the reach of many Kenyans who would be interested in such activity.

But will *Kwani?* be able to shed the stereotyped image of Africa as a continent of disasters, violence, corruption or evil. That Binyavanga himself has had to write the ironic piece *How to Write about Africa* suggests that despite the attempts often to present the *Kwani?* project as transcending the discourses of cultural nationalism in the arts, which characterized the writing of the immediate post-independence era, an Africa writer is still generally circumscribed by his racial and ethnic identity, which is also the primary category that defines his/her art as well. Yvonne Owuor too muses about this intractable/unresolved African identity in most writing about Africa in the West (and other parts of the world) in a commentary "Contemporary Projections: Africa in the Literature of Atrocity (*Aftrocity*)" (2009). One wonders if *Kwani?* will not eventually succumb to the need to produce 'truly African stories' that are generally assumed to be characterized by poverty, violence, savagery, disease and death – if it has to retain its non-African audience which has been weaned on such a literary diet. The other risk is that the periodical could end up being accused of not being truly representative of Kenya/Africa should it continue to project itself as writing and translating beyond the nation.

Also, to what degree can *Kwani?* claim to have democratized the literary and cultural space in Kenya considering that most of the contributors to its five issues so far seem to be from the same circle of friends, mostly based in Nairobi or circulating globally? The sixth issue has been an exception as it received and published contributions from across Kenya and Africa. The claim to liberalizing the literary and cultural worlds in Kenya is probably an attempt by individuals, most of who reside beyond the boundaries of the defined intellectual circles in Kenya, to stake their claim as cultural producers of significance and (public) intellectuals as well.

Indeed, as Maurice Amutabi notes about intellectuals, artists and writers can be conceived of as generic or general intellectuals and therefore their works shape a society's behaviour (2007, 208). To be an intellectual or opinion-shaper may not be an identity that an artist or writer would consciously adopt or proclaim, but history may bequeath it to them. And as evident in the two issues of *Kwani?* 5, those who are actively involved in collecting and archiving the experiences of individuals and communities that suffered during the December 2007 post-election crisis will proclaim themselves as 'historians of the moment.' In this endeavour they will partially be attempting to do what Dan Ojwang' sees as determining "why 'Kenya' remains an elusive fiction" (2009, 37). Literary and cultural works often tend to provide the forum for the dissemination of the fictions of statehood, nationhood, identities and life in general. *Kwani?* can be read as a platform for new fictions of being Kenyan in the late 20th and early 21st century – fictions that celebrate the presumed 'freedoms' that came with the end of the Moi and KANU rule in Kenya. Indeed the sixth edition of *Kwani?* invited fiction and non-creative fiction from young Kenyan and African writers to write about the "Kenya I live In" or the "Africa I live In", on the one hand suggesting the diversity of experiences of the writers whilst at the same time seeking to produce some 'collective' Kenyan and African identity.

In conclusion, available evidence suggests that the *Kwani?* project, the periodical, the Kwanini series, the literary/news blogs, open-microphone poetry reading, writing workshops and literary festivals, have re-energised literary and cultural production in Kenya. But the claim to being revolutionary cannot be evaluated on the basis of the output so far because, for instance, the journal itself has not been released regularly enough and the focus on creative non-fiction undermines its literary identity, making it read more like any other popular magazine; its reliance on donor funding and its seeming bias towards urban and transnational identities could also hamper its claims to meet the need for localness and literary/cultural egalitarianism. In the meantime the rhetorical stance assumed in the title *Kwani?* remains an unanswered question, and may remain so for quite some time in the future.

## *Note*

1.  Taban resurrected this topic recently in "An Open Letter to Phillip Ochieng' from Taban lo Liyong." Ochieng is a Kenyan journalist who writes for the Nation Media Group. In the letter Taban decries what he calls 'the call to worship the god of mediocrity' and the apparent fallen status of literary studies. By publishing his misgivings about African literary output and scholarship on the *Kwani?* weblog Taban seems to be endorsing its status as a new literary force in Kenya and Africa. Refer to : http://kwanionline. blogspot.com/2009/11/circa-1969-death-of-english-department.html

# Chapter 3

## THE POPULAR PERIODICAL AND THE POLITICS OF KNOWLEDGE PRODUCTION: LOCATING *JAHAZI*

### Garnette Oluoch-Olunya

### INTRODUCTION

*Jahazi*,[1] a Journal of the Arts, Culture and Performance lays claim to an illustrious, and entangled literary heritage. Through a rereading of the significance of *Transition*, and gesturing to such literary precursors as *Présence Africaine*, this chapter demonstrates the tensions that persist within the power structures, the social hierarchies, and discursive platforms, both as a legacy of colonialism, and as carried within postcolonial formations. *Jahazi*, conceptually cushioned, selects as its focus the gap between the world of scholarship and the world of Art; the meeting point between the abstraction of ideas, and their enactment in daily life. A vessel plying the sometimes choppy waters in between the self-appointed Islands of performance, of the visual arts, and of the literary, it enables meetings, convening conversations that might not otherwise occur in spaces which although closely related, are yet quite rigidly demarcated, and policed. It itself carries a nefarious history in its manifold uses, one of which was the facilitation of the Arab trade in slaves on the Indian Ocean, and of course, immigration from the Indian subcontinent. In the first Issue, its aim is stated, in part, as 'to harness the wealth of artistic and cultural synergies that have emerged and continue to emerge from Kenya and the East African region for posterity...

to expand the parameters of artistic and cultural analysis...archiving and chronicling...'

By its third Issue, *Jahazi* had captured a rare instance of intra- and cross-cultural dialogue—but also dissonance—celebrating, and provoking reflection on some of the compelling issues that have characterized, and that continue to inform the Eastern African literary and intellectual landscape.

## A BRIEF CONTEXTUAL BACKGROUND

> Literary magazines in Africa are faced with burdens and responsibilities that their counterparts in other countries do not have to shoulder. On the one hand, they are meant to be alive, alert, gay, and (we hope) sometimes frivolous, casually and uninhibitedly recording the lyricisms and laments of their times. On the other hand, like the eldest son of a family where the father has suddenly died, they have to show maturity and responsibility. (Neogy, 21)

> Magazines are also like cultures: they are progressive, conservative, radical, puritanical, slowmoving, or vigorous. At their most aware, they reflect the qualities or weaknesses of their societies...But the Ultimate purpose of a Literary Magazine will always be to herald change, to forecast what new turn its culture and the society it represents are about to take. (Neogy, 18)

*Jahazi* can be read within the context of such journals that have preceded it as *Présence Africaine, Black Orpheus,*[2] or *Transition*. Indeed, it is as part of this tradition that it can be best appreciated, even as it sets its own agenda and deals with issues in its own time. This chapter reflects on the role and impact of these precursors, so as to establish the function of this medium in the unfolding of the intellectual tradition in East Africa.

We begin by looking briefly at *Présence Africaine*, arguably the first journal of its kind. It was established as bilingual in 1947, in Paris, by the respected Senegalese, Alioune Diop. It was also broad in scope, and a representative forum for political and cultural intellectual exchange across the diaspora. Its aims, which have only increased in relevance and resonance with the passage of time, were outlined by Kofi Awoonor to a symposium in Seattle in the mid 1970's. He emphasized the importance of language and literacy, nurtured by vibrant 'original and expandible ontological systems...that define man, his world, time, place, events.' He noted that 'the literature of the Diaspora does not begin with the written text,' (thus prefiguring the centrality of Oral forms), and stressed that much work addressing the complicity between culture, politics and the arts already existed autonomously, in indigenous languages.

*Présence Africaine* was, of course, established as a marginal forum for black writers, away from the *Pléiade*, 'one of the standards of admission into the privileged canon of French letters,' for which works from such places as Africa and the Caribbean, seen as *'connexes et marginals'*, as marginal dependencies, could only be "an exotic footnote to French literature" (Benson 1986, 19). The eminent poet/president, Leopold Senghor, assimilated across this barrier, best demonstrates the privileging of culture over politics for the French. Inducted into the *Academie Française* for his contribution to French language and syntax, it was said of Senghor that he "has become so much of a European...that he can criticize European culture from the inside" (Benson 1986, 26). Russel Warren Howe notes that "[a]fter World war II Paris embarked on a daring and innovative gambit. Rather than encourage the dangerous notion that Africans could govern themselves, the French would offer an African elite the opportunity to govern France" (2001, 39).[3] Whilst other African countries were, in Nkrumah's words, seeking first the political kingdom, Senegal, for economic reasons is said to have had independence thrust upon it by the French, to whom it remained but a *departement*, its leader a member of the French parliament.

Meanwhile, in 1956, at the Sorbonne, the World Congress of Black Writers was convened by *Présence Africaine*. It is here that Ulli Beier, of German/Jewish origin, then based in Nigeria where he had started *Black Orpheus*, and Jahnheinz Jahn, a German scholar keen on black art met, and impressed by the literary energy generated by *Présence Africaine*, determined to inspire the same in Anglophone West Africa. Undaunted by lack— "it was not widely conceded that Anglophone black Africa *had* any modern art or literature" (Benson 1986, 19)— *Black Orpheus* set about cultivating, and generating the same. Against charges of poor grasp of the English medium, mediocrity and lack of standards, Beier pressed on. A significant cohort of writers and artists nurtured here were to overlap into *Transition*.

*Transition* was to play a unique role, not only fostering and capturing philosophical and literary milestones as it set the stage and agenda for subsequent journals in the region, but also because of some of the compelling concerns its very presence provoked, in terms of agency and place, in the context of a racialised[4] East Africa just emerging from formal colonization. It is a misconception that freedom necessarily, even naturally follows colonial rule. Much as the very title, *Transition*, signals change, it suggests not the torsion but rather just such a gentlemanly shift, and compared to Kenya and Tanzania, whose histories are punctuated violently by Mau Mau, by Maji Maji, and Hehe, Uganda did appear to glide into independence. But beneath the tranquil surface lurked turmoil—the Asian question, soon 'settled' in 1972, but more importantly for Government, how to bring the Kingdom of Buganda, rudely sovereign, into concert with the rest of the new nation. Both these, sharp markers of separation and difference at the local and broader levels distinguish Uganda as a microcosm, portending what the jostling for space, both spatial and discursive would mean in the postcolony.

Neogy's engagement with the political was robust—even then president, Milton Obote was a self-confessed keen reader of *Transition*. In the absence of an official Opposition, Neogy routinely gave Government the right to respond to issues raised in the magazine, and it was on the back of two of these, one related to matters of the Constitution, and one to ethnic privileging (Africanisation of the judiciary had to be deferred because the only qualified applicants were Baganda), that Government engagement subsequently broke (Benson 1986, 180). Mahmood Mamdani speaks of the tensions attendant on relating to power as an intellectual, between relevance and independence, between critique and service (Vasquez 2000, 139-40). Neogy's detention, and his self-exile, on which we now reflect, exemplified just this tension. A graduate of the University of London (Makerere was set up a little later, for Africans), Neogy, a Bengali was seen by the majority of the Africans in Uganda as part of the oppressive class: the colonial class (Benson 1986, 104). In Uganda, a British protectorate, white presence was thin on the ground while the Asian, representing and controlling business, was visible, and seen to be oppressive. Neogy was one of the first casualties of what eventually hardened into policy in Idi Amin's time, to expel the Asian, with local support.[5] The British, on a dare to repatriate all Asians who were officially British, deferred the issue, underscoring what has come to be read in postcolonial studies as their in-between status. Neither belonging here, nor there. Referring back to Neogy's opening quotation on magazines, even as he demonstrates the coming of age of the magazine, his own agency is tainted: he is the 'illegitimate' son, what Paul Theroux has referred to as the stepson: enjoined, but removed *Transition's* influence was monumental. Theroux has said, 'It is hard to imagine a little magazine that was so generally influential on such a vast continent, but that is what happened with Transition. Rajat began his magazine at just the right time, and it became a rallying point throughout the 1960s. It helped that Rajat *was a local boy*, with Africa inside him *as well as the experience of a British university* (Theroux 1996, 4 emphasis added).

That he was *not* a local boy was soon to become apparent. And the huge influence that the high quality publication he started was to have is in no doubt. *Transition* was concerned with largely ideological issues located around the axis of the Cold War (1945-1989), but also the unresolved tensions of colonialism one of which, the Asian question, was to eventually lead to Neogy's own exile from Uganda. Meanwhile, Neogy asserted the discipline of the academy over his practice at *Transition*, courting established and emergent scholars and writers at Makerere and beyond. There was emerging a cultural elite at the time who could 'approach with equanimity the demands made by an intricate piece of poetry and the subtleties of unknotting the threads of political factionalism', and one with a broad range of intelligence, and interests. Theroux sees the moderation by a British University as crucial to the success of *Transition*; and for Neogy, his western training was the very preparation that enabled his conceptualization of a Literary magazine predicated on the availability of an elite audience. As he said, if *Transition* only performs the "one function of catering fully to the intellectual needs of Africa's new men, it will have justified its role in existing at this time, in this century, in what is almost certainly an era of cultural and spiritual renaissance".

Having at its inception posited the need for a magazine to be able to regenerate itself beyond its genesis (ibid., 21), Neogy was however said to have been extremely uncomfortable with the elitist and broad bent of the new *Transition*, and unhappy with its success. [6] Based at Harvard, at the W.E.B. Dubois Institute, it is subtitled *An International Review*. Indeed, its editorial board, chaired by the Nobel Laureate Wole Soyinka and boasting such well-respected names as Aimé Césaire, Toni Morrison, V Y Mudimbe, Stuart Hall, Dennis Brutus, Micere Mugo, Paulin Hountonji, and more, and edited by Kwame Appiah and Henry Loius Gates, Jr. might be enough to reassure any start-up editor that he had succeeded beyond measure. Neogy's discomfort might have been prompted by the memory that Wole Soyinka, who had served as guest editor in the Accra years instead of Neogy's choice, Kofi Awoonor, was also the one who gave up the funding from Ford. Painstakingly negotiated by Neogy, the loss of this support led to the folding up of that chapter of *Transition*. Awoonor had not stood a chance against Soyinka's "more fund-raising name" (Benson 1986, 237). But even more importantly, alienation from home was no doubt painfully underscored by the very unboundedness, the internationalness of his 'baby' as to colour any notions of its success elsewhere. As Paul Theroux notes in eulogizing him, "After he left Africa, he was not the same" (Theroux 1996, 7).

Through the years *Transition* has succeeded in reconstituting itself, charting out a remarkable trajectory that has secured its place as one of the most important voices even today. Its success in establishing a platform on which rigour and excellence could be achieved in addressing questions concerning culture, writing, the arts, and of course, politics is borne out by the fact that for *Jahazi*, this confluence is assumed. The most significant departure is in its relation to politics. Coming after 2002 when Kenya enjoyed unprecedented optimism and freedoms after the defeat of the despotic president Daniel arap Moi, and with the emergence of a watchful civil society, for *Jahazi* the new tension is rather that between the different practitioners of the arts themselves: between those in the more informal sector, largely self-taught, and practitioners in the formal institutions of learning, for the most part perceived by the former as elitist. And while Neogy was not based at the University but drew from it, *Jahazi* was deliberate in locating itself away from the Institution. Its reasons were two-fold. Even as the editor himself was suspicious of the prescriptive nature of such centres of power, well-known for conservatism and conformity and in Kenya shamelessly compromised by Moi,[7] the funder, Ford was intent on building innovative institutions away from just such strictures.[8]

*Jahazi* deliberately set out to seduce. Using an attractive format suggestive of the more popular publications, it draws from the idea in *Transition* of carrying graphic Images along with text. In terms of layout and choice of font, it set out to enjoin artist and scholar, with pieces set out in random counterpoint, and concert. In putting together the first Issue, scholars and artists were invited to an open forum so that there was interaction and discussion in a workshop. Some participants had been asked to prepare short presentations on their specific areas so as to open them out, and provoke thinking and discussion around ways in which cross-fertilisation might occur. The meeting brought out the urgent need for such dialogues, and confirmed the necessity for just such a forum for both demystifying and reinforcing knowledge production as *Jahazi* planned to provide.

## MONEY MATTERS

One of *Transitions* most enduring legacies is the focus it brought on the question of funding. It had failed to survive on advertising and it was in seeking support elsewhere that it faced its most significant test. It was discovered that, through the Farfield Foundation, it was supported by the CIA. For a self-proclaimed independent journal in the context of the Cold War, this in itself was suicide.

And yet the way in which these funds were made available epitomized the best in terms of intellectual networking and cross-fertilisation. Rajat Neogy had met Ezekiel Mphahlele in 1962, at the Conference for African writers of English expression, in Kampala, Uganda, to which I shall return. Mphahlele was based at the Chemchemi Institute in Nairobi. The Institute was a grantee of the Congress for Cultural Freedom, an organisation covertly linked with the CIA. When *Transition* ran out of money soon after this meeting, Neogy was offered some on Mphahlele's recommendation.[9] John Thompson, Executive Director of Farfield saw in Neogy someone who shared his aims to strengthen in Africa "multi-party democracy; freedom of speech; the predominance of intellectual over bureaucratic, political, military, and traditional tribal elites, and a continued cultural interchange with, *and allegiance to, the West*" (Benson 1986, 162 emphasis added). As Peter Benson notes, this Africa was considered "so backward and remote, and the amounts actually needed were so small" (ibid.), Thompson made his decision almost unilaterally. In the big scheme of things, *Transition*—"the singlemost important magazine on the continent" (Benson 1986, 171)—was small. It is arguable that Thompson, himself an academic, was also driven by "an idealistic belief in the universalism of art and literature if only it could be given free reign—in its ability to serve as the foundation for a cultural unity that would also perpetuate democratic institutions" (Benson 1986, 169). The underlying ideology here is, of course, assumed; and it is intrinsically good.

Benson's soft lens focus on the CIA suggests a benign concern where "political affiliation and ideology were not in question", the fear being that "political independence might bring instability; a cohesive intellectual elite might be a stabilizing force" (Ojwang 2009, 38). But thinkers can be problematic, as was one Patrice Lumumba of the Congo.[10] Even more telling was Neogy's own reaction once this link was established. "(T)he grubby money dispensed by the clean hands of the Congress for Cultural Freedom" is said to have been responsible for his near breakdown.[11] The Congress was generous, and had in its stable other such reputable journals as *Black Orpheus, Africa South, New African* and the British radical journal *Encounter,* although it has been argued that at least one of the editors of *Encounter* knew of, and courted this connection. It also supported such groups as the Mbari Writers Club in Nigeria (most popularly linked with Wole Soyinka), as well as acting as clearing-house for other foundations, such as Rockefeller, Carnegie, and according to Mary Stonor Saunders, Ford.[12] This whole covert type of operation stems from the infamous McCarthy years, when the US Government, purportedly fighting Communism, resorted to witch hunting 'subversives' and suffered such a serious loss of credibility it could not legitimately support anything, and subsequently its funds were filtered through such organisations as the CIA. It was on the back of the funding issue that the original *Transition* was first compromised, and then eventually collapsed.[13] It is imperative to remember that ideology then was everything. After the Cold War, new global political and economic imperatives in the apparently seamless, transparent bubble enabled by technology might suggest a radical shift in North/South relations.[14] Yet particularly today, with the triumph of Capitalism, the question of who holds the purse strings remains sensitive (although for Michael Vasquez, recently editor of the Harvard-based *Transition*, all money is good). The spectre of patronage and influence is nevertheless in constant tension with such notions of agency as independent thought, and action.

The 1962 Conference of Writers of English Expression held at Makerere is widely read as marking a watershed in the development of African literature. Most of the emergent writers in English at the time were there. What I want to emphasize here is the role that *Transition* played in establishing this contribution. Aspects of the meeting were reported in *Transition* 5, and subsequently read by Obiajunwa Wali, then a graduate student at Northwestern University in the US. In refocalising what we have come to refer to as the Language Question in his response in *Transition* 10, titled "The Dead end of African Literature", Wali highlighted a problem that remains fundamental to the writing of African literature today.[15] One can argue that such careers as Ngugi wa Thiong'o's (also in attendance) have been made on the back of just this question, debated at the conference, that Neogy credits with the birth of African literary criticism itself. He observed in 1963,

> Literary Criticism is a comparatively new phenomenon. It is a new discipline which is just beginning to grow. Its seeds

were planted at the writers conference at Makerere last year,
where, as any participant would agree, a critical toughness
and ruthlessness of a kind no writer had experienced publicly
before accompanied each discussion of his work (Quoted in
Theroux, 3).

What Neogy did with *Transition* cannot be replicated: his remains a
remarkable legacy, born out of unique circumstances.

It is into this impressive but by no means homogeneous palimpsest
that *Jahazi* inscribes itself. It is curious that even whilst gesturing back
to *Transition* as model, *Jahazi* was fully funded by Ford, maybe suggesting that the anxieties around money, as indicated by Vasquez, are
indeed different today. I now trace this relationship.

I want to suggest that the founding editor of *Jahazi*, Bantu Mwaura[16]
brought a singular quality to the two worlds he inhabited, that of Scholarship (for which he retained a critical suspicion), and arts practice so
that he was able to see clearly the ever widening gap between these two
worlds that ideally should be mutually reinforcing, and powerful.

He was distressed by two things: having come to the academy late
(he had first trained as a school teacher), and progressed through it in
a non-linear fashion, with enriching practical pauses in-between, he
found the Institution sadly closed in. And popular theatre, from whence
he came was loosely organized and haphazard in its approaches. It had
failed to establish itself as a viable life-, and self-sustaining discipline
in Kenya. In a fortuitous convergence, changes at the Ford Foundation
itself favoured the arts. Bantu had applied to Ford after a frustrating year
when no one would touch his 'ambiguous' venture. In 1999, a new portfolio, Media, Arts Culture was introduced. This segment had previously
been under the Human Rights and Social Justice Portfolio, where its role
was to disseminate advocacy messages to support the Human Rights
Agenda. Now, with a budget of two and a half million dollars, and under
the umbrella of Alison Bernstein in New York, whose own, broad portfolio, 'Knowledge, Creativity, Freedom' underwrote its agenda, a new
period began. Where other funders were traditionally cautious of taking
risks, under the new portfolio, Ford was able to take big risks, and could
work with areas others were afraid to touch, what Rob Burnet, the first
program Officer to hold the Media, Arts and Culture docket at the time
terms 'the lunatic fringe'.[17] The endowment fund had grown, Ford identified a gap, and in 1999 moved into Nairobi, into Cairo, and into Lagos
with this program (South Africa has an active National Arts Council, so
Fords role here was not as muscular.) As with its previous support of the

Human Rights agenda, (and the arts in the sixties) there was the underlying assumption that the Arts and Creativity are linked to Democracy, and must strengthen democratic values. This is as far as it went in stating an overtly political agenda. And just like the other portfolios were charged with the building of Institutions, rather than giving grants to individuals, the Arts were to be no different. A few exceptions were made, however, in relation to building individual capacity where needed. Two notable individuals who received such support were Gichora Mwangi, himself a theatre man and scholar, and Bantu.

Driven by the desire for a 'good quality, original Kenyan script', and wanting "none of this British farce rubbish" (Salmon, 2003) which was the staple in theatres like the Phoenix in Nairobi, Gichora started the Karamu trust in 2003 with a grant of US$175,000 from the Ford Foundation. It set out "to support the development of vibrant playwriting in Kenya and East Africa by providing writers with a forum and to help muster any resources that will be of benefit to all writers".[18] Bantu was partially supported towards the completion of a PhD in Performance Studies at the New York University through a small Ford grant administered by Twaweza. He was at the same time determined to start an interdisciplinary journal that would bridge the rifts that had occurred between the different types of practitioners in areas of arts and culture, all the time engaging these two sectors on a shared, well-articulated platform, in both English and Kiswahili. It would capture and record, in whatever form the artefact might present itself, and then through editorial or whatever necessary interventions, create a platform as well as an archive.

It is in this context that *Jahazi* was funded, under Twaweza Communications, whose Director, Kimani Njogu shared this passion for interaction and dialogue across and outwith the disciplines. Burnet is arguably instrumental, with others at Ford and more generally in Nairobi, in underwriting much of the cultural revival we are enjoying in East Africa today. Himself for years an artist and arts administrator (he played the Harmonica in a Rock band), he had founded Kuona, an arts trust, which subsequently served as a kind of blueprint for growing the sector by keeping the door open to artists, and creating structures that enabled mobility. Twaweza Communications organized the first Linkages workshop. Here, artists and scholars thrashed out the cultural, and leadership agenda, to come up with the Art, Culture and Society series, which has so far published three books, and four journals. The books are *Cultural Production and Social Change in Kenya: Building Bridges*; *Culture, Performance and Identity: Paths of Communication in*

*Kenya*, and *Getting Heard: (Re)claiming Performance Space in Kenya*. The journal, *Jahazi* has tackled three similar themes. The next Issue, on 'Knowledge, Culture and Memory' is a commemoration, of Bantu Mwaura, and of E.S. Atieno Odhiambo, eminent Professor of History at Rice University in the US, who both died in 2009.

## 'IN THE PICTURE'

Both africanists and African scholars have condemned the execrable representations which the media deploy to reduce a landmass ten times the size of Europe into a veritable unknowable (Enzewor 2006, 12).

The postcolonial paradigm in Africa, more than being a historical and temporal gauge by which to acquaint ourselves with political and social transformation, perhaps indicates something else: the rupture in decolonized subjectivity and how the national cultural discourse that emerged from decolonization continues to plague the conception of a singular cultural identity. In this sense, the postcolonial helps us to imagine, and to negotiate the cultural plurality of the continent and the inherent multiplicity of African identities (Enzewor 2006, 23).

There has been an upsurge of interest in the visual medium, with a renewed focus on Photography as a form of representation. In Nairobi alone within the past year are numerous examples. *Kwani* Trust launched two projects in 2008, GenerationKenya: Self-Narrative through Photography' featured in *Jahazi*3, and dedicated to reflecting on, and archiving post-colonial social production to mark Kenya's 50th anniversary in 2013; the second, 'Nairobi 24', a 24 hour pictorial of Nairobi exhibited at the National Museum, additionally featuring 3D animation by Just a Band, and now the book *24 Nairobi* (2011). In the same period, *Awaaz Voices* 3 (Nov-Feb 2008-09) was dedicated to 'Photos and Photographic Memories: The old photographic studios; reliving an era'. It twinned with a photographic exhibition that launched at the Samosa Festival (Asian and African Cultural Festival) that ran from the 15-30th of November, 2008. And there are others, like 'Pigapicha' at the Goethe Institute, the Godown Art Centre's 'Kenya Burning' Exhibition, and book, at once controversial, and necessary, yet somehow escaping the police wrath visited on a similar photographic exhibition, 'Picha Mtaani', also on post election violence in February 2010 in Nakuru. 'Picha Mtaani', facilitated by the United Nations Development Program (UNDP) as a peace-building initiative, was different from 'Kenya Burning' only in that while it used the open street as exhibition space, Kenya Burning utilized contained space, which is much easier to control. While the controversies over the graphic portrayal of the violence that engulfed Kenya continue to rage, with audiences at 'Picha Mtaani' insisting that 'that thing' be taken off the street, I will step back briefly, and contextualise the drama.

Traditionally, the controversy has been of a different kind. According to Okwui Enzewor in *Snap Judgments: New Positions in Contemporary African Photography*, "no other cultural landscape has had a more problematic association with the photographic medium: its apparatus, various industries, orders of knowledge, and hierarchies of power" (Enzewor 2006, 13). He notes the persistence of this fractured vision of an Africa ten times the size of Europe (2006, 12-3). The idea is that of inscrutable Africa, unknowable Africa, mythic Africa. When Africa is as it were 'in the picture', Enzewor reads the primitivising capacity of the Peter Beard type of photography of Kenya, for instance, kicking in, as "graceful and unpredictable animals and Africans are commingled in a disjointed colonial fantasy". This troubling imagery is the stuff of glossy coffee table books, which take up whole sections of bookshops, both local and elsewhere, at once combining "pastiches of wild edenic Africa and the cultivated languor of settler lifestyle..." Indeed, "from the earliest recorded history of the photographic encounter Africa has made for a fascinating and elusive subject, at once strange, intoxicating, carnal, primitive, wild, luminous" (ibid.).[19]

Above, we visit the same visual violence on ourselves, and allow it to be reinforced by others.[20] This kind of voyeuristic gaze on the grotesque is an extremity, twin of the fawning over grace. *Jahazi* operates in this fractured terrain. In its third Issue it carried the remarkable pictures of the arts event hosted by Kuki Gallman in Laikipia, where an admixture of local and international artists converged to celebrate Aqva, a conservation event. Held in the wake of the election violence, some of the artists defied travel advisories from their governments to come and support Kenyan artists, and Kenya. Showcased in a 'coffeetable' *Jahazi*, how does one read such an event, within a former settler Colony that has a sizeable settler community still, and one struggling with the residual colonial legacy. Already read as an Expatriate writer in literary classification (she has written *I Dreamed of Africa,* itself turned into a successful film featuring Kim Basinger with Vincent Perez), do we collapse organizer Kuki Gallman, this late Italian (not British) immigrant, into the context of Peter Beard, above? And yet

> The idea that race is socially constructed implies that it can and must be constructed differently in different historical moments and in different social contexts. And one of the implications of taking seriously this historicity of race—that

> there are historically specific "racisms" and not one singular
> ahistorical racism—is the analytic necessity of exploring how
> racial phenomena articulate with other social phenomena.
> (Holt cited in Garuba 2008, 1644).

This appreciation of the nuanced nature of relationships is imperative in a space like Kenya, where it is easier to generalise rather than to
problematise. Neogy's painful example serves to remind us that these
are just some of the tough questions, most concerning belonging, that
we must raise as we constitute our landscape, as we determine the elements we claim as moulding our tradition.

I recall bumping into an elated Bantu at the Zanzibar film Festival (ZIFF) in 2006 soon after he interviewed Melvin Van Peebles, who
was celebrated Chief Guest and recipient of the Lifetime Achievement
award that year, for the first Issue of *Jahazi*. It resonated with him that
this Godfather of Independent American Film, here generously sharing
his skills had learnt his craft 'on the job'. One of the things *Jahazi* hopes
to achieve by facilitating dialogues through cross-fertilisation is, indeed,
to provoke curiousity across fences, precipitating interaction such that
film, for instance, speaking to the written word recognizes the imperative of telling a good story even as they draw on whatever singular techniques in their area.[21]

In the same Issue *Jahazi* carried the work of the Kenyan sculp-
tor Gakunju Kaigwa, not as well-known outside art circles in Kenya
perhaps, but whose award winning piece 'Dog Walking Man' tapped
neatly into the cultural seam of Scottish society, and was mounted in
the town square in Dundee, Scotland. The second featured cartoons by
the redoubtable East African cartoonists Maddo (Paul Kilemba), Gado
(Godfrey Mwampembwa), and Frank Odoi. The third issue carries photographs from the Earth Festival. Featuring Water, *Aqva*, it is organized
by the writer and environmentalist, Kuki, and her daughter Sveva Gall-
mann at the Laikipia Nature Conservancy in Kenya. I refer to this above.
It also carries the accomplished work of Magdalene Odundo, Kenya's
finest ceramicist, who lives and works in the United Kingdom. These
different forms demonstrate a fascinating heterogeneity, each speaking
to the reader in its own language, on its own terms, and yet interfacing
with the rest of the Journal as testament to a creativity, the depths of
which are as yet untapped. As Enzewor reminds us,

> Because contemporary African art is varied and sometimes
> contradicts even the most stable indicators of its means and

aesthetic distinctiveness, attempts to circumscribe the art of
the continent inevitably run up against its dispersed practices
and references, its formal and aesthetic concerns, its conceptual and historic address. (2006, 23)

Does the appeal to cultural diversity disguise the reluctance for
social change? Are pre-existing hierarchies being maintained under
this pretext? (Huggan 2001, 27). Against a broad diaspora, it is the
case that in establishing our intellectual traditions, we are hostage to
an impressive bricolage. *Présence Africaine* serves as a case in point,
to help us reflect on our entanglements, which further serve to embed
us with every gesture. From the devolved centre, Paris, Alioune Diop
started a revolution that has inspired against, as much as it has demonstrated the binding power of the colonial project. Under one of its
guises, boldly labeled Assimilation by the French, Martiniquéan Aimé
Cesaire released the first salvo, *Retour au Pays Natal*, first published
in the French periodical *Volontes* in 1939, and Négritude was born.
*Présence Africaine* notably published the first translation into English in
1968. A lifetime later, quite literally (he died at 94, in 2008), Césaire now
on the editorial board of a reconstituted *Transition* housed at Harvard
was given a state burial by France over five decades after the event that
inspired freedom fighters of the stature of Frantz Fanon. Even as we celebrate the seismic shifts that have occurred in the ways in which we do
knowledge production, right from conceptual approaches, in our interrogation and apprehension of epistemologies, and paradigms, the contexts out of which we shape and frame have a notable effect on outcome.
Nevertheless, the magazine/journal has lived up to its purpose, in many
cases responding to political processes and signaling renaissance in the
arts, and in culture.

## Notes

1. *Jahazi* is Kiswahili for 'Dhow'.
2. Ulli Beier & Jahnheinz Jahn, 1957-1967. There have been several attempts
   to revive it.
3. Compare the recent State funeral of Aimé Césaire, pioneer of *Négritude*,
   whose *Retour au Pays Natal* inspired many anti-colonial movements. He
   served Martinique, a *Departement* of France, until his retirement in 1993,
   and was buried with full honours, by Nicholas Sarkozy, the French president, in 2008. In Partington, 'Poetry and Pride', 64–66.
4. For a thoughtful discussion on the contexts of race and how race functions
   in modernity see Garuba, 'Race in Africa', 1643–1648.

5.  Vasquez, "Hearts in Exile",, 135. Mamdani was alarmed on his return to Uganda in 1986, that local people did not regret Amin's action, and instead thought it justified.

6.  Okello Ogwang of Makerere University made this observation at the "East African Literary & Intellectual Landscapes: Rethinking Eastern African Cultural and Intellectual trans/national legacies through History" Conference, University of the Witwatersrand, Johannesburg, 23-24 October, 2009.

7.  On the beleaguered role of the University, see Ojwang, "Kenyan Intellectuals", 22-38.

8.  In an Interview with Rob Burnet, 10 February, 2010.

9.  Ntongela Masilela reads Mphahlele as coming from an already established tradition, the Sophiatown renaissance where he was the Literary editor of *Drum*. According to Masilela 'one of Mphahlele's incontestable merits within the Sophiatown Renaissance was to draw or trace the complex map of black intellectual heritage in the 20th Century in which the Drum Literary School could find sustenance.../to establish the lineages of Black international culture in the 20th Century as a systemic process.' Masilela, 'Black South African Literature', Lecture.

10. In information declassified in 2000 American President Dwight Eisenhower quite directly ordered the CIA to 'eliminate' the problematic Patrice Lumumba. This evidence was uncovered in the investigation into the assassination of JF Kennedy.

11. Dan Ojwang's observation that the more overt links in this age of democracy and Human rights are any less damaging for their being obvious does not reckon with the sinister intent, and indeed, action in that period. (see n.28).

12. In Saunders, *Who Paid the Piper*, 1999. See also Wilford, *The Mighty Wurlitzer*, 2008. Its analysis is, however, not as crisp.

13. Soyinka stayed with it for ten years, leaving in 1973 having seen the last issue transition to Ch'Indaba.

14. The President of the United States, Barack Obama, whose father was Kenyan further complicates a myopic viewpoint.

15. Achebe insists that one can write in whatever language they chose.

16. Bantu Mwaura, a Kenyan scholar and theatre man (subsequently referred to as Bantu), with Kimani Njogu, professor of Kiswahili and founder of Twaweza Communications came up with the initiative for *Jahazi*, as a platform for dialogue between scholars and arts practitioners.

17. In an interview with the writer in Nairobi on 4 February, 2010.

18. Allen, 'Dr Gichora Mwangi', 2004. http:/www.playbill.com/news/article/88807, accessed on 10 February, 2010; INTERNET.

19. Ibid., 12-13. The most successful film this season, for instance, James Cameron's *Avatar* (2009), combines just these qualities in its depiction of the

mythic foil to the North American invaders to Pandora, figured as Africa. The hero, a disabled American marine, severally called 'moron' by his own easily triumphs over the superior Na'vi.

20. Boniface Mwangi has photographs in both exhibitions. There are other photographers, however.

21. Just as the very techniques of making 'film', such as the shift to Digital modes, are evolving, so also has the way in which scripts are written.

# Chapter 4

# INTERVENTION THEATRE TRADITIONS IN EAST AFRICA AND THE PARADOX OF PATRONAGE

*Christopher Joseph Odhiambo*

## INTRODUCTION: PATRONAGE AND ART

The Literature available on art history, (Bauman 1990; Gombrich 1996; Hollingsworth 1994, 1996; Kempers 1992; and Kent and Simons 1987) explicitly reveals that the relationship between the arts and patronage (here referring to those who consume works of art as well as various supports that are extended to artists by the public and private institutions) has always been symbiotic. A number of these studies indicate strongly that patronage of the arts can be traced back to royal or imperial systems or aristocracies which controlled a significant share of resource.[1] Indeed, rulers and the very affluent in such socio-political systems have been known to use patronage of the arts to endorse, promote and even legitimize their political ambitions, social positions, and prestige (Foss 1971; Kemper 1992; Verschoor 2009). Literature also shows that it was only with the emergence of capitalist modernity in the 19th century that European culture moved away from its elitist patronage system to the more publicly-supported system of museums, theatres, mass audiences and mass consumption that we are familiar with in the contemporary art world.

The term *patronage* used in this chapter comes from the *Longman Dictionary of Contemporary English* where it is defined as the support given by a patron and where a patron is a person or a group that supports and gives money to an organization or activity that is regarded as valuable or deserving support. With regard to intervention theatre, patronage refers simply to the direct support (often financial) extended to an artist-facilitator or a team of artists-facilitators to create a work of theatre expected to transform the consciousness of a target community or a specific category of people in society. On the other hand, *intervention theatre*,[2] in the context of this chapter, refers to those kinds of theatre practice such as theatre for development, theatre of the oppressor, liberation theatre, among others. The purpose of intervention theatre is to deliberately catalyze change and transformation on target communities; raising consciousness and conscientization in communities perceived as vulnerable.

Although this discussion is about the traditions of intervention theatre in East Africa and the paradoxes of patronage, it is perhaps imperative at this point to demonstrate how patronage has intersected with art in Africa. In *Sundiata: An Epic of Old Mali* (1960), D. T. Niane, for instance, implies that unlike today, the griot was then under the patronage of the King when Niane proclaims that:

> If today the griot is reduced to turning his musical art to account or even to working with his hands in order to live, it was not always so in ancient Africa. Formerly 'griots' were the counsellors of kings, they conserved the constitutions of kingdoms by memory work alone; each princely family had its griot that kings used to choose the tutors for young princes. (Niane 1960, viii)

David Kerr (1995, 12) also acknowledges the symbiotic relationship that exists between wealthy patronage of the ruling class and the arts. Drawing examples from performances of *Alarinjo* and *Egugun,* he describes how this relationship became symbiotic and manifested itself in pre-colonial traditional society. Drawing from the research work of Adedeji on the form of professional Yoruba theatre , Kerr (1995) records that *Alarinjo* started in Oyo court of Alaafin Ogbolu in about 1590, thus in terms of origin, the *Alarinjo* was a courtly entertainment under the patronage of the Alaafin. An interestingly symbolic patronage, according to Wole Soyinka, exists between artists and the Yoruba god of creativity, Ogun. He describes this metaphysical relationship in the following terms:

> The shard of original Oneness which contained the creative flint appears to have passed into the being of Ogun, who

manifests a temperament for artistic creativity matched by technological proficiency. His world is the world of craft, song and poetry. The practitioners of *Ijala,* the supreme lyrical form of Yoruba poetic art, are followers of Ogun the hunter. (Soyinka 1976, 28)

Rose Mbowa echoes this view in her accentuation of Luganda theatre and its audience by drawing an example from a popular royal song: *Ffe basajia ba Kabaka/ffe tumulya mu ngalo* (we are the Kabaka's men, we eat from his hand), argues that there has always been an established system of patronage between performing artists and royalty in the traditional Baganda Kingdom (1999, 229). Robert Serumaga (1974) poignantly captures what happens to the traditional artist when the patronage with the royal/chief's court ceases. The consequences become tragic for the traditional artist. For example, in the play *Majangwa,* Serumaga dramatizes how modernity destroyed the traditional socio-economic and political infrastructures that ensured the survival of the artist through patronage. The following conversation between Nakirijja and Majangwa, the traditional artists, captures this shift quite aptly:

Majangwa: It's a good road. It can't stay empty for too long. I've been on it before. Long before I met you, I was on it. Travelling. A young man and his drum playing at weddings across the country, at chiefs' parties. A good drum and fingers to go with it. (gets his drum) Mellowed over the years.

> Nakirijja: Years of nothing.
> Majangwa: It wasn't always like this. You forget. I wasn't always like this.
> Nakirijjja: Nothing. With a future we can't see and a past we would sooner forget.
> Majangwa: Forget? How can I forget the road? Majangwa, yes, that's me. (pause) I remember them, admirers; lovers of the drum and the lyre and the fiddle. There was the honour at the chief's court. (Emphasis mine) We gathered to make songs and meanings and connect our souls to the earth. You could hear the dead whisper above the sound of drums and in the voice of the man with the fiddle. Sekinoomu, Temutewo Mukasa, Namale. Honour at the chief's court... Those were the times when a man knew if he planted a seed in the ground, it would grow.
> Majangwa: A plant, and then seeds. Yes, you were there at the wedding as I played. Majangwa the great! Later I meant to retreat to my room. Hot water for my limbs, chicken in

> banana leaves, and a dancer or two dancers carrying echoes
> of drums into the night (Serumaga 1974, 24-5)

Majangwa recalls nostalgically the honour of the performing artist as a result of the chief's patronage. However, this honour/relationship is obliterated with the emergence of the capitalist modernity which reduces the performing artist to a pauper. Capitalist modernity coerces the artist to sacrifice his artistic aesthetics to satisfy the base instincts of his new patrons. He must now perform according to the whims and perverted tastes of patrons influenced by the consumption of modern art, especially pornographic cinema. The dialogue, once again, of the two traditional artists vividly witness this new patronage that denies the artist his honour and dignity.

Nakirijjja: Does it make it grow? I see that I knew it would happen. When I think back, I see that I knew. And I told you: don't give in to the crowds. Don't pander to the whims. Stick to the drum I said, and I to the dance. But no. You had to start. Plays you called them, funny words and actions. In between the songs, you talked and played with me. It was alright at the beginning, but the crowds taunted us and asked for one more inch. Then your embraces became kisses, in public, till even these could not satisfy the devil in the audiences. Your speech was gone, together with the drum and song. After that it was only a matter of time before I had my back to the pavement.

> Majangwa: It wasn't as simple as that, was it? You simplify
> things.
> Nakirijja: What's the difference?
> Majangwa: Times were hard. What about that, eh? Don't
> you remember I was proud, and honest and talented, and I
> carried my drum?
> (Serumaga1974, 30-1)

This dialogue between Nakirijjja and Majangwa is a metaphor to some extent of the patronage relationship in the contemporary post-colonial Africa between intervention theatre practitioners and the donors. As Lenin Ogolla (1997), one of the foremost post- Kamiriithu interventions theatre practitioners reminds us that:

Often the donors have their own agenda and the artist/educator finds himself completely limited in terms of how much he is really able to do. And any theatre that places the donor at the centre and not the people is simply beautiful propaganda...

> True enough, the donor and the NGO's are the major active players in facilitating development to the people. And granted, no artist has the capacity to implement and manage long term projects without co-operating with the donor. Yet the donor should be more discerning, the artist more honest if this partnership is to make meaning in the people's lives... (1997, 27)

The issues that Ogolla points out are echoed by Vicensia Shule (2008), Viv Gardner (2005), are elaborated on later in this chapter. Similarly, Osita Okagbu (cited in John Tiku Takem 2005, 165) also closely resonating Ogolla's when he reminds us that:

> One of the key problems confronting Theatre for Development programmes and projects seems to be the often inevitable but usually problematic alliance between Theatre for Development practitioners on the one hand and government and non-governmental organizations on the other. The problem is almost always one of funding and very often it is a relationship that becomes reduced to the cynicism and impotence of the proverbial 'He who pays the piper calls the tune; a situation in which the theatre project is expected to be the mouthpiece or a medium for government or the funding agency's propaganda.

From Okagbu's concern, it can be deduced that patronage compromises the efficacy of intervention theatre practitioners quite considerably. Yet, funding to put on the threatre is needed hence there is a paradox.

Among the Luos of Kenya, patronage for the arts has always exhibited itself in various economic, political and socio-cultural activities. For instance, traditionally, the *nyatiti* player, that used an eight-stringed instrument, that archetypal troubadour, in a traditional set-up, traveled to perform in different places and functions where he was generally well taken care of by the homestead that hosted the particular activity. More importantly, the patrons who, for instance, wanted to be mentioned in his lyrics used a tradition of *pakruok* (praise) which meant giving offerings as an emolument for the nyatiti player and his coterie of performers.[3] In this tradition of patronage, the patrons support the musician indirectly through the tradition of *pakruok*. At other times, a patron can stop the music by giving some amount of money and the music can only continue when another patron offers more money. All this money goes to the musician. This tradition of patronage is still in vogue even among the contemporary musicians in Kenya.

The continuation of this tradition in the contemporary Luo music scene is exemplified by the following song by one of the most popular Ohangla music performers Jack Nyadundo. In the song 'Obama" in which he sings in praise of United States of America's President Barrack Obama, Nyadundo mentions a number of patrons who have assisted him in many ways. For instance, he mentions a prominent lawyer in Kisumu Olago Aluoch whose generosity he highlights by announcing how this Kisumu based lawyer has helped him while he (musician) is still alive. He praises the lawyer for offering him a ride in his car when he was traveling to his home in Kisumu. He claims that through Olago's patronage he has had opportunity to relish the kinds of food he had never tasted before, drunk so much beer than ever before as well as seduced the most beautiful women than he had ever imagined he could. He also praises another patron, Ogweno Ajosi, whom he praises for having bought him an air ticket to travel to Europe, the land of white people, where he played his music to white patrons. The song actually becomes a profile of patrons who have supported his music career by consistently attending his performances.

## BER PINY: INTERVENTION THEATRE AND CONTRADICTIONS OF PATRONAGE

From the foregoing discussion it is evident that patronage and performance art are compatible bedfellows. But this compatibility becomes problematic and complicated in the realm of intervention theatre. Intervention theatre is a theatre practice that became extremely popular in the third world countries especially in this era of the HIV-AIDS pandemic. But of course, it needs to be acknowledged that all works of art to some extent do participate, either consciously or unconsciously in intervention. This role of intervention in art is well articulated by Okot p' Bitek when he argues convincingly that:

> The artist uses his voice, he sings his laws to the accompaniment of the nanga, the harp; he twists his body to the rhythm of the drums, to proclaim his rules. He carves his moral standards on wood and stone, and paints his colourful 'dos and donts' on walls. And canvas. In these and other ways, the artist expresses the joys and sorrows of the people. What is joy? What is sorrow? These questions are meaningless if the philosophy of life as created and celebrated in art, is not clear. What is happineness? What is sadness? Surely, these ques-

tions do not make sense unless the human situation is what it
should be. *Ber piny.* (1986, 40)

It is through the works of two Brazilians, the liberation pedagogue,
Paulo Freire and the 'theatre of the oppressed' connoisseur Augusto
Boal that p'Bitek's philosophy of art in facilitating *ber piny* has gained
currency among practitioners of intervention theatre. It is this theatre
that seeks to intervene in transforming the world into a better place
for mankind by drawing our attention to the ways that intersection
between art and patronage becomes paradoxically complex. Intervention theatre tradition has a long history especially in Africa, as p'Bitek
and Ngugi wa Thiong'o have always reminded us: "art always played
an intervention role."[4] Among the Luo of Western Kenya, there is this
axiomatic expression, *Iming' ka manene ok onindo e siwindhe* (You are
uneducated, like one who never slept in *siwindhe*[5]) lucidly summarizes
the intervention nature of the performance arts. This is because, ideally,
in the traditional Luo society stories are performed in *siwindhe*, and the
narrations are instructively supposed to intervene in the socialization
of the young people in the society. As such narratives and other related
genres are morally committed and didactic in their messaging. Indeed
this explains why the elderly persons in the community provide the necessary patronage for these performances (Ogutu and Roscoe 1994). For
Soyinka, the performances associated with mimetic rites of *Ogun* also
constitute this sense of intervention. He notes about these dramas of
gods thus:

> The points which concern us here are (1) the recognition of
> the integral nature of poetry and dancing in the mimetic rite,
> and (2) the withdrawal of individual into an inner world from
> which he returns, communicating a new strength of action...
> The community emerges from ritual experience 'charged
> with new strength for action' because of the protagonist's
> Promethean raid on the durable resources of the transitional
> realm; immersed within it, he is enabled empathically to
> transmit its essence to the choric participants of the rites-
> the community. Nor would we consider that such a commu-
> nicant withdraws from conscious reality, but rather that his
> consciousness is stretched to embrace another and primal
> reality. The communicant can effect on the audience which
> is the choric vessel and earthing mechanism for the venturer
> is not a regression into 'the subconscious world of fantasy'.
> (Soyinka 1976, 33)

This ritual performance is characteristically akin to intervention theatre, in Soyinka's interpretation, effects transformation in the participants as it sharpens their consciousness and as such transports them beyond mere fantasy. Kerr also reveals the existence of intervention theatre in pre-colonial Africa (1995, 3). Making reference to the work of James Brink who studied the *Kote-tlon* theatre of the Bamana people of Mali, Kerr outlines the intervention traits of this theatre. He notes that *Kote-tlon*, improvised young men's comedies, are frequently moralized performances on techniques of agricultural production used to ridicule/parody the anti-social elements in the community. In fact, the most common target in the Bamana plays is the wicked or lazy millet farmers.

Although the relationship between intervention performances and patronage in pre-colonial Africa appears to be unproblematic, Kerr accentuates instances where patronage conspired to manipulate and control the performance arts (1995, 12-4). He points out in particular the case of the *Egungun* cult leaders who attempted to keep some control over the *Alarinjo* professional offshoots, but the *Alarinjo* performers showed their independence by satirizing some of the solemnities of the cult.

In fact, the intrigues playing out between the various inflections of intervention theatre and patronage become more complex in the colonial and post-colonial periods. This is more so because a clearly defined form and practice of intervention theatre emerged during the colonial period. This was through the patronage of the colonial system of administration. This nascent practice of intervention theatre would later be popularly referred to as 'theatre for development' (TfD). What is of interest here, is the way that colonial patronage would deliberately determine how this intervention theatre was framed and deployed to relay messages to their subjects. Researchers and scholars of this theatre tradition such as Chris Kamlongera, A.K.Pickering and W.H. Taylor have noted that this theatre actually manifested itself in some parts of East Africa as early as the 1930s and that it was intended to convey messages specifically targeting literacy, agriculture, health and sanitation. Kerr notes that during the colonial period, intervention theatre tended to be ambivalent especially in the British colonies because it was meant, for instance, to create a class that would participate in the modernization of the colonial economy but not create political consciousness amongst the colonized populations to critically challenge the colonial hegemony (1995, 31-2). For example, in Kenya, an agricultural campaign during the 1930s was supported by dramatized versions of indigenous folk-tales. One of the observers, W.H. Taylor, enthused over the way drama could support the work of the Jeans schools of proselytizing such ideas as 'Better Homes', Healthier Children and 'Better Gardens and Plantations' among the pagan population'. From Taylor's observation, it is apparent that the colonial administration as the patron of this kind of theatre was very cautious in the way that the transformation in the colonized persons was to be undertaken. The framing of this rudimentary form of intervention theatre was deliberately meant to ensure that the colonial hegemonic ideology was insulated from any subversion or challenge. As Kerr rightly argues:

> In a colonial context, however, this transformation was not one of a radically progressive kind; the relationships between the agencies of social change and the African peasantry were vitiated by the exploitative relations inherent in the colonial system… 'Their messages emerged not from a genuine popular viewpoint but were imposed by an alien force, one that took from the masses effective instruments of knowledge.' The peasants did not participate in the campaigns, they were the passive objects of a communication system designed to make them conform to strategies pre-planned by remote and administrators. (1995, 32-3)

From the above quote, it is obvious that the patronage by the colonial structures to the intervention theatre provided subtly determined its framing in respect to both the material content, performance aesthetics as well as to the ideology that it circulated.

This relationship between patronage and intervention theatre in East Africa indeed became more explicit in the period after independence. This begins with the Universities free traveling theatre tradition that found its genesis at the Makerere University in Uganda then spread to Dar-es-Salaam University in Tanzania and University of Nairobi in Kenya, The literature on this intervention theatre movement tradition indicates that its patrons were mainly expatriate English teachers who were brought up on classical Western theatre traditions (Mlama 1995; Kerr 1995; Ngugi 1981). According to Kerr, the Makerere Free Travelling Theatre was initiated by two expatriates, David Cook and Betty Baker (1995, 135). Therefore these teachers were naturally inclined to introduce the same theatre traditions to their students at the expense of the local performance aesthetics. Support for the theatre came from the University itself (with the extra mural departments in the provincial areas being particularly useful), the Ministry of Planning and Community Development and British Council both of which lent Landrovers),

Esso, which provided some petrol. Penina Mlama (1991) particularly finds the intervention of this theatre tradition problematic for a number of reasons go on to illustrate this point. Mlama observes that one major weakness of this theatre was that it leaned more on the provision of entertainment, and therefore, to a large extent, was not only emulating the bourgeoisie theatre that it emerged out of, but was also circulating the culture and ideology of that socio-economic class. It is in this regard that Mlama deduces that Universities' Free Traveling Theatre therefore failed to bring out the fundamental ideological functions of theatre. Implicit in this observation is that this theatre practice, most probably because of its association with a particular kind of patronage, failed to recognize the potential for theatre as an apparatus for analyzing socio-economic and political problems and as a critical form of intervention. From this, Mlama concludes that since the University Free Traveling Theatre was framed within Western theatre traditions, it went "contrary to the character of the popular theatre forms in the villages which normally combine entertainment with education for critical analysis of their socio-economic and political circumstances" (1991, 65).

From Mlama's observations and arguments above, it emerges in very subtle ways, that patronage especially when it commissions works of art, may use their influence entrench a particular ideology and thus instead of intervening, ending up reinforcing the same hegemonic ideologies which the theatre practices had intended to disrupt.

## INTERNATIONAL DONORS, NGOS AND INTERVENTION THEATRE

Although patronage is important for the realization of intervention theatre projects, as noted previously, serious questions of ethics regarding mostly its manipulative, controlling, and authorizing nature. This is analogous to the investigation by Graham Hancock (2007) of his criticism of humanitarian industry in the third world. The relationship between international patrons, especially from the Europe and North America and the intervention theatre practitioners are in many ways analogical to the North-South cultural economic and political dynamics. This is aptly captured by an example that he (Hancock) provides to reveal the arrogance and paternalism of the North towards the South. He notes:

> At the root of these is the humanitarian ethic itself in which
> aid becomes something that the rich compassionately bestow

upon the poor to save from themselves. Britain's Prime Minister Margaret Thatcher best summed up this patronizing attitude when she said of Ethiopian peasant farmers: 'We have to try to teach them the basics of long-term husbandry'...Mrs. Thatcher's thinking on the subject, however, is indicative of the manner in which aid becomes transformed to the strange alchemy of mercy from mere neutral material help into something that 'we', the rich, do to 'them' the poor. (Hancock 2007, 22)

Hancock's position is reiterated by Tim Prentki (1998) when he notes that many Southern NGOs (many of which support intervention theatre enterprises) have adjusted their policies, visions and mission statements, and organizational frameworks to align themselves with those of the funding Northern NGOs and agencies.

Mlama points out these ethical aberrations when she recalls how external patronage influenced the framing and execution of a children's intervention theatre in Kenya in 1986. She notes that:

[I]n 1986 the Goethe Institute in Nairobi sponsored the staging of three productions of unadapted and to a large extent irrelevant plays for children from the German Gripps Theatre repertoire. Jorg Friedrich, the director of the Gripps Theatre, was flown in to conduct a workshop for theatre artists from East Africa on how to direct such play. The three plays directed by Kenyans and acted by Kenyan children formed the basis of the workshop. It became very apparent during the workshop that both directors and the actors, only half understood what the plays were all about. The productions were mechanical reproduction of the scripts. (Mlama 1991, 59)

Since intervention theatre is about creating awareness and reflecting on the meanings generated by a piece of theatre work, from Mlama's observation, this obviously did not take place. Instead, the productions remained mechanical reproduction of the scripts. In short, both the directors and actors did not understand the meanings inherent in the scripts that they presented as stage performances.

Reporting on her personal experience of a Ugandan production of Bertolt Brecht's *Mother Courage and her Children* as an intervention/educational theatre project, Viv Gardner (2005) provides an interesting insight of the paradoxical relationship between donor's patronage and intervention theatre in Uganda. She describes with much vivacity how the competing interests of different external funding agencies, each with a different agenda, affected the objectives of this performance and in the process took away the 'agency'-that very ability to take action leading to change-from the Ugandans. According to Gardner, this project came to be known as the *Maama Nalukalala N'zzadde Lye*, was initially a collaboration between the Ugandan National Theatre and Theatre Guild and the Royal Theatre in London. The production was a translation of Brecht's *Mother Courage and her Children* into Luganda. The production of the play in 1994/5 was significant in terms of intervention and civic education as Uganda was just emerging from a long period of violent civil war. Thus, the play as Gardner observes had "particular resonance for both the players/performers and its spectators" (2005, 177). Gardner records that this production was then funded by the Arts Group and the Social Development section of the British Council, who were more interested in the wider implications of cultural identity in socio-political and economic development. Gardner further observes that because of the cultural identity as the central organizing theme of the play, the World Bank and Policy Center Inc. became excited about the production and decided to fund its tour of Uganda and to the National Arts Festival in Grahamstown, South Africa.

However, the paradox of patronage in the arts, according to Gardner became obvious when "the objectives of the *Maama Nalukalala* company had to be realigned to meet the objectives of the funding bodies, the World Bank and PSC" (2005, 185). During the six years of its existence, Gardner notes, "the Company had always determined the agenda for its project. But now the donors were taking away this power/agency from it. The new funders insisted categorically that the production had to be linked in a 'concrete' way to 'development' and 'poverty alleviation; and must address social development objectives—including HIV/AIDs education and the inclusion of the poor" (2005, 185). The irony here is that Uganda was just coming from a long period of civil war, as such national healing and reconciliation was a precursor for development. Yet the funders could not envisage this as a priority. The other irony was that the donor patronage insisted on privileging poverty alleviation as one of the productions themes and at the same time insisted that the Company had to reduce its cast from twenty-five to six actors and singers therefore denying about twenty Ugandans a source of livelihood. Gardner, laments that donor's patronage imperatives eventually led to the near demise of the Company's project.

Also, Gardner (2005) notes that the funders insistence on a more quantitative monitoring and evaluation instead of a qualitative one that would be more amiable to the artistic production, created accountability problems for the project. She notes:

> It seems ironic though, that a project that had engaged so masterfully and so actively with issues of language and identity, of political and image, should have ended with words that were designed to obfuscate rather than communicate. It also seems A shame that the World Bank –like many other funding bodies—was not able to recognize—to see and to hear—that in the *Maam Nulukalala Ne'zzadde Lye* project we have a project that can fulfil…wider 'vision of sustainable development' as one that must have a cultural content, that recognises that governance and institution building, and enhance human capacities are all central parts of development process and may, in fact, be the *keys* that undergrid economic well-being' (cited in Nash, 1998, p. 6). And that insisting on a set of schematic criteria they were/are unable to embrace the 'evident, erratic and obstinate' that is at the core of creative cultural practice. (2005, 186)

From Gardener's description, it is possible to claim that in a number of intervention theatre projects the agency was taken away from both the artists and the local community by the source of patronage. Thus, patronage becomes a 'patronizing' agent instead of a partner in the development of art. Frank Marion also reports a similar case in regards to AIDS Campaign Theatre in Uganda where the Government Organizations (GOs), NGOs and international organizations put pressure on the intervention theatre practitioners to produce results (1995, 69-70). Marion reports that these results were based not on medical or theatrical but on administrative or political criteria: that the most important thing was the number of people who attended the performance. This affected the framing of this intervention theatre because the only way to get big audiences was to organize for huge festivals that could attract media attention. A similar case is also reported from Tanzania by Paul Nyoni as read in Odhiambo Joseph (2008). In this particular incident, Nyoni laments at how the intervention theatre facilitators were frustrated by the sponsors of the project. He notes that as intervention theatre animators they were commissioned to facilitate a theatre project in Rukwa in Tanzania by the Integrated Food Security Programme (IFSP). Although the funders contracted them to work in collaboration with the community using theatre for development techniques and methodology to identify problems facing the community, when they presented their findings, the donors simply ignored those findings and went ahead to implement projects that had not been considered as priority by the community. In regard to the way the patron-donor treated the intervention theatre animators, Nyoni concludes that:

> Employing Theatre-for-Development as a participatory planning process was just a means to justify their presence than a process of democratization of thought that aims at empowering the rural masses… (Odhiambo 2008, 66-7)

Vicencia Shule (2008) in a paper: "Tanzanians and Donors: Opposing Audiences in Public Theatre" gives yet another intriguing account of the relationship between donor patronage and intervention theatre in Tanzania. Using two cases as illustrations: Tanzania Theatre Centre (TzTC) established in 1997 and Eastern Africa Theatre Institute (EATI) established in 1999, he shows how donor patronage has affected the efficacy and autonomy of intervention theatre. Shule, for instance, observes that donor patronage has to a large extent compromised aesthetics and sense of ownership of this kind of theatre practice. Shule argues that before the proliferation of donor patronage, intervention theatre in Tanzania, at its inception in the 1970s was decidedly involved in social and political emancipation as it overtly incorporated ideas and philosophy from revolutionary theatre. However, with the emergence of external donors' patronage in the 1980s after the introduction of International Monetary Fund and World Bank Structural Adjustment Programmes (SAPs), the ideology of theatre in Tanzania was radically changed. The agenda of this theatre changed from people-driven to donor-driven. But more disturbing, theatre began to privilege a global agenda instead of the local ones. This situation is well delineated when Shule laments on this relationship as follows:

> At the beginning of 2004, the Swedish International Development Agency (SIDA) officially changed its funding policy to focus on livelihood enhancement for the poor i.e. poverty reduction. Since it was not communicated earlier, EATI and TzTc were direct (sic) affected by this abrupt policy change. Most of their activities were not funded under new policy. Since there were no options, the Organizations had to restructure their objectives to focus on poverty reduction so as to fit within the new global development policy known as Swedish's policy for Global Development (PGU), passed by Swedish parliament in 2003. (Shule 2008, 5-6)

These intervention theatre organizations did not only forfeit their autonomy of setting their programmes agenda but also, as Shule notes, the donor patronage also affected adversely other fundamental dimensions of this theatre: for example the entertainment aspect of it was suppressed at the expense of the message; aesthetic value of the performances were also watered down drastically because they were shown free as donors had sponsored them; because donors prescribed the themes of this kind of theatre, a particular theme was repeated several times leading to monotony and consequently to audience fatigue.

There is also an interesting case reported from Kenya. This is about a group of teachers from Sigoti in Kisumu province who started an educational intervention theatre group known as Sigoti Teachers' Group in collaboration with a theatre-educator from the Netherlands. In their endeavor to intervene on wastes brought about by the 'wrong' disposal of plastics and batteries, the group sought for funders, and their partner Colijn traveled to the Netherlands to explore possible sources of funders and funding. However, the response she got from the anticipated patrons is a classic example of how patronage undermines intervention theatre programmes. The documenter of this experience relates that:

> When Joyce returned to the Netherlands she wrote an extensive proposal for the first programme of the project, the one on the waste. With it she visited many organizations in order to get support, either financially or materially. Although quite a number of organizations were enthusiastic, they...felt that the project did not comply with their objectives. *Some proposed that we should change the focus of the project to agriculture or try hygiene.* Even when given the explanation for the difference in approach, the organizations insisted on the direct approach if they were to sponsor us. Finally some funds came from a private company who (sic) had read an article about the project in a local Dutch Newspaper. This at least made it possible for us to run the first programme. (Okolla and Colijn 1995, 90-1)

This citation shows with much clarity the dilemma facing intervention theatre programmes and practitioners who are aware of the problems facing their communities and yet can not intervene, because many a times they are forced to recast their agendas to suit those of the patrons. This situation is well critiqued by Prentki (1998) when he notes that because theatre for development (TFD) is perceived to belong to the arts most development agencies therefore do not include it in their list of development priorities. This is what makes the intervention theatre practitioners look helpless because they must wait for NGOs to get money from donors and then contract them to implement the contracting agency's agenda. This dilemma of the intervention theatre practitioner in the South is well captured by Kerr when he reminds us that:

> The question mark in my title is meant to raise doubts in the minds of those who, like myself, have been enthusiastic practitioners of participatory popular theatre-doubts about whether such drama forms might not sometimes be abetting the same process of dependency noted by Nkrumah, rather than helping de-link African societies from Northern dominance. (1991, 55)

The paradox of patronage in the realm of intervention theatre becomes more vivid when one critically unpacks the relationship between them. For instance, in Kenya, the entry of sponsors in Kenya Schools and Colleges Drama festival was heralded with a lot of enchantment but patrons' have in some way shifted the philosophy of the festival to reflect their commercial interests at the expense of pedagogical and entertainment values. The role that Kenya Schools and Colleges Drama Festival plays in socio-cultural, economic and political intervention and transformation obviously can never be underestimated. This perhaps explains why so many corporate bodies are offering patronage. But these patronages apparently come 'with strings attached'. For instance a number of them hold the right in the contract to decide what kind of content they want the performances to privilege. For instance, Kenya Anti-Corruption Commission provides awards for performances that have effectively interpreted the theme of corruption. While on the one hand, NACADA, a government advocacy organization against drug abuse, rewards only performances which highlight the dangers of underage smoking. On the other hand, Equity Bank gives sponsorship to schools whose performances propagate the virtues and benefits of indigenous enterprises. Equity Bank is an indigenous bank. The irony is that, sometimes, a performance that is aesthetically mediocre will be rewarded so long as their message is in alignment with the agendas of the patrons.

Patronage has had both positive and negative effects on the festival as an intervention theatre enterprise. Negative effects, in the sense that sometimes the burning issues of the day, are not explored by the participants because those issues have not attracted sponsorships and will not therefore earn them any monetary or material gains. For instance, Sidho Girls High School neighbouring ICIPE (a research centre in Mbita District in Nyanza) was given sponsorship in 1998 to participate in the drama festival but they had to do a play that aligned with ICIPE's advocacy programme on malaria prevention called the *Mosquito Mask*. One can argue that even if the school wanted to perform a play about some other issue that might have competed more favourably at the festival, they could not do so because the sponsorship was very specific about the message of the play that they had to produce. They did produce the play but it did not perform very well at the festivals.

Ideally, the main patron of the school festival is the ministry of education. During the reign of the former President Moi, this patronage ended up as a censorship board and ensured that performances at the festival were politically correct. Since the provincial education office sponsors schools within their jurisdictions, schools whose performances were perceived as critical of the then KANU government and its autocratic policies were usually barred from proceeding to the next levels of the festivals. For example when the Musingu Boys High school from the Western Province of Kenya put on their play: *The Press*, it was barred because it was deemed by the provincial education office to be critical of the government as it was interpreted, as implicating the government in the death of a catholic priest who was known to have been critical of corrupt government officials. However, this is not an unusual practice when the Ministry of Education is the patron.

A number of patrons tend to censor the content of intervention theatre. For instance in 2002, a sponsor advised the CLARION theatre team that was touring intervention theatre on civic education to reframe their performances to be more allegorical because she thought they were too direct in the manner they addressed the question of land grabbing within her region. With this allegorical framing, the plays were performed without getting into trouble with the government security agents. Similarly, an international organization working with rural women, that had commissioned Moi University theatre students to produce a play on gender violence, insisted that some sections of play had to be deleted because they were "un-African".

## CONCLUSION

Although patronage is an important component in Intervention Theatre because, unlike mainstream theatre, it does not have the benefit of box office ticket sales to sustain it. It is evident that the agenda of patronage(s) need to be interrogated more critically by theatre practitioners if the practice is expected to achieve its objectives of intervening to, create awareness to that would bring about urgent social transformation. As it has emerged in this discussion, different forms of patronages have had different impacted on this intervention theatre in a number of the interventions/ performances that we have witnessed in the discussion had to change their objectives to suit those of the sponsors.

What this implies is that the intervention that was intended by the performers on the target society is, more often than not, not achieved. Unlike in the traditional set up of theatre where patronage was given as a token of appreciation, in the modern capitalist systems, patrons tend to impose their agenda on the theatre practitioners.

The relationship between intervention theatre practitioners and their sponsors, in a sense, is a reflection of the unequal relationship between the poor South and donors from the developed North. Maybe the intervention theatre practitioner should borrow from the experience of Ngugi wa Thiong'o's intervention community theatre at Kamiriithu where without any external patronage, the community did set its own agenda leading to radical socio-economic and political transformation. In addition, governments in the developing world, where intervention theatre has become a significant tool in both development communication and implementation should design policies that would protect the practitioners and by extension, the art form of intervention theatre as democratic right of civil expression from undue manipulation from funders and sponsors. In addition, this policy is also crucial because most of the performing artists in East Africa are vulnerable because they were unemployed and joined the theatre as a response to unemployment. This situation makes them vulnerable to any source of manipulative patronage.

## Notes

1. For more details see Ruth Finnegan *Oral Literature in Africa* (1970) especially chapter on 'Poetry and Patronage' pp.81-110.

2. For details of intervention theatres see Kerr(1995); Mda (1993); Odhiambo (2008); Mlama (1995)

3. The symbiotic relationship between *nyatiti* player and patronage is well archived in Finnegan (1970) pp. 99-102, 120.

4. See Ngugi *Decolonizing the Mind* and P'Bitek *Africa's Cultural Revolution*

5. *Siwindhe* is the house of a grandmother where traditionally Luo narratives were narrated. It is in this house that Luo girls and boys gathered in the evening to be taught the cultures and beliefs of the community.

# Chapter 5

# THEORISING CRAFT: READING THE CREATIVE THROUGH THE CRITICAL IN THE WORKS OF OKOT P'BITEK AND NGUGI WA THIONG'O

*Susan N. Kiguli*

## INTRODUCTION

In exploring the development of the East African literary tradition, this chapter investigates the forms of 'dialogue' between the creative and the critical in the works of the two writers. I argue here that Okot p' Bitek and Ngugi wa Thiong'o's creative works express their respective positions namely: Cultural Nationalism-cum-Nativism for Okot and Marxist Cultural Nationalism for Ngugi. Even as I use these labels, I am aware of the contradictions, inconsistencies and ambiguities they carry sometimes in reference to the authors or in reference to the wide application of such terms to African Literature.[1] Ngugi has been said to move from liberal humanism, to Marxism then to radical nationalism as his current persuasion. I do want to note that there is an expected reluctance to refer to Ngugi's Marxist views now with the less popular position of Marxist theory. Alex Callinicos notes in an evaluation of the position of Marxist theory that:

> Marxism also finds itself forced onto the defensive as an intellectual tradition...This is a time to keep Classical Marxism alive, not by retreating into a watch-tower or an ivory tower,

but by bringing it into contact with the forms of resistance through which the working class is responding to the myriad of attacks it is suffering around the world...The future of Marxism will be settled by whether or not it is able to connect with and grasp the logic of the struggles through which the domination of capital is tested. (Callincos 1996, PE-9)

In general, my view is that throughout both his creative and non-fiction work, Ngugi sees real value in connecting and harnessing the power of what he refers to as the African peasantry who are the essential producers of labour in their context. In this light if the future of Marxism as Callinicos observes is going to be settled by its ability to "connect with and grasp the logic of struggles through which the domination of capital is tested", then I would argue that Ngugi still holds Marxist views even when he never names them as such.

Ngugi in a rare moment of labeling himself states thus:

I am a literary humanist and democratic ideals appeal to me.
At the heart of democratic or any political process in society
is the question of power (2009, 16).

Ngugi's apparently unequivocal statement strikes me as deeply problematic. This label of his ideals himself seems to me vague by expressing an inclusive interest in all aspects in the study of "humanities" from a literary point of view. Thus, I find that this label does not elucidate Ngugi's position rather it further complicates it. Ngugi's linking of the democratic ideal to his use of the term literary humanist may point to his desire to ascribe to a form of humanism that liberates the mind from accepted *status quo* of society's manipulation of power and consequently of the democratic ideal while at the same time it celebrates the aesthetic ideal the literary humanism evokes. In Ngugi's representation of himself as a literary humanist, I would surmise that it may be possible that his intention here was that he wants to show his devotion to the struggle for the survival of human values and emphasise its link to the literary and culture as a whole. In examining Ngugi's ideological stance, both in his critical and creative work, one cannot disregard what Claudio Gorlier terms "the complexity of his theoretical stance and the multivalence of his literary discourse" (2002, 98).

As part of the process of thinking through the corpus of the creative-critical-dialogue, I examine the 'double-ness' and ambiguity of text as a discursive and critical literary tradition in East African writing in the works of these two authors. Given the central role and position of these two writers as both creative and critical figureheads in the literary tradition of East Africa, I contend that they may be seen as trailblazers in the development of the East African literary–critical tradition. I am also attempting to call attention to the interplay of the historical, political and contemporary in East African literary Aesthetics.

Okot p' Bitek and Ngugi wa Thiong'o are two of the most celebrated writers of the post-independence era who showed keen interest in connecting the writer and society. They were adamant in their claims, each in his own right, about the intimate link between literature and the community from which it springs. For Okot p' Bitek, literature was a product intimately concerned with actual performance, involvement and enjoyment. For example Okot commented in the preface to *Horn of my Love*:

> When, recently, my friend Taban wept bitter tears over what he called *the literary desert in East Africa,* he was suffering from acute literary deafness, a disease which afflicts those who have been brainwashed to believe literature exists only in books. Taban and his fast dwindling clan are victims of the class-ridden, dictionary meaning of the term *literature,* which restricts literary activity and enjoyment to so called literate peoples, and turns a deaf ear to the songs and stories of the vast majority of our people in the countryside. (1974, ix)

I think Okot's remark is important in this discussion in two ways. Firstly, it introduces a book which is a compilation of the poetry of the Acoli, in which Okot pays tribute to the literary revolution which in his own words "demolished the English department and replaced it with the Department of Literature, the central core of African Literature" (1974, x). He presents the book as a contribution to that revolution. Secondly, it introduces an approach which is instrumental to Okot's critical practice that sees literature as a deep sharing of the values, knowledge of the societal symbols and situations of a community; in essence literature is a product of meaningful relationships set up by the solidarity that characterises the cultural environment, writer-composer, author and audience (1973, 22).

Similarly, Ngugi sees the writer as part of a context and has variously advanced the argument that the writer cannot exist in a vacuum and to read/write about the present, the writer has to talk about the past. Thus in his book of essays *Homecoming* in the essay 'The writer and his Past' he remarks:

> The novelist is haunted by a sense of the past. His work is often an attempt to come to terms with 'the thing that has been', a struggle, as it were, to sensitively register his encounter with history, his people's history. (1972, 39)

Ngugi wa Thiong'o's *Homecoming* demonstrated his attention to Black/African Literature both in Africa and beyond. It also revealed an ideological position that ties strongly with Fanon (Ogude 1997, 94). Later on his work drew from Marxist theory although, as I have mentioned before, Ngugi never directly acknowledges his indebtedness to Marxist ideology. Ngugi argues in the above quotation from *Homecoming* that perceptive writers must have a keen sense of history and therefore literature must be linked to the people, their history and values. This point relates to his argument in *Decolonizing the Mind* where he states:

> The whole point of a neo-colonial regime imprisoning a writer is, in addition to punishing him, to keep him away from the people, to cut off any and every contact and communication between him and the people. (1986, 64)

I suspect that in my attempt to see how these two major East African writers established a collaborative relationship between the creative and critical traditions, questions on whether creative work has to be a product of a deliberate critical programme may arise. I am aware that it would be reckless to read creative work strictly according to particular critical concepts, particularly in the light of the argument that creative work cannot be limited by critical readings and theory especially if this is combined with the suggestion that we often have no way of uncovering/disseminating/interrogating/ telling the writer's intentions.

Despite this I still think that since many of the celebrated writers on the African continent are also some of its best critics (Olaniyan and Quayson 2009, 101), this sets up the partnership between creative and critical works in African literary discourses. Okot and Ngugi articulated distinct ideas and thoughts in their essays that could act as part of a critical framework in which we could examine their creative work usefully. In exploring the relationship these writers set up between their creative and critical works, we can also begin to explore the trend of the East African creative and critical work. In examining ideas about the understanding and function of literature, these two writers also imaginatively explored the aspirations of their people and a primarily East African consciousness which may have strong connections with the rest of Africa.

# THE RELATIONSHIP BETWEEN OKOT P' BITEK'S POETRY AND HIS CRITICAL IDEAS

Okot p' Bitek is regarded as the first major East African poet writing in English. He is celebrated for drawing extensively on traditional modes of expression. Okot has been hailed for starting the 'Song School' in East African poetry whose influence is still indirectly evident in poetry produced in East Africa. Emmanuel Ngara identified Okot with the movement of Cultural Nationalism because of his demonstrably serious concern with African culture and advocacy for a close association with oral literature and performance (1990, 60). Okot is also seen as one of the early writers from East Africa to carry out a blunt and critical examination of the post-independence state therefore promoting the trend of Africa speaking to itself rather than addressing the West through the voices of Lawino, the prisoner and Malaya. He addresses the outrageous loss of freedom for the African citizens and the political fortunes of bloodthirsty tyrants on the African continent. He is also concerned through particularly *Song of Prisoner* with the cultural desolation of the post-independence state.

Okot is preoccupied with the idea of a literature that reflects the philosophy and the reality of the people. In his essay in *Artist the Ruler: Essays on Art, Culture and Values*, "What is Culture?", he argues that the Western tradition has instituted an artificial dichotomy between philosophy and culture:

> This view of culture as something separate and distinguishable from *the way of life of a people*, something that can be put in books and museums and art galleries, something which can be taught in schools and universities for examination purposes, or enjoyed during leisure time in theatres and cinema halls- the Western tradition which regards culture as something that can bought and sold , where the artist is some very special fellow who is paid with money for his works - is entirely alien to African thought. (1986, 14)

This idea is echoed in a number of Okot's essays and also comes out strongly in Song of Lawino. For example, Lawino pleads with her doubly alienated husband who is estranged from his wife and his culture:

> Listen Ocol, my friend,
> The ways of your ancestors
> Are good,

Their customs are solid
And not hollow
They are not thin, not easily
Breakable
They cannot be blown away
By the winds
Because their roots reach deep
Into the soil. (1972, 41)

In this section and throughout the poem, Okot argues for the understanding of a people's values and roots, for the anchoring of people in
their own world view and suggests that despising one's roots is stupidity
which warrants forgiveness from the respected elders of the community:

Ask them to forgive
Your past stupidity
Pray that the setting sun
May take away all your shyness
Deceit, childish pride and
Sharp tongue! (1972, 119)

Okot asserts in both his essays and the poem *Song of Lawino* that a people's philosophy of life provides the basis for their behaviour and must
not be easily uprooted or dismissed. Continuing with this thought, he
suggests in his essay from *Artist the Ruler* "Man Unfree", that the people
while being seen as individual are also socialized into being members of
their society. According to this argument:

Man has always asked the most terrifying questions... And
according to answers provided by the wise men which have
been accepted, society is then organized to achieve these
ends. It is these fundamental ideas, the philosophy of life,
which constitute the pillars, the foundations on which the
social institutions are erected. Some have called these ideas
*myths* or world-views; others refer to them as ideologies...
Man cannot, and must not be free... permanent bondage
seems to be man's fate. Because he cannot escape he cannot
be liberated, freed. The so- called 'outcast' is not a free agent.
Being 'cast out' from society, for a while, does not sever the
chains that bind a man to society. (1986, 19-20)

It is through this poem *Song of Malaya* that one can appreciate this view
more fully. In Okot's philosophy:

> The African tradition lived and lives in the thick of battle of
> life, here and now... It is the living and celebrating of these
> fundamental ideas which constitutes culture... The true
> African artist has his eyes firmly fixed, not to some abstract
> idea called beauty 'up there' as it were, but on the philosophy
> of life of his society. (1986, 21-3)

The startling and subversive voice of the prostitute cynically brings to
life the reality as the artist observes it. It points to the hypocrisy and
pretentiousness of all those who actually want to deny her existence in
public but then associate with her in private. The poet poses a moral
question and looks at life in the view of the 'here and now' discussed in
his essay. The bold brazen voice declares:

> You black bishop
> Preaching morality...
>
> But your father
> Had six wives
> Your mother
> Was not one of them,
> Was she? (1971, 161)

One can argue that Okot had a knack of writing attention-grabbing
lines but more importantly I would argue that his poetic persona's voice
is fresh because he believes in what speaks most immediately to other
human beings and asks disturbing questions such as "What is morality?" In essence he asks the reader to pay attention to what he terms in
his own words the philosophy of life of a people.

In Okot's poems, I sense a quality of the personality of the artist
behind them. In the final analysis these poems are gripping because
there are about connections between men and women with each other
and about their environment. These are immediate issues and arguments which point us to one of Okot's central preoccupations, the
paradox of post colonial existence. Out of this feeling, I argue, came
Okot's strongest and most vivid and disturbing poem *Song of Prisoner*.
In exploring the post independence situation, Okot crafts the violent
images of *Song of Prisoner*:

> Look at the laughing wound
> In my head...
> Brother,
> How could I

So poor
Cold
Limping
Weak
Hungry like an empty tomb
A young tree
Burnt out
By the fierce wild fire
Of Uhuru

How could I
Inspire you
To such heights
Of brutality? (1971, 14-5)

In this extract, Okot plays with the oxymoron of 'laughing wound', one would perhaps expect an angry wound but a laughing one evokes the most troubling paradox of excessive pain that mocks the abuser back and asserts that the prisoner will not be destroyed. The poet uses adjectives such as poor, cold, weak and hungry to show the frailty of the prisoner. The language in this poem is on the whole less idealistic, more raw and violent, less personal and more bitter even if perhaps less moving than *Song of Lawino*. Okot feels keenly the distress and humiliation of the ordinary person. Okot's argument that literature is anchored in participation in a people's culture is strong here. I read a sense of personal disquiet in what we can term a public poem. The prisoner seems even more symbolic than the voice of Lawino and Ocol because his ethnic identity is more ambiguous, more tinged with the sense of displacement.

In reading Okot his concluding remark in the essay "African aesthetics- The Acholi Example" is relevant:

> It is only the participants in a culture who can pass judgement on it. It is only they who can evaluate how effective the song or dance is; how decoration, the architecture, the plan of the village has contributed to the feast of life, how these have made life meaningful. (1986, 37)

I want to point out that Okot in his writing particularly as reflected in *Song of Lawino* regards the artist to be a guide. He later articulates this position in *Artist the Ruler*. Whereas I do not claim there is a linear and straight forward relationship between his essays and his creative work, I would like to contend that these interconnections are strong.

In emphasising the role of the artist and the art, Okot takes the argument to another level where, I think, it is beyond simply politicking or even instruction. It becomes a human and humane project. In a way then the artist's work cannot easily fit into a narrow social, political or even historical context. When Okot argues for culturally committed perspectives, I would like to think that he opens up the argument especially since culture as has been repeatedly stated, is not static and can be influenced by different elements such as time, events and meaning. In *Song of Lawino*, although Lawino does not understand the white person's culture, she insists that she does not despise it and directs her focus on what she understands: her culture. One of her arguments is that if Ocol despises what he was groomed in and what he is familiar with, how then can he claim knowledge of new ways? The fundamental question of identity and of re-positioning one's self in both the local and larger contexts becomes important. Okot addresses this question in his article "Theatre Education in Uganda" when he states:

The cultural renaissance that is being witnessed in Uganda is part of a powerful movement sweeping the entire continent of Africa and Asia: a reaction against foreign-imposed culture, a deep search into the soul of men. The question of "Who am I?" is being answered in a dynamic style in Uganda through a cultural revolution. (1968, 308)

In the above quotation, Okot alludes to the Black Aesthetics movement which spurred on a period of artistic and literary development among African Americans and Africans in the 1960s and early 1970s. The Black Aesthetics movement was closely linked to anti-colonial movements in Africa and the civil struggles in the United States (Neal 1968, 29-30). Okot in step to the fray with what he termed a "cultural revolution" recognized the major role culture in form of both oral and written literature plays in shaping sense of self and, at the risk of being accused of stretching beyond its limits what Okot was doing, sense of both ethnicity and nationalism. In reading Okot particularly *Song of Lawino*, he regards the revitalization of the specific culture, in his case Acoli culture as a catalyst for creating a sense of the nation. In celebrating Acoli ways, Okot did not seek separateness or uniqueness rather he viewed it as beginning of unity in diversity.

Okot occupied many positions: he was a poet, dancer, cultural critic ethnographer, story teller, theatre director and cultural critic[2] and this makes his work quite complex and multi-layered.

## NGUGI WA THIONG'O'S VISION

Ngugi wa Thiong'o has been recognized as one of Africa's prolific writers and East Africa's major fiction writer to- date. Ngugi positions himself as a writer who is consistently attempting to reflect and interpret social and political history and its impact on the present and future. In his essays and his fiction, his struggle is to interpret the often unmapped but deep aspirations of his society. He embarks on this in his writings by seeing colonialism beyond the racism to the economic and social factors. He steeps his critique in Fanonist and Marxist ideology combined with what some scholars have termed Linguist Nativism.[3] He states his view in *Moving the Centre: The Struggle for Cultural Freedoms* in the essay "The role of the Scholar in the Development of African Literatures":

> My view is that scholarship will be able to contribute to the development of African literatures only if scholars manage to free themselves from limiting angles of vision. To accomplish this they will have to adopt a social base that enables them to see, hear smell and taste more accurately... A consistent anti-imperialist position – that is, a position that struggles against or that exposes the continued neo-colonial control of African economics and cultures by Western bourgeoisie- is the minimum necessary for a committed, responsible scholarship in Africa, or anywhere in the Third World. Certainly both African literature and Afro-European literature cannot be understood outside the framework of consistent anti-imperialism. (1993, 86-7)

Ngugi sees in his society the forces of "historically changing economic, political and cultural practice." He examines the colonial, neo-colonial era and the class divisions within the society that produce the woes of the post-independence era. He describes "the dangers posed by the mediators or collaborators between the "imperialist bourgeoisie and the mass workers and peasants". According to Ngugi:

> To the majority of African people in the new states, independence did not bring about fundamental changes. It was independence with the ruler holding a begging bowl and the ruled a shrinking belly. It was independence with a question mark. The age of independence had produced a new class and a new leadership that often was not very different from the old one. (1993, 65)

This quotation explicitly points out the tension between what is expected of the new order and what has been delivered so far. Ngugi explores this conflict in both his fiction and essays. It is an anomaly that Ngugi sees as inevitable because of the mindset of the new greedy leaders who deliberately turn their eyes away from the people they are supposed to lead.

In his novels beginning particularly with *A Grain of Wheat*, without seeking to reduce the novels to the same level,[4] Ngugi explores the chaos of the emergency, the role of violence, and it is in *A Grain of Wheat* that the ironies of independence the uncertainties begin to take shape in the readers' minds. The people's apparent hero is guilt ridden and the struggle for independence has produced tension, guilt and rivalry among a number of characters. *A Grain of Wheat* shines a torch onto the independence period. In *A Grain of Wheat* as Ngugi seems to be beginning on a loftier stylistic journey, he is also at the same time establishing a very distinct way of seeing in his critical essays. In the author's note in *Homecoming,* he remarks:

> The present collection of essays is an integral part of the fictional world of *The River between, Weep Not Child* and *A Grain of Wheat.* Most of them were written at about the same time as the novels; they have been products of the same moods and touch similar questions and problems. There are differences. In a novel the writer is totally immersed in a world of imagination which is other than his conscious self. At his most intense and creative the writer is transfigured, he is possessed, he becomes a medium. In the essay the writer is more direct, didactic, polemical, or he can merely state his beliefs and faith: his conscious self is here more at work. Nevertheless the boundaries of his imagination are limited by the writer's beliefs, interests, and experiences in life, by where in fact he stands in the world of social relations.

The main point I would like to emphasise here is that the writer self-consciously points to the link between his fiction and essays even when he is conscious that they do not operate in the same way. In his somewhat tacit prose, Ngugi presents the character of Mugo and from the description, the reader can tell the stalemate of political change being portrayed. The narrator describes Mugo's actions:

> He liked porridge in the morning. But whenever he took it, he remembered the half-cooked porridge he ate in detention. How time drags, everything repeats itself, Mugo thought: the

day ahead would be just like yesterday and the day before. He took a jembe and a panga to repeat the daily pattern his life had now fallen into since he left Maguita, his last detention camp. (1967, 3)

Mugo's life reads like a metaphor of the complexity and tension between hope for change and the stark reality of failed dreams, the consequence of the ironic order that brought 'independence'. Ngugi mentions in his essay: 'Toward a Pluralism of Culture, the times in which he produces *A Grain of Wheat:*

> I mention the novel because in so many ways *A Grain of Wheat* symbolises for me the Leeds I associate with Arthur Ravenscroft's time, which was also a significant moment in the development of African literature. This was the sixties when the centre of the universe was moving from Europe or, to put it another way, when many countries particularly in Asia and Africa were demanding and asserting their right to define themselves and their relationship to the universe from their own centres in Africa and Asia. Frantz Fanon became the prophet of the struggle to move the centre and his book, The Wretched of the Earth, became a kind of Bible among the African students from West and East Africa then at Leeds. (1993, 2)

It is apparent that Ngugi links his thoughts and ideas in his essays to the imaginative world of his fiction and thereby providing explicit support for specific interpretations of his work.

Petals of Blood and The Devil on the Cross explore and articulate more systematically and passionately the idea of neo-colonial regimes as repressive and in partnership with the international and national structures of exploitation and oppression. Ngugi's main argument in his essays that the neocolonialism is driven by what he terms imperialists' forces, and that the real power lies within the people is prominent in his fiction too. In *The Devil on the Cross*, Ngugi vividly creates the characters that represent the ordinary exploited citizens. Jacinta Wariinga suffers at the hands of exploitative and hypocritical men. She is sexually harassed by Mr. Boss Kihara who fires her when she refuses his sexual advances. When she relates the incident to her young lover, John Kimwana, he also rejects her on the pretext that he believes she has been sleeping with Kihara. Characters of Wariinga's class suffer incredible injustice and exploitation. The ordinary characters in the novel often parallel the lives of ordinary citizens of the Kenyan society who are pitted against the rich who are backed by the international exploiters. In the novel, the feast of the thieves and robbers, the leader of the foreign delegation takes a higher seat than the others. The description of the foreign delegation is telling;

> There were different in the suits they wore. The one worn by the leader was made of dollars, the Englishman's pounds, the German's Deutschmarks the Frenchman's francs, the Italian's lire, the Scandinavian's kroner and the Japanese's delegate's of yen. (1982, 91)

They are evidently representatives of their countries' interests and they make no effort to disguise that. In the end Wariinga kills her oppressors and no one stops her although she walks on knowing "with all her heart that the hardest struggles of her life's journey lay ahead…"

Ngugi also categorically states that a writer's task is to highlight the plight of the people. He states in *Homecoming* in the essay "The Writer in a Changing Society":

> I believe that the African intellectuals must align themselves with the struggle of the African masses for a meaningful national ideal. For we must strive for a form of social organization that will free the manacled spirit and energy of our people so that we can build a new country, and sing a new song. Perhaps, in a small way the writer can help in articulating the feelings behind the struggle. (1972, 50)

I want to suggest that Ngugi's creative work, at one level, illustrates in recurrent themes and images the ideas in his essays. In an interview with D. Venkat Rao, when asked about the consistency in the themes he explores against the formal experimentation with different literary forms; Ngugi responds:

> The themes are created by historical situation in Africa- colonialism and resistance against colonialism are persistent themes; in the present, neocolonialism- they are constant themes, part of the history against which I am writing. A writer changes also in terms of how he or she approaches the same historical moment. (1999, 163)

In his own words Ngugi is constantly "evaluating his themes" and I propose he does this partly by discussing his ideas in his essays and creating a critical framework from his own standpoint. In building up this critical–creative relationship, Ngugi is taking up what he considers a major challenge to African scholars and writers to build up a body of work that can enable a construction of a consciousness that will help people to discuss and deal with their problems.

Working from a marxist nationalism persuasion, Ngugi draws on two binaries in his analysis of the conditions of his society in his own words "the democratic and socialist forces for life and human progress and the imperialists' forces that are reactionary and oppressive". Gikandi (2000) and Ogude (1997) have noted that Kenyan history as recounted in Ngugi's creative work is guided by his own vision of the Kenyan nation which in my view, he also clearly articulates in his essays particularly in his rendition of the Mau Mau struggle encapsulated in the movement's linking of the ideal of freedom to land. Ogude has pointed out that in Ngugi's desire to privilege the history of the oppressed specifically in Kenya and Africa in general has led him to make misrepresentations of the realities of Kenyan history to the extent of reducing what is a much more complex history into the binary of oppressor against oppressed:

> Ngugi is a prisoner of the broad perspective of dependency. In most of his works, he creates simplistic binary opposition between oppressor and the oppressed, which he precludes any possibility of conflicting interests within these broad social categories. (1997, 101)

This flaw in Ngugi's approach stems from his impassioned belief in the writer and intellectual's role in working with marginalized people to achieve a liberated consciousness. In *Petals of Blood*, Ngugi depicts Karega as the progressive organizer who works for the liberation of the people. Karega is symbolic of an organized intelligentsia that is ready to work with the people for freedom. In an interview with D. Venkat Rao he states:

> ...See my own practice as a writer...I must look at everything from the standpoint of the most oppressed center in society... In other words, I try and judge the progress of any society from that standpoint. (Rao and Wa Thiong'o 1999, 166)

His essay "The writer in a Neocolonial State" focuses on this point as central in Ngugi's literary practice:

But as the struggle continues and intensifies, the lot of the writer in a neo-colonial state will become harder and not and not easier. His choice? It seems to me that the African writer of the eighties, the one who opts for becoming an integral part of the African revolution, has no choice but that of aligning himself with his the people: their economic, political and cultural struggle for survival. In that situation, he will have to confront the languages spoken by the people in whose service he has put his pen. Such a writer will have to rediscover the real language of struggle in the actions and speeches of his people... A people united can never be defeated and writer must be part and parcel of that revolutionary unity for democracy, socialism and the liberation of the human spirit to become even more human. (1993, 74-5)

Ngugi's much debated decision to write in Gikuyu language is a part of this deliberate effort to speak for and with his people as he argues in *Decolonising the Mind* language is inseparable from who the people are as language is part of a people's self definition and history. In deciding to write in Gikuyu, he sought to focus on the question of language. He has referred to the choice of Gikuyu as the language of his work as an "epistemological break" although scholars such as Gikandi have questioned that claim. Ngugi as writer and critic has made it clear that his decision to change from writing in English to writing in Gikuyu was an ideological shift for him that showed his commitment to community instead of giving lip service to this idea. For Ngugi the language question has to do with what he terms as moving the center from the West to the "multiplicity of centers all over the world" (Rao and Wa Thiong'o 1999, 165). He sees this decision as 'a point of no return' even though it is also evident that he is aware of limitations attached. He has observed:

> ...I had to shift the language to Gikuyu...when you use a language, you are also choosing an audience...When I used English, I was choosing English-speaking audience... Now I can use a story, a myth and not always explain because I can assume that the [Gikuyu] readers are familiar with this...I can play with word sounds and images, I can rely more and more on songs, proverbs, riddles, anecdotes... (Rao and Wa Thiong'o 1999, 163)

Ngugi sees writing in what he terms "marginalized languages" as way of restoring the marginalized heritages which for him "it goes to the very heart of our being and existence" (2000, 9). Ngugi see his development of form in fiction as linked to his writing in Gikuyu. He feels that he can utilize the orature of his people more freely in his fiction. Even with the complications that go with Ngugi's strong and rigid belief to see issues from a specific angle, his conviction in both his fiction and essays that writers interrogate as well as contribute to keeping alive a people's values and identity is a compelling position.

## CONCLUSION

These two important East African writers emerge as emphasising the role of the artist and therefore the energy invested in expression. I am aware of the arguments against Cultural Nationalism for which Okot p' Bitek has been criticised. For example, Anthony Kwame Appiah has strongly argued that it is necessary to move beyond what he calls the "nativist hand waving" and understand the tools that we use to analyse literature. Whereas these ideas are valid in their own right, the complexity of the forces that the writers like Okot p' Bitek felt they were rallied against is important to acknowledge. With the changes in the world order Ngugi's Marxist Cultural nationalism presents its own challenges but I think Ngugi makes a pertinent point when he points out that the particular for example Gikuyu connects with the universal and the attendant benefits/threats of globalisation. Yet the particular is extremely important in the imagining of a people's life because usually a novelist starts from the particular which they know and use it to ground their narrative in the larger context. The perspective is quite fluid in this regard and as Ngugi notes:

> Literature is not only a question of the primary texts of study, specific novels, poems, dramas, and essays: it is also the criticism that goes with it. (1997, 23)

I conclude it is important to acknowledge how Ngugi and Okot p' Bitek have galvanised the literary debates in East Africa and Ngugi in particular. In addition, this debate has provided a substantial collection of essays which are associated with his fiction and with the developments in the literary tradition in East Africa. While a number of scholars have traced the contribution of Okot and Ngugi's contribution to African literature,[5] my focus here has been to contribute to an awareness of the legacy of these writers in setting up an active creative-critical dialogue in East Africa. While I am not suggesting that the writers deliberately set out to establish a direct relationship between the ideas in their critical/polemical and their creative work, I am drawn to the strong connections (conscious and unconscious) between the two. I contend that while the connections are not without contradictions, there are dominant convictions that run through their works. Okot argues for literature that is rooted in the lives of the people, this is demonstrated more vehemently in *Song of Lawino,* the latter works show more awareness on the part of the author of the inevitable tense relationship between tradition and modernity to borrow J. H. Kwabena Nketia's (2004) words "without masking my African voice or losing my African identity". On his part, Ngugi has argued consistently that it is important to monitor and to work towards empowerment of ordinary people in terms of encouraging them to have a grasp of their own resources as a community. One of the persistent themes in Ngugi's work is his criticism of the colonial and neo-colonial regimes in both his creative and nonfiction work. It is important to emphasise that although the degree and approach has varied over the years but the rallying point has remained and is the desire to work with the ordinary people to gain control of "the means of imagination" (Rao and Wa Thiong'o 1999, 163). In his effort to contribute to the struggle of keeping the marginalized cultures alive he took up the language question in his essays by writing his fiction starting with *Devil on the Cross* in Gikuyu. In some measure, Ngugi is aware of the complications involved with this decision but as he says he is determined to hold on to his decision: "now I cannot go back" (2000, 9). Ngugi in fact sees the decision to write in marginalized languages as part of the endeavour to move the center and empower marginalised languages and communities.

Both Okot and Ngugi's urgent concern was to get African intellectuals and writers talking to the wider group of ordinary people. This has remained Ngugi's major concern and in his taking up the directorship of the International Center for Writing and Translation at the University of California, with the irony of it being so far from home and the hurdles that poses, where he sought primarily to "encourage a model of cultural conversation through which marginalized languages can be in contact with one another" (Rodrigues and Wa Thiong'o 2004, 162). Both Okot and Ngugi aspire to promote cultural understanding among their own people as a means of liberating African people and cultures from colonial and neo-colonial projects and agency. This conviction manifests itself both in their creative and critical work and in my view their deliberate effort to state this in all their work sets up a dialogue between their creative and critical works.

# *Notes*

1. A number of scholars have specifically discussed Ngugi's theoretical stance and tried to account for his ideological shifts over the years. See Simon Gikandi (2000); James Ogude (1999); Carol . M. Sicherman (1989) and David Cook and Okenimpke (1983). Others have engaged more specifically with the controversies and significance of Marxist theory both in African Literature and in Ngugi's writing: Claudio Gorlier (2002) and Ayi Kwei Armah (1984).

2. A number of critics have observed and discussed Okot's versatility in cultural, intellectual and the arts fields. (see Peter Leman(2009), Lubwa p' Chong (1986), Angela Smith (1989) and Ogo A. Ofuani ( 1985).

3. Linguist Nativism refers to Ngugi's argument that unless writers develop their languages by writing in them, the languages will stay marginalised and the people who use these languages will remain subjugated. There are questions concerning this label. Simon Gikandi for example does not identify Ngugi with Nativisim. The position is more complicated by what Gikandi has called Ngugi's return to English in writing *Moving the Centre,* the revised edition of *Writers in Politics* and *Penpoints, Gunpoints and Dreams.* Gikandi points out that Ngugi's "break" with English is made ambiguous by his operating within "the very Western Establishment whose policies and practices he had previously attacked." Simon Gikandi "Travelling Theory: Ngugi's return to English", 196.

4. Ngugi himself points out what he sees as the differences and development in his fiction. He points out this development in interviews and in his essays. In an interview with D. Venkat Rao (1999) he says that he is aware of the developments in stylistic forms because he is consistently evaluating his themes even those there are persistent themes he explores. He details from his own point of view the differences between his novels. I agree with Ngugi's view that there is continuity as well as shifts between his novels and I also recognize that because the shifts and continuity co-exist there is bound to be contradictions and ambiguities in these texts.

5. I will mention a few although the list particularly in Ngugi's case is endless: Edward Blishen (1971) , G.A. Heron (1972, 1976), Ogo.A.Ofuani (1985), Carol Sicherman (1989), Angela Smith (1989),Patrick Williams(1999), James Ogude (1999) and Simon Gikandi (2000).

## Chapter 6

# HEIRS OF TRADITION OR VEILED ANXIETIES? ROMANCE, SEX, AND MARRIAGE IN CONTEMPORARY UGANDAN WOMEN'S SHORT STORIES

*Lynda Gichanda Spencer*
*Stellenbosch University*

## INTRODUCTION

Ugandan literature is today the site of feminist insurgency. At the core of this literary insurgency is a new generation of women writers.[1] The early 1990s saw the emergence of women's writing in Uganda under the auspices of FEMRITE Publications Ltd. This publishing house, which grew out of the Ugandan Women Writers' Association, has contributed significantly to the expansion of the Ugandan women's literary corpus. It is a Ugandan based, non- profit making association which was born out of the need to organize literary women writers nationally and internationally, collect and disseminate information on gender related issues, advocate for increased women's literacy programs by incorporating literature generated from local communities, while simultaneously encouraging a positive portrayal of women by promoting gender sensitive literature in society. This essay focuses on the emergence of FEMRITE as a site for the articulation of a feminist critique and comments on the various forms of cultural and political marginalization of women located at the intersection of modernity and tradition. The argument is put forth that in the short stories selected for commentary, romance, sex and marriage represent contradictory demands and conflicting desires, on the one hand, projecting a traditional view of marriage, and on the other hand, challenging traditional patriarchal power by constructing alternative forms of female subjectivity.

Prior to 1985, only four women writers had published creative writing in Uganda. Thus, while a number of male writers have secured their place in the African literary canon, their female counterparts have lagged behind (Kimenye et al. 2008, 194). The male literary tradition includes writers such as Cliff Lubwa p'Chong, Byron Kawadwa, Eneriko Seruma, John Nagenda, Peter Nazareth, Robert Serumaga, Pio Zirimu, Okot p'Bitek and Okello Oculi.[2] Despite their under-representation, women have nonetheless been a powerful presence in Ugandan literature, perhaps most memorably in the figure of Okot p'Bitek's fictional matriarch, Lawino. In 1966, Okot p'Bitek one of the most prolific writers to come out of Uganda — published his lyrical poem *Song of Lawino*.[3] Although he was not the first Ugandan writer, p'Bitek was one of the first poets in post-independent Africa to draw heavily on the elements of the oral tradition. Indeed, *Song of Lawino* was originally written in Acoli and then translated into English. In p'Bitek's emotionally charged monologue, Lawino, the female persona, an illiterate village wife, laments the loss of her husband Ocol, who having gone to the city to get a Western education, rejects the traditional Acoli ways. In the song she speaks as a representative of traditional African values, begging her husband to stop mimicking the Western way of life and to return to his indigenous culture, which, she insists, is not as primitive as Ocol thinks it is. Throughout the song, she laments:

> Listen Ocol, my old friend,
> The ways of your ancestors
> Are good,
> Their customs are solid
> And not hollow
> They are not thin not easily breakable
> They cannot be blown away
> By the winds
> Because their roots reach deep into the soil.
>
> (p'Bitek 1966, 41)

As Carole Boyce Davies has argued, women in the African literary tradition, especially in male-authored texts, are defined in relation to men. They are always regarded as someone's wife, mother, daughter, mistress or concubine. As a result, the African female character tends to fall within specific categories or stereotypes. She is either seen as an idealized figure, the Great Mother, endowed with eternal and abstract beauty, embracing each and every nation to emerge as Mother Africa, or as the good-time girl or the prostitute (Stratton 1994; Boehmer 1992; Boyce Davies 1990; Ogundipe-Leslie 1987). In *Song of Lawino*, although we hear the voice of a woman, the concerns of women tend to be on the periphery, as in most male-authored texts from Uganda. The ambiguity of Lawino's legacy is that p'Bitek, the nationalist writer, is ventriloquising through her voice to articulate his concerns about the tensions between tradition and modernity, effectively reiterating the classical nationalist patriarchal trope of women as carriers and custodians of culture.

Yet if we read Lawino as a literary foremother in the characterization and representation of women in Ugandan letters, it would seem that contemporary Ugandan female writers are ambivalent heirs to this iconic figure. Arguably the first literary character to initiate a dialogue on the position of women in polygamous relationships within the modern Ugandan context, Lawino, who may be illiterate, but is highly intelligent, refuses to veil herself in silence. Various male characters may have drowned out Lawino's voice, but women writers in Uganda have heard this whisper loudly and clearly, and they are unequivocal when they address women's issues in their texts. Lawino's voice resounds in contemporary women's writing from Uganda. This voice of protest and resistance has been given a new lease on life through the writings of several Ugandan women writers under the umbrella of FEMRITE. Yet it is clear that the voice of protest that emerges in these texts is firmly grounded in the new social cultural context that is the outcome of colonial modernity. Lawino's concern is colonial modernity as such and the FEMRITE authors focus on the subsequent problems generated by the socio- historical moment that Lawino was speaking to and about. The female characters portrayed by Ugandan women writers, who can be read as Lawino's fictional daughters, are shown struggling to come to terms with colonial modernity and its side effects on various institutions and experiences such as marriage, romance and sexuality.

The Uganda Women Writers Association uses FEMRITE Publications as its mouthpiece in establishing a distinct female literary tradition by creating space for women writers in Uganda. This particularly gendered project, with distinctively gendered subjects, began in July 1997, assisted by the non-governmental organization HIVOS, with the launch of FEMRITE's first publication, the now defunct monthly maga-

zine *New Era*. The magazine was regarded as a medium of conscientization of the association, which aimed to reach out to ordinary women
and men, to encourage a reading culture, to portray positive images of
women, and to change the negative attitudes and biases towards women
and accelerate socio-cultural transformation. In April 1998, FEMRITE
ventured into fiction, when it published four titles.[4] The Royal Netherlands Embassy, which provided the financial assistance, stipulated that
a thousand copies of each title were to be donated to women empowerment groups in the districts of Soroti, Lira, Moyo and Adjumani. In July
1999, five additional titles were launched.[5] In an attempt to generate a
reading culture, particularly among women, FEMRITE, encourages its
writers to create reading materials with a typical "Ugandan touch", so
that their readership is able easily to associate with these narratives.
The association challenges primary school teachers to encourage their
pupils to read these stories, which are relevant to their experience, and
to use these narratives to promote functional literacy among adults.
FEMRITE is conscious that the majority of their adult readership is
semi-illiterate, and therefore writers are encouraged to use an idiom
that is easily accessible.[6] Furthermore, FEMRITE challenges women to
transform their own negative self-images, which are a consequence of
centuries of internalization of the ideologies of patriarchy, gender hierarchy and colonial modernity. It aims to fill this void by exposing stereotypes and placing the concerns of women at the centre of its writing.
As Davies puts it in so doing it is "making 'visible the invisible woman',
or audible, the mute, voiceless woman, the one who exists only as tan-
gential to man and his problems" (1990, 15).

Ugandan women writers do not attempt to rewrite figures of women
encoded in the male literary tradition. Instead they engage in dialogue
with male writers, offering an alternative to male-authored fiction.
FEMRITE recognizes that patriarchy manipulates various aspects of
custom, religion and tradition to subjugate and intimidate women. By
approaching gender from a different standpoint, women writers challenge such biases by addressing the needs and concerns of women. By
constructing a world of women and women's experiences, they are able
to use their writing to negotiate their own space in society. The portrait
of the female that emerges in these texts does not posit a simple, passive,
submissive female character, but re-defines the female as an individual
who appears to be shifting, contradictory, complex, ambiguous and
paradoxical. These images of Ugandan women and tensions of their
existence as women, had been previously been neglected and silenced,
or rendered inaccessible or simplistic, by male writers. Since women

writers in Uganda are concerned with interpreting their experience from a female perspective, they begin by extending the range of female characters marking the heterogeneity of women, a departure from the homogenous woman figure that was portrayed in texts written by men writers; finding spaces within the male authored narratives and opening them up to include the female experience. As Stephanie Newell notes, instead of openly challenging or subverting masculinistic narratives, or writing from marginal or socially outcast perspectives, "women writers are positioned *within*, taking up commonly acknowledged interpretive positions and exploring the flip-side of male-authored narratives" (1997, 397).

The very first collection of short stories written and published by Uganda women is *A Woman's Voice: an anthology of short stories* (1998). This anthology is significant in that it provided the platform from which various unpublished writers were given the space to articulate the experiences of women in a modern urbanized society. In its genesis as a collection, the stories attempt to represent the conflict and tensions between FEMRITE's political agenda and the realities faced by various women in Uganda. The themes in *A Woman's Voice* include teenage pregnancy, marital infidelity, domestic violence, the lack of sex education, the dilemmas of a modern polygamous marriage, the importance of educating the girl child, and the impact of HIV/AIDS on women. The female protagonists in the stories are continually required to deal with various socio-economic issues that affect women in the city. V.Y Mudimbe contends that the African city is an intermediate place

> between the so-called African tradition and the projected modernity of colonialism. It is apparently an urbanized space in which ..."vestiges of the past, especially the survival of structures that are still living realities (tribal ties, for example), often continue to hide the new structures (ties based on class, or on groups defined by their position in the capitalist system)". This space reveals not so much that new imperatives could achieve a jump into modernity, its precarious pertinence and, simultaneously, its dangerous importance. (1988, 5)

The city tends to be envisaged as a place of opportunities. People flock to it harboring high expectations of drastic improvement in their personal, social and economic lives. However, the city is an unpredictable, highly competitive milieu with scarce economic resources, and for uneducated women in particular, most of these hopes and dreams are often left unfulfilled. In order to survive in this hostile environment, women who lack the relevant skills may resort to romantic relationships in pursuit of success. An analysis of the stories 'Joanitta's nightmare' by Hope Keshubi, 'The last to know' by Violet Barungi and 'Where is she? by Philo Nabweru, expose the numerous expectations and accompanying dilemmas that challenge women in the city. The selected stories are representative of the key thematic concerns that are explored in the anthology *A Woman's Voice*. Although the authors use romantic love as a starting point, romance, sex and marriage veil the anxieties that are suggested by the titles of the stories. In other words, romance, sex and marriage are symptoms of contradictory demands and conflicting desires that manifest as the authors attempt to critique a traditionally oppressive society while interrogating women's roles in that society. One could argue that these female characters can, to some extent be seen as the daughters of Clementine, Lawino's arch rival in as far as they inhabit the urban space. Nevertheless, in the poem Lawino the matriarch is dealing with the same troubled relationships as the protagonists in the FEMRITE stories. Insofar as Lawino simultaneously enables and contradicts a feminist voice, the female characters in the short stories tend to echo and contrast her concerns. The three female protagonists expect to find personal fulfillment in their respective intimate relationships but, these expectations are nothing more than wishful thinking. Instead, they come up against real social problems and suffer various forms of gendered oppression. Through romance, sex and marriage, the authors signal an external shift that needs to take place in society both politically and socially before women can begin to feel at ease in their different environments.

## THE ANXIETIES OF TEENAGE PREGNANCY: 'JOANITTA'S NIGHTMARE'

In 'Joanitta's nightmare', Hope Keshubi exposes societal attitudes towards young women who fall pregnant outside of marriage. The female protagonist Joanitta meets Jackson for the first time at an inter-school drama festival. The two are instantly drawn to each other. This physical attraction leads to a date, which ends in the two engaging in sexual intercourse. Unfortunately for Joanitta, her ideal romantic relationship turns out to be the beginning of her nightmares when she finds out that she is pregnant and has to deal with the consequence of the sexual liaison on her own. A disappointed headmistress reluctantly takes Joanitta, one of her brightest students, back to her parents' rural home, where she faces the wrath of her father who reacts violently:

> He dashed to the bedroom and grabbed his hunting spear. On his way from the bedroom, he stormed to the kitchen, grabbed Joanitta's mother with his free hand, and dragged her to the sitting room. ... He grabbed [Joanitta], threw her onto the ground, face upwards, and placed the sharp end of his spear shaft on her belly. "If you don't want me to use this spear to rip your stomach open and remove this unwanted bastard, name the man responsible ... .(1998, 36-7)

Her father with his phallic spear, a traditional symbol of patriarchy, is the villain of the story. He epitomizes all patriarchal hardships that women constantly have to endure. Because she has brought dishonor to her family, Joanitta's only option is to escape the wrath of her father by finding refuge with her maternal relatives. However, as an unmarried mother, her relatives take advantage of her vulnerability and turn her into their house-slave.

Keshubi's views seem to be articulated by the headmistress, who is conscious of her own complicity in an oppressive patriarchal society that prescribes specific values and norms for women. Although she is disappointed that one of her promising pupils is pregnant, her disillusionment is directed towards a society that is unnecessarily punitive towards young girls. Both the family and school system fail to provide any form of sex education, yet when teenagers engage in sexual activities, the female body becomes the site to which societal condemnation is directed because it bears witness to the sexual liaison, while her male partner is absolved of any responsibility. It is these contradictions and tensions inherent in society that the headmistress undermines by offering a counter critique. Firstly, she deliberately flouts the school regulations that demand that she publicly shame Joanitta. Instead, she secretly takes her back home, and even offers her the rare opportunity to continue her studies after the birth of the child. Secondly, she issues a stern warning against backstreet abortions. Underlying this advice is a veiled criticism of repressive patriarchal laws that impede and control women's bodies by criminalizing the termination of unwanted pregnancies while refusing to offer viable alternatives, compelling desperate girls to carry out illegal abortions that are extremely dangerous to them.

The story suggests that Joanitta's pregnancy closes off all her options. In a move that marks her distance from Lawino, Joanitta steps out of Lawino's legacy as her daughter. After the birth of her daughter, Joanitta realizes that there are no possibilities for her in the village, so she moves to the city in search of better opportunities for herself and her daughter. However, the legacies of colonialism and traditional patriarchy have shaped a gendered city that is hostile to women. During this period, attempts were made to keep single women out of the urban areas, because they were regarded as a corrupting influence on the male migrants. Florence Stratton quotes Christine Obbo who reports that in Kampala during the 1950s,

> there were laws requiring the repatriation of all single women found 'loitering' in town. All single female migrants were branded as 'prostitutes' or 'loose' women who were intent on satisfying the sexual needs of the male migrants and consuming some of their money, but who were not destined for marriage. (1994, 16)

Although the modern city may offer alternative possibilities, it is a space of crises and contestation.[8] People migrate from the rural areas in hopes of making a success of themselves, but the city only provides an illusion of material and economic success. The harsh reality is that all it can offer is a cycle of deprivation, social and cultural alienation, and general moral degeneration (Odhiambo 2005, 47). The modern city is a competitive environment, with scarce economic resources and chronic unemployment for Joanitta, who has no money, no educational qualifications, no job prospects, and no social support structures. Her chances of surviving in the city are virtually non-existent. In the absence of legitimate employment she has two options that may generate an income, sex work or employment in the informal sectors of the city. Her destiny is reflected in the life of Nambi, the female character in the story 'Looking for my mother'. Like Joanitta, Nambi is an uneducated woman who comes to the city in search of greener pastures, but soon finds out that, without any skills, the only way in which she can survive is by selling cooked food. She says: "Everyday I had to wake up at 5:00 am in order to start working. My work at that time consisted of cooking food and supplying it to the market vendors at Shauri Yako" (Tindyebwa 1998, 3). At best, this is how Joanitta can expect to survive in the city. Florence Stratton argues that,

> the patriarchal situation ... puts the African woman in a particular kind of double bind. For if, in order to improve her economic status, she chooses to migrate to the city or seek employment, she is labeled a 'prostitute' or singled out as

the cause of national 'indiscipline.' If, on the other hand, she elects to stay in the village or be a housewife, she is economically marginalized. (1994, 17)

The city may promise the individual opportunities for prosperity, but this is only an illusion. Veiled within this promise is an anxiety. For Joanitta to survive in this urban space, she needs to have what Tom Odhiambo, in a different context, describes as the skills and resources that will enable her to participate in social and economic exchanges (2005, 51). Since Joanitta does not possess any skills or resources, one can only conclude that she is going to be as frustrated as she was in the village. In charting this 'transitional moment' between the rural and the modern, new systems which need to be recreated in the urban space have not yet been established.

This initial sedate aura of romance and hopes of personal fulfillment with which the story begins gives way to realities of female vulnerability. Keshubi uses Joanitta's story to capture the social realities and marginal status of women in both the traditional village and the modern city. The issue of teenage pregnancy and its effect on young girls acts as a site for the critique of the breakdown of social morality and the distressing condition of women. During the shift from the rural tradition to the urban, various social systems of sexual education that used to exist in the rural areas, and that would have precluded pregnancy, seem to have been lost, eroded and forgotten in the modern milieu. The story is also an indictment of rigid education policies that only serve to reinforce gendered norms while failing to give information on sex education and the various birth-control methods that are available to provide teenagers. Joanitta warns young girls who may be carried away by their unrealistic views of love and romance:

> I am a living example of how teenage pregnancy causes interruption in education, puts the health of both the mother and the baby at risk, and adds to the economic burdens of the extended family. (Keshubi 1998, 40)

Joanitta's story is an example to young women illustrating the various complexities, tensions, anxieties and contradictions that they have to confront in their daily lives. By creating awareness of the burdens and social injustices facing women, for Keshubi the very act of writing then becomes as Bukaayi puts it, a "silent revolution of protest against the position of women in society" (2009, 158).

# THE DILEMMAS OF FEMALE AUTONOMY:
## 'THE LAST TO KNOW'

In 'The last one to know', Violet Barungi reflects on the sacrifices that women have to suffer in their pursuit of financial independence. After completing high school, Ruth, the female narrator, is romantically involved with John Agaba, a man twelve years her senior. Like Joanitta, Ruth is enticed by love, as well as by the material possessions that John generously purchases for her. When Ruth finds out that she is pregnant out of wedlock, John marries her. In a sense, Ruth's story can be seen as a wishful fulfillment of Joanitta's desire for a stable loving relationship. Nevertheless, the unplanned pregnancy and marriage at an early age mean that like Joanitta, Ruth is forced to sacrifice her education to become a dutiful wife and mother. As a wife, she realizes however that John is not as generous as he was during their courtship. He turns out to be niggardly with his money. Since Ruth has no academic qualifications, she is financially dependent on him, which gives him the power to control her. In the beginning of the marriage, Ruth chooses to ignore this imbalance in their relationship, because she is convinced hers is a marriage based on love, mutual trust and respect. However, the confidence that she exudes veils her anxieties about her personal goals and aspirations. The cracks in her perfect relationship begin to manifest in respect of money. This intensifies her desire for financial autonomy, so when John loses his job, she seizes the opportunity to take control of her finances:

> This was the chance I had been looking for, the golden gate to the El Dorado of my dreams. More and more women were venturing into the business world and making a tremendous success of it. ... I felt excited and confident that things were about to change for the better in the Agaba family. (Barungi 1998, 56)

Ruth's naivety blinds her from the realities of her situation. In the patriarchal society she inhabits, marriage as an institution is viewed as an honour, and being married carries with it a privileged status.[9] It is a society that socializes men and women to perform different roles in a marriage. According to gendered divisions of labour, men tend to occupy the position of the provider and protector a position that is authoritative and assertive, while women are the care givers and nurturers, a role that limits and restricts their mobility to the domestic space. When these roles are reversed in the Agaba household, the minor cracks in the marriage expand into wide crevices. John's patriarchal views that the responsibility of his wife is to stay at home and take care of her husband and children become progressively more pronounced. Financial autonomy provides Ruth with a sense of self-worth and dignity, but it comes at a price, because her husband finds it extremely difficult to reconcile with her success. As John gradually feels disempowered, he seeks validation elsewhere in the arms of Monistera the domestic help, who has increasingly become more involved in the daily running of the house, to the point where Ruth admits that, Monistera "knew more about [her] children's needs and desires; [her] husband's tastes and idiosyncrasies than [she] did." (Barungi 1998, 58) Like most women, Monistera has been taught how to manage a home. This involves how to deal with domestic affairs and prepare food, how to behave towards men and look after husbands, and how to care for children. (Bukaayi 2009, 145) She epitomizes the submissive, obedient, domesticated wife that John desires. The affair, which transpires in Ruth's house, represents John's attempt to regain his perceived loss of masculinity. Barungi is critical of John because he manipulates traditional polygamous institutions to gratify what Ramatoulaye in *So Long a Letter* calls polygamous instincts. Traditional polygamous marriages endeavored to maintain equity, justice, fairness, harmony and shared responsibility within the family (Nnaemeka 1997, 173). In a polygamous compound, each wife was entitled to her own house, a small garden, a share of the livestock, and recognition as the first wife or co-wife (Bekou-Betts 2005, 22). However, modern polygamous arrangements appropriately called 'formalized concubinage' by Obioma Nnaemeka (1997, 174) result in women feeling psychologically and emotionally fragmented.[10] It is this type of polygamous relationship to which that Lawino reacts. Both Lawino and Ruth are humiliated, deceived, betrayed and abandoned by their husbands. The critic Mbye Cham maintains that this

> [a]bandonment is a social disease. It is the cumulative result of a process that could be referred to as the gradual opening and enlargement of emotional/sexual circle that originally binds two partners (a husband and a wife) to introduce and accommodate a third partner in a manner so devious and deceptive that a new process is set in motion. This new process itself culminates in a state of mind and body that forces the first female partner to reevaluate the whole relationship by either reluctantly accepting or categorically rejecting the enlarged circle. (1987, 92)

101

As a woman who experiences conflict and tensions between family and professional responsibilities, Ruth positions herself as a victim of both Monistera and John. She is unable to understand John's betrayal. In spite of her success, she has continued to perform the role of the subservient wife by including John in all her business ventures.

Barungi is problematising the price of female success while commenting on the patriarchal attitudes that Ruth holds towards Monistera. Ruth believes that an unattractive Monistera is not a threat to her marriage, and is only useful insofar as she performs her domestic chores. Meg Samuelson argues elsewhere that women's success is made possible by the presence of a 'wife figure' in the form of a domestic worker who absorbs all the domestic duties (2007, 207).[11] Given that Monistera manages the household efficiently, Ruth moves out of the domestic to the public space to conduct her business, confident that all her wifely duties are being performed to satisfaction. The author implies that as the third partner in this marriage, Monistera is a victim of male lust and female subjugation she chooses self-immolation to escape her oppressive circumstances.

At the beginning of the story, it appears as if Ruth is more fortunate than Joanitta who is abandoned and left to struggle in the city as a single mother. However, like Lawino, she realizes that the secure environment that the institution of marriage seems to offer veils anxieties of the actual experience. Marriage can be a confining space in which women continue to feel marginalized. Romantic love may seem idyllic, but it can also be restrictive, and destructive. Through romance and sex the author explores the unequal gendered power relations that women experience in marriage. She is offering a case study of the contradictory demands that women in the urban spaces deal with in their quest to be economically independent. Ruth's story explores the difficulties that women face as they attempt to negotiate a balance between marriage and financial autonomy. The authorial voice suggests that women should be financially independent without being regarded as a threat to their husband's masculinity. Society needs to recognize that women's economic independence is not linked to power and control, but is a way in which women feel validated and are able to accomplish their personal goals and aspirations. Barungi does not provide any solutions, and the reader is left pondering whether women in Uganda can strike a balance between marriage and economic independence. The paradoxes and contradictions that Ruth has to negotiate, reflect the experiences of women in Ugandan women's writing.

# THE VAGARIES OF WIFEHOOD AND MOTHERHOOD: 'WHERE IS SHE?'

In the short story, 'Where is she?', by Philo Nabweru explores the constraints of dominating and coercive abuse confronting women in intimate relationships. The female focal character, Migisa Anne, like Joanitta and Ruth in the previous stories, has a whirlwind romance with Mugurusi, who fulfills all her prerequisites of the perfect partner. While they are dating, he takes her out for dinners, dancing, and parties, and showers her with expensive gifts. The romance blinds her to advice from her family who warn her against marrying him. The first three years of her marriage prove her detractors wrong, because Mugurusi treats Migisa Anne with love and respect. However, the birth of her first son, which should be a happy occasion, exposes the true identity of her husband. She begins to realize that she married a possessive man, who is so consumed with jealousy that he is resentful towards his own son: "He could not bear those kisses she bestowed on the angelic face of their son. He could not tolerate the love, all of it, was his. He was not ready to share it with anyone ... not even with his first born child" (Nabweru 1998, 69). This resentment towards his own son eventually progresses into physical violence against his wife. In a society where a first-born son is regarded as a prized possession, Ruth is at loss as to why her marriage is falling apart. Marrying a man of her choice does not offer her marital and emotional fulfillment, instead romance and love, are replaced with pain, anger, fear and frustration. While Lawino has to deal with verbal abuse and abandonment, Migisa Anne faces emotional and physical violence from Mugurusi. Unlike Lawino, who vociferously speaks out against Ocol's transgressions, Migisa Anne turns into a timid shell of her former self.[11] This emotional confusion and inner turmoil is a result of being in an abusive relationship.

Nabweru portrays Migisa Anne as a woman caught in a double bind. Since most Ugandan societies are patriarchal, women's social existence is defined in relation to men. Women tend to be defined by their roles as wife or mother. Migisa Anne has fulfilled these dual roles. She is the dutiful wife and loving mother who diligently attends to all her familial obligations, but in spite of this devotion she still finds herself in an abusive relationship. As a woman subjected to frequent violent abuse, Migisa Anne experiences battered wife syndrome. Cipparone defines the psyche of a battered woman as follows:

[she] often believes that no one, including even herself, will be able to resolve her predicament. This feeling of helplessness stems from, among other things, society's reluctance to involve itself in marital affairs. ...The process of victimization experienced by a battered woman may be perpetuated to the point of psychological paralysis: even where options of escape exist, the woman may be unable to act or even perceive the existence of such options. (cited in Tibatemwa-Ekirikubinza1999, 162)

Migisa Anne looks at her situation but she is psychologically paralyzed, preventing her from seeing what options are available for her to break away from her conflict-ridden marriage. Apart from her tumultuous state of mind, I would also argue that there are a number of cultural, socio-economic and legal factors that appear to work against her. Culturally, marriage is regarded as a status symbol in most Ugandan societies it provides men and especially women with an elevated status. Both Migisa Anne and Ruth remain in unhappy marriages because society does not allow them to see themselves as independent beings separate from their husbands. Firstly, their identity is linked to their marital status, and so they find it difficult to see themselves outside that marriage. Secondly, because Migisa Anne marries amidst strong objections from her family, when her marriage begins to fall apart she is too proud to approach them for support. In addition, she cannot turn to her father because he is dead, and her widowed mother can barely take care of herself, so her only option is her brother. In the traditional milieu, it would be his duty as heir to try and resolve her marital problems. If he is unable to find a solution, it is his responsibility to protect his sister by offering her and her son a safe environment in which to reside until she can support herself. But her brother is concerned that she will be a financial burden to his family and refuses to offer support. Mudimbe argues, "one could regard the social disintegration of African societies and the growing urban proletariat as results of a destabilization of customary organizations by incoherent establishments of new social arrangements and institutions" (1988, 4). Her final resort is to turn to the church, which has supposedly replaced the traditional support structures. However, the Catholic Church to which she belongs is full of contradictions. Although she is frequently abused physically, the church offers her no assistance and yet it will not grant her a divorce. Instead of protecting women in accordance with biblical teachings, the church would rather defend the sanctity of marriage. In this case it is done at the expense of a vulnerable woman. Through Migisa Anne's experience, Nabweru is attempting to problematize the various forms of domesticity that entrap women. These domestic traps derive from both colonialism and traditional society:

> Historians have ... pointed to domesticity as a prime example of how foreign values were imposed by colonialism upon local people, inculcated mainly through ducational institutions. In Uganda, however, the Christian and colonial emphasis on women's domestic roles served to intensify values and patterns already in place in most of the country. In the eyes of the British, marriage, motherhood, and the domestic sphere were linked to notions of respectability and gentility, but these class-based definitions would not have been accepted so readily in Uganda had they not accorded with the existing social hierarchy and attitudes towards women's roles. (Grace Bantebya, Kyomuhendo, and Marjorie Keniston McIntosh 2006, 56)

Apart from cultural reasons, there are also socio-economic factors that prevent Migisa Anne from leaving her abusive marriage. Lillian Tibatemwa-Ekirikubinza comments that, "[i]n a patriarchal society, the socio-economic order makes women dependent on men and on marriage. For many women in Uganda, the only economic security they can ever have is a man" (1999, 232). As a housewife and mother Migisa Anne, like Ruth, is economically dependent on her husband. This is in direct contrast to Lawino who has access to a piece of land on which she can grow her own food, which means that she is self-sufficient and not entirely dependant on Ocol for daily existence. These are some of the problems associated with colonial modernity. In the city Migisa Anne is forced to perform a particular kind of domesticity that shuts off some of the opportunities that were open to Lawino. Like Joanitta, she does not have the proper educational qualifications that would enable her to find employment in the formal sector. Even if they both had the necessary qualifications, the colonial education was mainly designed by missionaries and focused on "the idea that good women would remain in the home, concentrating on their husbands and children and utilizing their practical skills as housewives, [which] was a bulwark of middle-class patriarchy in late Victorian Britain and on much of the European continent." (Kyomuhendo and McIntosh 2006, 54)

Migisa Anne is forced to stay in her marriage because of cultural and socio-economic reasons. However, as Lillian Tibatemwa-Ekirikubinza argues, there are also legal reasons that hinder women like Migisa Anne and Ruth from leaving their marriages. Until 2004, the Divorce Act was biased in favour of men. In the case of divorce, adultery by a wife was adequate grounds for a court to grant the husband a divorce, "but a wife could not divorce an adulterous husband who had not, in addition to the adultery, either deserted her or been cruel to her, or committed bigamy or had an incestuous relationship" (Tibatemwa-Ekirikubinza 1999, 95). In other words, for Migisa Anne, physical and emotional cruelty alone is not sufficient grounds for divorce. This divorce law, which was introduced by the British colonial government, illustrates how existing traditional oppressive patriarchal attitudes and colonial practices contribute to the marginalization of women.[12]

In addition to their roles as wives, women like Migisa Anne and Ruth see themselves as mothers. However, since most societies in Uganda are patrilineal, Migisa Anne is aware that if she is to divorce her husband, she cannot take her son with her, because children supposedly belong to the father. In addition to these biased cultural norms, Ugandan law in the majority of cases grants fathers legal custody of the children. Therefore, as Lilian Tibatemwa-Ekirikubinza points out, motherhood

> leaves women vulnerable to patriarchal power because society and individual men hold women's children hostage in order to force women into obedience. A woman's duty to her children plays a critical role in her subordination. Society expects her to sacrifice her joy and freedom to remain in a violent home for the sake of her children. Society requires that a woman's obligation to her children should always take precedence over her own independence and safety. (1999, 9)

Through Migisa Anne's story, Nabweru exposes a society that condones violence against women and shows how complicated it is for women in abusive marriages to escape because of the various cultural, socio-economic and legal restrictions that force them to remain married.[13] Her husband, family, the church, and society have all conspired against her and want her to suffer for the rest of her life. With all her options exhausted, she turns to extreme measures too try to stop the abuse before it kills her. Her marriage is one of pain and suffering, and the broken bowl at the beginning of the story symbolizes her shattered self, a self that cannot be pieced together. Since society does not look kindly on women who have left their marital home, the only way for Migisa Anne to escape from this prison of womanhood is too resort to violence. As a woman who is trapped in a physically and psychologically abusive marriage, Anne is driven to violence in an attempt to protect the self. Anne's attempts to kill her husband, son and herself are a direct result of having been subjected to a prolonged period of physical abuse. This story is an exemplar of the significance of what Nnaemeka means when she describes "personal traumas and disorders [as symptoms] of broader issues of post-colonial dislocations and cultural hemorrhage in an environment where internal systems are undergoing self-induced and externally enforced rearticulation" (Nnaemeka 1997, 187). The romantic love that Mugurusi offers at the beginning of their relationship turns out to veil a destructive infantile obsession, which deteriorates into violent abuse and ends in tragedy as Migisa extrapolates herself from this abusive relationship by disappearing into the night brandishing a knife. With all the disappointments that she has experienced, one can only conclude that she is going to commit suicide and end her torment through the only choice available to her.

## CONCLUSION

The protagonists in these stories have inherited her Lawino's fears and anxieties; and share her disillusionment of marriage and romantic relationships. Romance, sex and marriage veil the harsh anxieties that women have to confront in their everyday lives. 'Joanitta's nightmare' problematises the issue of teenage pregnancy; 'The last to know' offers a complex debate on the tensions that women face as they grapple to balance marriage and economic independence; and 'Where is she?' focuses on the ways in which marriage as an institution entraps women. On the surface, the stories may appear explicitly didactic, but a critical interrogation reveals that they are more nuanced and complicated. The authors appear to represent stories of failure, but each character is provided with a form of agency. Joanitta fully recognizes the hardships that await her in the city, but she is determined to confront any hostilities that she may encounter in order to improve her and her daughter's lives. Ruth loses all her material possessions and her dignity when Monsitera burns herself in her house, but she is determined to rebuild her business and be financially independent. Migisa Anne refuses to remain in an emotionally and physically destructive and damaging marriage. To some extent they may seem unsuccessful, but these silent forms of protest expose the conflicting voices that emerge to challenge the perception that the characters are hapless victims unaware of their oppressive situations. In other words, the writers use their characters to problematize womanhood in Uganda. As African writers, they are taking up Mariama Bâ's call, in a different context, to "paint a realistic picture" of the Ugandan woman's condition (quoted in Juliana Nfah-Abbenyi 1997, 13). As women writers, they are disrupting deeply entrenched patriarchal attitudes and social constraints, which women come up against in their daily lives. They "speak from the position of women's lives, identities and subjectivities that are constantly changing, within specific social locations. We see how most of the characters have to strive for agency within each social location or gender relation in their bid to construct subjectivity" (Juliana Nfah-Abbenyi 1997, 151). In Uganda women's writing, women's voices that had been subsumed by the male literary tradition move from the periphery and are placed at centre stage. By defining women's stories in their own voices, women writers offer the female articulation of the Ugandan experience.[14] Writing creates the space for Uganda women writers to focus on various thematic preoccupations that reflect the experience of female marginality. It gives them the opportunity to "explore more personal experiences, to allow for desire that goes unarticulated indeed, unvoiced in the other forms. The very act of writing for a woman, then, can be seen as [a] transgressive [subversive and empowering act]" (Julien 1992, 47). Although they are limits to this feminist imaginary, there are also numerous possibilities, the major contribution of the female literary tradition in Uganda has been to foreground issues for debate that for a long time have been ignored, neglected silenced or inaccessible.

## Notes

1. I would like to express my sincere gratitude to the Five Colleges African Scholars Program, especially Katwiwa Mule, Samba Gadjigo and Andrea Rushing who read and commented on early drafts of this essay. I also appreciate the suggestions and feedback received from Karen Scherzinger, Meg Samuelson, Nwabisa Bangeni, Ralph Goodman, Louise Green, Tina Steiner, Grace Musila and Dirk Klopper.

2. Because of Uganda's multiple legacies-colonial, cultural, social, educational etc.- the lists of Ugandan writers have mainly been dominated by men. They have traditionally had more access to the country's English-based educational system than women, and they have consequently had more opportunities to express themselves in creative writing.... In the writings of male writers like Robert Serumaga, David Rubadiri, Peter Nazareth, Davis Sebukima and Godfrey Kalimugogo for example, women are assigned peripheral roles. There are even some embarrassing cases in which some novels (by male writers) do not have a single female character. Abasi Kiyimba, "Male Identity and Female Space in the Fiction of Ugandan Women Writers," *Journal of International Women's Studies* 9.3 (2008):194.

3. The Acoli title is *Wer pa Lawino*

4. *Memoirs of A Mother*, by Ayeta Anne Wangusa; *The Invisible Weevil*, by Mary Karooro Okurut, *A Woman's Voice: An Anthology of Short Stories written by Ugandan Women* and *The African Saga*, a collection of Poetry by Susan Kiguli.

5. *Cassandra*, by Violet Barungi; *Silent Patience* by Jane Kaberuka; *No More Secrets by* Goretti Kyomuhendo; *A Season of Mirth*, by Regina Amollo; and *No Hearts at Home*, a poetry collection by Christine Oryema Lalobo. This was followed by the second anthology of Short Stories; *Words from a Granary* which was released in 2001. In 2003, *Tears of Hope*, life stories of eight rural women from western Uganda was published. In 2004, Banannuka Jocelyn Ekochu published *Shock Waves across the Ocean*.

6. The following are blurbs that describe the idiom used in FEMRITE fiction; "Words *from a Granary* and *A Woman's Voice* are inspiring stories *written in a crisp, short style* that is pleasant to read. The stories have unforgettable characters that make us rethink the value systems in our society." (Wordwrite December 2003:32) "*A Season of Mirth is written in simple language,* enriched with proverbs and humor and has characters that come across as real." (Wordwrite July 2004, 21) In *African Saga*, Kiguli *uses simple everyday language* that transforms poetry from the realm of the abstract to the comprehensible without diminishing the spontaneous enjoyment of her message." (Wordwrite April 2003, 15) (Emphasis mine)

7. The first collection of short stories published in Uganda was *Kalasanda* (1965), written by Barbara Kimenye. It is a collection of eight inter-connected short stories based on Kalasanda, a typical village in Buganda. These are stories of ordinary village life, each story tells of an incident in the life of one of the residents of the village, which range from witchcraft, to the visit of the *Kabaka* (King of Buganda). However, *A Woman's Voice* (1998) was the first anthology of short stories published by FEMRITE Publications. The two collections are dissimilar, in that *Kalasanda* was written by a Muganda woman; all the stories in *A Woman's Voice* are written by women from different ethnic groups, their diversity reflects the complexities of post-colonial Ugandan society. In addition, *Kalasanda* is about people in a traditional setting.

8. In order to survive in the city, you have to do the same thing. You have to constantly make sure that you create and invest in certain networks, which are no longer the network of the household, maybe, or of your ethnic group or your village, but different kinds of associations, different kinds of groups of cooperation - maybe a gang, maybe all kinds of groups. But you constantly have to invest, you constantly have to be present, constantly have to exchange, constantly be "in touch" with others. In order to survive in the city you have to know how to do that. When people speak of the city as forest, they refer to a specific kind of forest. It's a forest in which you can become modern, where you can attain and access a certain modernity,

even if it's only in imaginary or oneiric form. Rao, Vyjayanthi. "In conversation with Filip de Boeck and Abdou Maliq Simone Urbanism beyond Architecture: African Cities as Infrastructure," in *African Cities Reader*, ed. Edgar Pieterse et al. (Cape Town. African Center Cities and Chimurenga. 2009), 30-1.

9. In Ugandan society, marriage is a status symbol and it adds value to a woman's worth, not only in the eyes of society but also in the woman's own eyes. A married woman considers herself and is considered to be an appendage of her husband. She will always introduce herself and be introduced by others as her husband's wife. Her whole identity is derived from her marital status. Perhaps this is understandable in a strongly patrilineal society where residence is patrilocal. Marriage submerges a woman's individual identity. A wife hardly considers herself as an autonomous individual separate from her husband. Lillian Tibatemwa-Ekirikubinza. *Women's Violent Crime in Uganda: More sinned against than sinning,* (Kampala: Fountain Publishers, 1999), 233.

10. [T]he "modern," urban (but not so urbane!), African man juggles and manipulates different, sometimes conflicting, systems in an attempt to enjoy the best of all possible worlds. In many ways, the so-called modernity has intensified the masculinization of the African tradition, thereby deepening the marginalization of women and creating instances (for women in particular) where tradition is progressive and modernity reactionary. Obioma Nnaemeka. *The Politics of (M) othering: Womanhood, Identity and Resistance in African Literature.* (New York:Routledge, 1997),171.

11. Retaining a woman to fulfill the wifely duties associated with the private sphere, Ramphele frees herself to operate unhampered in the public sphere and prevents herself from being reproduced as an embodiment of Home. She usurps what she identifies as the 'privileged access to the services of their wives' that has 'freed men to succeed outside the domestic arena.' Meg Samuelson, *Remembering the Nation, Dismembering Women? Stories of the South African Transition,* ( Pietermaritzburg. University of Kwazulu-Natal Press, 2007), 206.

12. The abused wife undergoes a personality change as abuse increases. She becomes frightened and unable to project her thinking into the future. She lives her life from one beating to the next and her thoughts relate solely to her efforts to avoid the next beating. The wife is usually hopeful that if she pleases the husband, the abuse will stop. Lillian Tibatemwa-Ekirikubinza. *Women's Violent Crime in Uganda: More sinned against than sinning,* (Kampala: Fountain Publishers, 1999), 162.

13. 'Physical abuse is for wrong doers' and 'the purpose of the beatings' is to correct the wife' ... the general view was that there must be a reason why a husband beats a wife, so the solution does not lie in divorce. The woman should improve her ways and discard that which provokes the husband in order that the marriage stabilizes. A woman who is beaten for doing wrong

has no justification for leaving her husband. If she provokes her husband, she should endure the abuse. Lillian Tibatemwa-Ekirikubinza. *Women's Violent Crime in Uganda: More sinned against than sinning*, (Kampala: Fountain Publishers, 1999), 41.

14. Goretti Kyomuhendo says "To me, making women the central figures in my stories was, and still is, natural. It is spontaneous! By making them the protagonists, the heroines in the stories I tell, I feel like I am finally according them what they deserve, and have been worthy of for a long time. I grew up perceiving many heroes, but lacked a role model to admire and identify with. By making a female character take on my voice and carry the narration, I am able to make her perceptions an essential part of the message itself. I also realized that in order to write well, one needed to write about a subject one was familiar with, and to me, being a woman is something with which I am existentially bound." Goretti Kyomuhendo. "To be an African Woman Writer: Joys and Challenges," in *Words and Worlds: African Writing, Theatre and Society*, ed. Susan Ardnt et al. (Eritrea. Africa World Press, 2007), 189.

# SECTION II:
## The Eastern African Canon and Postcolonial Imaginaries

# Chapter 7

## RECONSTRUCTION OF THE SUBJECT AND SOCIETY IN NURUDDIN FARAH'S *LINKS* AND *KNOTS*

*Fatima Fiona Moolla*
*University of the Western Cape*

### INTRODUCTION

The abiding concern of the Somali writer, Nuruddin Farah since the publication of his first novel, *From a Crooked Rib*, in 1970 has been how the individual is influenced by power and also how the individual is a source of social transformation. In his early career, Farah did not consider himself a novelist, rather a dramatist in chrysalis, a conviction which led him to submit the first draft manuscript of *From a Crooked Rib* with stage directions and asides. This chapter suggests that, in part, it is the centrality of the individual in Farah's thought which ineluctably draws him to the genre of the novel. The novel is the foremost cultural construct within which the concept of the person as individual has been articulated. But the potential of the form of the novel has been a paradox. In Farah's work, the novel emerges as the genre which best expresses individual freedom but which also ironically precludes the utopian social horizon crucial to the writer's vision. This occurs since the novel originates in and cannot escape the assumption of philosophical individualism contained in formal realism. The constitutive individualism of the novel genre unavoidably disengages the subject it represents from a social code. Farah has written ten novels to date, which, since his very early novels, have taken the form of trilogies. The trilogy, Farah has suggested in interviews, is the novel convention adequately expansive to the full development of an idea. The title of the first trilogy, "Variations on the Theme of an African Dictatorship", clearly captures the issues explored in its constituent novels. "Blood in the Sun" is the title of the second trilogy. What connects these three novels, *Maps*, *Gifts* and *Secrets*, which make up the second trilogy is the figure of the orphan. The orphan in these novels is not only parentless, but also without clan. The social and cultural bonds embodied in clan organization forge the Somali worldview. Ironically, manipulation of a rigidified concept of clan in the colonial and independence eras has led to social fragmentation. In Farah's novels, clan is the one idea which is not open to debate. *Links* and *Knots* are the first two novels of the third trilogy, titled "Future Imperfect", which will be completed with the publication of the novel, *Crossbones*. These two novels are concerned with the reconstruction of self and society in the Somali civil war context. However, it is not only the civil war which makes reconstruction necessary. The reconstruction which forms the project of *Links* and *Knots* is made necessary by the dissolution of the individual to which the novels of the previous trilogy lead. The fragmentation of the superficially unified subject represented by formal realism is the inescapable outcome of the founding contradiction within the novel form. The novel originates as the genre which narrates personal development generated wholly out of the hero's inner resources. Ironically, however, in closure, the protagonist inevitably appears to accept the social role from which he was escaping, but he accepts it, crucially, *of his own free will*. This idea is explored more fully in the next section.

What makes Farah noteworthy among contemporary writers worldwide is the fact that his *oeuvre* traces the trajectory of the history of the novel. His novels move from the proto-realism of *From a Crooked Rib* to the modernism of *A Naked Needle* and *Sweet and Sour Milk* to the postmodernism of, in particular, *Maps* and *Secrets*. This development in the genre of the novel appears to be the necessary resolution of its founding contradiction in formal realism, exemplified especially in Farah's first novel, *From a Crooked Rib*: In this narrative the egregious heroine escapes the oppression scripted by the novel into the concept of tradition, symbolized by the countryside, for the freedom symbolized by the postcolonial city. The heroine flees the countryside to escape marriage to an overweight, elderly but wealthy man arranged for her by her grandfather. Ironically, in the city, the heroine chooses of her own free will a "husband" who is as fat, old and rich as the one she rejects in the countryside. In closure, thus, the heroine "freely" submits to the social role her escape from the countryside was meant to avoid – this is what Joseph Slaughter economically designates as the "tautological-teleological complex of inherency in becoming" which marks the *Bildungsroman*, the defining sub-genre of the novel (2006, 1405-1423, 1415). The move inscribed in the novel "dramatizes" the move which for Canadian philosopher, Charles Taylor (1989), makes modernity wholly distinctive from any other worldview. The novel embodies the relocation of the external social ethical sources constitutive of the person *within* the disengaged, disembedded subject or "individual."[2] The novel in its realist moment generates irony to resolve the contradiction at the heart of individualist subject formation. Irony quite clearly attends closure in *From a Crooked Rib*. The heroine sardonically reflects on the fact that wifehood in the city is not markedly different from wifehood in the countryside, but consoles herself with the idea that at least her "status" is the object of free choice. Modernism, in general, and the modernism of some of Farah's subsequent novels allow irony to reflect on itself. In *A Naked Needle*, the novel which follows *From a Crooked Rib*, the step into a social role is presented ironically. Here, however, ironic resolution distances itself from itself by presenting itself as pure textuality. The end of the novel circles back to the beginning, producing a vortex of textuality. The effect of textuality is to make the tension of irony self-reflexively resolve itself as parody. This development also registers as a critique of the sovereign, rational, Cartesian subject, but it is a reaction which proceeds from the model of the subject as individual which effaces itself. The consequence of this move for the subjectivity inscribed in the novel is fragmentation of the self. In particular, *Maps* and *Secrets* in the second trilogy take this development to its vertiginous conclusion. The virtually complete dissolution of the subject in these novels will be briefly outlined in this chapter with a more detailed consideration of the subject's reconstruction in the third trilogy. The return to a relatively coherent form of subjectivity is, however, demanded by Farah's social concern.

## THE DISSOLUTION OF THE SUBJECT IN *MAPS* AND *SECRETS*

Farah's most self-conscious postmodern novels, *Maps* and *Secrets*, explore and celebrate decentered or fragmented identity in various ways. What this chapter suggests is that these forms of "schizophrenic" identity do not constitute a radical critique of the autonomous subject "tautologically" and "teleologically" constituted in formal realism, outlined in brief above. What dominant interpretations of schizoid identity efface is the disengaged, autonomous subjectivity upon which the celebration of the schizophrenic is premised. As Louis Sass (1987) suggests, schizophrenia is not the escape from the authoritarianism embodied in the autonomous, sovereign subject, it is the pathological consequence of too intense a focus on the atomic identity. As suggested above, it is the figure of the orphan that thematically connects the novels of the second trilogy. The orphan symbolically comes to represent autonomy to the extent that the parentless child is free of what Edward Said refers to as "filiation." Being orphaned need not be construed as a misfortune. Quite the contrary, on a refracted view, once the question of whose son I am is sublimated into the unconscious, the orphan is paradoxically an inheritor of freedom. At a symbolic level, the orphan is free from the "Law of the Father". The concept of the "Law of the Father" developed by psychoanalyst, Jacques Lacan, regards entry into the symbolic order of language as simultaneously a process of submission to a patriarchal order. Questions of identity only partially exposed in the earlier novels are made explicit in *Maps*. "Who am I?" is a question Askar asks himself and others ceaselessly from the time that he can speak. This existential question is also central to *Secrets*. Kalaman, the hero of *Secrets*, is conceived when his mother is gang raped. The leader of the rapists is known only by the initials Y.M.I. – "Why am I?" But in both novels, questions of identity are ultimately sucked into a self-destructive vortex where the question itself and the subject the question is meant to reveal disappear into an abyss. At the end of *Maps* the question remains unanswered since the narrative returns to the beginning. The concept of the secret, which centrally is the secret of Kalaman's identity is destabilized in the final novel of the trilogy. The secret at the heart of *Secrets* is that there are no secrets since every secret seems to be revealed to those from whom the secret must remain most hidden. The dissolution of the subject thus inscribed in the second trilogy is presented as liberatory. Dissolution is scripted into the body politic of Somali society in the form of the civil war whose beginnings we witness at the end of *Secrets*. But dissolution on a social scale is not liberatory. Dissolution when it tears apart family, clan, city and nation is disastrous. The narrative imperative in the third trilogy thus is reconstruction, drawing together what has been rendered asunder, as suggested by the titles of the first two novels, *Links* and *Knots*.

## *LINKS*: TOWARDS RECONSTRUCTION

Recouping some form of centered subjectivity is paramount to Farah's project as it develops in response to the unfolding of turbulent political and social realities in Somalia. Above all else, Farah remains a highly political and socially concerned writer.

However, it is impossible to base a politics on the model of the schizoid subject, since the pathologically fragmented identity lacks agency. Purposive action requires a relatively coherent actor. Clearly in *Links*, "innovative self-destruction," to quote Marshall Berman (1983, 98), quoting a 1978 Mobil oil advertisement, no longer is an option. As Christopher Lasch suggests, "Escape through irony and critical self-awareness is ... itself an illusion", providing "only momentary relief." Lasch suggests further that "distancing soon becomes a routine in its own right," and ultimately "inhibits spontaneity" becoming "as constraining as the social roles from which they are meant to provide ironic detachment" (1976, 96).

*Links* tells the story of the exile, Jeebleh, who returns to Mogadiscio after almost twenty years in New York where he has established a family and a career. Jeebleh returns to Mogadiscio ostensibly to locate his mother's grave. His mother had died nine years earlier. As in many of Farah novels, motives are never uncomplicated. It would appear that Jeebleh also returns to Mogadiscio, the city of death, in the hope that he might "disorient death", as the character himself suggests about his motive. He has had a close brush with mortality before in an accident involving a taxi driven by a Somali immigrant to New York. But these may just be rational justifications for Jeebleh's "true" motive. He may have been drawn to Mogadiscio to settle scores with his "step-brother" and lifetime enemy, Caloosha, the perpetrator of numerous criminal and cruel deeds and the person responsible for the detention of both Jeebleh and his best friend, Bile, who is also Caloosha's brother. Jeebleh also "coincidentally" returns to Mogadiscio at the same time as the mysterious disappearance of two young girls, Raasta and Makka, who may have been kidnapped by Caloosha and whom Jeebleh hopes heroically to rescue in the process of exacting revenge upon his enemy.

In Jeebleh's return, a number of motifs come together symbolized by the title of the novel, *Links*. In coming to Mogadiscio, Jeebleh re-establishes a "link" with the homeland, which simultaneously is a voyage of self-discovery, allowing him to connect with himself and with other like-minded characters, who attempt to reconstitute the body politic. Here, dissolution is read only pathologically, a symptom of the collective insanity of the nation. Schizophrenia and madness are read as psychological responses to a society self-destructing, no longer as a liberatory release from a repressive autonomous self. On witnessing social fragmentation in the city, Jeebleh repeatedly refers to the "borderline schizophrenia" of its inhabitants (Farah 2003, 125, 137). The father of one of the missing girls appears to have a schizoid personality (226-7), similar to the guilty conscience of a Lady Macbeth, at being a passive witness of the slide into anarchy. In an Islamic take on Lady Macbeth's obsessive hand washing, Faahiye, Raasta's father, compulsively performs the ritual of ablution in an attempt to purify himself of guilt. Faahiye personally has not transgressed any legal or moral code. His symptom, in terms of the novel's analysis of the civil war, symbolizes the individual embodiment of the guilt of each and every Somali. Every Somali, on this analysis, is guilty of the horrors of the civil war through an act of omission. Jeebleh's best friend, Bile, appears to suffer from a "mental imbalance" (282) for which he requires "chloral anti-depressants" (296). In the next novel, *Knots*, it is clear that medication is insufficient to compose Bile's disintegrating self.

Allusion, in the specific form of intertextual reference served in earlier novels to suggest the literary "constructedness" of a self which had no stabilizing core: The case of *A Naked Needle*, where in closure in particular, the protagonist is revealed to be a pure textual construct has been explained above. In *Links*, by contrast, allusion serves to give depth and authenticity to a centred protagonist. The texts alluded to fairly explicitly in the novel are Dante's *Inferno*, the Faust myth, Conrad's *Heart of Darkness* and Defoe's *Robinson Crusoe*. Interestingly, Ian Watt (1997) identifies Faust and Crusoe as two of four "grand" mythical figures of individualism, central to the constitution of the European sense of self. (The other two are Don Quixote and Don Juan.) Dante, whose Thomistic conception of man's relationship to God, is shot through by a hitherto unknown focus on the self, is the subject of the claims of both Medieval and Renaissance scholars. Dante locates the source of his subjectivity in a pre-Renaissance conception of the centrality of God but Dante, unlike any other author of the Middle Ages, makes the self the focus of sustained attention. For Jacob Burckhardt in *The Civilization of the Renaissance* Dante is "the most national herald of the time," as a result of "the wealth of individuality which he set forth" (1945, 82). Or as another Dante scholar asserts: "At the same time, Dante is the supreme example in literary history of the writer who, at every important turn, is seeking himself (humanly, morally, psychologically, imaginatively), finding himself, defining himself – in effect, telling his life story" (Lewis 2002, 100). Similarly, *Heart of Darkness* frequently is read as *the* paradigmatic text of modernist subjectivity.

There is a strong connection in *Links* with Dante Alighieri's *Inferno*, the first canticle of *The Divine Comedy*. In an interesting, ironic twist, Dante the Pilgrim descends into Hell and discovers that it looks remarkably much like his native Florence. Jeebleh, by contrast, returns to his native Mogadiscio and discovers that it looks remarkably much like Hell. Even if it were not for this superficial similarity, there are a number of other reasons why Farah might identify with Dante. Dante, like Farah, was an exile whose writing obliges him to revisit again and again the soil of his birth. The clan politics of Dante's Florence, strike one as remarkably similar to the politics of Mogadiscio. *The Divine Comedy*, which Farah has read in the translation by Mark Musa, appears to inform *Links* at numerous levels. It appears to be part of the mental universe of a number of the characters. When he arrives in Mogadiscio, Jeebleh is met at the airport by a character variously called Af-Laawe or Marabou. Interestingly, Jeebleh assumes that Af-Laawe has given himself this nickname, which means "No-Mouth" in Somali, as a deliberate reference to the character "No-Mouth" in *The Divine Comedy*. Jeebleh himself, we are informed in the text, while studying in Italy, did a Somali translation of the *Inferno* as a dissertation. Jeebleh's Irish friend, Seamus, who also studied with him in Italy, is quite unproblematically able to quote a Dantean verse appropriate to the Somali civil war.

But the *Inferno* is more deeply constitutive of *Links* also. In the structure of its plot, *Links* parallels the voyage of Dante the Pilgrim on his spiritual journey from being lost in the forests of despair, through the gates and all the circles of Hell to Lucifer's inner sanctum and out on the other side. Dante the Pilgrim is guided in his descent through the Inferno by the reliable, trustworthy pagan poet, Virgil, who represents Wisdom. In the same way, Jeebleh is guided through the hell that is Mogadiscio by the deceptive, corrupt, thieving Af-Laawe, who represents the antithetical wisdom of the streets. In *The Divine Comedy* when Dante first sees Virgil, he is described as a "shade." The first thing Jeebleh sees of Af-Laawe is his shadow: "Turning, he saw the stranger's late afternoon shadow" (11). Part of the inscription above Hell's gate in *The Divine Comedy* forms the epigraph to the first part of the novel in the later Duckworth edition.[10] It reads: "Through me the way into the suffering city / Through me the way to the eternal pain, / Through me the way that runs among the lost."

The allusions to the *Inferno* are dense and layered and cannot be fully unraveled here. However, Jeebleh's escape from his Mogadiscian hell requires consideration. With an economy and simplicity strikingly similar to the exit of Dante the Pilgrim from the Inferno, Jeebleh emerges from the hell that is Mogadiscio. Where Dante emerges from the crepuscular gloom to see the stars, Jeebleh emerges from the mist to see the sun. Dante's Hell "is shaped in concentric circles that spiral downward ever tighter, until you reach Betrayal" (Menocal 1994, xiv). Traitors are the sinners who keep the devil company. And, for a number of reasons, Jeebleh regards himself as a traitor since he abandoned his mother and his motherland. Betrayal similarly seems to occupy the very heart of the architecture of Mogadiscio as Hell. *Links* suggests that the civil war in Somalia needs to be understood as the betrayal of one Somali by another. Af-Laawe, Jeebleh's treacherous guide, observes: "In a civil war, death is an intimate … You're killed by a person with whom you've shared intimacies, and who may benefit from your death" (128). Af-Laawe underscores his point by referring to the Somali expression for civil war, "*dagaalka sokeeye*," which translates as "killing an intimate." Of all the explanations which have been offered for the Somali collapse, the text seems to suggest that at the heart of it all, lies the betrayal of one individual by another. At a personal level, Jeebleh suspects, agonizingly, that through his "brother" Caloosha's offices, his mother may have died thinking her son was a traitor. If Lucifer is the arch-traitor in the inner circle of Dante's Hell, Caloosha is the Devil in Farah's *Links*. The text quite explicitly identifies Caloosha as the source of whatever disharmony, violence, corruption, cruelty and brutality exist in the novel. Caloosha, the brother of Bile, who, it appears, murdered his own father and had a hand in his incarceration under the Dictator, is represented as pure, evil, a supporter of inter-clan strife, an oppressor of women and the head of a cartel dealing in body parts, a thoroughly disgusting, vile person.

There is, however, a highly significant difference between the *Divine Comedy* and its use in *Links*. Political analysis in Farah's novel distills down to the inherent evil in certain individuals, challenged, as we shall see, by the good in others, symbolized by the miracle child, Raasta. Evil and good exist as metaphysical categories, however, in an individualist philosophy which structurally cannot produce such ontologies. The structure of the *Divine Comedy* sustains a focus on the unique person, but each person is offset against a transcendental moral horizon. In the afterlife, each sinner is punished according to the nature and degree of his sin which is judged against an ontologically fixed moral code. The culture of individualism, the crucible which forms Farah's novels, exists, in Alasdair MacIntyre's terms, "After Virtue", since the autonomous disengaged self cannot construct a *social* moral code. *Links* thus is structured around a clear moral axis, which comes from outside of the individualist worldview of the novels. But in the process of the individualist "reinvention" of sacred eschatology, the *social* practices in which good and evil were constituted are lost. Good and evil exist in the novel simply as sensational elements in a world without a complex enabling social structure.

The myth of Faust is, for Ian Watt, another of the symbolic representatives of European individualism. The way Faust is used in the novel suggests another inherent problem in the manner in which the novel resurrects morality which is necessarily social, but elides the origins of ethics in a social paradigm. If Jeebleh's unacknowledged motive for returning to Mogadiscio is to kill the cruel and villainous Caloosha, then, like Faust, he has entered into a pact with the Devil. The novel progressively exposes how Jeebleh's story is drawn into the corrupt and corrupting influence of the civil war story. The text suggests that Jeebleh would not hesitate to kill to serve the ends of justice. Paradoxically for Jeebleh the quest for justice draws him closer and closer to the Devil, much like Caloosha's quest for power makes him evil incarnate.

What makes the analysis of the character of Caloosha problematic, and Caloosha is presumably the type for many of the warlords operating in Mogadiscio, is that his psychopathic behaviour appears not to be the consequence of a self-interest unchecked by societal control since Somali society is a non-functioning society. It appears rather to be the consequence of the fact that he is innately evil. In a sense, he is presented as a detestable Devil whose inauspicious beginnings – he was born in the breech position – very nearly kills his mother and fatefully determines his character. The evil that is Caloosha is epitomized by the anxiety of his own mother, who before her death, had remarked: "It's very difficult to rid yourself of the monster whom you've given birth to yourself, fed raised and looked after, and then let loose on the world" (156). Since *Links*, dedicated as it is to autonomous individuality, cannot construct a moral horizon since morality is necessarily social, it resorts in sensational terms to the moral vocabulary of other social codes, but without the complex social network of obligations out of which this moral vocabulary arises.

Numerous explanations for the Somali collapse have been proposed, sometimes as single factors and sometimes as a combination of factors. Many of these analyses are presented in the collection *The Somali Challenge: From Catastrophe to Renewal?*, edited by Ahmed Samatar.[12] Among these explanations are included: the destabilizing effect of colonial manipulation of tradition and the imposition of colonial national boundaries, the breakdown of civil society as a consequence of more than three decades of dictatorship, Cold War proxy rivalries and tensions, the sometimes deliberate and sometimes unforeseen effects of international aid; urbanization and unequal distribution of resources between the middle class and the unemployed and a host of other factors. Yet in *Links,* all this complexity is distilled down to the individual and issues forth in statements like: "... in civil wars, both those violated and the violators suffer from a huge lack – the inability to remain in touch with their inner selves" (69) and "Neither the city nor the nation had a unifying theme. We were headless as individuals..." (108). While not denying the factor of the agency of each person, it is misleading to locate all Somalia's ills only in the autonomous individual disengaged from its social circumstance.

It is precisely this limited and limiting view of the crisis which leads Jeebleh to his simplistic individual and, to a certain extent, megalomaniac solution. His singular intervention will save Somalia. *Links* thus goes well beyond resuscitating agency from the indecision which hangs over *Maps,* to an exaggerated sense of the significance of the individual intervention. To serve the greater cause of justice which consists in the liberation of the child of peace, Raasta, he feels justified in killing her captors, which in the actual outcome of the story proves unnecessary when Raasta, in circumstances which remain mysterious, is simply released.

*Links* shares a number of structural similarities also with Joseph Conrad's modernist *Bildungsroman, Heart of Darkness.* Early on in the narrative, reference is made to self-recuperation as forging "a link to the darkness at the centre of [one's] life" (55). This summary of *Heart of Darkness* (in part indebted to Michael Levenson (1991) makes clear its similarity with the plot structure of *Links*: A man leaves his home to travel to another country where he hopes to conclude unsettled matters. The country itself and the people he meets there disturb his moral certainties. As a consequence of his experiences, he finds himself adopting the distorted morality of the alien country. Despite his transformation, he is unable to remain in the alien country. He returns to the normality of his home, but will feel forever estranged among his acquaintances.

However, while the subjectivity Marlow discovers is "hollow" to the core, subjectivity in *Links* is centred, but within a moral horizon structurally outside of its own possibility. The character, Jeebleh, marks a return once again after *Maps* and *Secrets* to the relatively coherent self of literary realism. Jeebleh's development involves finding ways to connect with others without the ties which bind the autonomous self.

In the novel this involves affirming again the individualist truth of the disengaged, independent self; whereafter forms of association which leave the individual fundamentally free may be negotiated. Affirming autonomy takes the form of a parable, based upon Defoe's tale of *Robinson Crusoe*, one of Watt's "grand" myths in the formation of modern individualist subject formation. This allusion reverberates throughout in the text, not through the central character, Jeebleh, but through his best friend, Bile, whose importance is suggested by the fact that, apart from Jeebleh, Bile is the only other narrative focalizer.

Significantly, Bile's general factotum who "rescues" Jeebleh from the suspicious Af-Laawe is referred to as Bile's "Man Friday". This reference to Crusoe's colonial subject, Man Friday, alerts us to the ways in which Bile's story is modeled on that of Robinson Crusoe. Bile has been incarcerated under the dictatorship of Siyad Barre. When the dictator flees Mogadiscio in January 1991, the gates of all the prisons, zoos and madhouses are flung open, delivering their inmates into the streets. Bile experiences his release from captivity not as an exhilarating freedom, but as an experience as terrifying as Crusoe's shipwreck. Much like Crusoe who shuns social ties to pursue his agenda as *homo economicus*, Bile prefers remaining in his cell alone. Bile claims he cannot leave this "room of his own" since he has trouble walking as a consequence of muscle atrophy through lack of exercise in prison. Later he is forced to leave his cell. Like Crusoe, shipwrecked on the island, who fears attack from wild beasts and cannibalistic natives, Bile fears the people on the outside. He encounters, what he describes as a gang of marauding youths whom, surprisingly, contradicting his earlier claim about his incapacitated condition, he manages to outrun. Fortuitously, he comes upon an abandoned house evacuated by its obviously well-to-do owners. As he is fleeing from the youths Bile finds that he is alone in the house except for a dog, the analogue of Crusoe's parrot, which the owners have abandoned. This house is to Bile what the deserted island is to Crusoe. If Crusoe needs the deserted island in order to stage himself as the hero in a narrative about the virtues of economic individualism, Bile needs the empty house to compose himself as a hero of a slightly different sort. Bile composes himself, both in the sense of recovering after his frightening ordeal, but also in the sense of constituting himself as a kind of benevolent, philanthropic actor in the cause of goodness. In the house, Bile discovers a duffel bag filled with almost a million US Dollars. Having figuratively "pulled himself together," he ventures forth to construct the world anew. He uses the money to fund his experiment in imaginative social construction, called "The Refuge," for those dispossessed by war. He also constructs a hospital and a home for himself and his like-minded friends. These, to continue the insular motif are islands of hope in a war-torn land.

What often goes unnoticed in the myths of self-made men is the occluded extent to which they rely on the products of social endeavor. Crusoe, of course, is not wholly independent in the construction of his sovereign domain. As Christopher Hill observes, he relies on the products of a more social world, brought from the shipwreck: "It is thanks to the tools and commodities which Crusoe salvages from the wreck that he is able not only to survive but to prosper, drawing on the heritage of centuries of civilization" (1980, 12). What Hill refers to as Crusoe's "mental furniture," comes from a world in which the subject is embedded in social relations, not isolated on an island. Similarly, to construct his "islands of hope," Bile uses the money which is not the product of his independent labour. More importantly, however, he fosters in The Refuge positive social practices which have their source in precisely the traditional worldview Farah's novels critique. For example, Bile encourages the use of the *mayida* or tray out of which a number of people share food, on the belief that people who eat together will not kill each other. Harry Garuba notes that Bile's experiment "in creating a new kind of public" is anchored "on a traditional practice from the past" (2008, 193). What is also interesting in Bile's experiment in a new form of sociality which borrows from but tends to elide the past, is Bile's position as "benevolent sovereign", – he constructs a society which, curiously, he is not a part of. What is striking in descriptions of Bile's participation in the social and sociable world he constructs is that he seems to be alienated within it. The reader knows fatefully that Bile's projects will fail because it is suggested by the decomposition of his self which we observe at the end of the novel and which is corroborated in the subsequent novel.

This project of social engineering proceeds on the basis of the autonomous self that comes to be embodied in the miracle child, Raasta, whose given name, "Rajo," means "hope." Raasta has a preternatural facility for languages and draws people around herself together in peace. Garuba suggests that Raasta's body "becomes the site around which the conventional heterogeneity of city life can be performed" (193) and her gift of polyglossia is symbolic as "the abode of linguistic diversity" (194). Raasta is the wonder child conceived and delivered as opposed to the stillborn miracle children of the earlier novels, in particular, the foundling in *Gifts*. Unlike these other children who usher in a golden age, Raasta has "secular beginnings, and had nothing to do with the religious fevers that were part of the millennial hysteria presaging the disastrous end of the corrupt world" (276).

Raasta's Down's syndrome companion, Makka, by contrast, for Garuba, "represent[s] the arrested development of the country and the city and the potential locked away in its inarticulacy" (194). At a more primary level, of the subject who constitutes the public sphere, Makka may be read as an example of failed *Bildung*, akin to Askar of *Maps*, but with a significant difference. If perfect self-fulfillment for Askar is embodied in the solipsistic ideal of perfect existential certainty, "I am I," in the later text, the hermetically contained self becomes a problem. When Bile finds the orphaned Makka, she utters over and over to herself the Somali phrase, "aniga, aniga ah!" translated in the text as "Me, myself I!" (149), or in alternate translation, "I am it!". But clearly the self-constituting self here is psychopathic. Thus, while in the earlier novels, the self-generating, perfectly self-sufficient subject is presented as a utopian ideal, in *Links*, through the contrast between the prodigy Raasta and the abnormal Makka, a shift in the nature of subjectivity is signaled. Complete independence and self-reliance now are projected as pathological. The individual now needs to connect to achieve self-realization.

The transformed subject is the individual who can connect with other individuals, which breaks the curse of isolation, who can make "links" without losing the freedom essential to the autonomous self. *Links* is a novel about entering sociality, but a sociality quite unlike earlier forms of community, since sociality must not create obligation, Freedom, rather than duty, is the central virtue of a restored social world which consists of a collection of individuals. Raasta again is a symbol of the new public envisioned by the novel. Towards the end of the novel, after the girls have been found, Raasta's mother, Shanta, is distraught at the impending psychological collapse of her brother, Bile and her impotence to assist him. The mother is in tears in Bile's clinic. Expanding on the allegory of individual and collective contained in the use of pronouns which has been a sustained concern of the novel, Raasta overcomes her fear "of plurals," to draw those around her into a kind of mutuality: "Raasta now gave her mother a sweeter hug ... And Raasta talked to her mother, then to Makka, then to the little sick girl in an inclusive way, making them all think that there was fun in plurals" (284).

Raasta, in miniature, thus represents the protagonist, Jeebleh's, development. Jeebleh's self-realization involves much more than just the renewed link with the motherland. It involves, more fundamentally, finding ways to link with others which do not compromise the independent self. Jeebleh, seeing his reflection in the mirrored sunglasses of

Qasiir, the type of the new Somali urban youth, concludes "that he had changed a lot in the short time he had spent in the city of his birth" (292). The nature of this change involves the capacity of the autonomous, self-narrating subject to form associational bonds with other autonomous, self-narrating subjects: "My friends and I are forever linked through the chains of the stories which we share" (302). If, in closure of the classic realist novel, individual freedom is contained by the social bond of marriage, at the end of *Links*, a broader sociality is imagined which is lyrically and triumphantly articulated through the closing words: "And we!" (303).

Curiously, what is absent in closure is the irony requisite of the novel as a genre. Irony was generated out of the "tautological-teleological" compromise of individual autonomy with traditional morality. Irony is notably absent at the end of *Links*. The "neo-realism" of the relatively coherent, improvisational self seems to transform the novel more and more into romance, one of the sources out of which the novel emerged, as will be shown in the next section. Jeebleh, on this interpretation represents a kind of knight who rescues both the maiden, Raasta, and the common good. The romance dimension of Farah's neo-realism within which a relatively coherent subject is once again recovered, becomes apparent in the most recently published novel, *Knots*.

## *KNOTS* AND THE POSTCOLONIAL ROMANCE OF THE PUBLIC SPHERE

An incipient focus on alternative forms of community in *Links* is continued and is enlarged upon in the next novel, *Knots*. *Knots* tells the story of a diasporic Somali who returns from Canada to her native land. In this novel also, the personal developmental tale is inextricably connected with a broader story of development, but this time not of national development, as in *Maps*, but the development of a form of post-national community. Cambara, the protagonist, returns to Mogadiscio for a number of overlapping reasons; but chief among these is her secret and outrageous intention of taking possession of a property owned by her family, now occupied by a minor Mogadiscio warlord. Repossessing the mansion which her family let out to diplomats and dignitaries appears to be part of a greater ambition to construct a "counter-life" of peace in the war-decimated Mogadiscio. The family property acts in the novel as the symbolic locale for the reconstruction of Somali civil society. She knows that "as a woman alone, she stands no chance of survival,"[16] so she aligns herself with a women's mutual help network, which appears to operate throughout Mogadiscio. Cambara's ambition as Farah presents it is nothing less than to construct, single-handedly and at an oblique angle to Somalia's historical trajectory, a version of the modern public sphere.

The reading of this dimension of the novel relies on Jürgen Habermas's (1989) analysis of the version of the public sphere which emerges in late eighteenth century Europe. Habermas's understanding of the modern public sphere will emerge in the course of the interpretation of the novel. In *Knots* the reconstruction of Somali society, stateless since the flight of the dictator, Siyad Barre, in 1991, may again be contrasted with the earlier novel, *Links*. While *Links* seems to locate the potential for regeneration of Somali society in benevolent men, *Knots* locates the potential for reconstruction specifically in women. We encounter again in *Knots* the character, Bile, from the earlier novel. But Bile is completely war-traumatized, overdosing himself on Prozac generics to keep himself quite literally from coming mentally undone. Also abandoned in *Knots* is the idea of the transformation of Somali society by a miracle child of peace. In *Knots* the task of Somali reconstruction is left squarely to women and is given shape through the formation of Somali civil society. For this monumental mission, the almost superwoman status with which her author imbues Cambara is vital. Cambara jets in from Canada, a knife-wielding martial arts expert who is also a make-up artist, actress, distinguished journalist and soon to be playwright and theatre director.

While public spheres have existed wherever there have been communities, the public sphere envisioned by *Knots* is a variation of the public sphere which emerges at the end of the eighteenth century in Europe, analyzed by Jürgen Habermas. For Habermas, this public sphere embodies a utopian ideal, which in the course of history has not been realized. The bourgeois public sphere is a sphere of "private people [who] come together as a public" (Habermas 1989, 27-8) and engages in rational-critical debate which challenges public authority. By implication, the participants in the potentially utopian public sphere are the subjects of a "disenchanted" world, where the participants view the world in the light of reason procedurally rather than substantively defined. Procedural rather than substantive rationality is focus of the Cartesian conception of truth. The Canadian philosopher, Charles Taylor, makes clear the unprecedented nature of this public sphere in a qualification of Habermas's definition. The eighteenth century public sphere is "an instance of a new kind: a metatopical common space and common agency without an action transcendent constitution, an agency grounded purely in its own common actions" (Taylor 2004, 86). In other words, in the Somali context, a public sphere has always existed for public debate which was radically democratic in its (gendered) inclusiveness, symbolized by the tree beneath which participants came together. This Somali public sphere deferred to an "action-transcendent" code of virtue, embodied in Islam and tradition, the law of God and the law going back to time immemorial. The actors in the Enlightenment public sphere, by contrast, are autonomous, morally self-constituting individuals. The public sphere thus constituted is purely horizontal, constituting exclusively in its activity its own higher order or morality.

What is the nature of the Somali public sphere envisioned by *Knots*? If, as critics suggest, the reference to "private people" in the formulation of the bourgeois public sphere is a euphemism for propertied men, then by contrast, the private individuals of the public sphere in *Knots* quite explicitly is a sphere of propertied women. Somali civil war atrocities are symbolized by dirt, filth, ordure, graphically represented in virtually all of the male characters. Cambara, for example, finds Bile, the Robinson Crusoe figure in *Links*, physically unable to raise himself from his own excrement since he has fallen apart psychically. In the same way that Cambara cleans up both Bile and his apartment, the text suggests that women need to "clean up" what is rotten in the "state" of Somalia. The task of Somali reconstruction in this novel is presented as the task of women since even men with the will to challenge the civil war lack the capacity to effect any change.

Thus, *Knots* constructs *ab initio* a female public sphere. This female public sphere is not a *counter*-public sphere. In the civil war Somalia of the novel, there is no male public sphere. Since there is no state there is no public authority. The female public sphere is created in this vacuum of statelessness and social order. There is, furthermore, no sharp division as with the bourgeois public sphere, between public *activity* and private *deliberation*. The Somali female public sphere takes on what in Habermas's formulation would constitute the function of public authority, implicitly weakening the public sphere's capacity for political critique. The Women's Network takes the initiative for the provision of healthcare and acts as police, judge and jury in cases of the abuse of women.

Habermas's conceptualization of the bourgeois public sphere constructs the division between public and private so that traditional women's work and women's concerns fall into the realm of the private and thus are not open to political deliberation and transformation. The Somali female public sphere as presented in *Knots*, gestures towards opening up the sphere of women's work to public deliberation. There is a focus on traditional women's work which suggests that women's concerns will be part of a fundamentally restructured conception of the public sphere. Unfortunately, the novel draws in women's work in a way which seems to limit concerns to middle class consumerist worlds. This novel indulges in carefully crafted "throwaway" references to female attire, day and night creams, make-up and shoes. Cambara also invests an inordinate amount of effort cooking. In a variation of the adage that the way to a man's heart is through his stomach, Cambara cooks for the various child soldiers and battlewagon security guards to win them over. All of the principle female characters are professionals, but also mothers. Yet the novel's projection of a Somali female public sphere does not challenge in any fundamental way the division between female reproduction and male social subject production. The women of the Somali female public sphere bear and raise children, cook and keep house, but these are not the activities around which their public sphere is developed. Traditional women's work remains excluded from real debate even though it is brought out from what Habermas describes as the "shadowy realms" of the intimate sphere of the bourgeois household. The Somali female public sphere maintains the masculine division between public and private activity through locating the real work of a public sphere elsewhere, as we shall see. As such, the female public sphere presented by *Knots* appears merely to be a feminized version of the male public sphere.

It would appear that part of Cambara's mission all along has been to stage a play in the family property, repossessed from the minor warlord. Like Habermas's bourgeois public sphere, the Somali public sphere envisioned by *Knots* seems to consolidate itself through cultural expression. But there are also marked differences between the two public spheres. For Habermas, the private individuals of the bourgeois public sphere at the outset are a reading public. This appears not to be the case in the Mogadiscio constructed by *Knots*. A few of the male characters in the novel, through their dispositions and social conscience, act as token women. Bile is one such character. When she first meets him "...Bile is holding a book gingerly and using his index finger as a bookmark; ..." (169). Unfortunately, "...no matter how hard she tries, [Cambara] is unable to make out the title of the book he has on his lap" (169). Thus, while the bourgeois public sphere developed organically out of economic and cultural transformations of which letter writing, an improved postal service, burgeoning newspaper and periodical circulation, the development of the scholarly journal, the activity of the literary critic and widespread reading of novels were hallmarks, the private individuals of the Somali public sphere are not conceived by the novel as a reading public. No matter how hard Cambara tries, the book on Bile's lap cannot be identified and cannot come to occupy even a symbolic role.

Somalis, particularly Somalis who have remained in the Somali territories, constitute an oral rather than literate public. Paradoxically, although the public envisioned by *Knots* is not a reading public, the individuality displayed by its full members is an individuality derived originally primarily from books, particularly the novel in its fundamental embodiment as *Bildungsroman*. Cambara intends "to construct a counter-life dependent on a few individuals, namely Kiin, maybe Bile and Dajaal, whom she has cast in the likeness of reliable allies" (201). The characters whom Cambara is able to enter into association with, rather than those whose purpose consists in being functionaries, are all products of the formation ideal which is the project of all Farah's novels. But the focus in this novel falls on identity formation through theatre and the electronic media since Somalis remain predominantly oral.

Ironically, although the public to be incorporated by *Knots* is largely not a reading public, nevertheless, full entry into this sphere depends upon "full" individuality. As has been suggested earlier, the construction of such individuality relies in no small part upon the technology of the *Bildungsroman*. What makes *Knots* slightly different from the earlier *Bildungsromane* in Farah's *oeuvre*, is that, here, construction of "re-inventing" individuals for an imagined community is so deliberate. The centrality of the individual is foregrounded in ways characteristic of the novels of Farah. Farah's protagonists without exception reflect a consuming preoccupation with the self. Cambara is no exception. Securing the right allies and procuring the appropriate means of defence is a subordinate concern of Cambara's mission in Mogadiscio. More than anything else, realizing her ambitions depends upon the realization of a particular sense of self. It is an abstracted sense of self wholly disengaged from its context which exists as a defined object manipulated and structured at will by the radically reflexive mind. In order to consolidate and develop this "audience-oriented" self, Cambara displays the tendency to isolate herself. Like the individuals of the bourgeois home Habermas describes, Cambara repeatedly needs to withdraw into the private spaces of her bedroom or bathroom either at her cousin's house or at Kiin's hotel. Privacy figures in the novel not as the occasional need to be by oneself. Privacy appears to constitute a fundamental feature of how individuality is represented. The new subjectivity which comes to light is the identity which repeatedly privately rehearses its public roles before the mirror. Again and again in the text, the protagonist seeks out her reflection in perfecting the dramatization of character.

Not everyone in the novel, it would appear, is equipped with the appropriate individuality for its version of the Somali public sphere. Cambara seeks in Mogadiscio to replace the son she lost in Canada with other children. Two possibilities present themselves. The first is a child soldier that her cousin, Zaak, employs to protect his home and himself. The second is an apparently orphaned child whom Cambara finds hanging about outside the hotel where she stays. Although the first child is a product of the patrilineal, pastoral Somali clan system which values kinship to the extent that most Somali children are supposed to be able to give not only their own names but also the names of their forefathers right up to the higher reaches of the family tree, the child who appears to fulfill Cambara's maternal instincts is known only by a physical attribute. Because of his soft, wavy hair, this child is called SilkHair. Virtually without exception, those characters immersed in ways which could be described as traditional, appear to lack as individuals the uniqueness and rich interior world which would warrant their being given a name. All of these characters, who through the nature of their subjectivity, must remain incidental, are identified only by external attributes. The characters named only by physical attributes are fated through their lack of individuality to perform the roles of functionaries in the novel.

The orphan whom Cambara meets at the hotel, on the other hand, is not simply named according to some outstanding external feature. He is asked his name. It is Gacal. Gacal is a child born to expatriate Somalis who, though they have no Somali friends in the United States where they live, wish for their son to come to Mogadiscio to learn Somali culture. Gacal's father is killed and his mother's whereabouts are unknown. The cultivated Gacal, unlike SilkHair, displays a full individuality Cambara studies Gacal:

> She finds the observation most becoming, out of the ordinary: a boy, not quite ten by her reckoning, who displays a developed-enough personality and qualifies as no one's son … Gacal has the sort of flair you associate with the well-born. He carries himself with élan. It does not require much imagination to sense that he is of a different class, physically aware of where he is in relation to where others are. Not only does he surround himself with much space, but he is mindful not to encroach on yours. Does his behaviour point to a middle-class upbringing in his past? (229)

As if Gacal's development were not complete, Cambara gives him a video version of Carlo Collodi's *Pinocchio* to watch with Kiin's daughters. The novel foregrounds an interpretation of the children's story which highlights how, despite their circumstance, Good Bad Boys, as opposed to Bad Bad Boys can become well-adjusted. But *Pinocchio* is also a children's tale which, as many children's stories do, lays bare the mechanics often masked in adult fiction. *Pinocchio* is, of course, a *Bildungsroman* which reveals the developmental path by which a boy made of wood, a mere puppet on a string, subject to dictates which are not his own, can become a real flesh and blood, thinking, feeling, reflecting, rational being determining his own course. The class specificity of the individuality required for the novel's version of a Somali public sphere is apparent.

Through a noticeable attention to consumerism and life as "style," evident in the focus on clothing, shoes, make-up, table settings, food and the common leisure activities of a select group, the public sphere envisioned in *Knots* bears a remarkable similarity to the *lifestyle enclave* which as Robert Bellah et al suggest "celebrates the narcissism of similarity" (1996, 72). The question of "style" particularly in relation to the self is highly significant.

The focus no longer is, as it was in *Maps*, on the illusion of an autonomous self revealed to be an aesthetic construct. Rather, at this moment in Farah's career which reflects a global trend beyond postmodernist writing/thought, the focus is on how a relatively coherent, constructively self-reflexive subject "styles" itself. The concept of self-styling draws upon, but also misreads *gnothi seaton*, the Greek invocation to "care of the self," taken up by Michel Foucault in *The History of Sexuality*. The life of the individual here is presented as an "aesthetic or cultural project." In other words, where earlier the subject was projected as a literary construct, now the subject constructs itself as a work of art. Earlier in Farah's work, the moral horizon was projected onto the aesthetic; at this stage in Farah's exploration, to aestheticize one's life becomes the new moral horizon as the subject him/herself becomes the work of art.

An associated move in *Knots* is identified in the focus on performance - on theatre, masks and costumes and through performance on the idea of "performativity". The concept of "performativity" originates in the Speech Act theory of J.L Austin and has been developed by Judith Butler into a broader theory about the construction of identity. Austin's "performative" refers to words which in their utterance constitutively perform an action, rather than merely naming an action. Butler develops Austin's notion of the "performative" into the concept of "performativity" where discourse does not merely describe identity, but itself constructs identity. Butler's focus has been mainly on gender and sexual identities. The concept of "performativity" has been extended in the work of others, however, to explore questions of identity more generally. The use of the term has also been extended out of its initial context in the philosophy of language and is now used also in the context of theatre. "Performativity" has generally been presented as an understanding of identity which frees the subject from the restrictions of fixed roles which are culturally or biologically determined.

"Performance" of hybrid identity in the context of "nomadism" on an international scale is interrogated by May Joseph in *Nomadic Identities: The Performance of Citizenship* who in some ways interrogates the new cosmopolitanism of hybrid or fluid identity. Joseph suggests that:

> ... this new cosmopolitanism [is] often neither stable, easily penetrated, legal nor necessarily progressive in their internationalizing imperatives. On the contrary, the enticing logic of consumption as the great leveler of nations, national identities, and competing modes of citizenship conceals the exclusionary and nondemocratic tendencies embedded in this logic that contradict the hard-fought battles for alternative venues of public citizenship waged by various political identities. (1999, 8)

What is suggested thus is that in the context of global politics, the freedom assumed in the fluid, cosmopolitan understanding of identity as performance tends to exclude the struggles of those people who do not share this understanding of what it means to be a person.

The focus on performance is not a wholly new concern in Farah's novels. Acting, playing out a role, dramatizing the self is alluded to in the childhood games of the young Askar in *Maps*, and is the subject of more obvious attention in *Secrets*. By the end of *Knots*, it appears that staging a play in the ballroom of the repossessed family home is the true purpose of Cambara's return to Mogadiscio. In this context, she is able to construct an ideal non-authoritarian, liberatory community out of "like-minded" performative selves.

What the focus on performativity elides, however, is the prior, ideologically fixed concept of a disengaged "self" which scripts its roles for itself from the publicly available range of roles. The self-inventing, self-narrating subject is always already inserted in a broader ideological context. The broader context is a product and effect of the modern disengaged conception of identity. The paradox inherent in this idea of performativity is pointedly elicited in the "folk wit" cited by Steven Kellman in an overview of the self-generating artwork, to the effect that "Abraham Lincoln was born in a log cabin which he helped his father to build" (1976, 1251).

"Performativity" is connected in the novel to the idea of "self-styling". Both concepts proceed from the idea that a pre-discursive, fixed, unitary self does not exist. "Performative" identity suggests that the self is constituted out of a repertoire of publicly available roles. "Self-styling", however, conveys the additional sense of improving the self. The idea of "styling" the self is a contemporary aesthetic transmutation of non-modern forms of self-perfection. The person in the latter conception finds self-perfection in an idea of grace located in custom or the transcendant. The individual in the former conception locates refinement in the styles of a society which is defined as a collection of such individuals. The focus on style in *Knots* is apparent from the attention paid by the protagonist to clothes, make-up and hair styles which allow her to transform and perfect her identity. However, as with the concept of the "performative" identity, the focus on "styling" of the self, effaces the prior disengaged self which is always already "styled", but whose "style" is transparent.

What we witness in the novel, thus, is that *Knots* constructs a glowing liberatory post-national Somali community from the turbulent lives of a diasporic cast. In this respect, the narrative moves closer to the genre of romance. Michael McKeon (1987) identifies as "romance" those elements in eighteenth century novels which defy the formal realism attendant upon the individualism Ian Watt (1963) suggests is constitutive of the novel genre. The novel, Watt argues, gives literary form to the philosophical realism of Descartes and Locke, among others. The formal realism of the novel purports to present the world objectively. The novel hero develops wholly out of the dynamic produced by his rational interpretation of experience in the real world presented in the novel. Included under the rubric "romance", McKeon includes spirituality, stock situations and conventions, and traditional plot, among other elements. What McKeon identifies as "romance" is a version of what Taylor might identify as the "external morality" constitutive of the individual. In other words included under the rubric "romance" are those elements of sociality which novelistic individualism relies upon but must efface in order to come into existence as a genre. Romance or the external higher order of sociality is what Farah's latter novels tend towards. But, while closure in realism generated irony, romance in Farah's neo-realism negotiates subject constitution in such a way that irony is dissipated.

Fredric Jameson, in an essay on the importance of attention to the analysis of "the history of the forms," suggests that the fullest account of "romance as a *mode* has been given by Northrop Frye" (1975, 136, 138 emphasis in original). Frye defines the romance, the "mythos of summer", thus:

> The romance is nearest of all literary forms to the wish-fulfill-
> ment dream, and for that reason it has a socially paradoxical
> role. In every age the ruling social or intellectual class tends
> to project its ideals in some form of romance, where the vir-
> tuous heroes and beautiful heroines represent the ideals and
> the villains the threats to their ascendancy. [...] The perenni-
> ally child-like quality of romance is marked by its extraordi-
> narily persistent nostalgia, its search for some kind of golden
> age in time or space. (1971, 186)

The imperative of the postcolonial romance that drives *Knots* need not be rehearsed, since it is amply revealed in the desire for an ideal world symbolized by Cambara's family home turned theatre. What needs to be clarified, however, is the fact that romance, unlike fantasy, desires "a fulfillment that will deliver it from the anxieties of reality *but will still contain that reality*" (1971, 193 emphasis in original). In other words, the concern of romance is paradise, but the paradise it constructs is mundane. The hero of the romance according to Frye is a "mythical Messiah or deliverer," but on a human scale. In the earlier "Blood in the Sun" trilogy and the trilogy in progress, strong gestures are made towards prophetic deliverance through a golden child, but in *Knots*, this tendency is restrained. The new world envisaged is a secular one, con-structed by a woman in profane time. Absent in *Knots* also, is the irony in closure constitutive of the novel as genre, as discussed above. *Knots* thus circles back to the historical origins of the novel since it presents a relatively coherent subject much like the protagonist of the hero in realism. What makes the literary mode which *Knots* employs different from realism is that the novel seems to have effaced the paradox atten-dant on individualist subject formation in formal realism. This refers to the paradox where in the realist novel the hero comes to occupy a social role apparently of his own free will.

The ideal world created by *Knots* is constructed by metropolitan Somali intellectuals. The diaspora the novel has its eye on is not the members of the Somali diaspora in Kenya, Ethiopia, South Africa, Saudi

Arabia or the Gulf States. It is the intellectual, professional and business class diaspora in Canada, Europe and the United States. So, while one can choose to be whatever one wants to be, the range of subjects to whom this choice is open is radically limited. Some sense of the closed boundaries of a text which in other ways is nomadic on an international scale is apparent from the extensive, detailed and coldly efficient description of the security which surrounds Cambara's theatrical debut:

> To ensure that there are no lapses in security, which Dajaal has planned very tightly, Seamus has run the cables all the way to the checkpoints. There are several inner and outer circles and a minimum of three checkpoints... All manner of communication gadgets are in use: walkie-talkies, a landline telephone at the property, and several handheld mobiles. At each checkpoint , there are men with machine guns hidden from view, the second security ring having only the "technical" as part of a show of force, if it comes to that (415).

What is curious about the ending in *Knots*, is that concern with keeping others out does not register as ironic undercutting of closure. It is instead, merely a practical concern. The novel does not address the question of what to do with the barbarians at the gate. But by implication they must be permanently excluded.

The achievement of *Knots* is the modeling of a relatively coherent self on the template of Cartesian subjectivity, but without the founding paradox upon which the procedurally rational identity, associated with the Cartesian break, is based. When identity itself becomes aestheticized in the styled subject, a coherent identity is articulated in which boundless freedom need not be limited by paradox. But as *Knots* shows this boundless identity may be constituted only in a gated utopia.

# Chapter 8

## POST-COLONIAL PRISON AND COLONIAL VIOLENCE IN NGUGI WA THIONG'O'S *DETAINED*

*Isaac Ndlovu*
*University of Cape Town*

### INTRODUCTION

Ngugi wa Thiong'o's *Detained: A Writer's Prison Diary* (1981), is a narrative characterized by a defiant militancy and pulsating moral urgency. The title of the book suggests that it is a collection of diary entries of the year Ngugi spent in Remand Prison at Kamiti, Nairobi, in 1978. In reality, *Detained* explores, among other things, the role of colonial violence and the imposition of colonial culture during the late nineteenth century European invasion and conquest of Africa, and how Kenyans' resistance reached its zenith in the Mau Mau war that led to independence in 1963.

One of Ngugi's aims in *Detained* seems to be the excavation of the archive of colonial violence against the colonial subjects as a means of understanding his own imprisonment by a post-colonial regime. Ngugi makes this one of his urgent tasks because, as Makau Mutua observes, "there seems to be a rush of amnesia, a deliberate forgetfulness that wants to wish away this barbaric history" (2008, 33). In *Detained*, Ngugi reminds his readers of the brutalities of colonial rule so that they can see parallels with the postcolonial state's violent excesses. He exposes colonialism's savagery which was justified through the depiction of natives as savages who could only be subjected to humane European ways through the use of brutal force. Throughout *Detained*, Ngugi suggests that post-colonial violence has its roots in the tyranny of colonial rule. He argues that violence was not a temporary tool of subjugation, but rather, brutality was the very essence of colonial settler culture, and fear was its defining feature. Ngugi's aim in *Detained* is to show that the Kenyan people did not accept British colonial rule 'lying down', and therefore should not accept postcolonial abuse without resistance. He interprets his own imprisonment and prison writings as a form of participation in this resistance. Since colonialism was essentially a violent regime, Ngugi reckons that all the cultural productions of this system should be interpreted through the same paradigm of brutality.[1] He writes:

> For the settlers in Kenya were really parasites in paradise ...
> No art, no literature, no culture, just the making of a little
> dominion marred only by niggers too many to exterminate.
> (1981, 29-30)

For Ngugi, therefore, it is not so much colonial violence as the colonialists' lack of culture itself which was destructive to African social structure. It was this vast "emptiness," the inability to "produce a culture," which resulted in the colonialists' resort to violence and coercion, exemplified by the prison, as the principal means of rule. Ngugi says that it is this legacy of cultural emptiness which the departing Europeans bequeathed to the African "comprador bourgeoisie" that needs urgent attention. He observes that, since colonialism did not only use physical violence but also engaged in a systematic attempt to impose a culture of emptiness masquerading as the Rule of Law upon the Kenyan social sphere, true emancipation for Kenyans from the neo-colonial mentality lies in the revival of the Kikuyu cultural heritage, such as the use of Gikuyu and other indigenous languages in the arts and as language of instruction in academic institutions. Ngugi believes that this is one of the major ways of achieving an economically independent and culturally decolonized Kenya. His arrest and imprisonment by the postcolonial regime of Jomo Kenyatta, when he was engaged in what he perceived to be a Kikuyu cultural renaissance through the staging of Gikuyu performances of *Ngaahika Ndeenda* among the peasants of Kamĩrĩĩthũ, convinced him of the power of his people's culture in the fight against the forces of neo-colonialism. To prove his point that the repressive and violent postcolonial Kenya is an extension of the colonial regime, Ngugi gives numerous examples of atrocities that were committed by high ranking colonial officials against native Kenyans. One of the examples that he gives is a dispatch by an early colonial governor, Sir A. R. Hardinge. The governor wrote:

> These people must learn submission by bullets – it's the only school; after that you may begin more modern and humane methods of education ... In Africa to have peace you must first teach obedience, and the only tutor who impresses the lesson properly is the sword. (1981, 37-9)

Through this quotation Ngugi implies that colonial imprisonment was the violent means through which the native was taught 'obedience'. The governor's words also reveal not only the patronizing generalizations that facilitated colonial invasion and its attendant violence, but also the kind of power systems that characterized the colonial encounter. This shows how colonial rule was facilitated by an 'Other-ing' discourse that was pre-Enlightenment in nature and yet rooted in enlightenment thought. Echoing Fanon's argument that the colonial world is a "compartmentalized" and "Manichaean" world (2004, 3, 6), Edward Said helps us understand the colonial governor's almost unforgivable condescending arrogance when he argues: "Throughout the exchange between Europeans and their 'other' that began systemically half a millennium ago, the idea that has scarcely varied is that there is an 'us' and a 'them,' each quite settled, clear, unassailably self-evident" (1993, xxviii). It is also interesting to note that the governor believes that the colonized had to be subjected through two forms of power: first, the bullet which leads to disarmament and forced submission; and then the use of more enlightened and humane methods of education. On this matter, Rao and Pierce observe:

> The exigencies of governing the colonized ultimately produced uncomfortable similarities between the so-called barbarism of the native practices and the acts of terror and violence used to contain them. (2006, 2)

So it would seem that the Foucauldian formulation of the spectacle yielding way to disciplines does not necessarily fit the colonial situation. Foucault says that the Europe of Antiquity was a civilization of spectacle, and defines spectacle as "render[ing] accessible to a multitude of men the inspection of small objects" (1991, 216). Foucault points out that these spectacles were meant to unite people temporarily through the spectre of violence. He writes: "In these rituals in which blood flowed, society found new vigour and formed for a moment a single great body" (ibid.). For the colonial governor, the bullet represents an all-out war against the entire recalcitrant native population and not just the rendering of few objects to a multitude. The colonized population becomes fearful and submissive upon the realization that the colonizer has both the will and the means to exterminate them. Superficial peace and unity are achieved through the fear of being punished or annihilated at worst. By extension, then, Ngugi seems to imply that, in the post-colony, the 'colonial bullet' has been superseded by the prison as a symbol of all repressive state apparatuses and has become 'the only school' for those who oppose the neo-colonial state. The bullet and prison are brutal means through which precarious peace and unity are achieved and maintained both in the colony and the postcolony.

Interestingly, Foucault claims that in Europe, from the eighteenth century onwards, the spectacular exercise of power with its attendant violence was gradually replaced by the "disciplinary modality of power" (1991, 216). Foucault also refers to these dispersed modes of power which insidiously but systematically monitors its subjects through complex connections of disciplines, as a *capillary* form of power. For Foucault, this transformation in the functions and uses of power did not lead to a lessening of the grip of power over the individual but rather its intensification. He argues that the development of a disciplinary society "assures an infinitesimal distribution of the power relations" (ibid.). However, despite the development of the disciplinary modality of power, a careful reading of Foucault suggests that the exercise of power remains Janus-faced. He wrote:

> At one extreme, the discipline blocked, the enclosed institution, established on the edges of society, turned inwards towards negative functions: arresting evil, breaking communications, suspending time. At the other extreme, with panopticism, is the discipline-mechanism: a functional mechanism that must improve the exercise of power by making it lighter, more rapid, more effective, a design of subtle coercion for a society to come. (1991, 209)

In *Detained*, Ngugi shows that the new form of societal power relations which Foucault calls a capillary form of power was not exported into colonies because the natives were regarded as savages who only understood violence. He sets out to prove that the colonial rulers did not apply the European ideas of reform in the colony because Africans remained irredeemably 'other' even after gaining what the colonial governor calls more "modern" and "humane" methods of education in the excerpt quoted earlier. Africans represented an extreme form of the other, such that the sword and the bullet did not just precede the use of disciplines but remained a permanent feature of colonial rule. Ngugi observes that the colonial system produced "a culture of legalized brutality, a ruling-class culture of fear, the culture of an oppressive minority desperately trying to impose total silence on a restive oppressed majority" (1981, 34). The colonial prison clearly participated in this attempt at imposing total silence on the majority. Ngugi also demonstrates that in the majority of cases the British colonial commanders did not even make an attempt to hide their arrogance and utter contempt for Africans under the rhetoric of bringing enlightened civilization to Africa. For example, one British military commander, exasperated by the fierce resistance of the Kenyan Nandi guerrilla army against British invasion, wrote:

> I have used every effort to conciliate the tribes and have exercised the greatest forbearance in dealing with them ... but the ignorance of the people is so extreme that it is impossible to convey to such savages that the occupation of their country is not harmful to them. (1981, 41)

Ngugi argues that those controlling the colonial repressive state apparatuses such as the prison had a brazen and unquestioning sense of superiority over their colonial subjects. Logically, imprisonment was seen as a legitimate cure for the ignorance of savages. Ngugi forcefully asserts that the postcolonial Kenyan regime is a colonial mutant.[2]

In 1902, Kenyans may have lost the battle, but the war continued unabated through other means over the years leading to the Mau Mau war of liberation. After the initial violence of colonial invasion in Kenya, Ngugi shows that the coloniser continued to build upon this culture of legalised brutality against the colonised subject through the use of a racially biased penal system. Ngugi gives numerous examples of natives who suffered appalling injustices at the hands of respected white settlers after being accused of frivolous and ridiculous crimes. Ngugi notes:

> In March 1907, Colonel Grogan and four associates flogged 'rickshaw boys' outside Nairobi court-house ...Their crime? They had the intention of alarming two white ladies by raising the rickshaw shafts an inch too high! (1981, 32)

In another example:

> "In 1960, Peter Harold Poole shot and killed Kamane
> Musunge for throwing stones at Poole's dogs in self-defense"
> (33). [And] "[i]n 1918 ... two British peers flogged a Kenyan to
> death and later burnt his body. His crime? He was suspected
> of having an intention to steal property ... The governor later
> appointed one of them to be a member of a district commit-
> tee to dispense justice among the 'natives.'" (1981, 33)

Through these and other examples, Ngugi seeks to prove that the postcolonial Kenyan violence and arbitrary imprisonment of suspected
political opponents is a continuation of the British colonial culture.Since
colonial rule of law was essentially violent, Ngugi views the postcolony
as a transformed colony disguised by the black faces that now occupy
political positions. He shows that it is the colonial justice system which
Kenyatta and his colleagues have not only inherited but admired and
administered after the departure of the coloniser at independence from
1963 onwards. Ngugi strives to show that what Comaroff and Comaroff
call the postcolonial condition of endemic "criminality with violence"
was instituted at the colonial invasion of Africa and continued during
the entire period of colonial rule (2006, 6).

Like Florence Bernault, who argues for an inextricable link between
the development of prison practices and the European colonial project
in Africa (2003, 3), Ngugi locates the establishment of the prison in
Africa at the very beginning of the invasion of the continent because he
views all colonial institutions as violent. The prison is a typical institution in this regard. He writes:

> Detention without trial is part of that colonial culture of fear
> ... Detention was an instrument for colonial domination. In
> its origins and purpose, it is clearly a colonial affair. (1981, 44)

For Ngugi, the fact that the post-colonial Kenyan government continues to use the prison to persecute its critics is evidence that neo-
colonial conditions prevail in Kenya. He locates his own post-colonial
arrest as providing an unbroken link between the early detentions of
militant leaders of the patriotic armed resistance to British invasion at
the turn of the twentieth century.

## PRISON NARRATIVES AND THE EXCAVATION OF EMANCIPATORY HISTORIOGRAPHY

Ngugi's extensive quotations from colonial historiography should be viewed as a writer's attempt to lay bare the structures of power and knowledge which the African 'comprador bourgeoisie' and their former colonial masters would want to remain hidden and forgotten. The many citations of colonial historiography that Ngugi exposes and then challenges in *Detained* can be seen as performing a normative function to the biased version of history of Kenya, which he argues is perpetuated by the postcolonial administration. For Ngugi, it is this distorted history that prevents Kenyans from engaging in a protracted struggle that will lead to cultural emancipation and ultimately to a truly patriotic exercise of power by the ruling class, and to an equitable redistribution of the material resources of the country.

Ngugi insists that the coming of independence has not brought any change to postcolonial Kenya, as illustrated by the fact that both the colonial and postcolonial regimes use repressive state apparatuses such as the prison to gag dissenting voices. Ngugi's *Detained* seeks to show that the criminalization of a clearly political function of colonial prison regimes is maintained by Kenyatta's post-colonial regime, and this is what he refers to as a colonial affair. The banter that characterizes the exchange between Ngugi and one of his jailers who reprimands him for breaching the regulation of switching off all lights at midnight is illustrative of Ngugi's understanding of these disturbing continuities in the postcolonial modality of power. The dialogue goes like this:

> "'Professor ... why are you not in bed? .... What are you doing?'
> 'I am writing to Jomo Kenyatta in his capacity as an ex-detainee'.
> 'His case was different,' the warder argues back.
> 'How?'
> 'His was a colonial affair'.
> 'And this a neo-colonial affair? What's the difference?'
> 'A colonial affair ... now we are independent ... that's the difference ...' he says (1981, 4).

Ngugi narrates his imprisonment by these numerous detours into the colonial origins, and uses of prison and imprisonment, in order to show that both the Kenyan colonial and postcolonial prison regimes were and are used in managing restless populations. He debunks the concept of an independent Kenya by showing that it is an empty signifier.

145

Ngugi implies that the use of the prison by the British invaders is an indication that Kenyans did not welcome them with open arms as their long awaited saviours from the African forces of darkness, as subsequent European historiography would have Africans believe. The colony was founded on the blood of valiant Kenyans who were brutalized by the bullet and the prison of the colonizer into an uneasy submission. To substantiate his case Ngugi gives a long list of Kenyan warriors who valiantly fought the British invaders and were subsequently captured and killed in colonial detention camps and prisons. The first of these men was Waiyaki, who was imprisoned in the Fort Smith from 14 August 1892 and was subsequently shot and buried alive for his heroic defiance of colonial invasion. Then there was Nguugu wa Gakere, who was arrested and imprisoned in 1902 for leading his men against Nyeri Fort. He died in detention in 1907, still defiant of colonial rule. This list includes women. Me Kitilili led the Giriama people to resist and fight British colonial rule up to her arrest and imprisonment in 1914. Ngugi points out that his own arrest without charge was possible because: "by 1966 all the repressive colonial laws were back on the books [coated in] sweet semantics" (1981, 51). According to Ngugi, Kenyatta, who had previously fought against and as a result had been detained by the colonial regime, offers a bad example of individuals who were not only broken by prison, but were co-opted into the colonial system: a system which Kenyatta then perpetuated in independent Kenya under the guise of black rule. In summarizing the ideology that drives the Kenyan post-colonial regime Ngugi writes:

> Ideally, the authorities would like to put the whole community of struggling millions behind barbed-wire, as the British colonial authorities had once tried to do with the Kenyan people. But this would mean incarcerating labour, the true source of national wealth: what then would be left to loot? So then the authorities do the simpler thing: pick one or two individuals from among the people and then loudly claim that all sins lie at the feet of these few 'power hungry' 'misguided' and 'ambitious' agitators. (1981, 13)

Ngugi suggests that his imprisonment is a display, a means by which the ruling regime pummels the agitated masses into submission. He casts his arrests as a pre-emptive strike, an invisible spectacle, a Foucauldian rendering accessible to a multitude of men the inspection of small objects. Although not publicly displayed, Ngugi's imprisonment quickly became national and international news. Just as the bullet and imprisonment were to serve as violent and bloody instruments of submission for the colonial governor, secretly murdering political opponents and throwing some into prison becomes an important feature of the Kenyan postcolonial regime even after Kenyatta's death in 1978. Mutua observes: "[T]he state under Moi widely used extrajudicial killings, including the so-called ethnic clashes of the 1990s, to silence dissent" (2008, 286).

In the same quotation above, Ngugi suggests that the colony became an experimental space where the colonisers tried forms of coercion that had never been practiced in Europe. This is seen in Ngugi's reference to the concentration camps in which the British colonial authorities confined entire villages in an attempt to curb the Mau Mau war of liberation in the 1950s.[3] During the Mau Mau state of emergency, we see a manifestation of power which is neither spectacle nor panoptic. The Mau Mau phenomenon enables us to make sense of Bernault's observation that the prison was used as an early instrument of colonial conquest and in the subjugation of Africans (2003, 3). Ngugi suggests that both before and during the Mau Mau Emergency, Kenyans experienced the prison not "as the auxiliary of justice in pursuit of criminals [but] as an instrument for political supervision of plots, opposition movements or revolts" (1991, 215). However, the irony of the situation is that the colonial authorities never admitted to this political function of the prison, and they even denied that the Mau Mau phenomenon was a manifestation of any genuine political aspirations. Instead they chose to view Mau Mau members as misguided criminals who needed psychological and physical rehabilitation. This is seen from the fact that the Mau Mau detention camps remained under the supervision of the Kenyan Prisons Service well up to 1959 when they were eventually transferred to the Ministry of African Affairs (Kercher 1981, 27). Despite the subtle changes in the postcolonial regime and its penal system, Ngugi insists that it remains an unmitigated perpetuation of colonial rule. While the British colonial authorities had attempted mass imprisonment of all black Kenyans in the 1950s, Ngugi depicts his own imprisonment as an inverted spectacle of power. He writes:

> [D]etention without trial is not only a punitive act of physical and mental torture of a few patriotic individuals, but it is also a calculated act of psychological terror against the struggling millions. It is a terrorist programme for the psychological siege of the whole nation. (1981, 14)

Interestingly, Jeannine DeLombard (1995) calls Ngugi's imprisonment and that of other prominent figures in postcolonial Kenya "a spectacle of invisibility" (1995, 51). Probably, this is best illustrated by the fact that the police chose to arrest Ngugi at midnight on 30-31 December 1977 "with an incredible show of armed might" (1981, 15). He spent one night in the police cell and then the next day at noon was transferred to Kamiti Maximum Security Prison. What happened when the car transporting Ngugi arrived at the gates of the prison exemplifies what is referred to as the spectacle of invisibility by DeLombard. Ngugi writes:

> The whole area around Kamiti was immediately put under curfew – and this in the noon of day ... within seconds there was not a single civilian standing or walking in the vicinity of Kamiti Prison. (1981, 18)

This suggests that Ngugi's arrest was simultaneously a spectacle and also an attempt at concealing it from the public. This vacillation between the visible and the invisible was characteristic of colonial rule as well. The fact that the officers who come to arrest an unarmed academic do so with an incredible show of force, suggests a spectacularization of power. However, the fact that they do so at night with obscene and unnecessary display of power by the warders who declare a *de facto* state of emergency outside the gates of the prison, all point towards a regime which is trying to prevent its criminal acts from being publicized. Evidence indicates that early in his rule, Kenyatta combined imprisonment and lethal brutality as important tools of entrenching his corrupt rule. Depending on how dangerous his opponents were regarded to be, were either imprisoned without being charged or were assassinated.[4] It is ironic that Kenyatta is a perpetuator of the same brutality and injustices of colonial rule that he had been a victim of. Addressing the court which was about to sentence him and five of his colleagues on trumped-up charges of being leaders of the Mau Mau, Jomo Kenyatta expressed his feelings of helpless submission, rejection and resistance to the entire colonial legal apparatus when he said: "I am asking for no mercy at all on behalf of my colleagues. We are asking that may justice be done and that the injustices that exist may be righted" (Slater 1959, 241). With the benefit of hindsight, it is clear that as Kenyatta was verbally rejecting colonial justice or the so-called Rule of Law he was at the same time internalising its logic. This suggests that Kenyatta, and many other post-colonial political elite after him are at once victims and equally willing agents of neo-colonial forces.

Ngugi is at pains to show that postcolonial Kenyan regime's attempts of imposing total silence on a restless majority through imprisonment and brutality will not succeed, since the culture of Kenya from the time of the imposition of colonial rule is not one of passivity but of struggle which culminated in the Mau Mau war of liberation. He does not assume that agency and/or resistance is some "natural" human capacity that will inevitably emerge under oppressive conditions – instead, he locates resistance as part of a historical legacy in Kenya. After the Mau Mau war, Ngugi believes that the most potent tool for fighting neo-colonial forces are cultural productions in Kenyan languages such as the play *I will Marry When I Want*. Ngugi believes that this culture of defiance already exists among the peasants as demonstrated in their 1977 stage performances of his socialist play in Gikuyu. Ngugi views his books as cultural interventions meant to fight a post-colonial disciplinary modality of power, where power relations are now distributed in an infinitesimal and subtle way through the selective use of the prison, nepotism, tribalism and appeals to false sentiments of patriotism.

## FAULT-LINES IN NGUGI'S VISION

However, Ngugi's stance in *Detained* is problematic for a number of reasons. While he is at pains to show that the Kenyan postcolonial regime is caught up in a colonial binary thinking; he believes that the peasant and himself can or have transcended this binary condition. Ngugi seems to be advancing essentialist views. Like Ashcroft (2001), Ngugi believes in the resilience and transformative capacity of the colonised people's culture of resistance. Ashcroft says that colonial rule was not simply an unmitigated cultural disaster: rather, the colonized societies engaged and utilised imperial culture for their own purposes (2001, 2).[5] However, for Ngugi as we have seen, the struggle against colonialism did not just remain at a cultural plane or what Bhabha after Lacan describes as psychological guerrilla warfare, but involved what became a trademark physical confrontation which ultimately drove the colonizer out of Kenya in the early 1960s. Ngugi's *Detained* is an attempt to show the masses that Kenya has an unbroken history of physical struggle which started as early as 1895 during the British colonial invasion of Kenya, and continued well into the first two decades of the twentieth century, when the natives were eventually brutalized into submission by the superior firepower of the colonizer. Ngugi argues that this resistance reached its climax with the heroic exploits of Mau Mau fighters in the 1950s. In *Detained*, Ngugi appeals to the Kenyans

149

that this record of valiant struggle against oppression should not have stopped after the attainment of political independence in 1963.

In *Detained*, Ngugi somewhat problematically, assumes the role of a self-appointed representative of peasants, and the rest of the underclass. This position is complicated by factors which include his social position as a Western-educated university professor, and the fact that after his release from prison, Ngugi went into exile, first to Britain, and then to the United States of America where he still resides. Ngugi seems oblivious of the contradictions that his situation invokes. This can be attributed to the immense influence that Frantz Fanon's (1967) and Amilcar Cabral's (1973) works have had on him. While Fanon overestimates the cathartic value of anti-colonial violence for the colonized subject, Ngugi, like Cabral, overestimates the revolutionary capacity of anti-neo-colonial cultural strategies in eliminating postcolonial economic, social and political inequalities. Since he views himself as a soldier conducting a cultural warfare, he reckons that his geographical location is of no consequence. Peter Childs and Patrick Williams indicate that the position of an intellectual is one of power which the intellectual needs to be aware of (1997, 23). Ngugi's imprisonment was a profoundly traumatic experience and it also became a moment of loss of anchoring for him, particularly since there are clear indications that it intensified his anger and disillusionment with the Kenyan post-colonial government, which in turn led to the impairment of critical reflexivity and literary creativity on Ngugi's part. Although Ngugi may not regard himself as a postcolonial theorist, Kwame Anthony Appiah's (1992) description of what he terms the postcolonial theorist embraces some of the contradictions that Ngugi as a person and his work inhabit. Alerting us to the inescapable entanglements with Western epistemologies by even the most radical African writers Appiah argues:

> Even when these writers seek to escape the West – as Ngugi wa Thing'o did in attempting to construct a Kikuyu peasant drama – their theories of their situation are irreducibly informed by their Euro-American formation. (1992, 149)

Notwithstanding the anti-imperialist militancy of Ngugi, the fact remains that his considerable Western education and training means that his understanding of the Kenyan realities that he still so authoritatively writes about is partly informed by his location and his social position. The canonisation of Ngugi's writing in many institutions of learning in Africa and in many parts of the world, and Ngugi's own self-perception as a dissident and subversive writer, puts him in a paradoxical position.[6] Edward Said (1993) makes a perceptive observation about the difficulty of occupying one impermeable cultural position. He writes: "[A]ll cultures are involved in one another; none is single and pure, all are hybrid, heterogeneous, extraordinarily differentiated, and un-monolithic" (1993, xxix). This suggests that in one way or another, Ngugi's radical voice may have been normalised into the disciplinary modality of power without Ngugi even being aware of it. In the light of the above, one of the greatest ironies of Ngugi's *Detained* may be that while it circumvents the operations of neo-colonial operations of power in a number of ways it also exposes Ngugi as implicated in the disciplinary functions of power that he criticises so much. In *Detained*, Ngugi suffers the ambiguity of embracing what Spivak has famously called the position of the 'subaltern' and entirely rejecting the benefits that flow from being what Appiah calls the "comprador intelligentsia" (1992, 149). The three sections of the first chapter of *Detained* are an attempt to resolve this uncomfortable position. The first section of this chapter indicates that Ngugi is largely representative of the somewhat more privileged experience of political prisoners. He writes: "12 December 1978: I am in cell 16 in the detention block enclosing eighteen other political prisoners" (1981, 3). Ngugi's tone makes it clear that he accords political prisoners a superior status. Throughout his narrative, Ngugi gives the impression that "[i]t is the active few who, through their original ideas, leadership and guidance, transform the masses into creative agents, rather than the masses who, through their independent actions, transform the few into leaders" (Crehan 1995, 106). The peasants, he claims, literally took charge of the *Ngahika Ndeenda* failed to initiate new projects after his arrest, imprisonment and his subsequent self-imposed exile.

Ngugi also presents his one-year stay in prison as a moment of profound revelation. For example, Ngugi wrote his pre-prison fiction in English. By contrast, all his post-imprisonment novels are first written in Kikuyu, and then personally translated by the author into English. He attributes his transformed view of languages to the unsolicited lecture that he received from a Mugikuyu prison warder. The warder said: "You [educated] people, even if you follow Europeans to the grave, they ... will never let you into the secrets held by their languages" (1981, 129). Ngugi interprets the warder's words as an exposé of the betrayal of the people by the African western educated intellectuals who use European languages in their works of literature. The warder's words highlight an essentialist perspective which views language as an irreducible carrier of a people's culture. Curiously, the *warder* – who has power in the prison – becomes the voice of the ordinary African people. So it suddenly dawns upon Ngugi that to privilege the English language in the production of Kikuyu cultural experiences is to place Kikuyu culture and its historical experiences in an inferior position in comparison to English culture. However, Ngugi is only using this encounter with the warder, whether real or imagined, as a stylistic tool to explain his own rejection of the English language as means of expressing the Kenyan people's experiences and worldview. This is made clear by the fact that it was his pre-prison experiment with the Gikuyu play that sought to displace the hegemonic position of the English in the arts, and the fact that he took it to the exploited peasants, which led to his imprisonment in the first place. This suggests that his understanding of the subtle manner in which the colonial culture had entrenched itself, not only through brutal violence but also using cultural institutions was more of a gradual process, rather than the sudden moment of enlightenment implied in the above quotation. Ngugi constantly tries to attribute his journey of retracing his cultural roots back to the ordinary people as in the example of the warder's words above. Jennine DeLombard writes:

> As an imprisoned African former colonial subject who repeatedly has presented himself as an ally – if no longer a member – of the peasantry and the working classes, Ngugi is representative of a number of groups who have been marginalized in both political and literary terms. (1995, 52)

An example of this is when he attributes the final script and performance of *I will Marry When I Want*, which he co-authored with Ngugi Wa Mirii largely to the peasants of Kamīrīīthū. He writes:

> [T]he whole project became a collective community effort with peasants and workers seizing more and more initiative in revising and adding to the script, in directing dance movements on the stage, and in the general organization. (1981, 77)

A page before this statement, Ngugi tries to convince the reader that all his Western education had been of little consequence in comparison with the six months he spent with peasants preparing for the performance of the play. He says:

> The six months between June and November 1977 were the most exciting in my life and the true beginning of my edu-

cation. I learnt my language anew. I discovered the creative
nature and power of collective work. (1981, 76)

A little later, he makes the following self-deprecating comments:

> For myself, I learnt a lot. I had been delegated to the role of
> messenger and porter, running errands here and there. But
> I also had time to observe things. I saw how the people had
> appropriated the text … so that the play that was finally put
> on to a fee-paying audience on Sunday, 2 October 1977, was
> a far cry from the tentative awkward efforts originally put
> together by Ngugi and myself. (1981, 78)

Ngugi is trying very hard to prove that he has "shifted the centre
of vision because … [he is no longer] bound by the European Centre"
(1993, 53). For Ngugi, true knowledge comes from the peasants and not
from Western institutions of higher learning. But despite his assertions
that he represents the peasants' views, what Ngugi succeeds in offering
is often a constricted and deterministic socialist ideology and worldview,
notions which emanated from European Enlightenment. Some may also
find offense in Ngugi's naïve condescending attitude, arising from having
been alienated from the people in the first place, which now enables him
to find fascination and fulfillment from the peasants' awkward attempt
at scripting and directing a play. In the above quotation, Ngugi is speaking as an observer of peasants and not as being one of their kind. He is
also obviously writing with a Western audience in mind.

Throughout *Detained*, Ngugi pits himself against Kenyatta. Unlike
Kenyatta, who was broken down by the colonial prison to become a
member of the comprador bourgeoisie, Ngugi clearly points out that he
himself managed to resist Kenyatta's attempts to break him. But it can
be argued that just like Kenyatta, who was a member of the Western-
educated *intelligentsia,* and initially posed as someone who represented
the aspirations of the people only to turn around after attaining political
power, Ngugi's militancy is sustained by the fact that he is sidelined from
political power. Ngugi tries by all means to show that unlike Kenyatta,
he truly represents the aspirations of the subaltern. Curiously, though,
in order to illustrate that ordinary Kenyans realised the continuity of
the repressive colonial ideology in independent Kenya, Ngugi includes
photographs of Kenyan demonstrators who reside in London brandishing posters. One of them reads: "*Waingereza walifunga Kimathi …
Mzee anafunga Ngugi*" (The white man imprisoned Kimathi … Kenyatta
imprisons Ngugi). It is a painful irony that it is not the peasants of

Kamīrīīthū where Ngugi says *I Will Marry When I Want* was scripted and first staged, but the educated elite residing in the metropolis of the former coloniser who have the courage to protest Ngugi's arrest. This captures the contradictions that Ngugi has to negotiate in his quest to be both an equal and also a voice of the voiceless Kenyan masses.

One of the questions that seems to preoccupy Ngugi in *Detained* is how KANU (Kenya African National Union), a party that had shown a lot of anti-colonial zeal, quickly imploded into an oppressive machinery serving the interests of the ruling elite and those of foreign powers. He is of the opinion that when KANU took over power on 12 December 1963 it had a clean nationalist record. However, what baffles Ngugi is that "by 1966 all repressive laws were back on the books" (1981, 51). His answer to his own question: "What happened between 1961 and 1966 to make KANU reintroduce all these undemocratic, unjust and arbitrary practices?" (ibid.), is populist and informed by his unique Marxist understanding of history as having reached its consummation during the Mau Mau war of liberation. Since the masses had fought so valiantly to overthrow forces of colonial oppression, Ngugi puts the blame squarely on the "comprador bourgeoisie which had been growing in the womb of the colonial regime [and] desired to protect and enhance its cosy alliance with foreign economic interests" (1981, 53). According to Ngugi, this is the group of people who raised "Colonial Lazarus" from the dead. Other writers, however, have argued that Ngugi's Colonial Lazarus may not have died in the first place. For example, Neuberger argues that "KANU accepted the 'Majimbo Constitution' because that was the condition for independence" (1986, 175). This is an important observation because it suggests at least two things. While Ngugi paints a romanticised picture of the British who were vanquished and driven out of Kenya by the patriotic Mau Mau guerrilla forces, Neuberger implies that although the British may have been forced to the negotiating table by Mau Mau activities, Kenyan independence was by no means an unconditional surrender of the routed colonialists.[7] Historical developments also indicate that despite Ngugi's efforts to show that the interests of the African ruling elite always converge with those of their former colonial masters, this may not always be the case. In the Kenyan situation, British attempts to weaken KANU by imposing a federal constitution indicate that they viewed KANU as a threat to British settlers' commercial interests. As it turned out, KANU shrewdly played along with the British game as a means of attaining the control of the repressive state machinery. Once that had been achieved, within three years they imposed the unitary regime which the British had opposed in the first place. While Ngugi's claim that the comprador bourgeoisies' "political inspiration and guidance comes from outside the country" (1981, 56) may be partly correct, historical evidence paints a much more complex picture.

Robert H. Jackson suggests that right from its inception the post-colonial state has never enjoyed legitimacy and loyalty neither from its officials nor from its citizens, and as a result, its survival has largely been ensured by external factors and interests (1992, 1). According to this view, Ngugi's portrayal of Kenyans as a homogeneous rainbow nation torn to pieces by the greed of the ruling elite that co-operates with foreign multinationals has to be supplemented by a much more careful study of the African situation. For example, Ngugi accepts the principle of Kenyan nationalism and the notion of the state without interrogating their imperial origin. Interestingly, Mutua tries to get to the root of the problem. He points out that the arbitrary nature in which modern African states were created by European imperialism (for example Kenya has over forty ethnic communities) made most of these communities ticking time-bombs. T. O. Elias also locates the origin of modern African problems to the Berlin Conference of 1884-5, which apportioned the continent to competing European powers (1988, 37). This suggests that African problems and solutions thereof may lie deeper than Ngugi is willing to allow in his polemic prison narrative. Curiously, Ngugi depicts the unity of the Kenyan people in their fight against foreign invaders in exuberant poetic terms. He writes:

> [Kenyan history] is the history of Kenyan people ceaselessly struggling against Arab feudalists and slave dealers; against Portuguese marauders ... a history of Kenyan people waging a protracted guerrilla war against a British imperialist ... a revolutionary culture of courage and patriotic heroism ... A fight-back, creative culture, unleashing tremendous energies among the Kenyan people. (1981, 64)

As propaganda for spurring Kenyan people on in their fight against neo-colonial forces, this may be permissible. However, as a historical record, it is not very helpful because it is a blatantly romanticised version of history. The Kenyan people are described as "ceaselessly struggling" to fend off enemies of every sort. The British are called "predators ... with claws and fangs of blood" preying on innocent Kenyans who have "a revolutionary culture of courage and patriotic heroism". This descrip-tion negates the participation of Kenyans, no matter how negligible, in the oppression and exploitation of fellow Kenyans during these heroic battles against foreign invasions.[8] This is something that Ngugi is aware of, as his 1967 novel *A Grain of Wheat* shows. Ngugi also problematically depicts Kenyans as a homogeneous group united against invaders. Mutua (2008) acknowledges that during moments of crises, such as the fight against colonialism such moments of unity could have existed, but they never ran deep enough to sustain the de-colonised state. He argues that "beyond race and oppression African nations within the colonial territory did not have much else in common" (2008, 38). This suggests that instead of idealizing the African multifarious entities which are called 'nations' today, and which were essentially constituted through European colonial violence, Africans should probably rethink the notion of the nation and the concept of nationalism, and seriously acknowledge the central role that tribalism (both as a colonial construct and pre-colonial reality) has played in Africa's seemingly intractable problems. Still pursuing an idealized vision, Ngugi suggests that the common fate of political prisoners at Kamiti forged an unbreakable bond of unity among them. He writes:

> [W]e all shared a common feeling: something beautiful, something like the promise of a new dawn had been betrayed, and our presence and situation at Kamiti Maximum Security Prison was a logical outcome of that historical betrayal. (1981, 63)

If we consider Matua's comments, the unity and amicable relations that Ngugi says existed amongst political prisoners during his stay at Kamiti may be viewed as people temporarily united by tribulation. Significantly, Ngugi's vision of a people who share an intense feeling of oneness is only limited to fellow political prisoners. His vision is not broad enough to encompass the entire prison population. The collective pronouns "we" and "our" in the above quotation clearly refers to political prisoners who were Ngugi's only companions during his stay at Kamiti. Since in *Detained* Ngugi largely represents the experiences of political prisoners in the jails of postcolonial Kenya, it is important to ask how representative he is of other subaltern voices, such as those of common criminals, the peasants and the urban underclass. The problems presented by Ngugi's posing as a spokesperson for the feelings and views of other prisoners notwithstanding, the above quoted passage leaves the reader in no doubt that Ngugi assumes that this shared feeling of betrayal that he talks about also embraces the society outside prison. Ngugi goes on to assume that this feeling is deep enough in post-colonial Kenya to lead to a national unity and patriotism that would extricate the nation from its politics of patronage and oppression. However, the events after the successful 2002 democratic removal of KANU from power by the National Rainbow Coalition (NARC) for the first time since independence in 1963 indicate that tribalism still poses a serious challenge to Kenyan national development. Before it even started to govern, this unlikely coalition of numerous factions and leaders with competing interests and ambitions was fractured along two major tribal lines. There was the Kikuyu group of Kibaki, and the Luo party of Odinga. This duo was to lead to the disputed 2007 elections which turned bloody as people started to kill each other along tribal lines (Mutua 2009, 182, 287). In 1981 Ngugi had made the following prediction:

> One day these wishes (of freedom riding to liberty) will be transformed by the organized power and the united will of millions from the realm of morality into people's chariots of actual freedom from naked exploitation and ruthless oppression. (1981, 12)

Thirty years on after Ngugi's singing praises of the Kenyan people's deep feelings for national unity after their initial betrayal by the comprador bourgeoisie in his prison narrative, the bloody violence of late 2007 and early 2008 suggests that African problems need to be approached with caution and a soberness of mind. In the end, Ngugi tries to offer an inclusive solution to the Kenyan crisis of governance. He admonishes:

> Until democratic Kenyans, workers, peasants, students, progressive intellectuals and others, unite on the most minimum basis of a patriotic opposition to the imperialist foreign domination of our economy, politics and culture, things will get worse not better, no matter who sits on the throne of power. (1981, xv)[9]

This inclusivity remains at an abstract and problematic level. It remains unclear who these democratic Kenyans are almost thirty years since Ngugi penned the above words. What complicates the situation is that most of the so-called "democracies" which are in reality local autocracies that enjoy the political and economic patronage of most powerful Western nations. So, while Ngugi may be right in blaming Kenya's crisis on neo-colonialism and the predatory nature of the ruling elite, a theory that takes into consideration the changing dynamics of the internal structures of African societies, the impact of global forces on them, and the ways in which opposition politics and subversive discourse are constantly de-legitimated or co-opted into dominant discourses, is likely to lead to a more comprehensive explanation of Africa's problems. Probably to his credit, Ngugi refuses to engage with issues of confession and self-interiority that the prison aims to engender in its victims. He writes:

> A writer needs people around him ... In this literary target I was lucky to have for teachers, detainees and warders, who were very co-operative and generous in sharing their different mines of information and experience (1981, 8-9).

Although he emerges visibly more bitter and angry after his one-year stint in detention, he consistently places the prison at the collective, material and historical forces that led to its birth in Africa, and never at the individual confessional level. He argues that the imprisonment of an activist "is not only a punitive act of physical and mental torture of a few patriotic individuals, but it is also a calculated act of psychological terror against the struggling millions" (1981, 14). Post-colonial political imprisonment for Ngugi is "a terrorist programme for the psychological siege of the whole nation" (ibid.).

## Notes

1. This notion of colonial violence is emphasised by Frantz Fanon who argues that in the "colonies the foreigner imposed himself using cannons and machines". (*The Wretched of the Earth* 2004 [1963]: 5).

2. In a later section of this paper I criticise Ngugi for offering a linear relationship between colonial structures of power and those of the post-colonial state which may indirectly suggest that the post-colonial political class are victims completely lacking in agency.

3. At the onset of the Emergency, Kenya had 58 prisons and detention camps with a population of 9000 prisoners. By 1959 there were 176 prisons and detention camps with a population of 99 000 detainees. Leonard C. Kercher says the Mau Mau Emergency (1952-1959) was "a unique and aberrant experience in the history of the Kenyan experience" (*The Kenyan Penal System: Past Present and Prospect* (1981:23). While Kercher suggests that the Mau Mau Emergency was an anomalous mutation of the British colonial prison regimes, Ngugi, on the other hand, thinks that it was a logical climax of a colonial system steeped in violence.

4. For an account of these assassinations see Mutua 2008:286.

5. Similarly, in *The Location of Culture* (1994:109) Homi Bhabha argues that in the colonial set up "the space of the adversarial ... is never entirely on the

outside or implacably oppositional ... The contour of difference is agonistic, shifting, splitting".

6. In *Moving the Centre: The Struggle for Cultural Freedoms* (1993), Ngugi argues that early African post-colonial literature is "a series of imaginative footnotes to Frantz Fanon" (66). Notably, Fanon's work is characterised by its militancy against colonialism and all traces of imperialism, and Robert C. Young describes Fanon as the "father of anti-colonial theory" (1995: 161). Ngugi includes his own works alongside that of Fanon and sees it as participating in the struggle against neo-colonialism and imperialism.

7. This change of tactics by colonialist is something that Fanon had already noted in the *Wretched of the Earth* (1963) when he wrote: "When the colonialist bourgeoisie realizes it is impossible to maintain domination over the colonies it decides to wage a rearguard campaign in the fields of culture, values and technology" (9).

8. Moeletsi Mbeki captures these historical entanglements and the complicity of both ordinary and elite Africans to their own oppression and the continent's underdevelopment by relating his experiences when he visited the Slave House on Gorée Island, off the coast of Dakar, Senegal. The curator showed Mbeki a musket that was sold to Africans during the slave trade. Explaining the apparent contradiction, the curator points out that Africans "needed the guns to protect themselves against the communities they raided for people to sell" (*Architects of Poverty: Why African Capitalism Needs Changing*, 2009:x)

9. Karl Marx acknowledged the powerlessness and vulnerability of peasants and argued that they did not constitute a class. Marx declared: "They (peasants) cannot represent themselves, they must be represented". In Karl Marx. 1970: 170-171. "The Eighteenth Brumaire of Louis Bonaparte". *Selected Works in One Volume.*

# Chapter 9

## INFLUENCE OF MASHAIRI TRADITION ON CONTEMPORARY EAST AFRICAN POETRY IN ENGLISH

*Edwin Mosoti*
*University of the Witwatersrand*

### INTRODUCTION

The classical Swahili literary tradition continues to have a significant aesthetic impact on postcolonial literary productions (Mazrui 2007, 21). The works of Muyaka bin Haji, largely considered the father of 'modern' Swahili poetry, for instance, have continued to animate the poetics of contemporary poets of whichever medium of expression. Contemporary Swahili poets, most notably Shaaban Roberts, Kandara Saadan, Mathias Mnyapala and Sheikh Amri Abedi have appropriated and in some cases dialectically engaged with Muyaka with the aim of making his poetry and poetics fit into the nascent nationalist struggle as well as make his poetics accessible to the contemporary and growing audience of Standard Kiswahili (Biersteker, 1996). However, this inter-tradition dialogue is not limited to exchange between classical or Muyaka's poetics and contemporary poetry of Swahili expression only. Kimani Njogu has shown that antecedent ideas and style of composition are always being reworked by contemporary poets (2004, 65) irrespective of their medium or languages of expression, and hence interaction between temporally, culturally or linguistically separated discourses results in a 'contact zone.' Temporally separated classical literary tradition interacts and continues to shape contemporary output in East Africa, just as Swahili poetry in general interacts with English poetic texts written by authors from East Africa. However, this relationship is not unidirectional. Rather, a mutual or intertextual engagement exists where elements or 'texts' from both expressive forms crisscross and infiltrate the permeable boundary. As a mega-text, that is, a common pool or labyrinth of formal and textual resources and models for creative writers, Swahili poetry and poetics overarch and shape other poetic expressions in languages other than Kiswahili which is the dominant African language in the region. Using Julia Kristeva's (1986) concept of 'intertextuality' and Mary Pratt's (1991) concept of the 'contact zone', this chapter appraises the extent to which Swahili poetics have been incorporated or appropriated in English-language compositions. Coupled with the disturbing fact that contemporary East African poetry is rarely the subject of serious critical analysis Mwangi 2007, 41), the chapter uses a selection of poems from two anthologies *Boundless Voices: Poems from Kenya* (1988) and *Summons: Poems from Tanzania* (1980), and Marjorie Macgoye's *Make it Sing and Other Poems* (1998) to contribute towards bridging this gap and address the critical question of possible dialogue between Swahili and English poetry. I will make a brief exploration of the unique social-cultural matrix that Swahili poetic tradition has become in the region (in relation to output in English). I investigate why this tradition merits recognition as a mega-text – especially considering the asymmetrical relations between the two traditions, before identifying salient features of this tradition I consider as appropriated in English-language poetry. From Swahili tradition, poetry of English expression, I argue, appropriates a proclivity for storytelling and didacticism, its worldview, in particular, perception of the role of poets and language of poetry, its special choric devices and finally, its rigid prosodic patterns. I conclude that this overlapping of these two literary traditions anticipates a sort of third poetics or tradition that is neither wholly Swahili nor identifiably English in orientation.

It is paradigmatic to posit that the present attempt to explore how the two poetic traditions co-exist more specifically at the literary level will benefit from related developments at the linguistic level. Thus in tracing relations between Kiswahili and English in East Africa, Mikhail Bakhtin's notion of language becomes useful here because of its broad scope. The two languages are not simply communicative tools but systems embodying their respective cultural imprints, such as literature. Language therefore is envisaged in its broad sense, such that 'Kiswahili' also represents a distinct point of view characterised by its own meaning and value, in particular, to poetry as a genre which, relative to other genres, is more advanced, practiced and hence vehicle for much of Swahili consciousness. Its contact with English therefore implies a confluence of worldviews and negotiation of values embedded in the language. Considering that linguistic developments often precede literary contact, and since the linguistic realm has produced recognizable median, in-between forms such as *Sheng*[1] and or *Engish* – depending on the presumed dominance of either, how has the two literary traditions cross-fertilized each other, particularly, in poetry? The crux of this chapter therefore lies in interrogating the extent to which English poetic tradition may be said to be undergoing 'localization' or in the process of acquiring Swahili-ness, while Swahili poetry and poetics on the other hand, experiences 'universalization'. However, frequently, the relationship is appears as unidirectional with Kiswahili and Swahili literary tradition being presented as a perpetual passive receiver. As a point of departure, this chapter focuses on the role played by Swahili literary tradition in this virtual symbiotic relationship. Although literary sphere has not gone as far as its linguistic counterpart, that is, giving rise to a recognizable in-between, it is my conviction that evidence signals or anticipates such a development or evolution since there is every indication that the perceived boundary between them is not only permeable, but overlaps allowing cross-exchanging and intertexting. Bearing in mind that older, indigenous languages and cultures effectively overwhelm and dominate the younger, myopic, foreign ones (Pike 1986, 201-33) – socio-culturally, in spite of political interventions by colonialist discourses – and limiting textual evidence to poetry, it is possible then to argue that poetry in English from Swahiliphone parts of East Africa betray residual presence of dominant indigenous poetic practices and aesthetics such as Swahili poetry. Before delving into this, a brief note about sampled texts is necessary.

From the three collections, a general sense of poetry in English from this region may be deduced. The choice of the anthologies is not motivated by any particular literary merit or trend but serve as rough representatives of this repertoire. From the various regional anthologies such as *Origins in East Africa* (1965), *Drum Beat: East African Poems* (1967), *Poems from East Africa* (1971), *An Introduction to East African Poetry* (1976), *An Anthology of East African Poetry* (1988) through to the numerous 'national'[2] anthologies and individual collections, it is evident that the few (relative to West or South of Africa) poets writing poetry in English have been anthologised in most of these national or regional collections. A quick survey reveals that the works of prominent poets such as Okot p'Bitek, Richard Ntiru, Jared Angira, Marjorie Macgoye, Juan Mwaikusa, Everett Standa are duplicated in several of these collections. Considering that the anthologised poems later make up individual collections, in my view, anthologies offer a broader and fairly representative picture of poetic output from the region.

However, Macgoye serves as a bridge between the two traditions and therefore her work provides a site in which interaction between the two may be gleaned. John Kurtz (2002) describes her work as hybrid having 'crossed-over' and in my view, an instantiation of the interface between English poetry and poetry in English on the one hand, and indigenous African poetic expressions, here represented by the Swahili poetics.

## SWAHILI POETICS: A UNIQUE CULTURAL MATRIX IN EAST AFRICA

While written literary output, especially poetry, in Kiswahili in East Africa dates as far back as the 12th century, it was not until late 19th century that English became an alternative for poetic thought in the region (Gerard, 1981). From the onset, this places poetry in English in a relatively disadvantaged position where it had to compete with established traditions in African languages. Extra-literary factors or measures during colonialism were devised to impose hierarchies of languages and ensure that English and poetry in English occupied privileged positions in the colonies. Relations between literatures in African languages and those in the language of the colonial masters become clear when, for example, Taban lo Liyong's celebrated criticism obliterates the rich repertoire of poetry classics and manuscripts in Kiswahili from the region 1965, 5-13). However, in postcolonial times the interaction of a multiplicity of socio-cultural forces, as Mazrui (1998) points out, have ensured that, like the languages, their poetry play complementary and competitive roles and in the process acquiring both convergent and divergent functions in this region. Whereas the English language, and poetry in English, have become increasingly localized or domesticated, Kiswahili and Swahili poetry and poetics on the other hand have been seeking universalist credentials by appealing to audiences beyond Swahiliphone Africa. Certainly, asymmetrical but symbiotic relations exist between the traditions since different epochs have privileged different traditions hence there is a need to unpack this in relation to poetry and poetics. In most of postcolonial East Africa, Kiswahili became the language of politics and development (Blommaert 1999, 2). This meant that Swahili poetry took a different trajectory from that in English since contextually, the relatively limited use of English language implied an equally exclusive audience, and hence less practiced or developed as a creative or expressive form. In this regard, the Tanzanian context is particularly relevant. During the struggle for independence and the *Ujamaa* period of nation building, the government embraced Kiswahili as the socio-culturally and politically correct language for most Tanzanians, significantly reconfiguring relations between the two in the process. In post-socialist Tanzania, these two languages exist in unequal power relations, with English having significant dominance over Kiswahili as the preferred language of literary output. The promises of English in meeting the socio-economic ingredients (Neke 2003, 5) for advancement or development have profoundly altered the equation. As much as Kiswahili in the country is a deeply ideologically laden language, historically carrying with it particular socio-political and epistemological imprints (especially *Ujamaa* ideologies and associated socialist consciousnesses), English has come to be equated with, among others, knowledge, education, civilization and even development (ibid.) in a sort of reversal of hegemonic relations. As a tenacious residue of British rule in East Africa, poetry in English forms a substantial part of the creative culture in the region, alongside the pan-ethnic Kiswahili. A poet writing in English is therefore compelled to acknowledge these discourses, such that English is made to bear the weight of what Swahili poetry largely represents. Such imprints and consciousnesses can only be appreciated if one understands the tradition/s from which the poet is writing.

Although the genesis of Swahili language and literature is a subject of scholarly debates, it is often attributed to East Africa's triple heritage of the indigenous, the Islamic and the Western cultures. Looking at the Arab-Islamic contribution first, without imposing any specific order in this discussion, its contribution is credited for introducing literacy and for complementing and strengthening the long established oral tradition of Swahili communities. Much of the Swahili's expressive culture revolves around poetry which is divided into three categories – the *shairi*, a poem that has four lines in each verse; the *tenzi*, a long poem of three or four lines in each verse, with eight syllables per line and mainly composed as an epic and the *wimbo*, a three-versed poem composed to be sung. The three categories are not entirely distinct. While *wimbo* remained largely oral, *shairi* and *tenzi* – because of their religious function – flourished with the introduction of literacy and association with the ruling elite. What I designate as *mashairi* however is not merely the plural form of one of these categories, *shairi*, but rather a product of continuing overlapping between and betwixt these categories. As a contact zone where the three forms are engaged in continuous negotiation (Pratt 1992, 4), *mashairi* is thus envisaged as a sort of pedigree with elements drawn from these categories, whether oral or written, co-existing. In recent times, it is a poetic tradition solely relying on Kiswahili as medium of expression, and, therefore a product of what may be called modern Swahili culture – non-ethnically defined and need not necessarily be Islamic. In spite of drawing from African, Arab, Indian, and European cultures, Swahili culture remained confined to the littoral of East Africa, with pockets occurring along the trade routes of the hinterland until late in the 18th century. During its modern phase, Kiswahili therefore has benefited immensely from inland encroachment and interactions, colonial policies, and above all, post-independence decisions[3] which have given its language a pan-ethnic (nationalist) identity while its poetry retains its popular appeal in most of East Africa. The ubiquitous presence of *mashairi* derives from Kiswahili's status as a regional lingua franca in which it functions as the language of the work place, market place, educational systems and most of government business. Despite the fact that East Africa has literary works in English and some in the numerous indigenous languages, "the bulk of literary works; poetry, drama, prose and essays are now in Kiswahili" (Habwe 2009, 4). In much of postcolonial East Africa therefore, *mashairi* – like its medium of song – assumes a privileged if not hegemonic status beyond its "traditional skeletal boundaries" (ibid.). Although occupying a "traditionally complex hybrid space" (ibid.). Swahili poetry – like all other poetries – is also a living and dynamic art form. By envisaging its contemporary phase as *mashairi* the study recognizes the tradition's organic evolution in response to broader sociocultural, economic or political changes in society often manifested in form and content of literary output. In addition to transformations such as relaxation of rigid metrical patterns, mixing of prosodic patterns and incorporation of initially excluded thematic purviews, throughout its history, this tradition exhibits aesthetic preferences for cultural borrowing and appropriation of elements from other traditions. Undoubtedly therefore, *mashairi* interrogates and challenges essentialist designations of 'purity' since it has recontextualized its traditionally complex hybrid space into not only accommodating elements from other poetry traditions but also offering itself as a labyrinthine source for others – as evident in much of postcolonial or contemporary East African poetry. As a framework for analysis, *mashairi* may correctly be summarised as the spirit of creative experimentation arising from deconstructionist discourses of Kiswa-hili–such as 'de-coastalization', de-tribalization and de-Islamization of Swahili culture (Njubi 2009, 105-31), cultural and political decoloni-zation of East African countries and free verse movement in poetry – which have characterized and defined Swahili culture in general.

## SALIENT FEATURES OF *MASHAIRI* TRADITION

As a contemporary poetic style, *mashairi* issues from the continual use of meter and rhyme in a manner that is non-traditional, relatively more flexible or liberal and hence rightly captures the new literary spirit (Mazrui, 2007) which embraces both conservative and radical devel-opments within this tradition. In other words, *mashairi* echoes the post-modernist tradition of ruptures – especially from otherwise rigid, highly formalised and homogenizing conventions which underpinned classical Swahili poetry and most of the subsequent poetics. It embraces and typifies both thematic and formalist departures, the mood of the time, as well as continuities witnessed in most free-verse (*shairi huru*) as evident in various contemporary poetic evocations. Like other world cultures and literary traditions, Swahili has been engaged in a dialectical interplay between opposing forces of absorption and differentiation or conservative and liberalist politics. It is within *mashairi* that the struggle for artistic space is best negotiated (Njogu 2004, 73). These oppositional poetic forms coexist uneasily and innovatively enrich each other since *mashairi* remains both "classical" and "inventive" without being stilted (Gerard, 1981). What is considered as definitive of this tradition there-fore is a result of this negotiation of conservative and innovative forces.

The majority of poems in this tradition are based on telling stories. In particular, *tenzi*, which are narrative poems used to "explain stories" (Biersteker 1996, 171) or issues demanding depth and clarity (Shariff, 1988), constitute a major influence on contemporary poetics discussed in this chapter. I view the inclination towards narrative poetics in con-temporary poetry in English as a result of appropriating the *tenzi*-mode of *mashairi*. But more persuasively, since *tenzi* metre (eight-syllable lines) is used almost exclusively for narrative poetry, the word *utenzi* has come to mean "epic" (Knappert 1967, 6) and hence poetry that tells epic stories tends to appropriate the *tenzi* structure of poetics. By adapting *mashairi's* epic-like nature, the poetic space is conjured as a "clear medium for reflecting experiences" (Gregson 1996, 172) in a given society and not opportunity to abstract, engage in puzzling or indulge in gratuitous (self-) amusement. Hence, in using *tenzi*-formulae to approach content-form question, the poets often end up emphasising accessibility above linguistic or imagistic subtlety, manifested as preference for 'statement' to 'song' – and accompanying toning down of poetic language's complexity. Much of the epic-like character of poetry in English from East Africa emanates from reliance on *tenzi*-mode which imbues poetry with a predilection towards story-telling. To some extent, storytelling and didacticism are inseparable. This is why while surveying contemporary poetic trends, Tanure Ojaide reads didacticism in African poetry as inscribing a pattern of story-telling (1996, 22). In other words, *mashairi* adopted this proclivity for storytelling pattern as a result of its religious function within the Afro-Islamic society, precursor to modern Swahili. *Tenzi*-mode, together with attendant didactic emphasis results narrative poetics characterised by a sort of speaking-voice or generally folkloric approach. The poet is perceived "a vital agent in shaping social consciousness" (Amuta 1989, 10) and hence charged with the role of inspiring positive change in society. In narrative poetics, the poet is positioned as a moralist storyteller, while the poem is used as a medium for communicating moral lessons. The hallmark of the folkloric approach is a certain sense of urgency to make statements, to instruct ethically and morally, and in the process entertaining the audience. Unlike any other poetry, there is a great deal of moralizing advice conveyed via *mashairi's* metaphor-laden story-poems, with emphasis being placed on ideologically progressive content within Swahili tradition. I perceive this conceptualisation of the place of the poet and poetry as a key determinant and distinguishing feature since it eventually inscribes a particular poetics. The poet becomes a narrator arranging scenes, assigning characters typifying attributes and appropriate dialogue or actions, in a typical folkloric style. Even though they compose their poems in English, this consciousness underpins contemporary poets' choices informing both the content and form of emerging poetry. The foregoing echoes a widely held view that the most outstanding distinguishing feature of the poetry published in the late postcolonial period – which includes *mashairi* – is its populist Marxist tone and tenor (Kalu, 2003). However, rather than attribute this inclination to a manifestation of strategic interventions or the so-called alternative poetics, I regard this to be a carry-over from *mashairi* tradition in East Africa.

Although the *shairi*-form is typically marked by its flexibility that allows much variation (Shariff and Feidel 1986, 501), *mashairi* in general is distinguished by its specialized attention to a conspicuous choric device known as *kibwagizo* and prosody. As conceptualised in this chapter, *mashairi* tradition encompasses works inspired directly by Swahili folk songs hence embodies the folkloric approach typical of *nyimbo*. The manner in which *kibwagizo* and the prosodic patterns are deployed within Swahili poetry is not only regarded as the hallmark of the tradition, but is to a large extent an outstanding contradistinguishing feature from English poetry. The relatively rigid prosodic patterns together with pronounced rhyme schemes often ensure that the *kibwagizo* stand out whether in written or oral form.

## ASSIMILATION OF *MASHAIRI* POETICS

Although from what I have described here as significant in East African poetry one might argue that it is not unique to the region, it is possible that is true, but relatively, it is much more pronounced. Narrative poetics have defined modern African poetry since its inception and a number of African poets have told stories in their poems (Ojaide 1996, 22). For example, Steve Chimombo from Malawi deploys narrative poetics typified by folkloric approach in *Napolo and the Python* (1994) where the description of the encounter between Mbona and Mlawli alludes to oral tales. Much more profoundly, Mazizi Kunene's *Ancestor and the Sacred Mountain* (1982) reads like going through a collection of tales that reinforce the author's view of Africa's rich ethical heritage. But this is much more foregrounded in English-language poetry by poets from Swahiliphone parts. Moreover, whereas the motivation outside East Africa is often political – a gesture that oral traditions merit modern poetic spaces, storytelling and narrative poetics form the basic fabric of Swahili poetry. By appropriating the role of poetry among the Swahili, in particular its didactic function, resulting poetics inevitably leans towards the narrative. It is not mere transposition or simple continuity and carrying-over from the oral *nyimbo* tradition but a strategy resulting from negotiation between conceptualisation of the role and language of poetry in Swahili and English societies. A few examples from *Summons* will illustrate the point I am making. Richard Mabala, the editor and one of the anthologised poets in this collection exploits narrative poetics, in particular, narrative-story structure to critique contemporary socio-political and economic order in Tanzania. One of the most accomplished poets in using English from the country, most of his poems adopted a simple linear plot and folkloric pattern. In "A Village Song," Mabala chronologically recounts the fate of an *Ujamaa* village duped by their chairman into communal projects designed to enrich or "fatten[ing] the belly of a big big man" (1980, 72).

This is thematically and structurally related to Jwani Mwaikusa's "The Awful Dentist" – also a sharp critique of capitalist economic order and ideology which narrates the story of a dentist who, so eager to 'pull off' teeth, eventually exhausted all of the teeth out. Overzealous and clearly driven by the greed to amass wealth – just like the chairman in Mabala's – symptomatic of capitalism, as the persona laments, this short-sighted dentist in the end "had no teeth to attend to" (1980, 12). Both poets are appalled by the moral, spiritual and physical decay of their country, largely attributed to capitalist self-indulgent greed.

Mabala's poem proceeds from "last night" when the plot was hatched, recounts the actual implementation of the plan, production process, through to the damning revelation and eventual fate of the offenders, ending with a typically pronounced denouement. Reminiscent of *mashairi*, the poem is marked by the same striking metrical patterns and rhyme scheme. In spite of deploying typically prosaic language, this poem heavily relies on regular end-rhyme (-plot/-shot; - sold/-gold; - acres/-- makers; -white/- night; -flowers/-ours) considered essential to the genre. As already indicated, *mashairi* has a highly formalized poetics. This meticulous attempts to rhyme at all cost occasionally strangles meaning in the strings of rhyme schemes. It is common to forfeit standard spelling or orthography, syntax or phonology for the sake of rhyming in *mashairi*. This will become clearer when specialized repetition and Swahili refrains are discussed in the final section. In "Illegal Brew," a poem exploring the effects of alcoholism, the Mabala narrates what eventually becomes of a once "young and healthy" fellow "of favoured health." Deploying an admonishing tone, the persona details how it all started with a few sips. Alcoholism in this poem may be taken to symbolically refer to uncontrolled or unrestrained indulgence in potentially detrimental social pleasures. The poem adopts a typical oral story, aimed at conveying moral lessons to the audience and society in general. In an adroitly descriptive manner laden with anaphoric connectors and indicators, typical of Swahili epic poems, the poet narrates the events furnishing the reader with minute details relevant to the tale. It is this *tenzi*-mode modern poets appropriate into their relatively shorter poems, making them largely 'stories' about their contemporary socio-political existence, replacing heroic deeds with more immediate social issues. The once 'young and healthy' fellow is descriptively presented at the end of the poem as having his

> bowels visibly distended,
> his breath short
> and shallow,

he also drags thickly
swollen limits.

This heavily descriptive language parallels the unfolding of details associated with deeds of legendary figures in *mashairi's tenzi*. However,
unlike the Swahili epic compositions in English are shorter although
some unfurl into several pages.

In a poem dramatising the unchecked excesses of the post-socialist
government, especially in its critique of the policy's idea of state ownership of resources or nationalisation, Mwaikusa like his colleagues
adopts a simple linear and sequential pattern relying heavily on connectors and conjunctions. In "The Awful Dentist", the connector 'and'
is used over five times to establish causality and link events. The poem's
skeletal structure advances from "...*and* graduated...*and* he started work
(repeated twice) ... *and* they paid him...*and* so on went..." This echoes
*mashairi's* propensity to use the narrative morpheme -*ka*- which indicates successiveness.

In "The Fountain of Life", also a comment on greed-driven capitalism, the poet narrates how with time some so-called "fellows" filled
with greed decided that the communal fountain of life should belong to
a privileged class, made up of a few exploiters. Equally linear in plot, it
proceeds from the discovery, through a gradual growth of greed before
finally "a few united" and decided in "unison" "to dig a pool nearby"
the communal livelihood, symbolic of the insatiability that accompanies privatisation and nationalisation processes in most of postcolonial
(East) Africa. This resonates with the "increasing greed among middle
management Africans, especially the *wanaizi*, a category of people who
were appointed to posts vacated by Europeans and Asians through the
policy of "Africanization" shortly after independence" (Topan 2006,
112). These 'fellows' in the poem, like the *wanaizi* class, seize lucrative
opportunities or deals to accumulate wealth at the expense of the rest
in the community and its collective welfare. The poet-persona convokes
a community of readers interested in an imagined 'communal welfare'
and on whose behalf he speaks.

Similar narrative themes and poetics run through most of East
African poems. Apart from concerns with *Ujamaa* ideologies and governance issues, the concept of *jini* (also *djinn*) or sea spirits preoccupies
various East African poets. This ghost-like figure is a peculiarity of the
East African coast and finds its way into poetry in English. For example,
while steering clear of gnomic, cryptic poetics, Jwani Mwaikusa in
"Ghost Mystery" narrates:

Once I housed a ghost
And gave him food.
He ate it all
Convincing me he was a live human. (Mabala 1980, 12)

The persona convenes an imagined immediate audience listening atten-
tively. The rest of the poem details this 'ghost's' escapades in the persona's house – such as walking on high-heeled shoes; sternly refusing
to sleep on a bed on the floor, preferring to sleep on the ceiling and the
ghost's eventual disappearance. The story unfolds in the typical folkloric
manner with suspense as the ultimate prize, as the poem narrates what
become of the *jini* the persona sheltered, foregrounding the damages it
caused:

And so the ghost disappeared
And a good portion of my floor
Sunk after him. (Mabala 1980, 13)

The text is rich in narrative markers, such as dialogue and connectors ('and', 'after') used frequently to indicate linked 'minimal narrative
units' and hence the sequential pattern'. It further shows a preference
for other narrative, storytelling formal attributes and cues such as the
use formulaic beginning, "Once..." typical of tales. This is evident in
Mwaikusa's "Blind Struggle" which typically starts; "One day you will
learn that ..." and in Makande Mandia's "Doom Ahead" which can only
be appreciated if one has knowledge of *mashairi* poetics. It is common
within Swahili literary discourse to start with "*Siku moja...*" as a device
of de-contextualising and entextualising (Barber 2007, 74) a particular
'utterance' from the immediate social context to guarantee its applica-
bility in other situations besides the one in which it was first uttered.

The foregoing proclivity towards narrative poetics is not a peculiarity of *Summons*. *Boundless Voices*, a collection of poems from Kenya
instances a similar predilection. Like *Summons*, the poems generally confront disparate and diverse facets of contemporary life through largely
functional and transformative aesthetics. They attest to the preference
for narrative, didactic oriented poetics in handling mundane social
issues. From Everett Standa's "A Pregnant School Girl" and "Wedding
Eve", Jonathan Kariara's "A Leopard Lives in a Muu Tree" to Richard
Ntiru's "Twin Ceremony", inclination towards organising accounts of
varied experiences, events or series of events using chronological order,
with an explicit thread running through from the beginning to conclusion in poetic language abound. Standa's poem, for example, tellingly

opens with an unidentified 'he' paying for the protagonist a "seat in the *matatu*" before walking away, and conveniently disappearing "into the city crowd". From the second stanza, events at the bus stop are vividly recounted; passengers boarding, the cigarette smoking incident that triggers spitting and vomiting, then the nostalgic memories through which her (the 'pregnant school girl') predicament may be glimpsed. The omniscient narrator tells how the girl recollects events leading to her present quandary – "She remembers the warm nights" as well as the promises, the gifts, parties, and how "her classmates at school" envied her expensive shoes,/Lipstick, wrist watch, handbag" all which "she brought to school/After a weekend with him;" (Luvai 1988, 35). The narrative moves through into a gloomy and uncertain future in the last three stanzas

> The future stood against her
> Dark like a night without the moon,
> And silent like the end of the world;
>
> As the *matatu* sped away from the city
> She began to tremble with fear
> Wondering what her parents would say;
>
> With all hope gone
> She felt like a corpse
> Going home to be buried.

The linear thread is sustained by lexical items such as '*as* the matatu...' denoting continuity. The poem shifts tense from past, into the present before concluding with future all corresponding with major parts of any narrative; beginning, middle and ending. In Kariara's poem narrating the story about a leopard that "lives in a Muu tree" just outside the persona's homestead (Amateshe 1988, 110), a similar pattern can be discerned. While Standa's tale revolves around the issue of teenage pregnancy and attendant problems, Kariara examines infidelity within the institution of marriage. In this case, the persona is a victim of illicit relationships who expresses his concerns about his lineage and registers displeasure, noting that "the-one-from-the-same-womb," or the brother, blatantly fathers children with his wives or, as he puts it, "arches over my homestead". In a resigned tone, the persona details his frustrations saying his wives:

> ... fetch cold mountain water
> They crush the sugar cane
> But refuse to touch my beer horn.

> My fences are broken
> My medicine bags torn
> The hair on my loins is singed
> The upright post at the gate has fallen
> My women are frisky

Similarly, the surface simplicity emanating from the folkloric approach as discerned in most of the poems examined earlier is evident. The cumulative effect created by the piling of parallelisms to depict the persona's growing frustrations unfolds chronologically for emphasis in the ending. In Richard Ntiru's "Twin Ceremony", the paradox of human existence is also dramatised by the use of linear narration. A sense of overtly ordered chronological pattern can be discerned in:

> While the gay crowd exchange winks
> Wondering if he knows...
>
> Outside a draped coffin awaits the ultimate
> Blackmail – 'dust to dust' –
> As the businesslike gravediggers murmur (ibid.)

The contemporary East African poets' engagement with everyday, existential issues is unequivocal. Ntiru juxtaposes events evoking joy and sorrow, wedding celebration with funeral rituals, but chronologically links them using narrative lexical markers such as 'while', 'as' and graphological signal for continuity such as the three discontinuous dots. Partly, the folkloric approach adapted by these poets determines the nature of poetic language used. This is because a mutual relationship exists between theme and style as content tends to shape its medium.

With storytelling comes moralising and a distinctly reconfigured the persona and poetic voice – another poetic feature showing significant influences from *mashairi* literary tradition. Typical of a Swahili voice, replete with unending self-righteousness, exposing perceived evils and implying the necessity of a different moral order, most of the poems admonish their audience. Due to re-contextualisation of this tradition, that is, having to function beyond the confines of Islamic theology, capitalist ideology replaces the devil or *ibilisi* – the evil powers the audience is often cautioned against. In "The Awful Dentist", "The Fountain of Life", and in Kudi Faraja's "Saluting Ujamaa", just like Mabala's "The Socialists" and the highly allusive "Weeds", capitalism is presented in ghastly images aimed at exposing its negative effects on the welfare of post-socialist Tanzania. Like other East African poets, they sympathetically handle themes and ideas which expose and comment on such ills as economic disparity, social and political corruption, sexual immorality, de-culturization and the paradox of political independence. This characteristic focus demonstrates the poet's belief that they are writing poetry which, in keeping with the tradition of poetry in their society, expresses the people's collective reality, their plight and aspiration as well as extols their socio-cultural norms. Although a common phenomenon in postcolonial African arts with poets regarded as inhabiting a human society so beleaguered, this realist essence takes prominence in *mashairi*. From a Swahili worldview and philosophy, a belief shared by most African societies like the Akan of Ghana, the 'good' or ideal is synonymous with the welfare of society which in turn is expected to include the welfare of the individual (Gyekye 1987, 132).

This predilection towards didacticism, in my view, stems partly from *mashairi's* earlier religious function. *Mashairi* tradition has for long functioned as a narrative vehicle for religious and philosophical ideas especially within Islam, where the longer narrative and admonitory verses still serve as oral instruments for instruction. Appropriating this conceptualisation implies that poetry is positioned or redefined as an invaluable instrument of instruction, a tool and medium for persuading audiences hence vehicle for philosophical, theological or political ideologies. This is why, whether written in English or Kiswahili, poetry is postulated as a distillation and clarification of a community's thoughts and feelings in ways not as pronounced as in the poetry of majority of immediate post-independent Africa's poets. As the two anthologies and Macgoye's works demonstrate, contemporary East African poetry in English seems more concerned with its public role, and not so much with techniques of poetic craft for their own sake. As conceptualised among contemporary Swahilis, political action is considered a key aesthetic principle (Askew 2003, 6) of the genre. This means that when rendered in English, poetry from the region takes on the notion being 'art for art's sake' (Goodwin 1982, x) with a belief in the power of poetic language to catalyze change in society. The need to perceive the context of literature, its content and form as "dialectically interconnected areas" (Amuta 1989, 9) informs this poetics. Thus, *Mashairi* profoundly defines the literary context of East African output in English. It also maps into poetry form, in English, the prevalent ideologies embedded in Kiswahili and Swahili literary tradition. The dialectical interplay and resulting tension between the poet's political commitment or simply the message on the one hand, and textual form or aesthetic attributes on the other has shaped the discourse on the nature of poetry East Africa (Mwangi 2007, 138) as a literary region.

Some East African poets have also appropriated structural devices unique to *mashairi*, into English-language poetry thus introducing the formal textualities associated with Swahili tradition. As suggested earlier, there are certain special kinds of repetition characteristic and peculiar to *mashairi*. These poets appropriate *mashairi's kibwagizo* (also *kiitikio*) or refrain to provide a kind of thematic skeleton summing up or emphasising the central thematic concern. *Kibwagizo* provides a sort of lingering effect as it regularly punctuates the poem, opening and closing each stanza. Graphologically, the penultimate or final lines stand out from poem's body in a manner informed by *mashairi* tradition where, as the word suggests, they sign off in condensed line pregnant with the poem's focus. While it is more common to spread emphasis throughout a particular poem in English poetry, *mashairi* tends to rely on the penultimate moment or choric parts to deliver summative concerns of the poem. For example, Mwaikusa exploits this in "In the Moonlit Foyer" and "Blind Struggle". The later poignantly concludes; "One day you will learn/That I am just as human" (Mabala 1980, 140) to serve as a reminder of the persona's humanity hence deserving due dignity. With similar profundity, Manga Mmbagha winds up his three part poem with the lines "There is nothing sadder/Than the itching desire for freedom" (Mabala 1980, 139) which appropriately foregrounds the poet-persona's loneliness. Unlike the *mashairi* case where this often appears regularly at the end of each stanza, this regularity of pattern is often asymmetrical in poems written in English. By appearing in the penultimate or denouement group of lines, with some indented to jut out from the rest of the poem's main body, these lines carry thematic weight in an attempt to appropriate of use a refrain in a manner informed by *mashairi* tradition. This refrain foregrounds thematic concerns, wrapping up the poem by condensing – in terse lines – the poem's overall focus. More often than not, this is used together with the concept of *wasia*, an admonition, warning or reminder of the ethical and religious principles which undergird the society (Shariff and Feidel 1986, 504). As already indicated in relation to narrative poetics, storytelling in Swahili literary traditions – like in most oral traditions – is underpinned by moral lessons. The recurrent *Kibwagizo* and wisdom laden *wasia* combine to give *mashairi* rhythmic emphasis of didacticism.

In *Make it Sing*, Marjorie Macgoye (1998) not only uses Kiswahili to title some of her poems, such as "Shairi la Ukombozi" and "Shukrani" but integrates pillars of *mashairi* into some of her poems. It is significant that despite their titles being rendered in Kiswahili, not a single lexical item is used in the body of the poems. This is unusual because contemporary East African English-language poetry usually incorporates Kiswahili diction. But in this instance, Macgoye seems to signal the pre-eminence of this culture's language in the region. In "Shairi la Ukombozi", she demonstrates one of the most sustained attempts to echo *mashairi's* elaborate structural and rhythmic patterns, especially the *caesura* and the *kibwagizo*. She uses punctuation (comma and full stop) to divide each of the lines making up the five-line stanzas into equal hemistiches. This regularity is evident in:

> We miss a living voice, a dour and stocky presence,
> Abrupt in speaking, vivid, impatient of pretence,
> a heavy head, a heart heavy with understanding,
> We are too tame for lions. The pride has been disbanding.
> We miss a living voice, a dour and stocky presence. (Macgoye 1986, 76)

Note that typical of *mashairi*, the first line recurs again at the end of the stanza. This is a characteristic pattern used in the entire poem. Whereas the pattern in the first, second, sixth and tenth stanzas relies on repeating the first line in the last, the rest alternate to repeat the second (in the third, fifth and eighth stanzas), third (in the fourth and seventh stanzas) and fourth (in the ninth stanza) lines. Such regularity is common in *mashairi* where mid and end-rhymes alternate in a similar manner. Furthermore, the concluding stanza is made up of various *vibwagizo* (plural for *kibwagizo*) lines drawn from the rest of the poem, affirming the point made earlier that the final stanza is often designed to linger in the audience's mind. Therefore this poem is modelled on *mashairi* poetics. This is also the case in "To a Church Builder" where each of the six stanzas open and close with "if you must build...", (1986, 85-6) completed with different variants. Despite being common to all poetic traditions, the manner in which storytelling, repetition and the folkloric strategy are used within *mashairi* is arguably unique. It is this peculiarity that is appropriated in poetry of English expression, giving contemporary East African poems a unique texture. The manner in which narrative poetics, certain forms of repetition and prosody are deployed certainly alludes to or is informed by *mashairi's* conceptualization of poetic form. What emerges is not a Swahili poem rendered in English or simply a modern African poem appropriating indigenous literary traditions. Rather, it is a distinct poetics in which intertextual relations point to a sort of in-between, hybrid text requiring equally hybrid reading framework. As a mega-text, *mashairi* has continuously provided a reservoir from which a number of texts have found their way into poetry in English. The particular texts considered in this regard and have transgressed boundaries of Swahili poetics include *tenzi*-mode which inscribes storytelling poetics, the *kibwagizo*-type refrain as well the tradition's worldview which informs conceptualisation of the role of the poet and poetic language. The two poetic traditions, together with the numerous vernacular poetic traditions, coexist within the boundaries of East Africa, enriching and complementing each other. While the vernaculars remain embedded (in *mashairi*) or limited to predominantly oral realms, *mashairi* and poetry in English display intertextual symbiotic rather than antagonistic relations. This leads to exchange of textual resources between them, with poetry written in English exhibiting features largely regarded typical of *mashairi* as this chapter has shown. In this way, the role that storytelling serves in Swahili culture has been successfully appropriated into poetry in English. Just like the art of narrative which, when it was first transferred onto paper, did not cross-over as mere fictional stories, the poem-stories examined assume a different aesthetics. While the introduction of literacy transformed Swahili stories into 'histories of the Swahili, *mashairi* texts documenting various life experiences are de-contextualised and 'entextualised' from everyday existence to assume the status of models for the society to learn from. They are not mere fictive stories but 'real' life experiences providing templates for the society's moral code. Finally, rather than East African writers, as Peter Nazareth stated, being envisaged as falling victims of invisible colonial teachers, I have argued that an important 'visible' teacher is *mashairi* tradition. Poetry written in English from East Africa therefore should not be read as merely characteristic of "kindergarten type of simplicity" (Ugah 1982, 11) but rather, as approximating structures and conception of the poet and poetry in the region as evident in *mashairi* tradition. Read within the context of *mashairi*, Swahili poets downplay imagistic complexity associated with traditional English poetry. When poetry combines at least an idea and an image for the purpose of imposing and impressing an emotive force on the reader, provoke a sense of 'strange familiarity' or provide a spark of momentary surprise,[4] it fulfils the aesthetic role of art. Partly, East African poetry in English has intertextualised *mashairi* structure, and in the process merged the two literary traditions, anticipating a sort of third poetics or tradition that is neither wholly Swahili nor identifiably English in orientation.

# *Notes*

1.  See particularly Abdulaziz and Osinde, "Sheng and English: Development of Mixed Codes Among the Urban Youths in Kenya," in *International Journal of the Sociology of Language* (Berlin: Allemagne, 1997) and Githiora "Sheng: Peer Language, Swahili dialect or emerging Creole?" in *Journal of African Cultural Studies.* (London: Routledge, 2002) for details on *sheng*.

2.  'National' in the sense that all anthologized poets are drawn from a single geo-political location or country. Examples include *Uganda Poetry Anthology, Summons: Poems from Tanzania, Boundless Voices: Poems from Kenya,* among others either specific in gender or including other literary genres such as *Our Secret Lives: An Anthology of Poems and Short Stories* – by Kenyan women writers.

3.  Mulokozi, ibid. Specific policies which directly or indirectly impinged on Kiswahili include the adoption of Kiswahili as the national language in 1962, the adoption of the policy of *Ujamaa* and self-reliance in 1967, (the creation of factories, state farms and Ujamaa villages which brought together people from different linguistic backgrounds, hence enhancing the use of Kiswahili), the adoption of Kiswahili as the official language of government in 1967, the adoption of the policy of Education for Self-reliance in 1968 which included adoption of Kiswahili as the sole language of instruction in primary schools – entailed translation most of the existing government documents, forms, labels and designations into Kiswahili and Advanced Kiswahili Examination became compulsory for all senior civil servants who did not have the requisite Kiswahili language qualifications, the abandonment of the Cambridge School Certificate Examinations in 1970 which required a student to pass Kiswahili in order to get a certificate, and the adoption of the Cultural Policy (Sera ya Utamaduni) in 1997.

4.  In an interview accessed via http://everythinliterature.blogspot.com/2007_05_01_archive.html titled "Poetry is Demonized and Abused"

Chapter 10

# THE PLACE AND THEMATIC FUNCTION OF A PANEGYRIC IN SWAHILI SOCIETY: THE CASE OF SUFI AL-BUSIRI'S *KASIDA YA HAMZIYYAH*

*Tom Olali*
*University of Nairobi*

## INTRODUCTION

The *Hamziyyah* without doubt is a masterpiece of Swahili poetry, not only for bringing out the eulogy of the Prophet Muhammad in poetic expression, but also for serving as a treasure-house of old Swahili vocabulary of the kiNgozi dialect. The themes in the *Hamziyyah* provide the Swahili with a sure guide to life in this world and they are part of the required knowledge (*elimu*) for all who want to venerate the Prophet. For this reason, the Prophet's veneration has pre-occupied the minds of the Swahili and they spend many long nights discussing the image of the Prophet as versified in the *Hamziyyah* and regard the *Hamziyyah* as an epitaph, and a complete eulogy of the Prophet. Jan Knappert, who has worked intensively on religious Swahili poetry, confirms this fact. He asserts the following in regard to Swahili poetry:

> ....it deals with moral precepts and instructions regarding ritual, praise of God and His Prophet, the horrors of Hell and

> the pleasure of Paradise. Where the moral rules are not given
> directly, they are given, by implication, in the form of *historical
> sancta*, the legendary history of the Prophet and his followers.
> As such these legendary stories are of great importance to the
> members of the traditional Swahili society. [...] These legends
> are not entertainment, they are *elimu*, knowledge, required for
> all who want to lead a righteous life. Jan Knappert (1967,11).

In the *Hamziyyah*, al-Busiri does not arrange his ideas in any strict
thematic order but freely jumps from one theme to another, according to the spontaneous dictates of his poetic imagination. All his ideas
relate to the Prophet Muhammad. The *Hamziyyah* can be divided, for
convenience, into a number of sections. But the fundamental message
that runs across it is Muhammad's supremacy over the other Prophets.
The poet bases the panegyric on narratives from the Holy Quran and
religious stories which demonstrates his poetic imagination. Therefore,
the *Hamziyyah* is indeed a hagiography of the Prophet Muhammad,
which the Swahili refer to as *Sira ya Mtume*.

## THE THEME OF *SIRA YA MTUME* (HAGIOGRAPHY OF THE PROPHET)

The Swahili adore this theme because it includes the glorification of
the birthday of the Prophet, including his family, his lofty qualities, and
outward beauty. To them, the *sira ya mtume* is the core of the *Hamziyyah* themes. From it, they understand how the companions supported
and fought for the cause of Islam, and subsequently, it is incumbent
upon them to reciprocate. The companions emulated the Prophet by
spreading Islam after his death and each was given a duty to perform.
Allah is fully aware of their deeds and every deed will be sorted out in
detail on the Day of Judgement. Vv. 347 introduces the companions.

347.   *Na kwa swahabazo ambao kwamba wa baadaye
       Ni wasi zote ni ndugoze ya kula mema*

> The poet praises the companions of the Prophet who remark-
> ably continued to articulate and spread the message that
> Muhammad had begun to spread- the word of God

In addition, they learn from verse 347 that the caliphs were a good
example to be emulated by the rest of the world and that what they pos-

sessed in their hearts was very valuable to the people. The Swahili hold the view that God has promised success and prosperity to those who are humble, modest and lowly in the presence of their Lord. This is part of Islamic belief, the religion that the Swahili subscribe to.

349.    *Iwe ni wakwasi wa ithani ni fukarau*
        *Ndiyo maimamu maamiri ndiyo ulama*

> Although they were materially poor(the Caliphs), they were spiritually very rich in their hearts. That was the most important form of riches rather than earthly possessions. They were knowledgeable and were the best leaders.

They are reminded to copy the example of the Prophet just as people who were around him copied his example. In addition, they should be steadfast in their way of life and that they need not care much about material possessions. The following excerpt demonstrates this.

350.    *Waliwa mbele duniyani kwamba yowewa*
        *Kupondoke yao na kupenda kwao alama*

> Those who came after the Prophet were very steadfast and they never involved themselves with earthly possessions. They did not ask for signs to prove his Prophethood.

The poet continues to heap praise on the caliphs especially how they intervened in disputes, and fought in God's name and the blessing they received. This is mentioned in vv.351, 352, and 353. The Swahili ethos requires them to lead the right religious life. They believe that they need to acquire knowledge of right and wrong, as the companions did. As John Hick observes, goodness and love are generally treated as two further attributes of God (2010, 35).

## THE PHYSICAL APPEARANCE OF THE PROPHET

It is stated that the Prophet's physical beauty was praised as early as the period of his lifetime. The pioneer was the Prophet's poet Hassan Ibn Thabit( Mubarak 1943, 29-30). Hassan remarks:

> And a more beautiful than you, a woman has never borne
> and a more handsome one, have never seen my eyes.

Such praise of physical beauty was the mainstream of Arabic eulogy in general at that early period. As an example of these lofty qualities, consider al-Tirmidhi's description of the Prophet's appearance.

> Muhammad was middle-size, did not have lank or crisp hair, was not fat, and had a white circular face, wide black eyes, and long eyelashes. When he walked, he walked as though he went down a declivity. He had the 'seal of prophecy' between his shoulder blades [...] He was bulky. His face shone like the moon in the night of full moon. He was taller than middling stature but shorter than conspicuous tallness. He had thick, curly hair [...] His complexion was *azhar* (bright, luminous). Muhammad had a wide forehead and fine, long, arched eyebrows which did not meet [...] The upper part of his nose was hooked; he was thick-bearded, had smooth cheeks, a strong mouth, and his teeth were set apart [...] His neck was like the neck of an ivory statute, with the purity of silver. Muhammad was proportionate, stout, firm-gripped, even of belly and chest, broad chested and broad-shouldered. (Ahmed al-Tirmidhi 1859, 6)

We have quoted al-Tirmidhi here *in extenso* to demonstrate the different qualities he mentioned pertaining to the Prophet, so we can show how the poet has employed these descriptions and incorporated them in the *Hamziyyah*. In fact, all the poets who wrote panegyrics in praise of the Prophet, and came after al-Tirmidhi used these images in their poetry. On these looms of imagery, Aidarusi has woven the description of Prophet Muhammad with an array of coloured and lofty epithets. He writes:

12.    *Napendeza tena uso wako wingawi juwa*
       *Ufunukiweo ni usiku mwelupe mwema*

> The poet acclaims the face of the Prophet, saying that it was so bright after being shone upon by the light from the sun. The night was bright and beautiful. This was the night the Prophet was born.

More of Muhammad's beauty is narrated in vv. 153, 156, 158, 159,161, and 162.

He combines most of the lofty qualities enumerated by al-Tirmidhi. Aidarusi compares the Prophet's face to the moon and his smile to the luminous light. In v.156 he says;

156.    *Alidhihirisha kwa kupowa kovu ya uso*
        *Kana mwezi kwandha kuonyeshwa mwezi kwa wema*

> Despite the scar left on the Prophet's forehead during the battle of Uhud, most likely to make the Prophet's face look awful, it instead made his face look like the crescent moon at the beginning of the month.

This gleam or light is the Divine Light of God which shows the clear path; right from wrong, the truth from the false. The Swahili believe that this light leads them out of the ignorance of darkness and evil into light of goodness and piety. This Divine light offers a ray of hope to those who have lost their way in the wilderness of darkness. The Swahili believe that the Divine light originally radiating from God is understood as an eternal spiritual essence. In other words, as Muhammad was created from the eternal light, Muhammad himself is eternal—he is pre-existing, present from eternity to eternity. The Swahili endeavour to maintain Islamic way of life and they are concerned with Islamic solidarity and its symbols. Even when the Swahili perform their rituals, Islamic mores and attitudes continue to colour them. Literacy among the Swahili was through Arabic, introduced by the Muslims and therefore inseparable from Islam. Swahili had also compositions that were un-Islamic, although it, too, began to be coloured by Islamic ideas and attitudes when the Islamic way of life took firm root among certain social classes.

## THE SPIRITUAL QUALITIES OF THE PROPHET

In his discussion of the figure of Prophet Muhammad according to the popular literature of the Islamic people, Knappert enumerates some epithets which the Muslims have given to their Prophet. Among the Swahili, the spiritual *epitheta* that we can extract include: the Banner who will lead his community to paradise on the Day of Judgement. The Trustworthy one who will never forsake his people; the beloved; the closing seal of prophets; the shining lamp; the chosen one; the one full of mercy; and the guide on the right road (Knappert 1961, 24-31). Similarly, in the *Hamziyyah*, a common theme is the depiction of Prophet Muhammad as a Teacher, an Exemplar, an ideal man, and a Guide. V. (iii) written in Roman letters and which is the style used in the prologue mentions Muhammad as *mwenye makama* (the one of high rank). The poet summarizes all the spiritual qualities mentioned above. In v.iii Aidarusi says:

*(iii).*    *Sala na salamu za dawama mada dahari*
          *Zimutelele Muhammadi mwenye makama*

          Prayers and salutations should be plentiful for Muhammad,
          the one of high rank.

V.1 expounds on this rank, that the Prophet Muhammad is incomparable to any other prophet-past or future, and that Mohammed is the seal of Prophethood. It states:

*1.*     *Hali wakwelaye kukwelakwe michume yote*
        *Uwingu usiyo kulochewa ni muja sama?*

        The poet is asking a rhetorical question to the effect that how
        can any of the prophets climb to the seven heavens as did the
        Prophet during the *israi* and *miiraji*?

To the Swahili, as a teacher, the Prophet is envisioned as the perfect man who has all the noble traits of character and the knowledge from Allah. A man, who should be followed and listened to, and therefore, has to be venerated.

In verse 80, the poet says:

*80.*    *Kajulisha wachu mwenye enzi kwa tawhidi*
        *Nako kuwahidi ndio ndia walipo njema*

        He taught the people about the doctrine of One God and
        added that obeying this was the surest and straight path

The Swahili also see the Prophet as an Exemplar, honest, generous, and helpful to the poor. Verse 109 shows how helpful the Prophet is to the poor. This stanza is about *tamaa* (greed). Greed, especially for money is repeatedly condemned by the Swahili. First, one must repay one's debt, as it would be particularly inauspicious to die without first having settled the claims of others because they were trustful enough to lend their money. In addition, if one has lent money, one must not demand *riba* (interest). The same sum that was lent should be claimed but no more. Verse 109 clearly demands from man that he must not transgress the rights of his partners under any circumstances. The Prophet is humble and modest. He never tried to become rich. v. 117 says:

117.   *Kwa khuluku njema ya Mchume soyo karimu*
       *Kwa kuimisha yapo kwa sumuye soyo ajama*

       Because the Prophet was humble and forgiving, he forgave the woman who had tried to poison him.

In addition, humility is a quality expected of every Swahili. By being humble, one emulates the Prophet. In v. 118 the poet writes:

118.   *Lineemeshezo kwa fadhili Hawazini*
       *Kwamba paliwele kulewakwe kwao mapema*

       He freed those captured owing to his generosity and he let them go earlier than scheduled

The poet gives an example of one of the freed prisoners: he describes thus in v.119

119.   *Mateka yayile na mumule umbu la kwama*
       *na kuteka kwake kwa mahaba zima*

       One of the freed prisoners was his half-brother who was breast-fed together with him at Halima's place. He was ashamed so much when the Prophet captured him.

The Swahili see the Prophet as an ideal man, perfect man, who does not promise what he cannot deliver, and is the one Allah chose to be the seal of prophets and apostles. They see him as a Guide. They say he is the one whom Allah has chosen to bring the straying people back to the right path. He is also the spiritual leader who should be imitated and followed in all his deeds and sayings. In v. 140 He states:

140.   *Mshindi wa kwamba na vichendo mwema wa umbo*
       *Mulamuwa haki mambo vingi khuluku njema*

187

He is the leader in lofty qualities and beauty, honest and has many other admirable virtues.

## THE PROPHET'S MIRACULOUS BIRTH AND CHILDHOOD

Annemarie Schimmel (1985, 67) states that the Prophet's *miujiza* (miracles) are "deeds that render [others] unable to match them". On the day the Prophet was born, story has it that a bright light emanated from the star, and permeated the dwellings. Vv. 26 and 27 state:

26.    *Pakakurubiya kulokea nujumu mbazi*
       *Pakaacha mianga kaangali majimbo thama*

       There came near to where the Prophet was a brilliant star
       causing its luminous rays to penetrate in all directions.

27.    *Ziungu zayo zikaona zilizo Rumu*
       *Kuona ni alo nyumbani Maka mukima*

       The palaces of the Emperor, which are in Rome, became
       visible to the extent that even someone who was resident in
       Mecca could see them from his house

The Swahili hold the *imani* (belief) that the blessings of God, that is, His *fadhila* (favours) descend upon persons who sacrifice their lives and all their interest in the path of God, make a complete submission to Him and rein themselves wholly to His will and then supplicate Him to grant them all the spiritual blessings which man can attain of the nearness and union of God, and of speaking to and being addressed by Him.

Aidarusi describes the events occurring on the night of the Prophet's birth. His verses mention some of the natural wonders. He begins by saying that there was complete joy that day:

13.    *Usiku wa kuzawa na sikuye ambayo kwamba*
       *Pawele sururi na fahari ya dini sama*

       The night of the Prophet's birth was like a day when there was
       joy and pride for the religion all over the world

He adds:

14.   *Pakafuwacha na bishara za dilingano*
      *Kwamba uzaziwe Mustwafa mbili za njema*

      There followed the glad tidings of invisible voices, that
      Mustafa 'the Purified One' had been born and that the good
      things had come true.

His birth saw the main gallery of the Persian King tumble down while
the building from where he was born did not rock (v.15). It was a night
when every house saw the fire getting extinguished. This was the fire of
Zoroastrianism, a Persian religion. The extinction of it (the fire) demonstrated that the coming of the Prophet was to seal all the dominance of
the earthly kings who had established their hegemony over their people.
The extinction of fire symbolised the supremacy of God. Sovereignty
and power over the entire universe belongs to God alone. Therefore,
His law should prevail over all the affairs of the people. As He is the
Sovereign and the Ruler, His law stands supreme in the land and no
other lawmaker should be recognised besides Him. The following verse
further describes this scenario.

16.   *Pakaswirisapo kula nyumba moya ya nchu*
      *Lijalilingamo kwa luzima na baa nzima*

      And it happened that every fire temple was filled with grief
      because the fires were subsequently extinguished

Those who got a real set back were the Persians. Their vision was blurred.
They lacked knowledge to make any formidable decisions. They could
not understand what extinguished their power (fire). He says:

17.   *Micho ya Furusi ifusele hali pawele*
      *Kuzima kusoyo mocho wao wa wa kunguruma*

      The rivers of Persia extinguished the roaring fire

Verse 24 illustrates how the Prophet was born miraculously. It was not
usual for one to be born with 'his eyes looking up'. This 'act' symbolised
a sign of all good things. It symbolised the Prophet's submission to God.
He was to seek God's wisdom in every task he was set to do.

24.  *Amzazile atukule kitwa juu*
     *Na kutuwa ni ishara ya kula mema*

     She bore him, and he raised his head high, and in this raising,
     there was a sign of all good things to come.

He adds:

25.  *Matoye kianga uwinguni na malolo*
     *Yambao lake patukufu na pa adhama*

     The Prophet's eyes looked up to heaven and his glances to
     Him whose honour is elevated and of greatness

The following excerpt illustrates how the poet versifies the luminous stars with his birth.

26.  *Pakakurubiya kulokea nujumu mbazi*
     *Pakaacha mianga kaangali majimbo thama*

     There came near to where the Prophet was a brilliant star
     causing its luminous rays to penetrate in all directions.

In versifying the miracles of the night of the Prophet's birth, the
poet followed in the footsteps of other Muslim poets who had preceded
them. In an attempt to enumerate all the miracles that took place on
that night, the poet states:

18.  *Kuzawa kukulo paliwele kufa na wao*
     *Kuze ni zao kafiri waliko hama*

     This great birth meant death and disease for all those that
     had sinned.

Of all the miracles from the Prophet's childhood, the opening of
his chest is the one mostly spoken and discussed by the Swahili. V.41
illustrates the opening of the chest.

41.  *Pasuwa kuliko moyo wake chake kifuwa*
     *Kalifuwa nyama kuloshani aso dama*

> Where the heart was, his chest was cut open and by washing
> the black bile was removed from the flesh. This meant that
> the Prophet was purified from any form of sin

On the miracle of the splitting of the chest, Bahador Khan(1968, 348) explains that it is quite evident that, there is no mention of the incision made in the chest, its real (and figurative) meaning being, as most of the commentators have suggested: "enlarging it to receive truth, and wisdom, and revelation.". The poet illustrates how the miracle of the splitting of the chest happened, describing how Halima took him back to his grandfather after weaning him.

37.   *Kampelekeya jadi yake amzazipo*
      *Kama ni matungu ka fiswali yakimloya muluma*

> Halima sent the Prophet to his grandfather, when she had fin-
> ished nursing him, and for her, this was a harbinger of suffer-
> ing, since being with the Prophet meant having good fortune.

The *malaika* (angels) of God surrounded the Prophet during the opening of his chest and for a while he thought they were *majini* (jinns).

38.   *Wamzingilepo malaika yake Mulungu*
      *Kadhwani kwambao ni majini kwakeye mwema*

> The angels of God surrounded him and she thought they
> were jinns who had come near the most exalted one.

The angels are greatly revered by the Swahili. They believe that the angels are gifted with life, speech and intelligence. They are pure, free from darkness of desire and the disturbance of wrath and that they protect human beings and whenever a human being dies, they receive his soul. They believe that the angels are heavenly host side by side with Allah Himself. The involvement of *Malaika Jiburili* (Angel Gabriel) during the opening of the chest is captured as follows:

42.   *Fupile wachuwo mkono wa Jiburili*
      *Wisha zabayo akhabari kiza kusema*

> The hand of Gabriel closed the Prophet's chest and the tidings
> that were not revealed were placed in him.

This miracle, which was bestowed on the Prophet by God, is highly regarded among the Swahili. The literal meanings of the Swahili word *pasua* are rending, tearing out or opening. Another implication of this word is to open the heart thereby making the reality of a thing easily understandable.

## THE THEME OF THE HOLY QURAN

Every Swahili family is expected to possess a copy of the Holy Quran. It is an integral part of the *imani za Waswahili* (Swahili beliefs). They believe that no miracle can vie with the Divine Book revealed to the Prophet Muhammad. The most outstanding challenge to mankind is to produce a similar Book or a chapter.V. 187 expresses this view:

187.    *Ilimilizachu wato na majini ayaye moya*
        *Alifusahau kawaleche ayaye zema*

> Aidarusi says that no Jinn or mankind could compose a single line reminiscent to those of the Holy Quran, let alone composing just one of the verses in the Holy Quran.

To the Swahili, this challenge does not merely mean the writing of a book like this in style and in language. In fact, it means the writing of a book of a particular nature, grandeur, eminence, status and class in style, subject matter, chasteness, eloquence and rhetoric in any language. The miracle of the Holy Quran is found in v.184. Others are vv. 185,186, and 187:

184.    *Ajabu kufari wazidile dhalalo kwayo*
        *Yenye uongofu wa akili zilo salima*

> It is unbelievable that the disbelievers refused adamantly to listen to him despite the fact that he had shown them the physical evidence of his Prophethood.

The writer mentions that the Holy Quran has many miracles and those who read it would always find something new in it.

188.    *Miujiza mje wasumaji kula kutiza*
        *Waipelekee waisikize kulla yauma*

> Those who read it always come across a miracle while those who listen to it always get something refreshing and new

He discusses it further in vv.189, 190, 191 and 192.

The poet metaphorically says that the chapters of the Holy Quran reminiscences our faces that are all different from one another (v.193). In other words, the chapters in the Holy Quran have different thematic content and none is similar to the other just as the human face is distinct from the other. According to Aidarusi, in particular v.195, the verses contain vast knowledge and each chapter dwells with a particular body of knowledge and thought.

195.    *Kangapi yazo kuwadhihi elimu nyingi*
        *Kwa harufu chache kondoleza kwako alima*

        The verses in the Holy Quran contain vast knowledge such that each letter and chapter is a branch of a particular knowledge

The poet uses yet another metaphor and compares the benefits we obtain from reading the Holy Quran to a farmer who plants a seed and eventually reaps abundantly during harvesting time. That reading a verse of the Holy Quran results in bountiful benefits. To the Swahili, this is the only hope for the spiritual future of man, a cure for the lost and hurt souls, a guide for the evil and misled ones, and a joy for those who repent. This is metaphorically captured in the following verse.

196.    *Inga Kama punde na ukuzi ziajibuzo*
        *Mkulima kwazo zisikize vema na alama*

        The wonders that we obtain from those verses are immeasurable. It is like the farmer who plants a seed and later reaps a huge harvest.

The poet still laments and concludes that if the unbelievers still doubt the authenticity of the miracles and question the authority with which the Prophet carried out the miracles, then the best thing to do is to deny them (the unbelievers) any teaching relating to salvation. He laments:

198.    *Pindi miujiza ikitowa kufaa ajabu*
        *Kutaka kulwa kwayo tena ni shida nzima*

        If they cannot believe in this miracle (of the Holy Quran), Aidarusi states, then teaching them of the way of salvation is practically impossible

193

And adds:

199.     *Zilitwapo ndia zikajuwa ziso akili*
         *Mwenye kunusuhu unenane likawa hima*

         If God has devised ways of making them wiser then those
         who still doubt simply will not understand any Prophet

The Swahili believe that the Holy Quran will lead them to the right path,
and they must remain firm in that path.

## THE THEME OF *HIJIRA*

One of the most frequently repeated stories in the biography of the
Prophet is his Flight (*hijira*) from Mecca to Medina. The poet recounts
this story as follows:

66.     *Wamtolezele Maka pango ikamuweka*
         *Kamhifadhiye ndiwa manga mahala pema*

         When he fled Mecca he lived inside a cave. During
         this time, a pigeon looked after him well in the cave

People were in hot pursuit after the Prophet. Others who heard the
man advising a search of the cave laughed, told him that they would
not waste their time looking for him in a cave over the mouth of which
*matando ya ankabuti* (spider's web) unbroken was waving in the breeze.
The poet versifies this section as follows.

67.     *Kamtosheleza kwa chandule ankabuti*
         *Atoshelezayo ndiye ndiwa ya ivuzi njema*

         The spider made a web across the mouth of the cave while the
         pigeon took good care of him.

He describes how Abu Bakr, the Prophet's companion hid together
with the Prophet in the cave and that they could not be seen.

68.     *Kajisita kwayo kwa karibu ya kuonae*
         *Kudhihiri mno kuna masito kuu adhwama*

Muhammad and Abu Bakr could not be seen by their enemies since they were rightly protected from them. Their enemies assumed that there was no way someone could live in the cave with the spider web still intact around the door of the cave.

The miracles he performed culminated in the jinns singing his praises. Vv.70 is explicit.

70.　*Majini wakemba kwa sifaze chumwa ya mola*
　　*Zikapembejesha muumini zi nyimbo sama*

　　The Jinns sung in praise of God's Prophet and these songs subsequently impressed the believers

V.71 describes Suraqah, an enemy of the Prophet, who mounted a swift horse till he came quite close to him; but the repeated stumbling of his horse and his falling from it awakened him to the situation that it was a constant warning of God for evil design. He approached the Prophet with a penitent heart and begged him for forgiveness. The Prophet forgave him.

71.　*Suraka kampenda nyuma yake akamuacha*
　　*Kamba katumevu ivuzi njema*

　　A man named Suraqah followed the Prophet with an ulterior motive to maim him. Instead, he got stuck but was prayed for by Prophet and was later relieved

*Kusamehe* (forgiving) is one moral quality the Swahili teach their young ones. If for example somebody is forgiven on the right occasion, then one expects to find blessings from God. The most active opponents of Muhammad at this period were Abu Jahal, and the prophet's own uncle, Abu Lahab. The poet writes in vs.108

108.　*Na Abujahali awenepo shingo ya dume*
　　*Imtolokele ja unuki yenye adhwima*

　　And Abu Jahal saw a male neck (referring to a male camel), and he quickly ran backwards away from the camel

The other five enemies were Abdal Muttalib (v. 89), Manaf bin Zahara (v. 90), al-Walid bin Mughira (v. 91), al-As bin Wahil (v.92), and al-Harith (v. 93).

## *ISRAI* (NIGHT JOURNEY)
## AND *MIIRAJI* (ASCENSION) THEME

The Prophet's Night Journey and his ascension to heaven, is the story that recurs often in Swahili Islamic religious Poetry. *Israi* means night journey. Since this extraordinary event of transportation of the Prophet from the sacred mosque al-Masjid to the far-off mosque of al-Aqsa in Bait-ul-Maqdis, and subsequently to heaven occurred in the night, it is called *Israi*.

In *israi and Miiraji*, Muhammad flies across the skies on *Buraki* (a winged horse), while angels serve as his guides and explain to him all the phenomena of creation. The apotheosis of the story is the meeting face-to-face of Muhammad with his creator at a station where not even the angels can follow. For the Swahili, this theme has a personal significance; it is not just an interesting piece of Oriental mythology but also God's blessings to humanity (Yahya Ondigo 2006, 52). They consider the mosque at al-Masjid as the centre of the world( Challen Edward 2006, 18).They live with mounting tension through the episodes where Muhammad is shown the crowds of souls as he passes through one celestial gate after the other on his way up to the central light. The summit of the Prophet's ascent was *mkunazi wa mwisho* (the lote tree; ar. *sidratul muntaha*) ,beyond which is a hidden mystery, unknown to any save God. V.1 of the *Hamziyyah* narrates this episode.

1. *Hali wakwelaye kukwelakwe michume yote*
   *Uwingu usiyo kulochewa ni muja sama?*

   The poet is asking a rhetorical question to the effect that how can any of the prophets climb to the seven heavens as did the Prophet during the *israi* and *miiraji*

The journey from Mecca to Heaven via Jerusalem is to be found in vv. 73,74,75,76 and 77. When Muhammad returned and recounted this event to his Makkan opponents, they mocked him. However, the Swahili find it a source of joy and wonder, a confirmation of Muhammad's status as the seal of the Prophets. This can be found in the following excerpts.

78.  *Kudai wachume wenye shaka wasiwe ambao*
     *Hali pasalie na saili taka zikima*

     The Qureshi requested him to tell them more about Bait-ul-
     Maqdis (Jerusalem) because they cast serious doubts if he
     had indeed been there within such a short time.

79.  *Wakalingania kulekeya Muabudua*
     *Kufuru na pigo akashuku alama*

     Muhammad thanked God for what had happened during the
     *israi* and *miiraji*. On the other hand, the Qureshi continued
     to doubt if he had reached Bait-ul-Maqdis within a day.

The popularity of this theme among the Swahili might be due to the
supernatural nature of the journey. They see in it a model for the ecstatic
state in which the poet is transported instantly through space and time
and can see persons and things invisible to the naked eye. Among the
Swahili, the *miiraji* is recognition that Muhammad is the greatest of all
the Prophets and this is explicitly derived from the first stanza of the
*Hamziyyah*. They strongly believe that during the *miiraji* more than any
other aspect of the life of Muhammad, he takes the role of the guide on
the road to salvation and to the union with God.

## THE THEME OF *HAJJ*

Another outstanding theme in the *Hamziyyah* is the *hajj* (pilgrimage) to Mecca and Medina. As is the case with other Muslims, the
Swahili regard Mecca as the holy place where *kaaba* is located; Medina
is where the Prophet Muhammad died and is buried. The site of his
tomb is where the poet longs to visit. This is illustrated in the following
stanzas:

283.  *Maka alimbele mawaidi ya kumzuru*
      *Mwaka kuwafe waadui ewe ngamiya mwema*

      Al-Busiri's camel kept the promise to take him for visitation
      (pilgrimage) and truly, the good camel took him to Mecca

284.  *Nisiji kutile kwayo sumu matanganemwe*
      *Yakakuta kachikachi na kila hima*

The camel promised to complete the journey from Egypt to Medina. Al-Busiri longs for the camel to arrive there as quickly as possible.

285. *Kwa kukuziwiya Batwihau yamzajile*
*Nile imazipo kusudika ndani kwa dhwama*

The camel longed for al-Batha (Mecca).The Nile upset her.

Among the Swahili, *hajj* is one of the five pillars of Islam that they highly uphold. They see it, nevertheless, as a ritual event where they can 'visit' and 'see' the Prophet. They often mention that they are journeying to 'visit' the Prophet and that the longing for the Prophet is burning their hearts. For this reason, the *hajj* constitutes an important aspect of the life of the Swahili. Challen Edward(2006,35) argues that pilgrimage is the focus of the realized hope of the community. H adds that every hajj as the pilgrim is known, believes that his total act of dedication in the pilgrimage is the supreme means of obtaining the forgiveness of sins.

We encounter all the steps of the *hajj* rite of passage describing the longing for the Prophet and the arduous journey from home to *hajj* and back. The poet expresses his longing to "visit" Prophet Muhammad and to see the holy places.Vs. 301 states:

301. *Habadhaa! Habadhaa! Manzili yaliyo Maka*
*Urefu wa muda kwa udhuru zake alama*

After the *Hijja*, al-Busiri wishes to go to the Holy place in Mecca. It is a place that has since been and has remained so to this day.

Vs. 283, 284 examines would-be pilgrim's longing for the *hajj*, and progressing through the *hajj* rites and the pilgrim's return home.

283. *Maka alimbele mawaidi ya kumzuru*
*Mwaka kuwafe waadui ewe ngamiya mwema*

Al-Busiri's camel kept the promise to take him for visitation (pilgrimage) and truly, the good camel took him to Mecca

284. *Nisiji kutile kwayo sumu matanganemwe*
*Yakakuta kachikachi na kila hima*

The camel promised to complete the journey from Egypt to Medina.

with more excerpts found in vv.285, 286, and 304.

Fulfiling the *hajj* rites and "visiting" and "seeing" the Prophet are the expressed desires of the poet. V. 385 states:

385. *Chuliye uliko chuzilio kwa ufukara*
*Wachichukaliye ukasi dhaifu nyama*

> Al-Busiri says that they have come to where the Prophet is (his tomb) because of their poverty (their sins). He says that their weary bodies have come to seek God's blessings.

Although the required *hajj* rites do not include the visitation to Medina, where the Prophet's tomb is located, we find that most, if not all, the yearning expressed by Aidarusi is aimed at Medina. The motif of longing for the Prophet and for Medina is illustrated from vvs 306,313,314,322,323,324, to 325.

After completing the *hajj*, the epithet of *hajj* (for man) and *hajjah* (for women) is bestowed on the pilgrim. Finally, the pilgrims embark on the journey back home. Although the same as the outgoing journey, it is laden with different feelings and expectations found in vv.325 and 326.

325. *Chukarudi kwechu nyoyo na unguliko*
*Kulikoye Chumwa kwechu na isimu kwayo nyuma*

> The pilgrims went back to their homes half-hearted because they wanted to stay with their beloved Prophet.

326. *Chukamba kwa kichu hapakosi towa kipendi*
*Na bakhili kenda kwa dhwaruba kwambache njema*

> The pilgrims had come from someone that they truly loved, that is the Prophet Muhammad. Al-Busiri admits that if it were not for the families left behind, many could have chosen to go back to Medina.

The *hajj* is a great penitential act, which, if performed well, secures the remission of all former sins. It is an immense gathering which makes those who take part in it aware of the force of Islam, and though only a minority is in a position to make real contacts and have discussions, at least the majority of people who have embraced Islam can assemble together. It is an affirmation of the Muslim's singleness of mind and purpose designed to increase an awareness of Allah and gives a sense of spiritual uplift.

## THE THEME OF *JIHAD*

The other theme in the *Hamziyyah* is the conquest of Prophet Muhammad and his companions. For Swahili, it has a deep religious meaning. It was a vindication of the faith that had sustained the Prophet. The victory at Badr came to be regarded as the great deliverance God had effected for the Muslims, comparable to the deliverance he had effected for the Israelites at the Red Sea.

In regard to the battle of Uhud, the poet versifies how God defeated the enemies in various ways. Abdal Muttalib became blind (v.89), Manaf bin Zahara died from prolonged thirst (v.90), and al-Walid bin Mughira died of arrow wound (v.91). In addition, al-As bin Wahil was pricked by a thorn (v.92), and al-Harith died as a result of puss clot in his brain (v.93).

The poet continues in vv. 81, 82, and 83. The mention of the battle of Uhud is in v. 156

156.    *Alidhihirisha kwa kupowa kovu ya uso*
        *Kana mwezi kwandha kuonyeshwa mwezi kwa wema*

        Despite the scar left on the Prophet's face during the battle
        of Uhud, most likely to make the Prophet's face look awful,
        it instead made his face look brilliant and brighter like the
        moon

The Prophet was getting victories over his enemies and laughing in the process.

154.    *Mlipeo kuchana na jeishi kitekateka*
        *Pindi ghairipo ukuchano maso kalama*

        The Prophet never panicked when he faced his enemies.
        Instead, he would laugh when he came face-to-face with

them. Al-Busiri is longing to see the Prophet's face beaming with joy at such an occasion

The battle of Badr and Hunani (Hunayn) is referred in v. 144.

144.   *Latile zijiwe zikaswibu jeishi kuu*
       *Simbonitu ani na kutaka mukitazama*

> He threw pebbles to the mighty army during the battle of Badr and Hunayn. The pebbles vanquished the army. The pebbles did the same function like the Moses' rod splitting the Red Sea into two.

The Swahili believe that the souls of those killed in the *jihad* go straight to paradise. They say that those who fight in the *jihad*, not only by sacrificing their lives but also by giving all their property, will have their reward multiplied.

## CONCLUSION

In this article I have treated these themes as 'stories' rather than 'myths'. While the Swahili people of the Lamu archipelago view the themes in the *Hamziyyah* as factual, western folklorists and historians of comparative religion consider such stories to be legends, specifically saints' legends. Such a classification suggests that the stories are told as true but are actually untrue. The majority of non-Muslim scholars have also refuted the historicity of these stories and classify them as myth (*hurafa*). On the other hand, few Muslim scholars have sought not the literal, but the symbolic truth in them, especially in the account of *israi* and *miiraji*.

In contrast to the length of the stories that recount these miracles in Islamic history, the poet mentions them in cryptic or synoptic phrases. These allusions cause the Swahili to draw the motifs of the whole story from their religious repertoire of legends and stories about the Prophet's life. Considering the circumstances in which these themes emerged, developed and spread as well as their target audience, one must acknowledge that a deeper understanding and appreciation of the *Hamziyyah* can only be gained through exploration of its socio-historical context. The scarcity of biographical literature in Kiswahili tradition has already been written about. Obvious difficulties in placing the personality or character of an individual poet is obvious. However, the purpose of this paper was not to indicate this imminent gap, or to discuss the life and work of al-Busiri or Aidarusi. The aim was rather to call attention to existing textual evidence in the early poetic composi-tions like the *Hamziyyah* that may be used to denounce or debunk the notion that Epic form was not very popular in the traditional poetry of the Swahili. It is true that it was only used to highlight religious and quasi-religious topics after Islamic religion was adopted.

# SECTION III:
## Eastern African Diasporas

# Chapter 11

## SHIFTING PARADIGMS: THE INDIAN OCEAN WORLD IN ADBULRAZAK GURNAH'S *PARADISE AND DESERTION*

*Maria Olaussen*
*Linnaeus University*

### INTRODUCTION

The Zanzibari-born author Abdulrazak Gurnah approaches Eastern Africa as a part of the Indian Ocean World in several of his novels through the lens of transnational migration where Zanzibar and the East African coast are places of both arrival and departure within a history of shifting power relations. His work often deals with the experience of immigration to Britain that is set against a dramatic and at times also tragic departure from Zanzibar. The protagonists find themselves in situations beyond their control and express ambivalent attitudes towards the changes which they are forced to accept. The depiction of this ambivalence varies and is often expressed in terms of passivity and indecision on the part of the protagonists, who, in first person narratives, introduce themselves and their stories to the reader while reflecting on the circumstances which led up to the situations they find themselves in. In *Admiring Silence* (1996) we are introduced to the protagonist through his narrative of his life with a girlfriend and their daughter, both of whom leave him at the end of the novel. Throughout the novel, the narrator-protagonist has communicated only through the fabricated stories about his past in order to live up to the expectations of his British audience. As Tina Steiner points out, "the narrator becomes the agent of typical neocolonial discourse. He therefore joins the "us", if only temporarily and never completely" (2009, 104). The novel closes with the protagonist longing to both phone a friend and wanting to remain undisturbed at the same time. "But I am so afraid of disturbing this fragile silence" (Gurner 1997, 217). Saleh Omar, one of the character narrators of the novel *By the Sea* (2002) starts his narrative with a similar incident where he expects a visitor and both dreads her arrival and wishes to be left in peace. This novel addresses the question of ambivalence also through the theme of silence, an indecision about speaking which encompasses the actual telling of the story itself.[1]

Peter Kalliney describes Gurnah's work as characterized by their "refusals of nostalgia and invocations of a tense multicultural society" and therefore sees them as "the product of a global, diasporic, even postnational imagery, maintaining at best an ambivalent relation with the nation at large".[2] Gurnah's work is, however, not to be seen as simply a set of examples of a global imagery which challenges a world-view dominated by a European perspective. Rather, it is an articulation of the problems inherent in such a proposition. Gurnah's protagonists are often situated in Europe and from this position find themselves trying to recapture and re-articulate an Eastern African reality which, they realize, has suddenly been given a new meaning through a predominant racialised dichotomy. It is through this preoccupation with the problems of representation that Gurnah addresses East African realities within the history of the Indian Ocean world, and thereby, to paraphrase Gurminder Bhambra, refuses to write difference into a history already written (2007, 143).

The novels *Paradise* and *Desertion* express a concern with the connection between ambivalence and representation by drawing attention to the pre-colonial transnational realities of East Africa and the Indian Ocean world, as well as to the way these realities are subsumed and made to function within colonial representations of Africa. The importance of colonial representations can here be understood through Homi Bhabha's idea of cultural difference: "to see the cultural not as the *source* of conflict – *different* cultures – but as the *effect* of discriminatory practices – the production of cultural *differentiation* as signs of authority – changes its value and rules of recognition" (1994, 163). These effects are most clearly brought out in dominant views of the processes of modernity, which in the novel *Paradise* is represented through the intertextual replacement of the Koranic story of Yusuf by Conrad's *Heart of Dark-*

*ness.* It is in this replacement that the development of modernity is expressed as a deeply ambivalent but nevertheless conscious decision to identify with new masters and where the Eastern African coast is significant in its relation to the inland and the sea with a thematic focus on slavery and inland trade.

The connection between ambivalence and stories about transnational migration can be traced to the shifting influence of two different paradigms on the formation of these narratives. Isabel Hofmeyer (2007) suggests that the Indian Ocean be read as a paradigm for transnationalism in opposition to the black Atlantic. In Paul Gilroy's influential book *The Black Atlantic* black diasporic identities are seen as constituted through the triangular relation between the continents of Africa, Europe and America. Whereas Gilroy's focus is on the connection between the development of modernity and the slave trade and his argument is directed against black nationalism, the paradigm of the black Atlantic has been articulated in different forms by authors and critics on all three continents and has, in Hofmeyer's words come to encompass "the Atlantic seaboard as the site for the emergence of capitalist modernity as a transnational system" (2007, 4). Hofmeyer argues that one consequence of this paradigm is that the terminology employed around processes of globalisation, such as translocalism and transnationalism, place Europe or the West as central points of reference. Another consequence of this paradigm is that the understanding of transnational identities as opposition between settler and slave are racialised and static in the sense that they do not allow for shifts from one position to the other. This does not, of course, mean that the realities of the Atlantic slave trade is reflected through this paradigm but rather that this is how we have come to understand the history of the black Atlantic. Paradigmatically, however, the black Atlantic has formed ideas of the slave and the settler as dichotomies and racialised, unchangeable identities. Gurnah's work addresses the interaction between the two paradigms and shows how the history of the Indian Ocean World has been subsumed in representations of transnationalism dominated by the Atlantic paradigm. It is thus not a matter of reading Gurnah's work for a representation of the Indian Ocean World but rather of looking for articulations of the interaction between the two paradigms.

In placing the Indian Ocean World in opposition to the black Atlantic, Hofmeyer identifies the theme of 'people and passages' as one of the areas in Indian Ocean historiography which has the potential to challenge dominant ideas of transcultural migration. Studies of slavery, indentured labour and free migrants show that the movement of people across the Indian Ocean has evolved over a period of approximately four thousand years in multidirectional patterns of migration where the distinctions between slave, indentured labourer, convict and free settler have become blurred and do not follow clear cut racial or ethnic divisions. Although this could be said of many other areas of the world involved in shifting political, ethnic and religious patterns of dominance, large scale migration and changing economic conditions, the Indian Ocean world offers a particularly interesting examples of the complexities involved when power relations shift. Milo Kearney, in his study *The Indian Ocean in World History* argues that "significant participation in Indian Ocean trade as always been a major indicator of a state's or region's prominence and leadership from a global perspective" (2004, 1). Similarly, Sugata Bose shows that the Indian Ocean rim continued to be an important area of interregional area of exchange in both economic and cultural terms also in the nineteenth and twentieth centuries. In Gurnah's work, this history is present through the focus on shifting power relations and the influence of these shifts on Eastern African cultural expressions. As Hofmeyer points out, the Indian Ocean operated as a network in that "its unity resides in a myriad of factors: trade, capital, religion, war, pilgrims, ports, ships, slaves, indentured workers, clerics, sailors, creditors and commodities." Hofmeyer goes on to suggest that it has the potential to offer a site of "alternative modernities" through its combination of different intellectual traditions developed within a history of south -south patterns of exchange (2007, 13).

In my reading of Gurnah's texts, the most important aspect of this discussion concerns problems inherent in the representation of modernity as a European phenomenon and in efforts at re-conceptualizing this through ideas of alternative modernities. Gurminder Bhambra sees theories of modernity as referring to "the social, cultural, political, and economic changes that took place in Western Europe from the mid-sixteenth century onwards" and resting on "ideas of rupture and difference" (2007, 2). Bhambra further identifies a central idea on modernity across theoretical positions as "resting on the basic distinctions between the social formations of 'the West' and 'traditional' or 'pre-modern' societies" and relying on the Western experience as norm when describing "what it means to be modern" (2007, 3).

In Jeremy Prestholdt's words "the idea of 'alternative modernities' risks affirming the cultural and temporal singularity Westerners saw as their biological virtue, posing other visions as divergence from the (Western) norm, and reifying the Victorian notion of time as progressing in an evolutionary order" (2009, 168-9). Dipesh Chakrabarty's *Pro-*

*vincializing Europe* can be seen as one of the most important works articulating the challenges inherent in thinking modernity outside of the parameters which have posited Europe as universal and normative. Bhambra follows Chakrabarty when she argues for an approach which sees 'connected histories' as a starting point and which also demands a re-thinking of both current circumstances but also of how past events have been interpreted and theorized with relevance to the present. Gurnah's continued preoccupation with Europe in literary works set in East Africa can in many ways be seen as engaging with directly with these concerns.

## REVISITING SLAVERY AND FREEDOM: *PARADISE*

*Paradise* is Gurnah's fourth novel. It was short-listed for the Booker Prize in 1994 and is, unlike his other novels, set entirely in colonial East Africa in the early Twentieth century, and depicted the time where old power structures are replaced by new ones. It reveals the interrelatedness of religious and economic power structures by building on the well-known story of Yusuf who is sold as a slave by his brothers, found both in the Bible in Genesis 39 and in Sura 12 of the Koran, but uses this story in order to undermine its main message of how wealth and prosperity will come to those who lead honourable lives. The connection is established primarily in the seduction scene, known in the Islamic tradition as "Yusuf and Zuleika" and in the Genesis version as "Joseph and Potiphar's wife." The Persian poet Jami's rendition, dated to 1470, stresses the beauty of the young boy and the distraction this creates among women. Zuleika's husband is in this version the Asis Potiphar, the grand advisor of Pharaoh, a man she agrees to marry in the mistaken belief that he is the beautiful boy in Egypt that she has seen in a vision. The use of the names "Aziz" and "Yusuf" in the novel creates further connections to these stories and it also takes up the aspect of the beauty of the young boy but uses it to stress his vulnerability among the traders intent on sexually abusing dependent boys. The gift of dream interpretation, which is central in both the Genesis version and the Koranic version, is in the novel replaced by nightmares.[3]

The protagonist, Yusuf, finds himself as a young boy a pawn to 'uncle Aziz,' an Omani merchant, as settlement of his father's debts. In the second inter-text, Joseph Conrad's *Heart of Darkness*, is used to question the binaries between Europe and Africa in the section where the young boy participates in the trading expeditions to the interior and there comes to witness the violent hostility with which African villagers treat the Swahili traders from the coast as well as the ruthlessness of the racism on the part of the traders who see Africans of the interior as "uncivilized savages." Michael Pearson discusses the trade relations between the Swahili Coast and the interior from the early modern period onwards and shows how the opposition between inland people and coastal people, where the coastal people often claimed foreign origin, comes with a political agenda, particularly problematic when linked to the slave trade during the Omani period. During the colonial era, similar incentives existed for a continued reproduction of these ideas of foreignness (Pearson 1998, 25).

In *Paradise* the traders tell stories about the cruelty and the super-human qualities of the Europeans but, since these stories are exaggerated and embellished with details of magic, and since Yusuf's only direct experience of the Europeans consists of a dramatic act of intervention in favour of the traders, he is left with a sense of uncertainty when it comes to understand their position. In Aziz's household, Yusuf also experiences the powerlessness and degradation of dependent women and younger men within patriarchal structures. These structures are, however, also there to offer protection and possibilities. The ambivalence is further apparent when the young Yusuf is finally abandoned by Aziz and against his own wishes and interests is forced to join the German armed forces.

The ambivalence present in *Paradise* is not, as in Gurnah's later work, primarily concerned with historiography or with the form of the story itself. It is presented as a result of economic forces through the experiences and the limited knowledge of the young boy, who is excited at the prospect of escaping the poverty and dependence of village life and initially sees his servitude to Uncle Aziz as an exciting opportunity. At home there is only drought and famine:

> Sometimes they ate bones, which his mother boiled up to make a thin soup whose surface glistened with colour and grease, and in whose depths lurked lumps of black spongy marrow. At worst, there was only okra stew, but however hungry he was Yusuf could not swallow the slimy sauce. (Gurnah 1994, 2-3)

The hunger is relieved by Uncle Aziz and the "interesting morsels left over" (Gurnah 1994, 9) from the food he brings and expects to have prepared for him during his visits:

> Two different kinds of curries, chicken and minced mutton.
> The best Peshawar rice, glistening with ghee and dotted with
> sultanas and almonds. Aromatic and plump buns, maandazi
> and mahamri, overflowing the cloth-covered basket. Spinach
> in a coconut sauce. A plate of waterbeans. Strips of dried fish
> charred in the dying embers which had cooked the rest of the
> food. (Gurnah 1994, 8-9)

Yusuf's hunger for the world of Uncle Aziz is thus a literal hunger. The
fact that he is satisfied with the leftovers – his only concern is that his
mother insists on sharing them with their hungry neighbours – shows
how whole-heartedly he accepts the position of Uncle Aziz as their superior in his role of benefactor to the family. As several critics have pointed
out, the uncle is a central and recurring figure in Gurnah's novels.[4] He
often functions to displace the opposition between the public and the
private as changing power structures are introduced through the trope
of family relations. As Kearney argues, the case of Uncle Aziz presents
"a marvel of sustained ambivalence" (2006, 49). His refined manners,
gentleness and generosity towards Yusuf's family make Yusuf eager to
accompany him when Yusuf's father, who is no longer in a position to
repay his debts to Aziz, is forced to give him up as *rehani*.[5] It is only
much later that Yusuf overhears a conversation where the business
methods of Aziz are described and he understands that that his father
is only one among many victims: "if his partners cannot pay up, he takes
their sons and daughters as rehani. This is like in the days of slavery. It
is not the way honourable people should conduct themselves" (Gurnah
1994, 89). As soon as Yusuf leaves his family and joins his new household he is also told that Aziz is not his Uncle and that he should instead
call him "*Seyyid*."[6] What has been presented as business partnership
among equals is in fact revealed as a deliberate plan of bringing people
into servitude and financial dependence through the manipulation of
emerging economic power structures. Aziz stays ahead of the times
because he distances himself from the slave trade before it is outlawed,
keeping up the appearance of someone involved only in trade that is
honourable and lawful. "Trading in slaves is dangerous work, and not
honourable" (Gurnah 1994, 34).

In the same way as the truth about Uncle Aziz is revealed to Yusuf
only at a much later stage, Yusuf's departure from his family is initially
described as a welcome relief from the harsh treatment that he suffers
at the hands of his tired mother. But also through the foreboding that
the mother's silent tears communicate – tears that make his "heart leap
with terror" because their silence stands in stark contrast to her usual

loud wailing, making him remember "stories from other boys of violence and abandonment" (Gurnah 1994, 13). When he thinks back on the day of departure, however, he has no distinct memory of his mother:

> Later, Yusuf could not remember what his mother did or said, but he remembered that she looked ill or dazed, leaning exhaustedly against the doorpost. When he thought of the moment of his departure, the picture that came to mind was the shimmering road on which they walked and the men ahead of him. (Gurnah 1994, 17)

He makes no efforts to return to his parents but, on the contrary, hides on the floor of a railway carriage when he travels through his home village on his way to the interior with Aziz on one of his trading expedition. Yusuf does this in order not to cause his parents embarrassment but also because he feels ashamed about their rejection and confused about how he should act. At the return of the expedition led by the lecherous Mohammed Abdalla who openly lusts after him, after he has witnessed the brutal slaughter of his fellow-traders and seen many other die of disease and hardship, he reflects on his life and thinks about his parents with remorse rather than anger:

> Yusuf felt the reel of his life running through his hand, and he let the reel run without resistance. Then he rose and left. For a long time after, he sat silently with himself, numbed by guilt that he had been unable to keep the memory of his parents fresh in his life. He wondered if his parents still thought of him, if they still lived, and he knew that he would rather not find out. [...] Events had ordered his days and he had held his head above the rubble and kept his eyes on the nearer horizon, choosing ignorance rather than futile knowledge of what lay ahead. There was nothing he could think of to do which would unshackle him from the bondage to the life he lived. (1994, 174-5)

This passage suggests that the state of bondage is primarily economic but also social and emotional. The story of Khalil, the boy who introduces Yusuf to the life of a *rehani*, himself pawned to Aziz as a young boy together with his seven-year-old sister Amina, reinforces the interconnectedness of these aspects of the state of bondage which defies easy categorization. When the sister grows up, Aziz marries her and thereby also forgives the rest of the debt, leaving Khalil a free man with "nowhere to go" (1994, 207). Amina sees her life only as emptiness, as hell on earth, but likewise refuses to leave because her leaving would require Khalil to stay on to pay the debt. "This was the agreement, and this is what honour requires" (1994, 232). Like Khalil and Amina, both of whom find reasons for their continued enslavement, the old slave who works in the garden, Mzee Hamdani, also refuses to leave after he has gained his freedom, says: "They offered me freedom as a gift. She did. Who told her she had it to offer?" (1994, 223).

Yusuf's encounter with Aziz's first wife, who spends her days inside the large house, suffering from the pain of a disfigured face and the isolation of years without contact with the outside world, follows the seduction scene of the story of Yusuf in Sura 12 of the Koran. [7] As in the Koran, the attempted seduction ends with Yusuf turning to flee while "she clutched his shirt from behind and he felt it tear in her hands. As he ran out of the room, he heard her screams of agony but did not look back or hesitate" (1994, 236). The novel follows the Koranic version rather than the Genesis version of the story (where Potiphar refuses to believe Joseph and has him imprisoned) but tells the story about the torn shirt through the views of the cynical and frightened Khalil:

> 'She tore my shirt from behind. That proves I was running away from her,' Yusuf said.
> 'Don't be ridiculous!' Khalil cried, laughing with disbelief. Who'll have time to ask you that? Who cares? From behind?' (1994, 238)

But Aziz decides to let matters rest and Khalil, beside himself with happiness, is full of praise for Aziz:

> The seyyid is a champion, who can doubt that? He came back, took one look at the Mistress and thought to himself, *this crazy woman has been tormenting my pretty young man. These women are always trouble and mine is a top-class monkey, damn her.* Anybody can see she's crazy, with her whining voice and all that business about her wound. And your torn shirt! Oh your torn shirt! What a story! You have some fine angels looking after your affairs. (1994, 242 emphasis in the original)

In contrast to Khalil, Yusuf refuses to accept that his life should forever be ruled by the patriarchal authority extended by Aziz. More importantly, perhaps, his experience of trade in the interior makes him realize that the power of the merchant will not remain unchallenged.

Yusuf's attitude towards religion is deeply cynical and the trading expedition teaches him how desperately the Muslims from the coast hold on the idea of their superiority and how deeply they are hated by the Africans of the inland. Above all he is made to witness how Aziz nearly loses all his belongings when challenging the traditional ruler, Chatu, and how he is only saved through the intervention by a German government representative. Yusuf's dreams are frightening and they seem to contain a premonition of the future and point him towards the new sites of power and prosperity. When the German forces turn up with their *askaris* and their captives he recognises the dogs of his recurrent nightmares in the starving dogs who eat the excrement left at the site of the encampment. He imagines the dogs looking up at him in recognition: "Now, as he watched the obliviously degraded hunger of the dogs, he thought he knew what it would grow into. The marching column was still visible when he heard a noise like the bolting of doors behind him in the garden. He glanced round quickly and then ran after the column with smarting eyes" (1994, 247). Dianne Schwerdt reads the ending of Paradise in relation to *Heart of Darkness* and concludes that Yusuf here emerges as a young man "capable of making meaningful life choices" (2001, 32). Schwerdt also places the novel in a context which stresses the opposition between the African interior as "oppositional to the West" (2001, 36). This interpretation misses the crucial point that Yusuf's experience is not informed by Europe or the West but that it is an experience of servitude and dependence in a context of Indian Ocean power relations.

The use of Conrad's novel as an inter-text suggests that the understanding of modernity as simply generated through an opposition between the West and its colonies needs to be modified in order to adequately take into account the in the Indian Ocean context. The ending of *Paradise* returns to the issue of hunger and creates a further link with Conrad's *Heart of Darkness*, where hunger is similarly connected to dehumanization. In this passage Marlow imagines the hunger of the crew on the steamboat in his feverish fantasies about cannibalism:

> Don't you know the devilry of lingering starvation, its exasperating torment, its black thoughts, its sombre and brooding ferocity? Well, I do. It takes a man all his inborn strength to fight hunger properly. It's really easier to face bereavement, dishonour, and the perdition of one's soul – than this kind of prolonged hunger. Sad, but true. And these chaps too had no earthly reason for any kind of scruple. Restraint! I would

just as soon have expected restraint from a hyena prowling amongst the corpses of a battlefield. (Conrad 2007, 51)

What Yusuf's story articulates through the intertextual references to *Heart of Darkness* is the loss of an autonomous and independent means of self-expression. "What does slavery mean in this context? What does freedom mean? What is agency?" In asking these questions Isabel Hofmeyer suggests that novels, such as *Paradise*, are important because "they begin to open up the complexities of the Indian Ocean and help us understand the forms of modernity it produces" (2007, 15). These questions concerning freedom and bondage are addressed within the context of changing and mutually interdependent religious, economic and political realities, revealing how the acquisition of wealth and power depends on the power to define and utilise concepts such as honour and virtue.

## THE FAILURE OF LOVE STORIES: *DESERTION*

The Indian Ocean paradigm which articulates global flows free of racialised binaries is in the novel *Desertion* replaced and restricted by the dichotomies informed by the Black Atlantic. The novel exemplifies what Devleena Ghosh and Lola Sharon Davidson describe as

> formal and informal movements of peoples and ideas in imperial spaces force re-evaluation of the old binaries of colony and empire, home and the world, metropole and periphery, highlighting previously unexpected and uncovered connections and relationships between spaces that previously seemed discrete. (2009, 1)

*Desertion* consists of three parts. Part I contains the story of the arrival of the Englishman Martin Pearce to the small town on the East African coast in the year 1899: "There was a story of his first sighting. In fact, there was more than one, but elements of the stories merged into one with time and telling" (Gurner 2005, 3). The narrative is focalized through the Indian shop seller Hassanali and his family, his wife Malika and his sister Rehana, as well as through the views of Martin and his English host Frederick. The narrator is seemingly a third person omniscient narrator until the final chapter of Part I "An interruption" where he turns into a first person character narrator, Rashid, and comments on the narrative:

> There is, as you can see, an I in this story, but it is not a story
> about me. It is one about all of us, about Farida and Amin
> and our parents, and about Jamila. It is about how one story
> contains many and how they belong not to us but are part
> of the random currents of our time, and about how stories
> capture us and entangle us for all time. (2005, 120)

In Part II the story of the brothers Rashid and Amin is told in the third person. This chapter contains the story of their childhood and adolescence in Zanzibar as well as the love story between Jamila and Amin. Jamila turns out to be the granddaughter of Martin and Rehana.

Part III contains the story of Jamila and Amin narrated by Rashid and of Rashid's life in London narrated in the first person. Chapter 7 ends with Rashid receiving a packet from Amin with a notebook. Chapter 8 is Amin's story written after he has been separated from Jamila. The novel ends with the chapter called "A continuation" which is narrated by Rashid and which gives the background to his interest in the story about Martin and Rehana. This chapter reveals that Martin had returned to Britain, married an Englishwoman and continued his friendship with Frederick Turner. Martin's daughter and Frederick's granddaughter subsequently marry, and their daughter Barbara contacts Rashid and gives him a notebook written by Frederick Turner where the story of Martin and Rehana is written down. The novel closes with a suggestion of a relationship developing between Rashid and Barbara.

*Desertion* shows many similarities with M. G. Vassanji's novel *The Book of Secrets* (1994), especially in how the narrative evolves from the contents of a displaced notebook by a colonial officer. Other similarities concern the changing power relations and the complex family histories on the Eastern African coast. *The Book of Secrets* is, however, to a greater extent than *Desertion* part of a tradition which Fernando Rosa Ribeiro identifies as a common imaginative framework for "intimate relationships in creolised contexts" (2010, 104). Central to this imaginative framework is the "trope of the beautiful, sensual, mulatto woman" as well as the tragic ending of the love story (Ribeiro 2010, 114). But whereas the tragic family secret is the central narrative device in *The Book of Secrets*, *Desertion* shows how the possibilities of telling this story change with changing historical contexts.

Both the opening and the closing of Part I places the focus on storytelling and draws our attention to the fact that the narrative we have just read is structured from the point of view of Rashid and his experiences of life in England. What we have here is the predominance of the perspective of the Black Atlantic, superimposed on the history of ethnic relations of the Swahili coast. Towards the end of Part III we find Rashid's reflections about his arrival in England:

> I realised that I did not know very much about England, that all the books I had studied and the maps I had pored over had taught me nothing of how England thought of the world and of people like me. (Gurnah 2005, 214)

It is significant that it is Rashid's arrival in Europe rather than his experience of Europeans in Zanzibar which leads to this insight:

> So I had to learn about that, and about imperialism and how deeply the narratives of our inferiority and the aptness of European overlordship had bedded down in what passed for knowledge of the world. (2005, 115)

The most important lesson that Rashid learns in England concerns the dichotomies of racial belonging, a way of perceiving ethnicity which he is unprepared for but which he finally learns to accept:

> Soon I began to say black people and white people, like everyone else, uttering the lie with increasing ease, conceding the sameness of our difference, deferring to a deadening vision of a racialised world. (2005, 222)

What these statements suggest is the fact that neither Rashid's life in Zanzibar nor the life of his parents had prepared him for this particular way of viewing transcultural contact.

Part I of the novel, however, which tells the story of the arrival of Martin Pearce and the consequences of this arrival for Hassanali and his family, suggests the opposite. The focalization of the story creates a binary between the British District Officer, his friends and followers, on the one hand, and the Swahili inhabitants of the town, on the other. This opposition is particularly brought out in the scene where the District Officer and his servants burst into Hassanali's household:

> Where are his things?' Frederick asked. 'Property. Where's his property? His goods.' The wakil did what he could, but he could get nothing out of the dukawallah and his wife. The wakil shouted at them and wagged a finger dramatically, and Frederick guessed he was haranguing them for the robbery, or even more likely, making arrangements to ensure they would keep his share. He added a few sharp words of his own and

> scowled at the dukawallah, without producing the required
> result [ ... ] They would return for the property later, he told
> the wakil, when the poor man could give an account of what
> he had lost. (2005, 42)

While this scene develops as a result of the contempt and lack of knowledge displayed by the Europeans, their return is narrated from the point
of view of the Hassanali's wife, Malika, and his sister Rehana. They show
a similar tendency to dismiss those they identify as Europeans:

> The government European frightened them with his return,
> waving his whip impatiently at Hassanali and snarling at him,
> turning all of them into criminals. Never mind his return, he
> frightened her the first time he came, bursting upon them like
> that as if he had caught them in wrong-doing. Hassanali had
> hurried past to open the yard door, in his terror only man-
> aging to say *mzungu wa serikali amefika*. The government
> European has arrived. (2005, 56-7 emphasis in the original)

It is significant that Rehana sees Martin as a European only after the
District Officer, "the snarling figure from the stories, the destroyer of
nations," claims him as one of his own (2005, 57). At this point Rehana
and Malika dismiss him as a *mzungu*, thereby creating a clear difference
between themselves and the mysterious traveller:

> They had come to accuse them of robbing that ragged-look-
> ing living-death. The only thing they could have robbed him
> of was his soul, and who wanted to have anything to do with
> a mzungu's soul. (2005, 57)

When Hassanali first brings him into the household she sees him
"more like complication and confusion, a token of Hassanali's inepti-
tude with life" (ibid.). In her version of the story they had taken in a
dying man "out of kindness," she even, for a moment, believes that the
traveller is her long lost husband who suddenly, after many years of
silence, returns to them. Through this juxtaposition of Martin with her
husband she also places him in the context of men lost at sea, among
them her own grandfather, when they travelled across the sea on the
musim. This connection is further strengthened when Martin returns
on his own to thank Hassanali and his family and it is revealed that he is
fluent in Arabic and Kiswahili:

> 'Mashaallah, you have amazed us, o Sheikh mzungu. I have travelled from Lindi to Kismayu and even to Aden, and I never came upon a mzungu who spoke Arabic or Kiswahili. If you had spoken when we found you a few days ago, looking like a corpse, and had spoken to us in Arabic, and had spoken thus at that dangerous hour, I think we would have taken you for a servant of the infernal one. Tell us, ya Martin, how has this come to be and what brought you this way, walking in rags and so close to death. Tell us.'
>
> It could have been an opening to a new episode in One *Thousand and One Nights*, an invitation to begin a tale. So he did, keeping everything brief although he could see that his listeners had plenty of time and were eager for more details. (2005, 104-5)

The story about Martin and Rehana's encounter is, however, formed by Rashid as a narrator and by his experience of ethnic difference in England as one of "black and white," and, at this point in the narrative, we also realize that the omniscient narrator is, in fact, a character in the novel:

> I don't know how it could have happened. The unlikeliness of it defeats me. Yet I know that it did happen, that Martin and Rehana became lovers. Imagination fails me and that fills me with sorrow. (2005, 110)

Rashid's sorrow needs to be placed in the context of his efforts at reconstructing the encounter between Martin and Rehana as reflecting the possibilities of transnationalism in the Indian Ocean World, rather than the limitations of the European-African connections. What the failure of his imagination in the above quote suggests is that as he has been forced to accept the "deadening vision of a racialised world" and that he is unable to imagine the love story between Martin and Rehana in other terms, where "new knowledge sometimes obscures what was known before" (2005, 210). In his reading of the novel Erik Falk suggests that the final section of the novel, where Rashid presents an academic paper at a conference on "race and sexuality in settler writing in Kenya" and where he leaves out the story of Rehana and Pearce as being too improbable to be included in a scholarly work, is an indication of a self-reflective and deeply ambivalent attitude towards the power of fiction. According to Falk, "*Desertion* emerges as much as an investigation of the role of imagination in social organisation and subject formation as an affirmation of its power" (2007, 59). This ambivalence is, however, connected to the specific situation of the narrator as resident in Europe and the limitations that the conception of the racialised world imposes on his imagination.

In Part II of the novel, containing the narrative of Rashid's childhood and adolescence on Zanzibar as well as the love story between his brother Amin and Martin and Rehana's granddaughter Jamila, is similarly influenced by and narrated through Rashid's experiences in England. It is thus the history of European colonialism which comes to determine the narrative and it is through colonialism that he traces his family history as well. Alternative histories and value systems with their own hierarchies and power positions are present in the form of anecdotes about past generations who failed to realize that they had to adapt to the arrival of a new world order:

> Their father was forbidden to go to the college because his father was suspicious of colonial education: 'They'll make you despise your people and make you eat with a metal spoon and turn you into a monkey who speaks through his nose,' he said. Their father's father threatened and ranted in the way only a father of that generation could. 'They will turn you into a kafir, and we will have failed in our duty to God. You might as well escort us personally to the gates of Hell.' (2005, 138)

Against this interdiction his parents struggle for their education, become teachers with high hopes for their children and their future, but, because the stories of the parent's struggles are narrated in retrospect, their decisions seem equally ill-founded and naïve as those made a generation earlier. In contrast to Part I, which initially seems to be told by an omniscient extradiegetic narrator, the story about Rashid's childhood is self-consciously retrospective, described as life "in the interregnum [...] between the end of one age and the beginning of another" (2005, 150). The parents' opposition to the love story between Amin and Jamila is told as part of this misguided and outdated view of the world, a last tragic attempt at enforcing their values:

> Do you know who she is? Do you know her people? Do you know what kind of people they are? Her grandmother was a chotara, a child of sin by an Indian man, a bastard. When she grew into a woman, she was the mistress of an Englishman for many years, and before that another mzungu gave her a child of sin too, her own bastard. (2005, 204)

Amin's desertion of Jamila thus constitutes the final, tragic victory of the old order where Amin goes against his deepest beliefs and convictions out of pity for his aging and crippled parents. Amin stays with the parents when Rashid leaves for London and he is thus the one who both lives through the violence following independence and tries to communicate the news to Rashid.

Here *Desertion* addresses the same concerns as *Paradise* but partly from the opposite end of a spectrum: whereas *Paradise* places the story of Yusuf as an Eastern African experience firmly within a context of modernity without subscribing to the idea of belatedness in relation to Europe, *Desertion* points to the debilitating predominance of European ideas of travel, migration and change. What both novels do suggest, however, is that it is precisely in the engagement with stories that the opportunities for new understandings are born. As Gurnah himself puts it in an interview: "The narrative has slipped out of the hands of those who had control of it before. These new stories unsettle previous understandings" (Nasta 2004, 358).

## Notes

1. See, for instance, Cooper, "Returning the Jinns to the Jar," and Olaussen, "Refusing to Speak as a Victim" for a discussion of story-telling in *By the Sea*.
2. Kalliney, "East African Fiction and Globalization," 267. See also Kalliney, "East African Literature and the Politics of Global Reading".
3. See Shusheila Nasta's discussion of the context of the novel in the article "Abdulrazak Gurnah, *Paradise*."
4. See, for instance, Bardolph, "Abdulrazak Gurnah's *Paradise* and *Admiring Silence*."
5. An indentured servant or slave.
6. Sir or Master.
7. The version in Sura 12 reads: "The lady of the house where he lived tried to seduce him. She closed the doors and said, "I am all yours." He said, "May GOD protect me. He is my Lord, who gave me a good home. The transgressors never succeed."
   [12:24] She almost succumbed to him, and he almost succumbed to her, if it were not that he saw a proof from his Lord. We thus diverted evil and sin away from him, for he was one of our devoted servants.
   [12:25] The two of them raced towards the door, and, in the process, she tore his garment from the back. They found her husband at the door. She said, "What should be the punishment for one who wanted to molest your wife, except imprisonment or a painful punishment?"

[12:26] He said, "She is the one who tried to seduce me." A witness from her family suggested: "If his garment is torn from the front, then she is telling the truth and he is a liar.

[12:27] "And if his garment is torn from the back, then she lied, and he is telling the truth."

[12:28] When her husband saw that his garment was torn from the back, he said, "This is a woman's scheme. Indeed, your scheming is formidable.

## Chapter 12

# FARMS IN AFRICA: WILDLIFE TOURISM, CONSERVATION AND WHITENESS IN POSTCOLONIAL KENYA

*Grace A. Musila*
*Stellenbosch University*

## INTRODUCTION

In colonial Africa, the myth of white supremacy was legitimized and sustained by colonial state apparatuses – both repressive and ideological – including the law, the church, schools, colonial administration and a range of cultural productions such as literature and film – all of which policed the boundaries of what Mahmood Mamdani (1996) terms the citizen-subject axis. Through these apparatuses, the dividends of whiteness were assured, resulting in the accumulation of economic, social and cultural capital, all of which propped up and sustained white privilege. With the demise of colonial rule across Africa, these institutional and ideological infrastructures were to a certain extent dismantled. Yet, despite this, as Alfred Lopez notes, whiteness remains an aspirational ideal in the postcolonial world, while retaining much of the privilege it enjoyed at the height of colonialism (2005, 20) begging the question: how is whiteness constructed and performed in postcolonial Africa?

In her study *White Women, Race Matters: The Social Construction of Whiteness*, Ruth Frankenberg makes an important observation about the workings of whiteness: "the material and discursive dimensions of whiteness are always, in practice, interconnected. Discursive repertoires may reinforce, contradict, conceal, explain or "explain away" the materiality or the history of a given situation" (1993, 2). It is this interaction between the discursive and the material dimensions of whiteness that this paper seeks to explore, with particular focus on wildlife tourism and conservation in Kenya. Using a 1989 feature film on poaching set in Kenya, *Ivory Hunters*, narratives on the 1988 murder of British tourist Julie Ward in Kenya, and the 2005 and 2006 Tom Cholmondeley murder charges in Kenya, the paper reflects on wildlife tourism and conservation as important registers in the performance of certain strands of whiteness in postcolonial Kenya. Our key interest here lies in tracing these discursive tropes of postcolonial whiteness in Kenya. In what ways do they mirror the tropes of colonial whiteness? What are the implications of the continued deployment of wildlife tourism and conservation in the construction and performance of whiteness in postcolonial Africa?

On the face of it, the three sets of texts I examine here — narratives on the Julie Ward murder, the Cholmondeley case and *Ivory Hunters* — are unrelated. There are no explicit connections between them. But, part of the aim of this paper is to trace and surface the underlying connections between the three sets of texts, which I read as operating within a shared set of assumptions about the workings and constructions of whiteness in post-colonial Kenya, through particular relationships of ownership, control and conservation of land and wildlife. From this perspective, the centrality of land and wildlife as major co-ordinates in the three texts prompts me to set them in conversation with each other, not so much as representative of an overall discourse of whiteness in Kenya; but as offering important insights into one strand of postcolonial whiteness in contemporary Kenya; and its troubled reliance on a colonial archive of whiteness.

On 19th April 2005 Thomas Cholmondeley, great-grandson of pioneer Kenya settlers, Lord and Lady Delamere, allegedly shot dead Kenya Wildlife Society (KWS) ranger Samson ole Sisina on his Soysambu Ranch, in Kenya's Laikipia District. Faced with murder charges, Cholmondeley claimed that he thought ole Sisina was an armed robber. Little more than a year later on 10th May 2006, Cholmondeley allegedly shot and killed a second man, Robert Njoya Mbugua in the same ranch. Facing his second murder charge, Cholmondeley claimed Njoya and his friends had set their dogs on him and he had shot at the dogs, but accidentally hit Njoya. [I offer a more detailed description of the two cases shortly].

Close to three decades earlier, Kenya had witnessed another much-publicised death which was equally linked to wildlife: that of twenty-eight year old British tourist, Julie Ward. A passionate wildlife photographer, Ward was reported missing on 6th September 1988, in the Maasai Mara Game Reserve where she had gone to photograph the annual wildebeest migration from the Mara into Tanzania's Serengeti National Park. Six days later, her partly burnt remains were found in the bush. Julie Ward's death was a hotly contested matter with varied theories about how she had died. Eventually, an inquest revealed that she had been murdered. This finding was followed by a protracted search for her killers, who, at the time of writing this, are still at large. Ward's death and the search for her killers is the subject of three books: her father John Ward's *The Animals are Innocent: The Search for Julie's Killers*, Michael Hiltzik's *A Death in Kenya: The Murder of Julie Ward*, and Jeremy Gavron's *Darkness in Eden: The Murder of Julie Ward*. The third text in this study is a 1991 feature film, *Ivory Hunters*, which tells the story of the murder of an American tourist in a Kenyan game reserve, after she witnesses and photographs an illegal elephant poaching spree [I offer a more detailed synopsis of the film shortly].

In this paper, I bring together these three seemingly unrelated case studies in a reflection on wildlife tourism and conservation as important registers in the performance of whiteness in postcolonial Kenya. My key interest here lies in tracing the discursive tropes of postcolonial whiteness in Kenya. In what ways do these tropes mirror or contest the tropes of colonial whiteness? To what extent was Julie Ward's presence in Kenya, her death and quest for her killers mapped on to these grids of contemporary constructions of postcolonial whiteness? In what ways do the Cholmondeley killings signal particular grammars of whiteness articulated through white male authority and ownership of land and wildlife? What are the implications of the continued deployment of wildlife tourism and conservation in the construction and performance of whiteness in postcolonial Africa? These are some of the questions this paper engages with.

## LAND, WILDLIFE AND WHITENESS IN POSTCOLONIAL KENYA

Ruth Frankenberg's definition of whiteness as "a set of locations that are historically, socially, politically and culturally produced and [...] intrinsically linked to unfolding relations of domination" (1993, 6) captures this paper's interest in whiteness within the postcolonial context in Africa. Tracing its roots back to centuries of sustained construction of white supremacy, whiteness is primarily defined by its invisibility. For Richard Dyer, white claims to a normative position against which all 'non-whites' are measured and found wanting is founded precisely on the assumed "unraced" status (1997, 1), where, as Frankenberg notes, whiteness is viewed as non-racial or racially neutral (1993, 1). This claim to normativity in turn masks the social relations that ensue from it and the privileges that accrue to it. As Frankenberg argues, whiteness has a set of linked dimensions:

> First, whiteness is a location of structural advantage, of race privilege. Second, it is a "standpoint," a place from which white people look at ourselves, at others and at society. Third, whiteness refers to a set of cultural practices that are usually unmarked and unnamed. (ibid.)

Frankenberg here captures three definitive pillars of whiteness: raced privilege, assumed control of the gaze over others, (which simultaneously makes it invisible), and its sustenance through certain cultural practices.

One of the accepted truisms in whiteness studies is that whiteness manifests itself differently in different social, economic, political and cultural contexts. A second truism – which occasionally teeters dangerously close to the now-cliché idea that race is a social construct — is that definitions of who is white have historically been unstable, constantly changing, as illustrated by the Irish, Jewish and Afrikaner experiences in Britain, Germany and South Africa respectively. Despite this though, the myth of white supremacy over other races – largely hinged on proximity to blackness – has been a historical constant, prompting Frankenberg's reminder that whiteness is "intrinsically linked to relations of domination" (1993, 6). It is possibly in recognition of this that in much of postcolonial Africa, as Sarah Nuttall observes, "it is most often in terms of the 'settler' that white identity [...] has been given content and meaning" (2001, 116).

Nuttall underlines the limited reach of 'settler' understandings of whiteness in Africa, especially in contexts, such as post-apartheid South Africa, where white people are continually negotiating the shift from what she calls "the register of conquest" to "the register of negotiation" through a process of "mutual recognition that could lead to belonging" (2001, 118). Despite this though, in most African imaginaries, whiteness largely remains intimately linked to the terrors of slavery and colonial domination. Across the continent – South Africa included – what

Michael Chege terms "white Africans" (1998, 82, 85) remains a much contested identity, with popular imaginaries distinguishing between citizenship – i.e. being a Kenyan, Nigerian or South African citizen – and 'Africanness'[1] as a location anchored in particular histories of the raced traumas of slavery and colonialism.

In her essay, "Letting the side down: Personal reflections on colonial and independent Kenya," Celia Nyamweru underlines the difference between settler colonies and colonies of administration. As she notes,

> Colonies of administration, of which Ghana and Nigeria are the most significant examples in Africa, were those in which White people never acquired rights to land beyond residential plots. [...] Kenya, on the other hand, was a colony of settlement. From the late 1800s onwards, it was the avowed policy of the British government to facilitate White settlement in the cool highland areas. (2001, 171)

At the core of Nyamweru's distinction between the two colonial systems lie relationships with land.

In settler colonies, control and ownership of prime land was an important co-ordinate in the construction of white supremacy. This land was alienated from its owners in a process that was discursively mediated by the 'vacuation' of the land as large expanses of empty space without owners; in inadvertent or feigned ignorance of local land use and ownership cultures, which ostensibly gave the impression of 'unoccupied' land. In such contexts, Nuttall's description of settler whiteness holds true:

> The notion of the settler, which always also implies a native, carries with it in its originary sense a master-slave dialectic based on land - a dialectic, that is, in which the settler occupies a position of power based on the conquest and the ownership of the land through violent means, leading to the dispossession and subjugation of the native owners of that same land.... The settler, in this configuration, is marked as "coming from elsewhere" rather than being "of the place". The term *settler* shifts as the move is made from the politics of conquest and subjugation to the politics of negotiation and belonging. (2001, 118)

In Kenya, Nuttall's idea of the shift from the politics of conquest and subjugation to the politics of negotiation and belonging largely remains unmade for two reasons. Firstly, the white community in Kenya continues to form what Dane Keith Kennedy (1987) terms "islands of white" in his eponymously titled study of Kenyan and Rhodesian settler culture. Majority of the white community continues to live in its white enclaves which are largely exclusive and fairly disinterested in venturing into black Kenyan society. Indeed, one may argue that the illusion of multi-racialism in spaces such as the previously exclusive white leafy suburbs, schools and country clubs dotting all Kenyan towns in reality embody what bell hooks (1994), in a different context, refers to as "integration" of a select few black Kenyans into the existing masternarrative of white-ness; rather than a meaningful multicultural transformation. These spaces continue to uphold white cultural normativity, hardly displaying Nuttall's "politics of negotiation and belonging."

Secondly, there has been little negotiation of land ownership and a good percentage of white society in Kenya continues to own huge tracts of land dubiously acquired at the height of colonial settlement. One such example is the pioneer settler, Lord Delamere, whose Delamere Estates are currently owned by his great-grandson, Tom Cholmondeley. As Joshua Hammer writes in his article on the Cholmondeley killings, aptly titled "The Kenyan Cowboy",

> The Delameres are the most prominent members of an elite group of landowning families that profited from treaties forced on indigenous tribes by the British colonial govern-ment at the turn of the 20th century. Although many whites sold their land to black Kenyans decades ago, a few hundred big owners who remain continue to live in a bubble of wealth and privilege; even as the vast majority of Kenya's indigenous population is mired in poverty. (2006, 4)

Parselelo Kantai captures this situation in his observation: "The Dela-mere family owns 50,000 acres in the Rift Valley, in a country where people fight for a quarter of an acre. Their lives are a 1920s fantasy" (Cited in Hammer, ibid.).

It is almost impossible to discuss whiteness in Kenya – both colonial and postcolonial – without making mention of the Delamere family. In itself, this is an indicator of the continuities between colonial and post-colonial whiteness in Kenya, and not entirely on the basis of the fam-ily's cross-generational longevity. In fact, the Delamere prominence in Kenya illustrates the continued production of Nuttall's settler politics. As Elspeth Huxley's biographical portrait of the pioneer settler Lord Delamere suggestively titled *White Man's Country* presents him, Dela-mere was one of the architects of Kenya as white man's country.

Land annexation for British settlement in Kenya was undergirded by the colonial administrative apparatuses. Huge tracts of rich agricultural land were appropriated for settlement by white farmers in the so-called White Highlands, while the game-rich land in southern Kenya was converted into game parks and game reserves. One of the primary victims of this process was the Maasai community, whose land was rich in wildlife. Much of this land was turned into present day Tsavo, Amboseli and Maasai Mara Game Reserves and privately owned game ranches, including the Delamere Estates. In his incisive essay, "In the Grip of the Vampire State: Maasai Land Struggles in Kenyan Politics," Parselelo Kantai offers an account of the loss of the Maasai tribal lands to the British colonial administration. For Kantai, the Maasai presented a challenge to British settlement, in part because their legendary reputation as ferocious and war-like had preceded them; raising anxieties about British settlement as they "controlled a vast territory in central and southern Kenya that stretched into northern Tanzania [and] occupied the lands directly adjacent to those most favourable to European settlement: what would later become known as the White Highlands" (2007, 108). To solve the Maasai problem, the British persuaded Maasai elders to thumb-print two Anglo-Maasai treaties in 1904 and 1911.[2]

Against this background, the Cholmondeley killings were inevitably yoked into the Maasai land struggles, in a discourse that questioned the validity of Cholmondeley's ownership of the Delamere Estates, which remain one of the most visible chunks of the formerly Maasai-owned Laikipia lands. In view of this, three issues are of particular interest for us in this paper: the tensions between hunting, farming and wildlife conservation in colonial Kenya; the alienation of Maasai land for wildlife conservation; and the postcolonial tourism and wildlife conservation industry. These three issues have their roots in particular constellations of British economic and cultural practices in colonial Kenya.

Colonial Kenya attracted a particular calibre of British settlers. In his study *Black Poachers, White Hunters: A Social History of Hunting in Colonial Kenya*, Edward Steinhart writes that, in contrast with other British African colonies such as Rhodesia,

> Kenya attracted settlers of high social and economic status in their countries of birth, especially Britain. ....One clear mark of this background was the prodigious number of active hunters who came to settle in Kenya because of the hunting opportunities provided... Indeed, hunting in particular, and

> sportsmanship in general would come to be the chief feature
> of self-identification of the Kenya settler elite. (2006, 92)

Steinhart's description here outlines the twin attractions of Kenya to the settler community: farming and hunting. The latter resulted in the popularisation of Kenya as the hunter's paradise, which in turn laid the foundation for the subsequent branding of the country as tourists' paradise – a brand that remains to date.

An important figure in colonial Kenyan settler culture was the white hunter. A product of the outlined settler aristocracy, the white hunter in some ways embodied the dictates of the English hunt exported to the colony, which soon came to form a distinctive register of whiteness. As Steinhart explains,

> It was necessary to distinguish the Kenyan white hunter from other professional hunters who hunted for the market, either in meat, skins or trophies. Whiteness among these Kenyan professionals came to symbolize their virtues of honesty, probity and courage befitting sportsmen. [...] *Whiteness would be worn as a badge of honour, distinguishing sporting gentlemen from the lesser breeds outside the law and custom of the hunt.* (2006, 132 emphasis added)

Ironically, the subsequent turn to wildlife conservation in colonial Kenya (which was in some ways an outgrowth of these particular notions of white hunting) precipitated a layered contradiction between the twin settler pursuits of hunting and farming, and by extension, protecting the farms from wildlife. As Steinhart reminds us, "settler destruction of wildlife habitat through fencing, clearing and burning as well as intense predation, constituted white settlement as the single most important factor in the decline of game numbers during the first half of the twentieth century" (2006, 98). Yet poaching in Kenya has historically been framed as a black affair. Predictably, Steinhart notes, African conservation methods were totally ignored in the emergent game conservation enterprise. In a bizarre twist, Africans soon found themselves recast as the prime suspects in poaching, while wildlife conservation to date remains 'whitened,' an ethos signalled in the title of Steinhart's book, "Black Poachers, White Hunters", which uncannily captures the binary dimensions of the two Cholmondeley killings discussed below. This discourse laid the foundation for the appropriation of wildlife conservation as an important cultural practice of whiteness. Against this background, we begin to see the construction of the hunting safari and later wildlife photography, wildlife safari and wildlife conservation as white cultural practices in Kenya.

These discursive practices were continued in post-colonial Kenya; further deepened by the profiling of Kenya as a prime wildlife tourist destination for international markets. Indeed, wildlife tourism in Africa has historically been constructed as a white preoccupation at whose core lies what Steinhart describes as "the mystical oxymoron of safe-danger" (2006, 132).

The tourism industry in Kenya is officially touted as one of the key drivers of the country's economy. In popular imaginaries, however, the figure of the tourist is associated with whiteness, wealth and privilege. Indeed, in Kenya, as in many parts of Africa, wildlife tourism lay at the core of colonial leisure, and despite the gradual emergence of the black wildlife tourist, it remains embedded in white cultural bedrock.[3] Yet, despite the official promotion of the tourism industry in Kenya, there is bitter resentment towards tourists among the local populations living near key game reserves. This resentment is based on, among other things, perceptions of tourist arrogance; perceptions of preferential treatment of tourists; and feelings of exclusion from the economic gains of the tourism industry. As John Akama observes about the Maasai, for instance, they

> Incur immediate and direct social and environmental costs from tourism development and wildlife conservation; they suffer damage by park wildlife and forgo the opportunity of using this protected land for agricultural production; but insignificant amounts of the country's tourism receipts trickle to the Maasai in areas adjacent to the attractions. (1999, 716)

A Maasai elder Nkonina Songoi candidly captures this resentment of tourists and the tourism industry broadly:

> Tourists pass here constantly from one park to another. We have no relationship with them. They come and leave, knowing nothing of us. If someone is dying by the road, they don't stop. They knock down calves and goats and don't stop. These people must be human. It's our land they cross to get to the park. Surely they must stop and talk to us if they kill an animal. [In addition] wildlife coming off the parks, - particularly Amboseli – are all over our land now. They don't ask permission. But if we cross into the park, with our cattle, the Rangers chase us out with Land Rovers and helicopters. (Sayer 1998, 60)

231

In many ways, the postcolonial tourism and wildlife conservation industries continue the problematic master - slave dialectic described by Nuttall above, with Maasai participation confined at the very bottom of the food chain, as curio vendors, traditional dancers and exotic photographic subjects.

In light of this, the two Cholmondeley killings (both of which evoked the question of poaching and game conservation), the concern with poaching in the film *Ivory Hunters*, and the framing of the Julie Ward death along discourses of wildlife tourism and conservation speak to each other in ways that surface the mobilisation of wildlife and conservation as important vectors in postcolonial whiteness which remain haunted by the contradictions and tensions embedded in the formation of settler Kenya as "white man's country".

## POACHERS, MURDERERS AND CONSERVATIONISTS: IVORY HUNTERS AND THE CHOLMONDELEY KILLINGS

An important clue to understanding whiteness as a constructed cultural hegemon lies in remembering that empire "was an act, a theatrical performance staged before a captive audience of millions of colonized subjects" (Steinhart citing Cannadine 2001) or as Alfred Lopez puts it, understanding "the power of whiteness as contingent upon a performance of white power" (2005, 13). These observations speak to James Scott's (1990) idea of the importance of public transcripts in the maintenance of hegemonic power. As he reminds us, "if subordination requires a credible performance of humility and deference, so domination seems to require a credible performance of haughtiness and mastery" (1990, 11). One medium that has repeatedly lent itself to the construction and performance of whiteness as a cultural hegemon is film. The film *Ivory Hunters*, released a year after Julie Ward's death in Kenya continued this tried and tested tradition in the construction of whiteness in Africa.

Coupled with its reputation as a wildlife tourism paradise, is Kenya's reputation as a wildlife conservation site and a film location. Over the years, Kenya has produced dozens of conservationists and attracted an array of wildlife conservation projects and ranch-owning game farmers. Among the better known figures are Joy and George Adamson of the Born Free Foundation and Kuki Gallman of the Gallman Foundation. The three conservationists' work gained greater publicity through wildlife documentaries and feature films set in Kenya, among these Adamson's *Born Free* (1966) which tells the story of Elsa an orphaned cub that the Adamsons rescue from the wilds and nurse to adulthood. Kuki

Gallman's feature film, *I Dreamed of Africa* (2000) is an autobiographical narrative about her life in Kenya and her involvement in wildlife conservation. *Ivory Hunters* therefore continues a distinct, well-developed film genre in Kenya, which tells the narrative of white involvement in wildlife conservation. Over time, the white wildlife conservationist has grown into a stock figure in Kenyan white society; the white hunter reincarnate. Dr. Maria Edmonson in *Ivory Hunters* is moulded around such a figure, a fictional version of Kuki Gallman or Joy Adamson.

In *Ivory Hunters*, Dr. Maria Edmonson is a passionate wildlife conservationist, out to protect elephants from imminent extinction. Liz Page, an American research assistant to an American novelist Robert Carter, travels to Kenya, and goes to the game reserve to do research for Carter's next novel about the poaching industry. On a game drive alone, Liz accidentally stumbles upon elephant poachers in the act and takes their photographs. The poachers notice and capture her. Days later, her mutilated body is recovered. Eventually, her killers are arrested with the assistance of the novelist – now turned conservationist – and Maria.

Liz Page's murder in the film echoes aspects of the Julie Ward case. Liz's trip to the game reserve and her murder as she photographs elephants echoes Julie Ward's trip to Maasai Mara and her interest in wildlife photography. Further, the narrative in *Ivory Hunters* strongly echoes speculation about the circumstances surrounding the Julie Ward death and the possibility that she may have stumbled across poachers in the vast Maasai Mara Game Reserve. These close parallels and allusions to the circumstances surrounding Julie Ward's death make the film an interesting text to read alongside the Ward case. Despite the vast differences in narrative and the fiction-fact divide between Julie Ward's and Liz Page's murder, it is an important text in making visible what Gillian Whitlock calls "a paradigmatic circuitry" (2000, 116) that may shed light on our understandings of postcolonial whiteness in Kenya.

Having failed to catch the poachers who are decimating elephants at an alarming rate, the Kenyan police in *Ivory Hunters* decide to use captured ivory as bait, through Carter, who pretends to have turned from writing to enacting his protagonist's plan: stealing captured ivory from a warehouse in Mombasa. He therefore persuades the poachers to team up with him and steal this ivory. The poachers buy into this idea and are eventually caught and stand trial for murder and poaching.

Although the idea of baiting the poachers with captured ivory is initially conceived by the Kenyan Commissioner of Police, the ultimate victory belongs to Carter, to whom the film grants agency. The film evokes the Christian missionary interventions of earlier times. Under-

pinning this messianic intervention is a scripting of a proactive whiteness which stands in contrast with African helplessness. In the film, Liz
Page literally lays down her life in an attempt to protect the elephants;
and later, Carter risks his life as he sets the trap to catch the poachers.

The use of the trope of messianic intervention in African crises
in the film affirms what Lopez describes as "the self-sacrificing, self-
destructing white (fe)male rebel as a trope of the new postcolonial
whiteness; a paradoxically self-serving figure who would allow whites
to retain their central status as "emancipators" and thus their power
and privilege" (2005, 22). Citing Richard Dyer, Lopez underscores the
ways in which some white subjects adopt a distancing mechanism that
sustains a "collective willed blindness essential to both the maintenance
of white cultural hegemony and the avoidance of accountability" (2005,
22-3). As he writes

> Such distancing also allows for what Dyer calls the "exquisite
> agony" (206) of white liberal guilt, which likewise seeks to
> appease and appeal to the Other's capacity for orderly dissent
> while surrendering little of its own entrenched privilege.
> (ibid.)

Lopez and Dyer's ideas here underscore the mobilization of the messianic figure of the white wo/man in the construction of postcolonial
whiteness, and its continued maintenance of the privileges that accrue
from whiteness, at a time when colonial myths of white supremacy and
black inferiority are no longer viable. This figure of the white messiah is
an interesting example of the new grammars of postcolonial whiteness,
which re-invents the colonial missionary grammar, in its retention of
the stereotype of black passivity and need for redemption.

The messianic trope in *Ivory Hunters* stands in sharp contrast with
the portrait of whiteness painted by the Cholmondeley killings. Wildlife
feature prominently in the two Cholmondeley killings. According to a
report by the Law Society of Kenya,[4] ole Sisina had gone to the ranch to
investigate allegations of illegal trade in game meat on Cholmondeley's
ranch following a tip off. He was accompanied by fellow KWS rangers
Lillian Ochieng Ajuoga and Kushnow Mamo, and they had procedurally
logged their mission in the KWS offices. At Soysambu, they stumbled
upon a Land Rover pick-up carrying a just-shot buffalo to the ranch's
slaughter house for skinning:

> At the slaughterhouse, they [...] informed the group that
> they were under arrest. They rounded up the group and

handcuffed those who were restless... The manager wanted to inform his boss, Tom (Cholmondeley) about the incident but the KWS crew declined. ...Mamo and Lillian stayed in the slaughterhouse with the suspects while ole Sisina kept watch outside.... Lillian saw Tom who was holding a revolver rush towards the slaughterhouse. Tom saw Lillian. Tom is an honorary warden and knows Lillian personally because they had met on many work-related occasions. Lillian informed ole Sisina that Tom was coming and that he was armed. She then heard Tom say words to the effect of "What is KWS"? Immediately, Tom fired 4 rounds, in rapid succession at the crush...Mamo and Lillian, who were both lying flat on the floor, repeatedly shouted at the top of their voices the words "KWS! KWS!" ... Tom then told Lillian and Mamo that he had shot dead one of them... Immediately, Lillian called her superiors from her mobile to report. Tom ordered that Lillian's phone be taken away. Tom began making calls on his phone saying that he had killed an 'armed robber'. He called three of his security guards who brutally beat up Lillian and Mamo. (ibid.)

I have quoted the report at length because the circumstances surrounding this particular incident are important to our discussion in this paper. Further, although the case attracted a lot of media attention, the details of the circumstances were not public knowledge.[5] In the second case – barely a year later, Cholmondeley shot and killed Robert Nyoya, a resident from a neighbouring According to the 2006/2007 Kenya Human Rights Commission Bi-Annual Report (ibid., 72-4), Cholmondeley was taking an evening stroll in the ranch with his friend Carl Tundo when they bumped into Njoya and two other men from a neighbouring village. The three men were carrying a dead impala, which they had caught on one of the snares they had laid on the ranch. Allegedly cognizant of Cholmondeley's legendary wrath, the three men dropped their catch and fled. While his two colleagues escaped unscathed, Njoya and two dogs were struck and killed by bullets from Cholmondeley's game hunting riffle.

The absurd paradox in the case over the protection of wildlife would seem to reduce it to a question of contested ownership of the wildlife in Soysambu Ranch. In the first case, Cholmondeley shoots dead a KWS warden, in the process of arresting his employees on charges of illegal trade in game meat, seemingly with Cholmondeley's full knowledge. At the time, the KWS had banned animal culling in private ranches, as it believed private ranchers were exceeding accepted limits and threatening the wildlife population, but Cholmondeley allegedly ignored the KWS prohibitions.[6] For KWS spokesperson Connie Maina, "all the wildlife in the country belongs to the government and KWS is the custodian. You have to go with what is the law, but Tom Cholmondeley made his own rules" (ibid.). In the second case, Cholmondeley kills a man for poaching an impala on his Ranch. At the core of this conflict though, seems to be the old question of ownership of wildlife. This is an issue that has haunted wildlife conservation in Kenya since colonial times (Steinhart 2006, 212-4).

In both *Ivory Hunters* and the Cholmondeley killings, the masternarrative of wildlife conservation represents an important platform for the performance of whiteness in postcolonial Kenya. Like the white hunter described by Steinhart above, in postcolonial Kenya, the white conservationist too would seem to wear their whiteness as a badge of honor, now distinguishing animal conservationists from poachers. Thus, in *Ivory Hunters*, Maria with her doctoral degree and her sensitive passion for conservation, would seem to have inherited the mantle of whiteness from the white hunter, as she epitomizes animal conservation as an important marker of contemporary whiteness in which, as Whitlock writes in a different context, "humane feelings towards animals [are] associated with an enlightened view and a revolution in perceptions of relations between human and animal worlds" (2000, 136). On the opposite extreme are the poachers, who, in both *Ivory Hunters* and the Cholmondeley killings, are associated with blackness; itself a reversal of roles, when read against Kenyan settler history and settler involvement in wildlife extermination.

*Ivory Hunters* further speaks to the contradictions inherent in the modernity – savagery nexus that remains at the core of constructions of white subjectivities and their relationship with wildlife tourism in Africa. This is more so in view of Donna Harraway's reminder about "nature's discursive construction as "Other" in histories of colonialism, racism, sexism and class domination" (1992, 296). Harraway captures the tensions that lay at the core of wildlife tourism's fascination with 'safe danger', which in many ways replicates colonialism's ambivalent construction of Otherness as at once "an object of desire and derision" (Bhabha 1983, 19). The contradiction in Julie Ward's death, as in *Ivory Hunters*, lies in the intersection between fascination with the wild and the simultaneous construction of Africans as both living outside modernity and defiled by an aborted modernity. This contradiction illustrates the tensions that beset constructions of postcolonial whiteness using discursive tools carved out of colonial whiteness. But how did Julie Ward's presence, death and the subsequent quest for her killers as narrated in the three books speak to these discourses?

## JULIE WARD AND POSTCOLONIAL WHITENESS IN KENYA

*Ivory Hunters'* narrative reveals postcolonial whiteness to be preoccupied with the contradictions of modernity's claim to progress at the expense of the moral duty of protecting nature for posterity. In some ways, the film enacts a certain battle of conscience, a performed atonement for the destructive effects of modernity, which has created networks of markets for ivory. Yet, notably, this performed battle of conscience while interrogating the destructive aspects of modernity, simultaneously clings to the privileges afforded by modernity. In the film then, we see the deployment of Africa as a discursive terrain for dramatizing postcolonial whiteness and its moral anxieties. Whitlock captures this discursive capacity of Africa, in this case Kenya as a useable terrain for articulating these concerns: "the natural environment [in Kenya] is particularly responsive to very different kinds of intellectual and physical uses of Africa for the West:... the plains and the highlands, the vegetation and the variety of wild animals available for romantic visions of the loss or discovery of an essential life in nature" (2000, 113-4).

Elsie Cloete describes the pervasive representation of Kenya as an idyllic land in settler fiction, often captured in the "sense of landscape, location and space untrammelled by Europe's urban congestion" (2002, 9). These writings constructed African landscapes as Edenic wildernesses endowed with a certain savage innocence and beauty that the fast modernizing West yearned for.

Contemplating the Maasai Mara landscape in his book *A Death in Kenya: The Murder of Julie Ward*, Michael Hiltzik laments the desecration of the once-authentic primordial jungle that was the Mara, by the trappings of modernity:

> For all its fame, Maasai Mara is not exactly the place to contemplate nature in an atmosphere of serenity. The songs of hundreds of species of birds are often drowned out by the engine drone of aircraft .... It might even be true that some of the romance of seeing the wild animals in their natural habitat has been drained away by the Mara animals' easy familiarity with humans and their green tour vehicles. (1991, 70)

This fascination with pure wilderness unpolluted by modernity which lies at the core of African tourism can be traced back to the afore-discussed colonial leisure repertoire in which safari featured prominently. This repertoire mediated colonial knowledge of the people, wildlife and landscape of Kenya, which the tourists were seen to be capable of negotiating, photographing and describing. Travel and settler fiction writers such as Karen Blixen, Robert Ruark and Elspeth Huxley played an important role in the construction of this archive and with time helped to define and construct Kenya as a tourist destination.[7]

While tropes of exoticism and the purity of nature owe their genesis to settler representations of Africa, they have continued to be produced in post-colonial Africa as part of the commodification of African countries as tourist destinations. Tourism, an industry which primarily thrives on the admiring foreign gaze, has been a core contributor to the economies of many African states for a long time. In Kenya, there has been sustained marketing of the country as a tourist destination, a process that has coded the beaches, wildlife, cultural artefacts and various ethnic groups into the recognizable brand of 'tourist Kenya.' Wildlife tourism represents another face of postcolonial whiteness in Kenya, which rubs shoulders with wildlife conservation. Indeed, the two feed off each other and are largely mutually sustaining. The archive of tourist discourses about Kenya and Africa framed Julie Ward's presence in the Maasai Mara.

When she left Britain for Kenya on her first trip to Africa, Julie Ward told her parents she was going to Africa "to photograph the Jumbos" (1991, 23). On her third and last trip to the continent, Julie Ward was part of an overland trip from England, across the Sahara desert, down through central Africa, into Kenya. As a tourist, she was positioned within this web of ideas about tourist Africa; a positioning that both Jeremy Gavron and Michael Hiltzik reproduce in their respective reconstructions of Julie Ward's trip to Africa. In the opening chapter of his book, Gavron describes Maasai Mara National Reserve thus:

> [The Mara] lies towards the south-west corner of Kenya, just one hundred and twenty miles, but a different world from the capital, Nairobi. Its high grass plains and shimmering hills, freckled with flat-topped acacia trees, have hardly changed, tourist lodges and prowling prides of Land Rovers and minibuses apart, for a thousand years. During the day, a multitude of creatures – wildebeest, zebra, giraffe, elephant, lion, cheetah – swelter beneath the high, equatorial sun and a vast blue sky that seems to stretch up for ever. On moonless

nights, the darkness is so absolute that whole galaxies invisible in the European sky wink and glitter like dust caught in a distant shaft of light. (1994, 1)

In this opening paragraph of his novel, Gavron sets in place the lens of his Edenic Africa. This Africa retains certain purity, undamaged by modernity which seems to have clogged European skies.

A similar template is evident in Hiltzik's portrait of the Maasai Mara as "this place of primordial natural savagery" (1991, 4) a description that draws on a distinct lexicon in the grammar of African tourism. Hiltzik goes on to describe the impact of Africa on Julie Ward upon return from her first two trips to the continent:

> [Julie] packed the camera gear ...and went off to photograph animals in the best place on earth to see them: Kenya. When she came back to work a few weeks later, Rowland [Julie's boss] could not help noticing something different. There was a new glow in her eyes, as if she had discovered a new possibility in life. A year later, she took a second trip to Kenya, and this time she seemed entirely changed. "By the time she came back from that trip" Rowland said later "her heart was there. She had just fallen in love with it." (1991, 15)

From her experience, Kenya and Africa live up to the rejuvenating, healing power associated with it in colonial/settler literature and which remains an important attraction in postcolonial tourism. The landscape and wildlife seem to revitalize Julie Ward, putting a new glow in her eyes and opening up new horizons of possibilities in life. As her father observes, "Muff returned with a million magic memories of wild, remote places where at night huge stars hang low and bright in an unpolluted sky. A few of those stars stayed in her eyes" (Ward cited in Buckley ).

Years later, after the tragic death of his daughter in the Mara, John Ward offers a strikingly different account of the African night. Describing his stay at Keekorok Lodge in Maasai Mara on the night of the day his daughter's remains were found, Ward writes:

> I was in the farthest room from the lodge restaurant, across the large lawn. A native show was on that night and drums beat continually. Dancers with spears and painted faces stamped and pranced to the rhythm. Out beyond the lights, loud across the bush came the sound of animals as they snarled, roared and screamed through the darkness. To me,

the sounds were like some primitive prehistoric hell on earth.
How I loathed that place. (1991, 85)

Ward's loathing for the wilderness that had hitherto been eroticized, and which had attracted his daughter to Kenya and the Maasai Mara in the first place is striking. The continuity in Ward's thinking here between 'prancing' and 'stamping' natives, with the snarling, roaring and screaming wildlife just 'beyond the lights' in the bush is suggestive. But most interestingly, albeit inadvertently, Ward here captures the defilement of this Edenic tourist paradise.

In the discourse of wildlife conservation, twined with the vulnerability of the white woman, we begin to understand John Ward's framing of his text *The Animals are Innocent*, in ways that foreground Julie Ward's love for wild animals. This is captured in the iconic picture of the Julie Ward case, which shows Julie Ward hugging an orphaned baby chimpanzee at an animal orphanage in Cameroun. By selecting this as the emblematic photo of Julie Ward after her death, Ward underscores a shared vulnerability to black violence.[8] For Whitlock, Gavron further underlines this shared vulnerability by juxtaposing "the innocence of the animals and the white woman, over and against the preparedness of black men to slaughter both" (2000, 115) by drawing parallels between the 1988 burning of ivory captured from poachers in Kenya, with the burning of Julie Ward's remains in the wilderness. As Whitlock argues,

> the burning of the tusks episode in *Darkness in Eden* further harkens back to Gavron's graphic reconstruction of the burning of Julie Ward's body in the Maasai Mara by her killers, and so develops a further association between the woman and the wildlife as victims. (ibid.)

Incidentally, the ivory burning also features in *Ivory Hunters*, with similar echoes, as it reminds us of the cold blooded butchering of the elephants and the research assistant in a callous spray of bullets. Like Gavron, *Ivory Hunters*, presents the white woman and wildlife as equally susceptible to the same kind of (black male) violence.

It is unsurprising that the memorials to Julie Ward's life all had the theme of wildlife conservation at their core. Among these was a coffee table book of pictures of wild animals that she had taken on her last trip to Kenya and her letters to her family, as she traveled across the continent towards Kenya. The book, suggestively titled *Gentle Nature*, is published by the Born Free Foundation and proceeds of the book go towards the creation of a lion sanctuary in Uganda as a memorial to

Julie Ward. Her jeep was "converted into an open-top with her name on the side and donated to the Gallman Memorial Foundation [...] which provides sanctuary for wildlife" (Buckley n.p). The privileging of wildlife in all the monuments to Julie Ward's memory was consistent with the selective gaze that mediates the practices of African tourism.

## CONCLUSION

If the enlightenment project and broadly Western modernity implied containment, discipline and boundary erection, then this was fissured in Africa's wilderness by the aggressive masculinity of the black man. For Anne McClintock, British imperial conquest entailed "the feminizing of terra incognita [which] was, from the outset, a strategy of violent containment" (1985, 24). As she writes "land is named as female as a passive counterpart to the massive thrust of male technology (1985, 26). These dynamics of white male authority would appear to play themselves out in the Julie Ward case, *Ivory Hunters* and the Cholmondeley killings.

The figure of white male authority across the cases discussed suggests the preoccupation of postcolonial whiteness in Kenya with the re-insertion of white male authority. It is notable that the three sets of narratives – books on Julie Ward's death, *Ivory Hunters* and the Cholmondeley killings – all seem to figure white men engaged in a struggle with black men over wildlife and white women. Apart from the fact that all the three books on the Julie Ward matter are written by white men, her father, John Ward stood at the forefront of the quest for truth and justice, and found himself taking on a predominantly black male Kenyan state infrastructure. Similarly, in *Ivory Hunters*, Robert Carter is the one to take on the black male poachers, while the Cholmondeley killings would seem to have been as much about wildlife as about the contestation for authority between the white male Cholmondeley and the black Kenyan poachers, and KWS. But it is the later institution that draws interesting links across the three sets of narratives, primarily in the figure of another white male Kenyan, Richard Leakey.

In a curious, yet telling coincidence, both Gavron and Hiltzik close their books on the Julie Ward case by lingering on the appointment of Richard Leakey as the head of the KWS. The two reveal strong optimism in Leakey's capacity to bring back stability in the chaos of the tourism industry. Less than a decade later, the Moi government appointed Richard Leakey the head of civil service. Commenting on this, Apollo

241

Amoko (1999) notes the paternalist representation of Leakey as Kenya's messiah in British media.

On the whole, wildlife tourism and conservation emerges as an important platform for the performance of whiteness in postcolonial Kenya, yet this register has failed to break away from its colonial roots, which were mired in tensions and contradictions that were later to haunt the Julie Ward case. Further, as our discussion reveals, this postcolonial whiteness in Kenya remains a highly gendered one, at the heart of which lies a nostalgic struggle to affirm and restore a white male authority reminiscent of that of the settler colony.

## Notes

1. Admittedly, the notion of 'Africanness' is largely steeped in mythology, and often steers dangerously close to essentialism. Yet, at the same time, debates on skin-deep racial differences and African 'reverse racism' aside, white citizenship in Africa is often shot through with selective processes of laying claim to particular notions of Africanness while strategically retaining tenacious grip on various strands of 'Europeaness,' including European citizenship and cultural grammars.

2. Ibid. Kantai observes that, according to the Maasai, the second agreement ceded the Laikipia lands to the British for 99 years. The lease expired on 15 August 2005, and on this date, the Maasai community organised demonstrations in Nairobi, demanding their land back. However, the Kenya government argued that the second agreement ceded the Laikipia lands for 999 years and not 99 years as the Maasai believed. Although most of the land in question is in white ownership, the successive national elites have since laid claim to some of this land too.

3. See for instance Njabulo Ndebele's "Game Lodges and Leisure Colonialists: Caught in the Process of Becoming" (1999) for a fascinating reflection on wildlife tourism and black tourists' encounters with it.

4. Law Society of Kenya, "Human Rights Report of 2005/2006," 17-19.

5. According to the report, "The Attorney General entered nolle prosequi in the murder charge against Cholmondeley on the basis that there was insufficient evidence to support a murder charge" (Ibid, 73).

6. Hammer, "The Kenyan Cowboy," 6. Hammer's article sheds some light on the Cholmondeley – KWS conflict. As he writes, "Cholmondeley had been appointed an honorary game warden by the KWS in the nineties, and he and fellow ranchers claimed that he had the right to shoot wild animals that he deemed a threat to his property, his cattle, or his staff" (6).

7.  See particularly Karen Blixen's *Out of Africa* (1937), Robert Ruark's *Uhuru* (1962) and Elspeth Huxley's *The Flame Trees of Thika: Memoirs of an African Childhood* (1959).

8.  This coupling of both the white woman and wild animals as victims of the black man's violence can be traced further back to the writing of Robert Ruark on colonial Kenya. In *Uhuru* for instance, Ruark juxtaposes what he sees as African violence against animals - captured in the Mau Mau's oathing ceremonies, in which domestic animals are brutally killed - with their violence against white women, as seen in the decapitation of Katie Crane, an American tourist.

# Chapter 13

# GENDER AFFIRMATION OR RACIAL LOYALTIES? WOMEN AND THE DOMESTICATION OF HISTORY IN NEERA KAPUR-DROMSON'S *FROM JHELUM TO TANA*

*Godwin Siundu*
*University of Nairobi*

## INTRODUCTION

The quest for personal and communal identities play out powerfully in auto/biographical works, particularly those that articulate contestations with histories of dominance and oppression as in the case of immigrant communities. To a large extent, such works are male in orientation, subsuming experiences of female members of the immigrant communities in those of their male counterparts, and as such privileging men's experiences as the dominant, proper ones. Indeed, even with the few female-authored auto/biographies available, the tendency among scholars is to read them singularly within the separate trajectory of feminist concerns rather than as ones that deal with conditions of immigrancy. Some of them, like Rasna Warah's *Triple Heritage*, are viewed as undermining the male created works on immigrancy by exposing the immigrant communities to external gaze from non-community members. This gendered nature of immigrant literature needs further interrogation because they contribute to the archive of herstories and may thus lead to a more nuanced understanding of the wider discourse of immigrancy.

The purpose of this chapter is to critically read Neera Kapur-Dromson's *From Jhelum to Tana*, as an auto/biography that attempts to re-insert key elements of communal experiences within the wider matrix of the Asian diasporic narratives in the region, which I call a domestication of history. *From Jhelum to Tana* contains attributes of the autobiography because it is concerned with the personal history of an individual, but it also extends to her family through four generations and the entire community of immigrants to show how a personal narrative fits in its wider communal variants. In doing this, Kapur-Dromson combines narrative strategies of omniscience and the first person, to capture collective and personal experiences respectively. This is particularly important because autobiographical works form a basis for collectivising what may be individual experiences and comprehend them as communal concerns, particularly the quest for self-discovery and self-expression or affirmation. By narrating conditions of immigrancy from domestic spaces, Kapur-Dromson offers a new frontier in scholarship on East African immigrant communities, thereby inviting critical review of what has been taken for the known.

I am guided in turns by the literary theory of autobiographies as well as feminist and post-colonial theories that bring out various perspectives of marginality. Ultimately, I argue for a shift in analytical frame to look at female-authored works that interrogate history beyond the helpful yet limiting lens of feminist concerns; to broaden the spectrum as far as interrogating female authors' engagement with scholarly and experiential aspects of history, particularly its less written-about variants of the personal and social narratives as history. I designate this work as an auto/biography in order to signal the work's occupation of the unexplored space between biography – rendered from the all-knowing omniscient point of view – and autobiography – that is in the first person. It is because of this dual structuring of the work that I read it as representing the wider Punjabi and South Asian community currently resident in Kenya.

I begin by citing Rasna Warah's statement that resonates with Kapur-Dromson's *From Jhelum to Tana*. Warah avers: "I researched and wrote *Triple Heritage* out of anger and grief. Anger at the fact that despite being a fourth generation immigrant to Kenya, my status lay somewhere between citizen and refugee, of one not quite belonging anywhere" (1998, 6). This statement, besides signalling the complex process of searching for one's identities, brings to the fore one of the most dominant concerns that has driven not just literary and other artistic productions by East African Asians in the region and beyond, but also the critical responses to these works. Indeed, it appears as a natural expectation among readers that whoever ventures to study East African Asian literature and the arts must associate themselves with the group's concerns with identities, identifications, citizenship, nationhood and other related issues (Simatei 2001; Ojwang 2004; Siundu 2005; Herzig 2006). That this is the case could be both cause and effect of East African Asian writers' preoccupation with the same concerns, especially with regard to the place of the group in the making of contemporary Kenyan and East African histories.

Yet, for a long time, the discourses on immigrant literature – and its incursions into history – have taken on gendered characteristics, where the post-independence insider image of the East African Asian community is one offered by males. Which is why Warah's work from which I have already quoted is significant in marking the beginning of female writers' critiquing of mainstream histories of the region, but simultaneously offering an alternative insider view of the community; this time focusing on individual female members of the immigrant community as they grapple with the challenges of marginality. Scholars of East African Asian immigrants have acknowledged the centrality of history in understanding the context of being an East African woman of Asian descent, yet this has more often than not been political history, with names of key political or activist figures of Asian origin like Apa Pant and Pio Gama Pinto listed to acquit the entire Asian community against common place charges of complicity with the exploitative capital and political economies that were the ulterior drives of colonialism. While such focus may, admittedly, be correct, it freezes our understanding of the entire humanity of East African Asian immigrants to their political selves, leaving out significant parts of their essence, which includes domestic concerns and what one may refer to as social histories that focus on individual members of the community and how they shaped, and were in turn shaped by, national historical events. Such a strategy also brings into focus the intersection between fiction and non-fiction; especially how both are manifested in auto/biographical works from immigrant communities, as attempts to yield a more nuanced understanding of the said communities in terms of their values and the logic of their cultural bodies. Kapur-Dromson's work fits in this category for various important reasons: first, its auto/biographical structure imbues it with a reality that can be corroborated out by historical facts; second, that as a widely travelled female writer, she validates the authority of the claims in the work, making it a helpful starting point in such a feminist reading of the auto/biography. Third, its subject matter that engages in the social history of an immigrant community captures the various ways in which categories of gender, race, class and power intersect in fashioning contemporary identifications with and of difference, pointing to the complex position occupied by a female auto/biographer.

## AUTO/BIOGRAPHY AS HERSTORY?
## SOME THEORETICAL CONCERNS

In the Kenyan situation in particular, autobiographical works have been the most significant literary genre of female writers. While the autobiography in general weds literary and historical attributes, the female autobiography occupies a tentative space for lack of an established authorship and critical tradition, especially in the East African region where female writers – regardless of racial belonging – are perceived as latecomers. As Marta Piroli argues:

> [w]omen's autobiographical writing has not always been taken seriously by an essentially male criticism that restricted its interests to the lives of great men, considered more complex and appropriate for the literary canon. (2006, 11)

One should add to Piroli's view that the female autobiography has remained a blindspot for lack of adequate critical attention by both male and female critics, although this does not invalidate her well founded view that little criticism on the female autobiographies has been done. With regard to the suitability of female autobiographies as representative of an alternative view of the society, it is also about the unique psychological frame of womanhood which, as Mary Mason states, "comes to define itself in relation and connection with other people more than a masculine personality does. That is, in psychological terms, women are less individuated than men and have more flexible ego boundaries" (1979, 17). If we accept Mason's view, then, it is possible to examine a female autobiography as a quest for self-comprehension and extending to that of the entire community from which the female auto/biographer comes. I am further convinced by Susan Friedman's argument as read in Mason that:

[a] woman's autobiographical self often does not oppose herself to all others, does not feel herself to exist outside of others, and still less against others, but very much with others in an interdependent existence that asserts its rhythms everywhere in the community. (1979, 79)

If that be so, then one can argue that reading a female autobiography is like reading a communal narrative, even though it is often presented as personal, as in the case of Kapur-Dromson's work. Such a view is probably supported by Leigh Gilmore's problematization of the 'I' when she states that "[a]n exploration of the text's autobiographics allows us to recognize that the *I* is multiply coded in a range of discourses: it is the site of multiple solicitations, multiple markings of 'identity', multiple figurations of agency" (184). Hence, the female 'I' is devoted to the family, wife duties and 'I' as a human being with ambitions. I add then that while a female auto/biographer may, as Warah does, claim to be searching for 'self-discovery', such a venture is usually socially determined within the existing socio-cultural views of her community. It is then a 'communal' rather than 'self- discovery' activity.

When such female autobiographies are authored by members of an immigrant community, it becomes more representative because women have to deal with more forms of marginality/discrimination compared to their male counterparts. The scholars' attention in this field should thus focus on aspects of immigrant communities that had hitherto been either trivialised or simply ignored. Such include the immigrant communities' management of aspects of the "everyday life", to echo Michel de Certeau's phrase. Scholarly concerns with social history have largely deconstructed the authorized history on great politicians, often men, that tends to totalize experiences of entire communities made up of women and children also. Hence, social history as captured in autobiographies is a counter discourse that dwells on specificities of issue and personality, with a slant towards humanist history in the way Foucault (1972, 12) uses it, hence "making human consciousness the original subject of all historical development and all action" (in Green, 2000, 27). Thus the sub-title of Warah's autobiography – a journey to self discovery – can be said to be true of most female writers from the East African immigrant communities. This is important because the same works fit quite neatly within the recent scholarly concerns of literary revisionism.[1] In the recent past, revisionist enterprises have thrust themselves into the centre of scholarly engagements especially in the global south, where communal relationships have long been in the context of post-colonial discourses. Subsequently, revisionism deconstructs issues that have been presented and taken as commonsense, and for some beyond or beneath critical evaluation, thereby allowing longstanding issues of communal grievances – or feelings of the same – to be left unresolved. Indeed, the revisionist impulses of the hitherto marginalised voices across the disciplines have become a welcome challenge to the totalising tendencies of mainstream narratives. Whether from entry points of race, class, gender or ethnic community, the enterprises have been given impetus by the deconstructivist perspective to demand more from current meanings of historical and literary canons. And these tendencies have been attractive to actors whose consciousness motivates them to innovatively contest mainstream scholarly/disciplinary spaces in literature, history, politics and the wider spectrum of cultural studies. It is within the ambit of literary/historical revisionism that Neera Kapur in *From Jhelum to Tana* (2007) traces and presents the family history from the Indian subcontinent and its involvement in the making of contemporary Kenya's economic history four generations down the line, from 1898 to about 2004.

## NEERA KAPUR-DROMSON IN THE COMMUNITY OF EAST AFRICAN ASIAN WOMEN WRITERS

Clearly, other female writers like Rasna Warah (1998) from Kenya, Jameela Siddiqi (2002) from Uganda and Sophia Mustapha (2009) from Tanzania have already made valuable contributions in the trajectory of fiction and non-fiction, capturing the different ways in which historical occurrences in their respective countries affected them at various points in their lives. The thing about Kapur-Dromson is that she is the first female writer to my knowledge who has adopted a cross-generational approach to portraying the image of East African Asians spatial-temporally, making real and imagined return to the Indian sub-continent with a view to developing an argument in favour of East African Asians' claims to East African nationhood. Secondly, she foregrounds, for the reader's benefit, aspects of the immigrant communities' social histories and socio-cultural rituals that enhance the reader's understanding of the same communities' concerns that fall beyond political and economic histories. She thus domesticates history by acknowledging the struggles and challenges that confronted the average immigrants in the face of changing times. She appropriates the autobiographical mode to situate gendered and racial interests within already existing, if subsuming, mainstream histories, hence the acknowledgement of the many oral interviews with elders besides the intertextual referencing that is clearly evident in the work.

What is equally important is her decision to acknowledge and celebrate the value of 'oral history' and 'oral tradition' as theorised by Jan Vansina (1985).[2] That *From Jhelum to Tana* spans four generations of immigrant families makes such an approach by Kapur-Dromson acceptable as a means of research, because it fits within the Vansinian criterion of reliable oral data, especially how basic narratives generate others. One such is the way a portrait in the novel becomes the seed from which the entire narrative sprouts, and which I discuss next.

*From Jhelum to Tana* is a family story of Neera Kapur-Dromson back to her great-grand parents; Hardei, who courageously crossed the Indian Ocean to Kenya to search for her husband, Lala Kirparam. The patriarch, Kirparam, had in 1898 left "Karachi [Pakistan] to Mombasa in a dhow blown across the Indian Ocean by the northeast monsoon..." (23) in search of opportunity. That Hardei's sojourn occurred at a time when few women had dared to do so makes her a fascinating subject to Kapur-Dromson – and indeed the reader – because of what it reveals about family and community at the time. This story would remain in the minds of the second and third generations of the Kirparam-Hardei descendants, for it to be captured by Neera Kapur-Dromson, their great granddaughter. Kapur-Dromson employs omniscience narration to tell stories that largely focus on the experiences and fears of women characters in the wake of the many cultural and historical changes that the Punjabi and other immigrant communities encountered from the early 1900s to early 2000s. *From Jhelum to Tana* is a narrative that re-constructs the immigrant Punjabi and larger Asian memory through archival research, conversations and interviews with members of the community.

When Kapur-Dromson was forty-two, she visited a relative at whose home she encountered a portrait of her great grandfather, Lala Kirparam Ramchand, painted in oil colour by "an Italian prisoner of World War II" (n.p), which sparked her curiosity about the man. The portrait prompts her to ask questions: "Where did he come from? How did I, an Indian, come to be here among the vast lands of Africa? Why was my mother born here, as was my grandmother? Who was this man who started his life in Africa over a hundred years ago? I had entered my history midway, but I knew that there had to be a beginning some-where" (n.p). The portrait not only generates  Kapur-Dromson's soul searching and a desire to know herself and her people, it also marks the beginning point in both ventures. In a sense, then, the portrait rep-resents the population of pioneer immigrants whose historical signifi-cance is in their external engagements such as the construction of the

Kenya Uganda Railway, much more than in their domestic, social ones that led to the creation and structure of the Kenyan-Asian immigrant community. Put differently, the portrait is something akin to a monument and is also an important artefact here that celebrates social and familial rather than political or economic achievements. Monuments have for long been important artefacts in mobilising collective memory, simultaneously generating historical, cultural and political narratives even as they provide space for (re)inscription of similar and/or contesting narratives. In this sense, Lala Kirparam's portrait provides a bridge of engagement between the recent and the far past, and the present. In *From Jhelum to Tana*, Kapur-Dromson begins from this point in time to trace and narrate the economic history of her family from 1898 to early 2000s and in the process extends beyond the Punjabi community to enjoin the entire Kenyan Asian community in the mainstream colonial and post-independence Kenya's political and economic histories, in a process she views as "a re-creation of tradition" (xii).

Kapur-Dromson's assertion that "I caught snatches of his adventures from various people" (2007, 1) acknowledges the value of orality as a credible source of historical and literary narratives.[3] Yet her rendition – later in the auto/biography – of the same narrated in the first person acknowledges the necessary selection and re-ordering that gives these "snatches" coherence and meaning of a text, or its literariness, besides pointing out the historical value of the same "snatches" to her as an individual. The fact that she picked up the "snatches" from different people, and imbued them with meaning also signals the interlocking historical narratives of her ancestry and those of her wider racial community who had occasion to interact with Kirparam. The ultimate effect is the implied reflection of postcolonial/postmodern discontinuities that characterise contemporary literature that interrogates the current identities and their relational implications.

*From Jhelum to Tana* begins with an introduction to Hardei, the author's great grandmother, who is named after one of Indian god Krishna's many lovers. The mortal Hardei has decided, against cultural/traditional expectations and physical odds, to board a dhow with her son to Africa in pursuit of their husband and father respectively, who had reportedly left earlier for East Africa to seek employment as a manual labourer in the construction of the historical Kenya-Uganda Railway. From the text we note that:

> Hardei had also been waiting. Many years. For the man to
> whom she had been wed several years ago. Now she was

> waiting at the railway station. Perhaps six hours, maybe more. Her six-year-old son was becoming restless. He was hungry, so was she, *but they had very little money left. Moreover, they had never seen so many strange faces before. They did see some black slaves being brought in at the port when they arrived in Karachi, but she had not expected to see so many of them in this new country where she had just arrived. [...] it was the first culture shock* (1, my italics).

Here, Kapur-Dromson, through an omniscient voice, introduces history and racial/cultural difference in her narrative to imagine and capture the financial and cultural vulnerability that tormented the pioneer South Asian immigrants in Kenya. The "culture shock" and financial concerns dominate much of the story in the auto/biography, so much as to reflect the emptiness and anxieties of alienation from Pakistan, with all its challenges:

> Bag, baggage, burdens and family – he left all these behind. He came alone. Anew. A new place invited a fresh start. A dream. A quest. A search for himself. With very vague ideas about the future – if any. Actually, he did not even need a reason: it was a primeval urge. With just enough money to pay for his passage, Kirparam boarded the dhow (19).

This claim, however, is hard to believe, and indeed contradicts earlier and well argued theoretical analyses on immigrant discourses. Rosemary George for example avers that "[t]here are no wanderers, however impoverished, however sudden their eviction, who are cast out empty-handed or empty-headed" (1996, 28). As the autobiography later shows, for Kirparam and other pioneer immigrants, there was a strong spiritual attachment to each other and to the idea of India as 'home.' Hence, Kapur-Dromson's suggestion that some of the early East African Asian immigrants came into the region with absolutely nothing is a rather different, even strange, view of those pioneer Asians in East Africa. Dan Ojwang (2004) convincingly argues that East African Asian immigrants may have left a lot behind on their way to East Africa, but they retained their sense of commitment to community. Indeed in the narrative in *From Jhelum to Tana* some of these initial tensions in the immigrant communities are explored.

For instance, the author-narrator captures the extent to which the physical removal from India and Pakistan and their eventual arrival in Kenya precipitated a crisis of individual and collective morality.

Estranged from their autochthonous homes, most of the immigrants temporarily abandoned their communities' values and moral codes to engage in some licentious involvement with pastimes that would never be approved of back in Pakistan. "Some of the well-known Kanjariyam (prostitutes) – including Amma Motijaan, Rehmat Bibi (also known as Rai Rehmo) and Gulzaar – were accepted by society at large. Later they married and or adopted children, and were able to amass much land and property in the Pangani area. [...] It was in total defiance of all social norms and rules" (55). "Many nights she [Hardei] lay in wait for him. Eventually, in the wee hours of the morning, the smell of stale alcohol would penetrate the room" (65). Hence, indulgences such as drunkenness, prostitution and wild partying threatened communal values so much so that it was the arrival of immigrant women in large numbers and their determination to rehabilitate their men folk that restored some of the old values. In all this, women are shown to be patient and determined to moderate and restore their men and redirect their energies to their social and cultural responsibilities.

One of Kapur-Dromson's strengths in this autobiography is the intensity with which she describes the challenges that the immigrants grappled with on the domestic front. Because of the increasing populations and lack of proper planning, the health situation soon deteriorated into outbreaks ofhygiene related diseases. Kapur-Dromson captures these historical moments in her work, thereby introducing the domestic and health angle to the political and economic challenges that the immigrants faced:

> Yes, Nairobi grew, but its growth aggravated its problems of health and sanitation. Low on water after prolonged drought, the town was wholly supplied from Nairobi river. Contamination led to many diseases. The shops and stores that served as living quarters became an ideal breeding for rats. The plague had come. [...] The 'black death' started spreading with alarming speed. Workers, relatives and friends succumbed to the disease, one by one. As dangers from lions decreased, hazards from plague increased. Shops were closed down. Business came to a standstill. The first outbreak of the disease was in 1902. Fresh epidemics continued until at least 1913 (87 – 89).

Presented in such a realistic mode reveals the colonial urban planning that was shaped by the then logic of racial separateness, where the colonial urban planners zoned Nairobi into geographical quarters by allocating particular spaces to specific racial groups with a corresponding decrease in the availability of amenities of health, transport and security for Europeans, Asians and Africans in that order.[4]

Kapur-Dromson also describes the various communal social challenges that surrounded family life of the pioneer immigrants, especially the latter's deviation from long-held values on such issues as alcohol and prostitution. She writes that:

> [i]n the proximity and intimacy of their dark tents, the coolies relieved their sexual urges. They took young African boys, and African women. Others intermarried with them according to their ways and customs. In a community dominated by males, these men were not choosy about the colour of the skin of the women with whom they had sex. Nor did they ask after their caste. By 1904, prostitution was rampant [...] Unofficially, the brothels' existence was sanctioned (72).

An insightful view in the work is Kapur-Dromson's projection of the foregoing problems as the basis of the many stereotypical perceptions of Europeans against Asians. This form of textual violence would then be summoned to warrant the continued marginalisation of the Asians from the central spaces in urban Nairobi. "They called them backward. They called them unhygienic. They called them lazy. Now, after the plague, the Indians were insulted further. 'They are foul liars, drunkards and thieves,' said a certain Lord Cranworth. 'They live in conditions under which no English farmer would dream of keeping his pigs'" (98). For Kapur-Dromson, the conditions of squalor and the debasing attitudes of the British against Asians provoked the latter's racial pride that would later manifest itself in the struggle for respect, recognition, and their closing ranks with Africans to struggle against colonialism, especially post-1947 when the mother country, India, attained her independence. That Kapur-Dromson at this point lists names of Indian luminaries who assisted Kenyan Africans in various ways in the latter's struggle for independence – Apa Pant, Desai, Makhan Singh and Pio Gama Pinto – affirms her pride and that of the wider community. Indeed, the subterranean argument in the novel is one that attempts to vindicate Asians from the rather common view that many of them were complicit in the colonial exploitation of Africans, and projects both communities as having been equal victims of British colonialism, or at least having been motivated by other reasons in their treatment of Africans.[5] An interesting dimension here is how Kapur-Dromson sees the racial relations in colonial Kenya through more or less the same lenses as her male compatriots: Asians and Africans as equal victims of white colonialism with all its dehumanizing structures, thereby reifying racial experiences over gender ones. The implicit suggestion seems to be that on the domestic front, the excesses of patriarchy – widely documented in earlier male-authored novels – were almost non-existent, only the "bad graces" (71) of alcoholism and prostitution that could still be traceable to the colonial structures that necessitated such adulterations of character of many pioneer Asian male immigrants. Does this demonstrate Kapur-Dromson's wholesome embrace of earlier narratives by Asian male writers? This seems to be the case.

## NARRATIVE STRATEGIES

In capturing the intertwined nature of gender, race and history, Kapur-Dromson employs narrative strategies that reflect the dialogic nature of these discourses. This she does largely by relying on intertextual references that simultaneously capture the unique position of Asians in the region within a historical context, but also signals towards the existing theoretical material on the state of immigrancy and the fragmentation and other forms of violence that immigrants tend to suffer. One of the ends in using this intertextuality is to capture the inter-racial climate of suspicion and condescension that generated a host of stereotypical perceptions of the Asian immigrants. It is in this light that one reads such quotations as "[w]e, the women of Kenya humbly implore your assistance to protect us and our children from the terrible Asiatic menace that threatens to overwhelm us..." (101); "To be in measurable distance of an Indian coolie is very disagreeable', [...] 'most Indians belong to the lowest class and are prone to unsanitary habits.' Plague, venereal diseases and other contagious ailments were attributed to them" (98). Yet the auto/biography delves deep into the past in order to provide the historical origin and basis of the stereotypes – which is the division of labour along groups of the immigrants – as well as their violent ways of sowing differences among the various subgroups within the immigrants along the colonialist logic of dividing its subjects along racial and ethnic lines.

> Stereotypical images of the Indian as the dukawallah were already beginning to take shape. Clad in a white *dhoti* and tight-fitting black coat, seated on a low divan surrounded by his ledger and account books, was the Hindu money lender. The Bohra iron monger wore a long white coat and loose

trousers, while the bearded Sikh was the *fundi* – great with hands and physical strength – a mender of all kinds of things. The slim Goan was the chef, or secretary. Insisting upon Portuguese cultural ties, he spoke Konkani at home, but denied any Indian background. In fact, the Goan was neither put at par with the Indian, nor was he under British rule. He was a Portuguese of Goan origin, and therefore, slightly higher in status and esteem than the Indian. (2007, 54)

It is knowledge of such petty perceptions – reflected in the sarcastic view of the Goans in the quotation above – that also necessitated a deep-seated yearning to forge a community that could weather, or at least accommodate, the range of emotional responses to its presence in the region; that were at best tolerated and, at worst, contemptuous. In doing this, the East African Asian communities fashioned a desire to support each other through involvement in religious and cultural rituals, and in the overall creation of a community. Indeed, the entire *From Jhelum to Tana* is a work that deals with the various ways in which a whole community can face adversity to grow in numbers and economically prosper.

Hence, Kapur-Dromson eschews the usual tendency among scholars and commentators to view East African Asian immigrants as a homogeneous entity. Pascale Herzig avers that "[i]n the diasporic South Asian context the term 'community' refers to an organised social group, which is defined by religion and language or place of origin. In addition, a community is also based on caste or sect, race and class." It is "traditionally the primary frame of reference besides the family for the Kenyan Asians" (2006, 102). The Asian immigrants that Kapur-Dromson concerns herself with in *From Jhelum to Tana* attribute significant value to the importance of sticking to community affiliations for individual and collective identities. Yet, her critical presentation of the same concerns is such that her narrative is also punctuated by a focus on some of the intrigues within the community that are generated by differences in religious affiliation, area of origin in India and personal dispensation. Herzig's view after Nagar and Leitner that "community often evokes the erroneous idea of a homogeneous and harmonious group," and her caution that "a community is also characterised by dissension, disharmony, and power hierarchies that celebrate some people and groups [that] marginalise others" (1998, 102) comes to mind. Indeed, Kapur-Dromson, even in acknowledging the place of community in the individual survival of colonialism and its attendant exclusions, also captures some these intra-communal tensions that to a large extent allows us to peep into the East African Asian immigrant community that has been viewed as an insular one: "Gone were the days of familiarity, or of comradeship. Gone even were the days of a common language" (219). The variegations in language and the entrenchment of intra-communal differences further undermined the idea and value of community to the immigrants that Kapur-Dromson portrays in her auto/biography. Her further claim that "[d]isputes became ethnicity-oriented [sic]. Bitter at times, less easily brushed off, nor as jovial. They were less straight forward and less naïve. Incessant scolding and shouted instructions were heard at all times of day and night in different languages. It was like the tower of Babel" (221) reinforces this point. Her projection of the caste-based hierarchies where some members of the immigrant communities were even more marginalised by their fellow immigrants becomes the ultimate indictment of the undersides of 'community.' "*Chura* women, the lowest of the low, the outcastes, the cleaners of the night soil, orna-mented the bedroom door with a *Serha*. [...] *Churas* were not invited; they didn't have to be. Somehow, they just seemed to appear wherever there was a festive occasion in the family – an engagement, a wedding, a childbirth – trotting from one Punjabi house to another" (174). This portrayal of the immigrant community demonstrates a critical inward gaze by an insider, and indeed exposes some of the ironies of margin-ality as understood within the framework of post-colonial, minority discourses.

An equally important form of intertextual referencing relates to how she punctuates her entire narrative with proverbs from the Punjabi (*Dur de dhol subane*, distant drums sound better, (17)) and Maasai (*Elala Onu Ai*, the eye of *Enkai* [God] is large (41)) proverbs, as well as songs from the Gikuyu, Indian and Luhyia:

> *Andi a thii ino itakena ni imue menyaga wege ali*
> *Turi andi amme bururi witte ni wa ngai umme...*
> (The blood of all people of this earth is the same
> I know that we are one people).
>
> [Gikuyu Song, 322]

> *Meera joota hai Japani ye patloon Inglishtani*
> *Ser pe laal topi rusi, phir bhi dil hai Hindustani ...*
> (My shoes are from Japan, trousers from England,
> A red hat from Russia, but my heart remains Inaisn...).
>
> [Indian film song, 287]

> *Mama mbe tsi mbindi nzi kumitsa*

*Nzi nzi naikumitsa...*
(Mother give me chickpeas to plant
During drought we would starve to death otherwise ....
[Luhyia song, 313)

This strategy allows for a dialogue between the various communities that some immigrants have come into contact with, which also demonstrates the fact of the author's knowledge of some of the oral artistry of the communities involved. Other aspects of orality are captured in the rendition of some aspects of Hindu mythology such as the "Arya Samaj fire ceremony" (78) and the Hindu chant of "*Om vaangma aasyay astu*" (73), all of which contribute to Kapur-Dromson's efforts at creating a community. The desire to imagine a community with varied backgrounds and shared presence is also seen in the juxtaposition of these Hindu and Gikuyu myths of origin. Describing the town of Fort Hall, or present day Murang'a, the author retells the Gikuyu and Mumbi myth that lives in the oral narratives of many Agikuyu, and which has earlier been rendered in the novels of Ngugi wa Thiong'o, notably *The River Between*. One can read such a gesture as one that expresses the writer's desire – and by extension that of the immigrant community – to develop a greater intimacy with the Africans and the land around them.

Such a quest is further manifested in the way Kapur-Dromson invokes the use of a journey motif to capture the intricate relationships of geography, politics, religion and history. Under the various sections of "solitary sojourn" (1 – 16), "across the seas" (17 – 40), "another voyage" (287 – 299) and "epilogue: my journey to the ancestral land" (408 – 419), Kapur-Dromson captures the ways in which physical journeys open up possibilities for individuals to broaden their experiences with physical space, inhabitants of those spaces and the philosophies they espouse. Equally important is the suggestion that the same journeys provoke in the travellers the impulse to search for the meaning of their lives and their communities, ultimately emerging more spiritually uplifted and knowledgeable in the history and culture of their people. What is significant in this auto/biography is that, unlike other novels by East African Asian writers, Kapur-Dromson envisions the possibility of a physical return to ancestral India, albeit briefly, for purposes of making a symbolic homecoming for the pilgrims. Yet, the author portrays this homecoming as somewhat sterile because it confirms the sense of loss due to her immigrant status as permanent, never to be recovered even by physical return: "I am in a daze. It was all too short and too sudden. I was not even prepared. I had been so unsure about whether we would get here... but we did! *I don't know if I have learnt anything from this trip that is going to be useful to me. I certainly did not find a lead into my family roots, nor saw their* havelis [houses(?)], *nor identified their* mohallah [neighbourhood]. In fact, I didn't really expect to reach Bhera" (415, my italics). Her uncertainty regarding the knowledge value of her journey and her inability to locate the exact home or even neighbourhood of her ancestors therefore confirms the reality of her dislocation and re-directs her back to Kenya as the only physical home she can ever find.[6]

With respect to earlier journeys described in *From Jhelum to Tana*, Hardei's decision to follow her husband – in the chapter "solitary sojourn" (1 – 16) – in Africa captures the two levels of exposure to the outside world: first, the woman's decision to transcend the limiting economic conditions from which her husband had already fled and, second, the author-narrator's engagement with authorised history that had, according to the sociological norms of gender, remained 'outside' the scope of a woman. This is significant because it offers a complimentary view of immigrant life in colonial and post-colonial Kenya, not necessarily in refuting or otherwise contesting earlier accounts that had hitherto muted the woman yet purported to represent her interests as a member of a larger, marginalised, community. It does this largely by giving the woman voice to comment on history if only to broaden its scope sufficiently enough to accommodate domestic transformations.

By reinserting women into the centre of immigrant histories in Kenya, therefore, Kapur-Dromson manages to shift our attention to a fact that, though known to us in respect of other histories, is often overlooked as far as it relates to East African immigrant communities: that histories and politics are gendered disciplines. The same re-insertion is also a statement that what we have so far been engaged with – the idea of immigrant communities – in actual fact is based on the male Self and the family as the basic nucleus of communal organisation, both of which therefore need more attention in order to enable us understand what else they can reveal. It is this reality that can justify a project of this nature, where one can read individual/family histories as captured in auto/biographical narratives as possible commentaries on their communal and national variants. Such a position encourages impulses of socio-cultural and political collectivism, where the individual is implicated in the plight of the entire community and vice versa. This attribute is valid for it relates to the Asian community in which Kapur-Dromson grounds her narrative. This attribute also validates my decision to read the individual/family histories in an auto/biography as part of a narrative of a community in pursuit of self-preservation and advancement in the wake of many and varied challenges.

## BY WAY OF CONCLUSION: BUILDING ON THE PAST

What does *From Jhelum to Tana* add to our understanding of East African Asian community? The answer to this question ought to have been the thesis of my paper and should have, naturally, come earlier. But the fact of its contentious nature persuaded me to end my argument with it partly for the reason that the work plays a supplementary role to the existing archive of and on East African Asian literature, in the sense of acknowledging the past as a basis of any forward movement. Kapur-Dromson's view that "I realized that the past was not to be forgotten, but to be built upon" (x) is as paradoxical as it is true. Not just the past of political, economic and social histories need a more complicated interpretation but also critical and theoretical building up on the existing critiques. Kapur-Dromson's autobiography acknowledges, *ala* Langston Hughes,[7] the state of marginality that registers loyalty to a land/region that has only allowed her tentative admission into nativity but also resigns her existence to a borderline along two worlds: "India and Kenya together sustained my physical and spiritual being. I needed them both; I couldn't do without either. India and Kenya became states of my mind" (x). This echo of Iain Chambers definition of home also explains Kapur-Dromson's embrace, even privileging, of dominant male-authored narratives on the place of Asian immigrants in the region's politics, at the seeming expense of gender concerns as one would ordinarily expect. True, she foregrounds matriarchs as protagonists whose experiences in the domestic spaces are seeds for the larger narratives, but the matriarchs remain largely apolitical and, in line with cultural socialisation of the wider Asian community, defer to the authority and wishes of their husbands and sons.

Perhaps more importantly is Kapur-Dromson's success in showing the incompleteness of our understanding of the history of immigrant communities in general. By focusing on political and economic histories at the expense of their social variants, we tend to miss out on the humanistic basis of the political and economic aspects of the immigrants' life, thereby having only a two-dimensional grasp on their realities. It is in light of this also that Kapur-Dromson chooses to supplement the political histories of Asian immigrants in the region with the personal and social strands of their communities and gender.

# *Notes*

1. For a helpful theorisation of revisionism, see Michael Green *Novel Histories: Past, Present, and Future in South African Fiction.* Johannesburg: Witwatersrand University Press, 2000 [1997], pp. 26 – 27.

2. Accordingly, "oral history" refers to a verbal transference of a historical deed that took place within the lifespan of a people of the generation during which the deed took place, while "oral traditions" are verbal transference of the same beyond the generation in which the deed occurred, provided the same can be traced to the original, initial speaker or observer. See Vansina, 1985: 196.

3. The people are duly acknowledged on pp. xiii – xiv of the work.

4. For a detailed discussion of this urban zoning in Nairobi, see Joseph Slaughter, "Master Plans: designing (National) Allegories of Urban Space and Metropolitan Subjects for Postcolonial Kenya." *Research in African Literature* 35.1 (2004): 30 – 51.

5. The idea that Asians were simply trying to survive an oppressive colonial regime by seeming to acquiesce to its strategies dominates the argument in Rasna Warah's autobiography that I have already referred to. It is the same line of thinking adopted by many critics in the work edited by Yash Ghai and Dharam Ghai. See *Portrait of a Minority: Asians in East Africa.* Nairobi: Oxford University Press, 1970.

6. Mildred Mortimer has undertaken detailed study on the importance of journeys in exposing travellers to diverse experiences and ways of thought. See *Journeys Through the French West African Novel.* London: James Currey Ltd., 1990.

7. This has been one of the most stinging criticism of Langston Hughes' evaluation of the Black Americans in the United States of America. In the poem 'I, Too', the persona grudgingly accepts to defer to whiteness and as a second citizen of America. See 'I, Too', in *Selected Poems Langston Hughes.* New York: Vintage Books, 1959. P. 275

# SECTION IV:
## Performance and Media

## Chapter 14

# THE SERIOUS PEOPLE OF "*RAHA*": THE POLITICS IN THE ETHNIC STEREOTYPING OF THE LUO IN OKATCH BIGGY'S *BENGA*

*Tom M. Mboya*
*Moi University, Kenya*

## INTRODUCTION

In the following pages I read the engagement by the Luo *benga* musician Okatch Biggy (1954-1997) with the ethnic stereotype of the Luo as a people that are "extravagant, self-centred, and exhibitionist; that ... use[...] their money for show and not to improve themselves" (Odinga 1967, 77). Okatch Biggy was the single most dominant *benga* artiste of the 1990s (Oywa, 1997). Partly on account of Okatch Biggy's practice of it, *benga* was the most important genre of music in Kenya in the 1990s. There is need to emphasize that this view of the Luo has a long history, and that it is not only held by non-Luos. Such is borne out by the citing by James Ogude in "The Vernacular Press and the Articulation of Luo Ethnic Citizenship: The Case of Achieng' Oneko's *Ramogi*" (2001) of:

> One erudite reader, Z A Otieno K'Oloo, [from his name, a Luo; and who, writing in the DhoLuo newspaper *Ramogi* of 20 January 1959] warned that the Luo were being left behind in social and economic development because they wasted a major portion of their income on women prostitutes, alcohol and cars. (2001, 44)

The historian Atieno Odhiambo observed that this view of the Luo was widespread, commenting that the ethnic group was "renowned by their African and European detractors alike for their epicurean hedonism and no thought for tomorrow" (in Ogude and Nyairo, 2007, 162).

My reading of Okatch Biggy's *benga*, and especially of its ethnic stereotyping of Biggy's Luo people in the 1990s – itself a robust, deconstructive engagement with the ethnic stereotyping of the same people by their compatriots and by some of their own – will argue that the said stereotyping is sensitive to the political nuances attendant to the phenomenon of the modern Kenyan "tribe" and its necessary outflow, "tribalism."

## TRIBALISM AND ETHNIC STEREOTYPING

Even the most cursory perusal of Kenyan political news commentaries and analyses of the early twenty-first century reveals the importance of ethnicity – or, as it is more frequently referred to, "tribalism" – in the politics of this multi-ethnic post-colonial East African country at the time. Wycliffe Muga, writing in *The National Star* daily, captures the situation correctly when he comments that:

> [H]owever much we [Kenyans] may be ashamed of it, we are still so tribal in our voting that the foundation of political power at a national level is having a regional [that is polite for "tribal"] voting block behind you (2009).

This has been the case since Kenya – and indeed modern Africa – was invented. In his autobiography *Freedom and After* (1963) the Kenyan statesman Tom Mboya records that the problem of "tribalism" in Africa was discussed at length at the All-African Peoples Conference in 1958. Mboya reports that the participants in the conference, and he was one, "thought it essential to isolate what you might call 'negative tribalism' from tribalism in the form of customs and culture" (1963, 68). For Mboya, as correctly summarized by Goldsworthy, there was:

> 'negative tribalism' – tribalism in its competitive, xenophobic aspects, especially as harnessed by cynical leaders to their own material ends ... [and] the comforts, the stability, security, and communality, which 'positive tribalism' brought to masses of people living in difficult conditions .... (1982, 3)

In Kenya, discussions of "tribalism" – and ethnicity in general – have since, though in a somewhat simplified fashion, been framed by this notion of there being "positive tribalism" and "negative tribalism". But from the time of Mboya, "positive tribalism" usually refers to that which is also more often called ethnic nationalism: the taking of pride in and defending of one's ethnic identity. On the other hand, "negative tribalism" usually refers to, to quote Chinua Achebe's famous definition, *"discrimination against a citizen because of his place of birth"* (1983, 7, emphasis in the original – the "place of birth" being euphemistic for ethnic identity).

The favored scholarly explanation for the significance of ethnicity in Kenya's – and Africa's – political affairs goes like this. The partition of Africa – that "dividing up" and "sharing out" of Africa among European countries that was agreed upon at a conference in Berlin in 1884-85 and which was largely accomplished on the ground by the end of 1901 (Davidson 1983, 3) – literally brought into being a new social continent. In the practice of the colonialism whose promises motivated, and which actually set in on the heels of, the partition, new countries were constituted, and within them new communities were formed (as reported in, among others, Freund 1984, 154) even as a new economic and political order was imposed on the entire continent. These new communities were constructed as "tribes", ethnic groups that had distinct cultural and physical borders that they deliberately secured. Those older communities that they neighbored were also transformed into "tribes". This "tribalization" of peoples was a political act undertaken with the aim of controlling the colonized peoples (Mamdani, 2004). Expectedly, and as the case of the construction of the Kalenjin as an ethnic group in Kenya in the 1940s (Simatei, 2010) demonstrates, the emergent ethnic elites played a major role in the constitution of these new "tribes." The elites recognized the potential of "tribe" as a tool they could use to further their political ambitions in the new world. Gradually, as this chapter will suggest, the commoners started participating in practices that consolidated these new "tribes."

Within the new countries, later to be rather oddly referred to as "nation-states", the imposed economic and political order encouraged inter-"tribal" competition and thus defined the relationships among the groups. In the words of Basil Davidson:

> On one hand, there was the colonial organization of many old communities into fewer tribes. Each new tribe or grouping,

as well as older states or communities which had existed long before, naturally tried to advance its own interests. Often, it had to do this in rivalry with other groupings. That was how colonial rule worked: it played off one grouping or "tribe" against another. (1983, 68)

In short, the inter-ethnic competition gave birth to "tribalism". For the citizens of the new "nation-states" loyalty to "tribe" superseded loyalty to the state. The inter-ethnic competition gave birth to the practice of favoring people from one's ethnic group in a multi-ethnic context, by persons whose responsibility is to the state to which all (his "tribes people" and the others) are citizens. It is no exaggeration to posit that the average citizen of these "nation-states" was a "tribalist," a person who, in the words of the historian William Ochieng', "is devoted to his particular tribe against the wider, more approved aims of national unity, modernization and justice" (1989, 215).

"Tribalism" has survived the transition of these African countries that were created by Europeans from colonies to so-called independent nation-states. This happened chiefly because the transition was not accompanied by the radical reorganization of the colonial systems of governance that made the practice of "tribalism" both sensible and necessary. And so the post-colonial state reproduces the "tribes" that were created by the colonial powers.

The interest of this chapter is not in rehearsing the obvious benefits (in the context of early twenty-first century Kenya) of "tribalism" to members of an ethnic community whose sons and daughters find themselves in positions to distribute national resources and go ahead to do so by discriminating against compatriots who do not belong to their ethnic group. Neither is the interest of the chapter in the rehearsal of the equally obvious evil (in the context of early twenty-first century Kenya) of "tribalism" on the flip side of that coin, which is the lack of opportunity to partake in the national wealth for members of an ethnic community that does not have its sons and daughters in positions that distribute national resources. That official state corruption is often engendered by "negative tribalism", as the fear of being locked out of opportunities to enjoy the resources of the state in the future inspires ethnic groups in power to focus on "eating" rather than "producing" national wealth, has been explored exhaustively (Wrong, 2009; Ogude, 2009). The interest of the chapter is in the ethnic stereotyping that simultaneously flows out of and feeds "tribalism."

The further dividing of African peoples by the European colonialists was supported by and fed the constructions and consolidations of perceptions of "tribal" unity (one-ness) and difference (other-ness). Communities that now inhabited the same political space and had to compete against one another for economic resources, and the political power to control them, saw themselves as having characteristics (beliefs, values, practices, habits and histories) that were markedly different from, even irreconcilably antagonistic to, those of their rivals. The fact of citizenship to the same (colonial) state, and the increased movement of peoples and ideas that that implied, meant that these constructed perceptions of "tribal" unity (one-ness) and difference (other-ness) circulated quite a bit among the different peoples, most often as stereotypes. With these perceptions, and the attendant suspicions and mistrusts and even hostilities, the inter-ethnic competition gave birth to the extension and distortion of pride in one's ethnic identity to involve the favoring of people from one's ethnic group in a multi-ethnic context, by persons whose responsibility was to the state to which all (his "tribes people" and the others) are citizens. "Tribalism", in its turn, fuelled the perceptions of difference and highlighted, mostly obliquely, the economic and political bases for the hatreds. In this way, "tribalism" consolidated ethnic stereotyping.

Not surprisingly, in the *Uhuru* (KiSwahili for "independence") era, the "tribal" perceptions take on a vicious edge in moments of political contest. These are, of course, moments of struggle over the control of the resources of the state. In these circumstances, what Barack Obama has described as "the hardening of lines, the embrace of fundamentalism and tribe" (2008, xi) happens. Mbugua wa Mungai discusses this feature of the politics of the post-colonial Kenyan state in his interesting paper "'Made in Riverwood': (dis)locating identities and power through Kenyan pop music" (2008). Focusing on the music of two musicians who are both well known and highly regarded in their Kikuyu ethnic group, Wa Mungai shows how some members of this ethnic group defined their community and characterized the other communities in Kenya that they considered to be political rivals in the years 2003-2008. The musicians Wa Mungai studies construct the Kikuyu as the "natural leaders" of multi-ethnic Kenya, being "God's people", hard workers who heroically fought for the country's independence. Their competitors, on the other hand, are enemies, less than fully human, devils, hyenas, lazy, war-like people who, because they collaborated with the colonial authorities and (in the case of their perceived main rivals, the Luo) do not traditionally practice male circumcision, cannot lay any legitimate claim to the leadership of the country.

One does not want to belabor here the in/accuracies in the "histori-cal bases" of this kind of argument. (We know for a fact that decoloni-zation was a complex process and in Kenya it can be argued that most ethnic groups actively participated in it.) More important for the work at hand is the fact that these kinds of "arguments" have power and influ-ence perceptions, and thereby shape realities. In Kenya, such arguments feed people's understandings of who they are, of what it means to be human – in addition to positioning them politically.

The point explains why intra-group discussions of the identity of a "tribe" in Kenya are of necessity informed by the perceptions other "tribes" have of that ethnic group. The following words of Oginga Odinga, recalling the motivations for his economics-based project of Luo ethnic nationalism in the colonial era, bears out the point:

> We Luo had also to assert ourselves among the other peoples of Kenya. I was haunted by the view which other Africans had of the Luo people. I had been hurt at Makerere by the accusations of fellow students from other tribes that the Luo were extravagant, self-centred, and exhibitionist; that they used their money for show and not to improve themselves. The Luo needed to build a sense of unity, common purpose and achievement ... It was time to instill confidence; time to show we could stand on our own feet in the modern world. (1967, 76-7)

## POLITICAL LUO *BENGA*

Before I get into a reading of Okatch Biggy's engagement with the stereotype of the Luo as an "epicurean hedonist" (Odhiambo in Ogude and Nyairo 2007, 162), here is a brief description of the music form *benga*, with a word on political Luo *benga*. (For a comprehensive defini-tion of the genre *benga* and Biggy's practice of it, see Mboya, 2009.) *Benga*, which has been argued to be the "national music of Kenya" (Kariuki, 2000), is a music form that was created sometime in the late 1950s – early 1960s by peasant and fisher folk Luo youth based in what since the colonial times has come to be considered the "tribal home-lands" of their ethnic group, on the eastern shores of Lake Victoria, in Kenya and Tanzania. There is general agreement in the various myths of origin of *benga* that the "roots" – to use Barz's word (2004, 108) – of the form are in traditional Luo musical theory and practice even though the form itself is "modern", significantly impacted by European culture, a point that is signaled by the fact that the chief instrument of the music type is the guitar. (For narratives of the form's origins see, among others, Stapleton and May, 1990; Odanga, 1999; Barz, 2004; Osusa et al, 2008; Mboya, 2009; and Ndege, 2010). The key instruments used in *benga* are the lead (solo) guitar, the rhythm guitar, the bass guitar and the drum-set. In *benga* the guitar is played by plucking the strings, in the same manner that the strings of the traditional Luo lyre, the *nyatiti*, are plucked.

As is only to be expected, given what invariably happens in the career of any art form that attracts consumers and practitioners from generations, regions and cultures other than where it originated (as can be explained by the extrapolation and application of Edward Said's "Traveling Theory" of how ideas move from one setting to another – 1983), there have been several developments in *benga* over its half century history. (Mboya, 2009 gives an account of the development of Luo *benga* from the 1980s to the 1990s while Osusa et al, 2008 sketch a telling though limited account of the spread of the genre both within and outside Kenya). But there still remain some definitive features of the form, especially as practiced by Luo musicians. These are most clearly discernible in the variety that was dominant in the 1970s. In those years *benga* solidified into:

> [T]he authentic [*benga*] form, [wherein] the three guitars har-
> monized each other, but the more telling characteristic of [this
> authentic form of] *benga* was that the guitar chorus which
> comes at the end of the song has no relation to the rest of the
> arrangement. (Stephen Sakwa, quoted by Kariuki, 2000)

This guitar chorus is better known as the climax, and is meant as the vigorous dance section of the song. The "rest of the arrangement" in the two part structure of "authentic" *benga* is the song part and is structured in a call-response format. The high-pitched lead guitar "calls" by playing the (sometimes simplified) melody that the choral verse "answers" by repeating and elaborating. The lead guitar does not play when the chorus is on, and therefore separates the song verses. This is the traditional arrangement of the music of the single-string Luo fiddle, the *orutu*. And indeed, the *benga* lead and rhythm guitars reproduce the sound of the *orutu*. In terms of rhythm, the *benga* beat is fast, "pulsating", from start to end. It is the rhythm of the Luo *ohangla* drums. And there is the definitive driving, melodic bass line which, inspired by the sounds of the Luo lyre, the *nyatiti*, becomes a sort of secondary percussion instrument.

*Benga* was at inception the "fun" music of Luo youth. Conse-quently, and not surprisingly, the Luo *benga* song is predominantly a love song. Besides love, the musicians sing in praise of their (invari-ably male) patrons and friends (Okumu, 2005). Also not surprising, considering the "youth fun" origins of the form, is the fact that *benga* is typically performed live in the evenings in small pubs in towns and market centers in the countryside. This is space associated with the idea of the consumption of leisure that got established in the dying days of colonialism (Odhiambo, 2002), the time of the modern Luo youth that also originated *benga*. There is a sense in which the dominant subjects of *benga* and space where the music is performed greatly complement each other. It is all about a "feel good ambiance".

The musical genre Luo *benga*, then, is generally apolitical. Even so, and due mainly to the work of the late Daniel Owino "Mwalimu D. O. 7" Misiani (1940-2006), there is a significant tradition of political Luo *benga*. Misiani started his musical career just as the music genre that would later come to be known as *benga* was emerging. He then picked up the genre and in his practice helped define and popularize it. He became its most famous practitioner in the 1970s-1980s. The reason for Misiani's success was not only his musical genius. In the words of James Ogude:

> The popularity of Misiani's Shirati Jazz ... must be in large measure, attributed to his relentless engagement with Kenya's public sphere over the last four decades or so; specifically the political sphere which had been defined by repression and political intolerance in which all voices of dissent from within and outside the reigning regimes were eliminated. (in Ogude and Nyairo, eds., 2007, 175)

At the verbal level, Misiani creatively deployed fabulization, riddling and laughter to great effect in his Luo-centric critique of the Kenyan state (Ogude, 2007; Oloo, 2007; Amuka, 1992). The "dissident music" (Ogude 2007, 187) of D. O. Misiani and the consequences of its practice for the musician (like his run-ins with the Kenyan authorities) have deservedly attracted a lot of critical comment (Ogude, 2007; Oloo, 2007; Amuka, 1992).

Even though it is only Misiani of Luo *benga* musicians who so con-sistently practiced political *benga* to the extent that it is no exaggera-tion to describe him as a political Luo *benga* artiste, there have been, as is only to be expected, other political Luo *benga* songs. The defini-tive Luo *benga* convention of praise for friends and patrons has been exploited through the years as a doorway into political Luo *benga* by various artistes who have composed the odd political Luo *benga* song. Such musicians have extended the subjects of praise to include political figures. Raila Odinga, the most prominent Luo politician in Kenya since the reintroduction of multi-party politics in the country in 1992, has since the mid-1990s been a favorite subject of the Luo *benga* political praise song.

There is, then, a tradition of political Luo *benga* that allows for artistic flexibility. But, and however significant, it is a minority tradition. It may very well be that the treatment of Misiani by the state authorities has persuaded the majority of Luo *benga* artistes to remain true to the genre's roots as "youth fun" music. It can also be that a majority of Luo *benga* artistes simply stick to the genre's roots out of a puritanical impulse.

Okatch Biggy, who earlier in his career played the drums for D. O. Misiani (Juma, 2007), was in the 1990s obviously aware of political *benga*. Even so, Biggy is not a directly political musician. The political messages in his *benga* are embedded in the narratives of romance and personal friendship – his celebrations of "*raha*" – that make up his oeuvre.

## "THE SERIOUS PEOPLE OF *RAHA*"

In the 1990s Okatch Biggy brazenly celebrated a complex of characteristics that is often taken both by Luos and non-Luos to define Luo ethnicity. Indeed, it is this complex of characteristics that informs the dominant images of Luo-ness in Kenyan mass media. This stereotype is perhaps best embodied in the figure of the conspicuous consumer JVC (JaLuo Very Complicated [meaning: Ever complicated Luo]) that one encounters in advertisements, jokes, movies (like Luther, the main male character in *Malooned*) and popular music (a remarkable example of JVC's appearance in song being the character who stars in the intro to "Otonglo Tyme" by Poxy Presha).

The dominant impression created by the activities of the characters in Okatch Biggy's song-texts is one of people having fun or, as we say it in Kenya, of people "eating – or consuming – '*raha*'". "*Raha*" is originally a KiSwahili word for "pleasure" but it is now widely diffused into Kenya's other languages, DhoLuo included, in which it signifies a lifestyle characterized by a love for music/dance, liquor, fashion and sex.

The characters in Okatch Biggy's songs are either involved in love games (the love songs, which do not shy away from describing sexual play) or they are partying (the praise songs, which invariably include passages describing a feast hosted by the man being praised). The following excerpt from the song "Okello Jabondo", in which Biggy imagines how he would be eulogized upon his death, gives a snapshot of his celebration of the *"raha"* lifestyle:

*Aywagra Okatch*
I am weeping, Okatch
*To gima kiny akiya*
But I don't know what tomorrow holds
*Ka po akwongonu*
Should I precede you [that is, should I die before you]
*Chieng' ukowa Gem utim neno nyaka e liel*
Escort my body to Gem [his home], say my eulogy at the funeral
*Ne walemoga pamoja*
We used to pray together
*Ne wamethoga pamoja*
We used to drink alcohol together[1]
*To gima kiny akiya*
But I don't know what tomorrow holds
*Cosmos ne wayweyogae*
We used to rest at the Cosmos [a pub]
*Kisumu kanyo ne wamethoga*
We used to drink alcohol there in Kisumu
...
*Collee Mazee nuywaga*
Collee Mazee [a famous *benga* artiste, now deceased] you will mourn me
[that is, you will perform at my funeral]
*Kabasselleh Ochieng' nukowa*
You will escort me Kabasselleh Ochieng' [a famous *rumba-benga* artiste, now deceased]
*Owino Misiani nuywaga*
You will mourn me Owino Misiani [a famous *benga* artiste, now deceased]
*Ni wana ziki ema alosogo*
It is the musicians I am talking to
*To gima kiny akiya*
But I don't know what tomorrow holds

The *"raha"* lifestyle is about the enjoyment of alcohol, music, food, good clothes and sex – even, as in the above case, during the bad times. While Okatch Biggy's praise songs invariably have as their centerpiece a feast hosted for him by the subject of his praise, usually in the subject's home, his love songs delight in describing and hinting at sexual play. The following passage from "Nyathi Nyakach", which describes the welcome the lover (the character Okatch) is given by his beloved Nyathi Nyakach upon arrival in her home market center, Sondu, is typical:

> *Super, natimi nadi ma?*
> My Super, what will I do with you?
> *Sianda mabeyogi nonega nono*
> These beautiful bottoms will kill me "for nothing"
> *Sianda madongogi nowita oko*
> These big bottoms will throw me out
> *Sondu rach, to ng'iyo chuna nyaka abi* x2
> Things are bad in Sondu [it is the time of the politically instigated violent
> "land" clashes, and Sondu is a hot spot], but my relationship forces
> me to come x2
> *Jaber ogoyo sim, Toti wuondaga n'otuo* x2
> The beautiful one has telephoned, babe deceives me that she is unwell x2
> *Kara to Toti dwaro Biggy Okatch*
> But babe wants Okatch Biggy
> *Jaber okelo wiye n'odwa n'onena*
> The beautiful one stubbornly insists that she wants to see me
> *Atoti ogolo onyo kosiemo godo Okatch*
> Babe has cautioned Okatch
> *"Kileo Okatch Dola ok achak alimi"*
> "Should you fail to turn up, Okatch Dola, I'll never visit you again"
> ["visit" of necessity involves a sexual encounter in this context]
> *Ni "Kik iketh love wa"*
> And "Don't spoil our love"
> *Kara daleo nadi, ma?*
> But how could I have failed to turn up?
> ...
> *Kara natimi nadi, ma?*
> But what will I do with you?
> *To ka ne alor Sondu, Okatch*
> Then when I alighted in Sondu, Okatch
> *Rambanyana ma manyako ringo romona*

My girl with the beauty gap in her teeth runs to meet me
*Atwech nyaloyo atoti mula mos, to nyodha*
The sharp-dresser, champion-girl, babe, caresses me, then
kisses me
*Atoti nyodha mos, to kaya*
Babe kisses me tenderly, then bites me
*Atoti mula mos, to ndhuna*
Babe caresses me, then pinches me
*Toti tera dalagi*
Babe is taking me to her home
*Ni mondo amos mamane*
So I can greet her mother

The equating of *"raha"* with Luo lifestyle is, obviously, reductionist, stereotypical. But like all stereotypes, since despite their general arbitrariness they are attempts at understanding complex phenomena, the association is rooted in some (more often than not deliberately misapprehended) aspect of factual reality (Williams 2003, 129-36). In the case of the characterization of the Luo as a people who love *"raha"* one can point out that there is a strong epicurean strand in pre-colonial Luo culture (Mboya, 1997). Traditional Luo culture is rich in musical tradition, it that places a premium on ritual celebration, and valorizes good grooming.

I will now situate Okatch Biggy's celebration of *"raha"* in its historical context, and show how it is part of an engagement with the ethnic stereotyping of the Luo that has political connotations. Before I do so, I want to digress briefly and say a few things about the Congolese movement known as *"La Sape"* – especially the version of *"La Sape"* that was popularized and vigorously promoted in the 1970s-1980s by the Zairean (now Congolese) musician Papa Wemba – before I read the *"raha"* in Biggy's *benga*. It is my hope that in so doing my reading will be clearer.

*"La Sape"* celebrates sartorial elegance (Wrong 2001, 171-9). But "allegedly" does this in such a deliberate and sustained manner that its practitioners (*"sapeurs"*) consider it a faith, the religion of the cloth. It even has a quasi-church structure with saints, popes, bishops, etc. The definitive feature of *"La Sape"* is the glorification of Western haute couture fashion. *"Sapeurs"* dress in the most expensive stylish clothes from the Western world. Their lives revolve around the enjoyment of Congolese popular music.

*"La Sape"* is an interesting movement in that it holds sway in a generally poor society where the majority, most of the *"sapeurs"* included,

cannot afford to eat three meals a day. To understand its power one must go back to the context of its ascendancy, Mobutu Sese Seko's Zaire. The dictator Mobutu came up with a cultural policy that urged his subjects to take pride in their "real" cultural identities, their identities before their modification by their contact with Western culture. He encouraged the "updating" of these identities to suit the modern times, rather than the "uptaking" of Western identity. This policy Mobutu named Authenticity. Under it Zaireans had to drop their European – "Christian" – names. They also had to start dressing like "real" Africans. The men wore the "Abacost" [from "*Abats la costume*", French for "down with the Western-style suits (and neck-ties)"], a Mao-style shirt, usually in "African" print; and the women wore flowing "African" wraparounds. All the Authenticity was in support of Mobutu's warped idea of political organization, wherein unquestioning loyalty was due the "real" African leader, the all powerful chief who owned virtually everything and thereby controlled everyone – in this case Mobutu himself.

"*La Sape*" was a response to this political context. Directly, it was a response to the stifling strictures of Authenticity, and especially the narrow definition of "real" Zairean/African culture. The "*sapeurs*" opted to embrace Western culture, and specifically its most "decadent" – in the view of the proponents of Authenticity – expression. But, obviously, "*La Sape*" was also an expression of disaffection for the political organization in Zaire. It is this political angle that best explains the irrationality of the starving slum-dweller who insists on turning out in the most expensive clothes.

Exactly as it happens in relation to "*La Sape*", as the paragraphs immediately above make clear, reading the celebration of "*raha*" in Okatch Biggy's *benga* in its historical context gives us meanings that are not apparent when the phenomenon is apprehended ahistorically. When Biggy started recording his music in the early 1990s, about half a century had passed since Oginga Odinga had been "haunted by the view which other Africans had of the Luo people" (1967, 76-7), and which he had recalled and recorded three decades later in his autobiography *Not Yet Uhuru* (1967).

In the 1990s, also, competitive multi-party politics was being reintroduced in Kenya, with the real and imagined opportunities that the development afforded for "tribes" to secure control of the country's resources. As a result the country was being thrust into an era of intense political campaigning. For the Luo, who perceived that they had been politically – and consequently economically – marginalized in Kenya since Independence (Ogude, 2007; Oloo, 2007), the possibility of coming to power was especially exciting. These facts are pertinent when trying to comprehend the stereotyping of the Luo in Okatch Biggy's music. For, even though it appears to adhere to the subjects matter that defined the genre from the beginning, that is love and praise, Biggy's celebration of "*raha*" is in important ways a complex response to ideas such as those that Oginga Odinga responded to, to the ideas in responses like Oginga Odinga's, and to ideas like those propagated by the musicians studied by Mbugua wa Mungai.

The "*raha*" lifestyle that the male and female characters in Okatch Biggy's music lead superficially affirms the stereotype of the Luo as "extravagant, self-centred, and exhibitionist; that they use [...] their money for show and not to improve themselves" (Odinga 1967, 77). And yet not everything is as simple as it looks. For one, the participants in "*raha*" in Biggy's songs are not good-for-nothing loafers. These men and women are achievers. They are hardworking successful professionals and businesspeople. In that sense they are leaders, and not only of Luos. Their excellent work is acknowledged by non-Luos, including government agents (part of the praise for Agutu Nyowila in "Agutu Nyowila" is that: "*Tich kaka irito jiduto pako/ Kata D.O. bende oyie, D.C. bende oyieni*" [The way you do your job/ Even the D.O. and the D.C. acknowledge that it is good]), and even by "white people" – and so we hear in "Caleb Doctor":

> *University ne isomo doctor ema ne opuonji*
> You studied medicine at university
> *Caleb okalo e penj*
> Caleb passed his exams
> *JaUgunja riek to ikonyo oganda mayudo chandruok*
> The man from Ugunja [a place] is clever, and he assists those
> who are suffering
> *Nyaka jorachare gi yie*
> Even the white men know it.

Since the time of the struggle for *Uhuru* "hard work" has been valorized in the official Kenyan political speak. Jomo Kenyatta prepared his compatriots for the responsibilities of self-government with the slogan "*Uhuru na Kazi*" [KiSwahili: "Independence with hard work"] (Kenyatta 1968, 215-6). Just under a half a century later, both the main rivals in the hotly contested 2007 Presidential Elections used the idea in their slogans: Mwai Kibaki's Party of National Unity (PNU) had "*Kazi Iendelee*" [KiSwahili: "Let the hard work continue"] while Raila Odinga's

Orange Democratic Movement (ODM) had *"Kazi Ianze"* [KiSwahili: "May the hard work begin"].

Now, even though in Biggy's perception the Kenyan government mistreats the Luo by marginalizing them and denying them "development" (a point signaled in "Agutu Nyowila" when reference is made to the absence of a proper road to fish-rich Uyoma, which indicates government indifference to or stunting of the fishing industry on which a significant number of Luos depend), its agents cannot deny the obvious industry and good workmanship of the Luo celebrants of *"raha"*. The validation by the "whites" of Luo workmanship in its turn serves two functions: one, it is "objective", being removed from the "tribal" competition that clouds judgment in Kenya; and two, the "whites" are the "owners" of the modernity that Kenyan Africans aspire for (including the medical practice of the kind that Caleb is engaged in), and which makes the basis of judging others as progressive and therefore fit to lead or primitive and therefore only fit to be led. Not surprisingly, those who successfully embrace Western culture are singled out for praise. Thus we hear of Rose Nyar Yala in the song that takes her name for its title:

> *Rosemary nene ang'eyo ka pod somo*
> I knew Rosemary when she was still in school
> *Kor kwano nene ing'eyo gi kingereza*
> You were good at mathematics and English
> *Sport bende nene ing'eyo ne iyombo chwo*
> You were also good in sports, you beat men
> *Koda mon.*
> And women.

Mathematics and English are in this context the most modern of subjects. Excelling in them, and in sports which in Western formal education is seen as crucial to the edifying disciplining of the body, are indicative of a comprehensive immersion in Western civilization. Given that the embrace of the West is in Kenya taken for being modern (with connotations of "civilized") and is valorized, even the adoption of those aspects that other African nationalists reject is not frowned upon. In fact, far from it, it is praised. Thus we find Biggy singing approvingly of Adhiambo Nyakobura's beauty (in "Adhiambo Nyakobura"): *"Yie wiyi iloso adimba, ichal odiero nyar jorachar"* ["You have made your hair beautifully; you look like a white woman"].

As a result of their professional success Okatch Biggy's characters are materially comfortable. They are in a position to assist and uplift those of their "tribes people" that are struggling, and they do so (the praise songs). Hence the praise for Isaiah Ogwe's character (in "Isaiah Ogwe"): "*Kido no to ber, kido mapidho kiye, jo ma onge godo*" ["That character is good; the character that takes care of orphans and the destitute"]. The highlighting of the awareness of their social responsibilities by these people of "*raha*" further undercuts the notion that they, and by extension the Luo in general, are not a "serious people"; that they are not interested in "development". The notion is usually perpetuated with insidious intent, the logic being that not being "serious" the Luo should therefore not be entrusted with the political leadership of multi-ethnic Kenya. This is the political thrust of the "othering" in the stereotype of the Luo as a people of "*raha*".

More immediately, in the context of the politics of Kenya in the 1990s, the highlighting of the awareness of their social responsibilities by these people of "*raha*" sharply contrasts and critiques the insensitivity that had come to be associated with the Moi leadership in the Luo psyche. Okatch Biggy's most directly political song, which is also arguably his biggest "hit", "Nyathi Nyakach" dwells on the callousness of the Moi government. But by celebrating "*raha*" in the form of the feasting, Biggy is also affirming a value system that encourages social consciousness and responsibility. One is only a valuable member of the community if he or she contributes to its survival and general wellbeing. And this can be done by making it possible for the individual members of the group to bond.

With the endorsement of "*raha*" Okatch argues against the project to reconstitute the image of the Luo by the likes of Oginga Odinga. Biggy's is a deconstructive strategy not unlike that which the Negritudists undertook when they picked up the term used by "white" racists to abuse the "black" person (*negre*, "nigger"), accepted it as a proper term that refers to the "black" person and infused it with positive values (Loomba 1998, 211-2). Biggy agrees with those who characterize the Luo as "a people of '*raha*'", and then presents that enjoyment of "*raha*" as the sensible way of living. There is no apology being made; in fact, there is no reference to Odinga's "other Africans" (1976, 77) who took issue with the perceived lifestyle of the Luo in Biggy's songs. There is simply the celebration of "*raha*".

## CONCLUSION

Biggy, then, picks up a potentially politically damaging ethnic stereotype of the Luo that is already in circulation, as a "non-serious" boisterous "people of *raha*", and imbues it with positive connotations. In

Biggy's maneuver we see both the political motivation for and purpose of the celebration of the ethnic stereotype – by extension we see the political motivation and purpose of the project of ethnic nationalism or "positive tribalism". It stands to sense that a people that had been marginalized, and whose marginalization was often justified on cultural grounds, should react by defiantly embracing the demeaned culture and thus affirm themselves. An obvious "good" for the Luo ethnic nationalist in the celebration of "*raha*" in Okatch Biggy's *benga* comes from the fact that presented as a positive complex of characteristics, "*raha*" makes the Luo person unashamed, even proud of his/her ethnic identity in a polity where that identity is assaulted by others – by the ethnic group's "detractors" (Odhiambo in Ogude and Nyairo 2007, 162). Those who would attack "*raha*" are perceived to be continuing – whether consciously or not – the political project of devaluation, and resultant dispossession and oppression, that the Luo community has had to battle with in the state of Kenya. Following Steve Biko, I argue that this pride in himself then empowers the Luo "positive tribalist" (1978, 152-3), like Okatch Biggy: it positions him to be an agent in his/her political and economic affairs; it enables him/her to act.

The underside to this production of a positive ethnic stereotype in the context of early twenty-first century Kenya is, of course, the unwitting contribution by the "positive tribalist" to the continuation of the status quo in Kenyan politics. The end political result of the project of the "positive tribalist" – who usually is, in James Ogude's memorable phrase, "imprisoned within an ethnic paradigm" (2007, 176) – is a replacement of the political supremacy of one "tribe" with the dominance of a second "tribe". Since no fundamental transformation of the political system is envisaged by this "positive tribalist", the injustices that create the underdevelopment of the Kenyan state in the first place, including the "negative tribalism", are perpetuated.

## Note

1. In the live version recorded on video Biggy adds the line "*Ne wasero ga pamoja*" [We used to seduce women together].

## Chapter 15

# FROM DANSI TO BONGO FLAVA: POPULAR MUSIC AND POLITICS IN TANZANIA, 1955-2005

*Maria Suriano*
*University of the Witwatersrand*

## INTRODUCTION

Drawing on oral sources collected during various fieldtrips to Tanzania between 2000 and 2009 as well as literature on popular arts and power primarily by East African scholars, this chapter explores how the forms and functions of popular music have changed in tandem with the major political shifts in Tanzania (Tanganyika until 1964) between the mid-1950s and the mid-2000s.

In chronicling the major changes over time in the relationship between musicians and power in colonial and postcolonial Tanzania, I will first highlight popular singers' views on colonial rule. Then I will illustrate the links between musicians and Tanzanian politicians after independence. Lastly, I will examine the attitudes of *Bongo Flava* artists towards local politicians - and, to a minor extent, towards the elders - in the context of multi-partyism. I will theorize *Bongo Flava* as a particular democratic public space within postcolonial Tanzania.

The period examined can be divided into three phases: the "nationalist phase" (from 1954, when Tanganyika African National Union, henceforth TANU, was founded, to independence in 1961); the phase between 1961 and 1985; and the period of economic and political liberalization (from 1985 onwards).[1] In each of these periods, popular music has mirrored and produced Tanzanian broader socio-political reality.

Fabian (1978) has established that music and dance have the power to affect social and political realities. This insight has been pursued in more recent works which has shown that popular culture have shaped – not only reflected – the results of community-based socio-political struggles (for colonial Zanzibar see Fair 2001).

In Africa, perhaps more than in other continents, aesthetics, morals and politics are intimately associated, and there exists a long-standing connection between popular arts and political language. Besides being an attribute and symbol of power, art in Africa is an essential component of political landscape (Jewsiewicki 1988, 2). In Central and Southern Africa, the abuse of power has often been openly condemned in poetry and songs. African societies have sometimes tolerated and even welcomed such artistic forms "as a major channel of communication between the powerless and the powerful, the client and the patron, the ruled and the ruler" (Vail and White 1983, 887-8).

The terms "popular" and "politics" need to be briefly discussed. The complex and flexible term "popular" does not merely refer to "people" (as a group of citizens who constitute a community), but rather to the "masses" - often labeled as "common" or "ordinary" people, or "commoners", "subordinate", "marginalized", "disenfranchised", "subaltern" social groups – as opposed to educated elites (Bayart 1981, 74). However, popular artists in Africa have often created art which is commercial and at the same time well received by local elites and the masses (Barber, 1987). The urban masses, which first experienced popular culture (Fabian 1978, 315), do not represent a homogeneous category unified by a shared consciousness of their condition (Bayart 1981, 75).

As far as politics is concerned, as Bayart has pointed out in an influential article on politics "from below" in sub-Saharan Africa, according to conventional political science politics is carried out solely by the state and the ruling party, which are the *object politiques* (political objects) *par excellence* (1981, 68). Yet, political expressions (sometimes symbolic) through popular cultural forms have often been articulated beyond the channels of official politics (Bayart, 1981); they are characterized by a high blend of adaptation and resistance to the state system (Scott, 1990). Popular modes of political expression (or UPOs: "unidentified political objects"; Martin 2002) possess the quality of *politique* following the paradigm of Bayart (1981, 65). Moreover, the political potential contained in popular culture does not necessarily imply an open challenge to the system.

The "commoners" are not passive and submissive; instead to some degree they exercise autonomous action; even oppressive regimes have not been "totally insensitive to popular pressure and expressions of protest" (Jeffries 1978, 208 qtd. in Bayart 1981, 54). Popular forms of political expression are "a field within which the 'political' and the 'everyday' are mediated" (Kaarsholm and James 2000, 203).

## DANSI, NGOMA AND TAARAB, 1955-1961

In British Tanzania, the administration imposed various forms of censorship on musical performances on the basis on their "immorality" (Askew and Kitime 2006), and created a system of fees and licenses that regulated the organization of music performances and *vichekesho* (theatrical sketches). After 1945, the British also provided "detribalized" urban Africans with a number of Western-oriented recreational activities. These attempts to control popular cultural forms did not, however, prevent African musicians, dancers, poets and artists at large from delivering anti-colonial messages in their performances (for Kandoro, a poet and political activist in the Lake Province, see Kitogo 2002). During the struggle for independence, popular music turned out to be essential for entertaining, unifying, and politicizing Africans throughout the territory. In the mid-1950s, after the formation of TANU, popular cultural forms such as music were widely used to criticize the British occupation, as well as popularize Julius Kambarage Nyerere and other TANU leaders. Most songs were composed and performed in Swahili, which was widely spoken and understood by the African masses, therefore became the vehicle of the struggle for independence throughout the territory. My argument is that, far from being a harmless safety valve or an outlet for the voiceless masses, artistic creation actively participated in the transformations of late colonial political culture and practices.

The three main types of popular music in colonial Tanzania were *ngoma, dansi,* and *taarab.* The term *ngoma* (drum/dance) also refers to events involving drumming, singing and dancing. *Ngoma* performances originally took place in rural contexts, where most performances were associated with specific ethnic groups, while in urban contexts they were mostly multi-ethnic (Geiger, 1997).

The genre known as *dansi* or *muziki wa dansi* (literally means: dance music), associated with ballroom and couples dancing, appeared in the late 1920s and became popular after 1945 mainly in urban areas. Guitar music played by "jazz" bands, *dansi* was heavily influenced by various Afro-Cuban genres and other styles played at that time in other parts of the world. From the outset *dansi* was multi-ethnic and cosmopolitan.

*Taarab* is sung Swahili poetry that originated in Zanzibar at the turn of the nineteenth century, and encompassed African, Indian, and Middle Eastern elements (Askew, 2002). Initially associated with Zanzibar islands and the Swahili coast, in late colonialism *taarab* became increasingly popular in upcountry towns such as Mwanza, on the shore of Lake Victoria (*mzee* Sigda 2005).[2]

Despite colonial efforts to organize apolitical cultural activities for the colonized, in the 1950s these three styles turned against British power. Africans made deliberate use of relatively new popular music genres (such as *dansi*) to their own advantage, and attributed new meanings to older ones (such as *ngoma*).

According to *mzee* Mustafa Ally, despite the British ban on TANU activities in the Lake Province (to which Mwanza belonged) in the central years of TANU diffusion (1954 - 1958), *dansi* musicians in Mwanza still praised TANU leaders, producing "positive publicity to promote them", so that "people would become aware of what exactly TANU was" (*mzee* Ally 2005).

According to *mzee* "Kabwela" (literally means: proletarian), who participated in the independence struggle in the 1950s Mwanza, concerts and dance parties were used to collect money for TANU, mainly when competitions between two jazz bands took place (*mzee* Kabwela 2005). *Mzee* Kabwela also recalls that *taarab* songs performed in the 1950s Mwanza gave:

> hope, encouragement. Apparently [they expressed] just the joy of *taarab* music, but inside ... there was a political message: music united people, and induced them to perceive themselves as TANU members with a sense of belonging. Colonialists ... thought that [*taarab* bands] were just Swahili groups, playing some kind of music from the [Swahili] coast, which taught civilization [*ustaarabu*] to upcountry people, such as the renouncing of ethnic belonging. But within it there was a political message. Other songs praised Queen Elisabeth [II] and King George [VI?]; it was necessary to insert them in the repertoire. (*mzee* Kabwela 2005)

As the late *mzee* Hezronie Ndonho recollected,[3] while TANU was banned, the nationalist struggle was carried out not only through *dansi* and *taarab* performances, but also through *ngoma* songs (*mzee* Ndonho

2005). During *ngoma* performances and competitions, both in Mwanza and in its outskirts, someone would be in charge of selling TANU cards, and members of *ngoma* groups themselves made collections of money for the party.

Kaarsholm has argued that in Bulawayo, during the ban on political meetings (1960s and 1970s), "cultural activity took on a new significance as 'substitute politics'" (1999, 245). A similar mechanism took place in Mwanza nearly two decades before, due to the ban on TANU.

My interviewees in Dar es Salaam gave similar testimonies (*binti*[4] Ali (2000); *binti* Kamba 2000; *mama* Elisa 2000; Geiger 1997; Tsuruta 2003): by the late 1950s, almost all musicians carried TANU cards. Popular performers and their audiences, mostly illiterate or semi-literate, enthusiastically and intentionally contributed to spread the message of *Uhuru* (independence). Although uneducated people may have lacked "Western" political training, they did not lack political consciousness and acumen, and their "culture of politics" was central in building the nation.[5]

Moreover, oral data personally collected in Morogoro, Kilosa and Kimamba in 2000 suggests that patterns in minor inland towns and in major coastal cities were similar. Musical performances were tools to cover independence claims, encourage audiences to join TANU and unite people across the territory.

During the struggle for independence, popular music was not just a means of discussing the impact of power or a tolerated form of criticism. Rather, many musicians joined the main liberation party, and songs were active instruments in fighting British occupation.

This is not to say that popular music was used as a political tool only after the setting up of TANU. Amongst a number of East African cultural-linguistic groups, songs and performances have been used as a socio-political commentary since pre-colonial times (cf. Mwaura 2007, 201; Songoyi, 1988).

This close connection between popular music and the articulation of socio-political grievances can be observed in some semi-rural environments, where there is a long history of resistance through *ngoma*. Under German occupation (1886-1918), a type of *ngoma* known as *wigashe*, popular among the Sukuma communities (mainly in Mwanza region), were characterized by bold criticism of German officials (Songoyi 1988, 2005).[6] In Sukumaland, Gumha Misinzo, the first known Sukuma singer who openly attacked the colonial power, was threatened with arrest by German soldiers for his mocking songs.

287

During the 1950s another Sukuma songster, a peasant and TANU member, Kalikali Ng'wana Mbagule, openly sang many protest songs against the British occupation. Kalikali's main action was to use the *wigashe* tradition to mobilize the masses and fight colonialism. Although the language of these songs was Sukuma (thus understood by a rather limited number of people), not only did these performances invite rural inhabitants to join TANU, but they were used as a tool for encouraging Sukuma-speaking people to become aware of colonial injustices perpetrated against all Africans across the territory.

Among the aforementioned styles, *dansi* arguably played the most intriguing role. If *dansi* was initially associated with urban elites (Ranger, 1975), especially in the post-1945 period it was adopted by non-elite (mainly young) urban Africans. This relatively recent genre resulting from transnational musical connections was accompanied by Western style clothes and couple dancing. These elements represented a transgression to parental norms and at the same time allowed both musicians and listeners to acquire a modern identity.[7] As with cricket in India, *dansi*, besides being used for nationalist claims, became a tool for appropriating the "means of modernity" (cf. Appadurai [1996] 2005, 89-113).

## THE YEARS OF TANU-CCM, 1961-1985[8]

Looking at popular music and arts between independence (1961) and the end of socialism (1985), the most striking feature of this period is the effort put by Tanzanian leaders in creating the nation, and their endeavour to control popular music in order to carry out the process of nation building.[9]

The Ministry of Culture and Youth – formed by President Nyerere in 1962 – deemed arts to be a means of educating the masses (cf. Songoyi 1988). Cultural policies implemented during this period required full compliance to the one-party state established in 1965.

*Mzee* Ndonho bemoaned that prior to independence, the singing of political and anti-colonial songs was an initiative of the musicians, who were not influenced by politicians (*mzee* Ndonho 2005). A point on which Ndonho and other interviewees agreed on is that soon after independence, the state bureaucracy "made use" of musicians to foster the purposes of endorsing the ruling party (*mzee* Ndonho 2005; *mzee* Masunga 2005; *mzee* Ngoffilo 2005). In other words, having witnessed the potent impact of popular music in the late colonial years, postcolonial policy makers turned popular songs into a tool of communication to spreading the TANU political agenda.

In this context, and despite being a TANU member, the Sukuma composer Kalikali in 1963 again used the *wigashe* tradition of musical challenges, by observing in song lyrics that his fellow villagers continued to live in poverty while local leaders had became wealthy. In another song he openly deplored political corruption, mocking the politicians by making reference to their fat buttocks due to the money they had stolen. Having ignored repeated warnings from government officials to stop singing anti-government songs, in 1965 Kalikali was jailed for two months. He apparently stopped criticizing the state power for a while, but later on he composed another song against the forced relocation into *ujamaa* villages, emphasizing the violence of this political operation.[10]

Likewise, another Sukuma composer, Saidi Budelele, bitterly derided the way in which local Division Executive Officers carried out the villagization, without taking into account that many Sukuma people had lived in their "traditional reserves" for many years. Kalikali also sang about his disappointment with the Minister of Finance, Paul Bomani, the former founder of the Victoria Federation Cooperative Union, a peasants' cooperative union. African cotton growers expected Bomani to be aware of the difficulties they experienced, but he failed to take heed of their struggles. Again, Kalikali was warned to stop attacking TANU officials. Once again he blatantly continued singing (in Sukuma) that he did not mean to oppose TANU, but was only asking for a better price of cotton.

This is one case of an artist who in independent Tanzania expressed criticism towards the state authority and paid the consequences for his boldness.

The Arusha Declaration, proclaimed in 1967, marked the beginning of socialism, during which culture brokers saw art which aimed "at entertaining without teaching" as "no worthwhile art" (Ruhumbika and Mbughuni 1974, 284).

In the previous year Nyerere had remarked that political goals should be given priority over freedom of opinion. As a result, after 1967, Tanzanian singers were openly directed to compose songs with themes relevant to party events, and celebrating TANU policies. For example, Super Vea, a jazz band from Mwanza, composed songs such as *Pongezi kwa Rais Nyerere* (Congratulations, President Nyerere), and *Operation Vijana* (Operation Youths).[11] Similarly, the *taarab* singer and composer Shabaan "Sigda" of Mwanza during the war between Tanzania and Uganda composed a song against Idi Amin; he was not formally "asked" to write such a song, but he was somehow "expected" to do so (*mzee* Sigda 2005).

Nevertheless, as with any public action in postcolonial Africa, Tanzanian popular music may have been reshaped by both musicians and members of the public:

> There are as many meanings that can be constructed from a piece of music, as there are listeners. Hence, attempting to understand a song in relation to the initial motives of the composer only provides one of the many possible meanings. (Nannyonga-Tamusuza 2002, 138)

In other words, audiences generally get more meaning than what musicians aim to communicate, and tend to be more politicized than the performers, thus they are likely to read political meanings even into non-political lyrics.

As far as musicians are concerned, it seems that in Uganda under Idi Amin popular music has been a political field in which "performers could use gender metaphors to load their music with subversive messages of resistance to the state" (Ssewakiryanga and Isabirye 2006, 4).

Jewsiewicki and Moniot (1988) have argued that the political content of artistic creation is inversely proportional to the legal possibility of political participation. In some independent African countries, what maintained a political space within the consciousness of the masses were not the governmental policies, nor the formal action of the opposition, either legal or illegal, but rather mocking words and derision (Ellis 1989; Toulabour 1991) against the power. For the powerless, *le mot* (the word) has probably been the only means of reaction and way to distance themselves from oppressive and authoritarian regimes (Toulabour 1991).

The last points about audiences' and musicians' respective manipulation of song lyrics raise the questions: can we make similar statements about socialist Tanzania? Can we argue that, in spite of tight political control by the ruling party, various Tanzanian social groups found their voice through arts, primarily through popular music? Besides an analysis of songs as media texts, oral sources seem to be the only data available for this period. According to all former *dansi* musicians interviewed in 2005 and 2009 mainly in Dar es Salaam, Mwanza, and Tanga, in addition to songs that praised TANU, many *dansi* songs were about love; at that time there was no opposition or hidden meanings or metaphorical subtexts whatsoever, and everybody unquestioningly supported the one-party state. Nor do audiences seem to have manipulated the meaning of popular songs released during the socialist period. Yet, despite my interviewees' memories, some artists and audience members might still have found veiled ways to express their criticism. Love songs may have been a form of escapism from the one-party state (TANU and – after 1977 - CCM), a sort of "option exit" as opposed to "option voice" (cf. Hirschman 1970). This choice may have been partly motivated by artists not taking the risk by singing about issues that could be interpreted as a critique of political power.

Some performers *on stage* may have used subtle sub-textual language with hidden meanings to comment on the political situation. It is also possible that Tanzanian audiences subtly appropriated the lyrics of some songs and attributed different meanings to them. In the realm of musical and more generally cultural production, it is unlikely that Nyerere's ruling party managed to provide Tanzanians with a complete sense of devotion towards the state. More research is needed on the socialist period.

## THE RISE OF *BONGO FLAVA* AS A DEMOCRATIC SPACE, 1980S-2000s

When Nyerere retired from the presidency in 1985,[12] the International Monetary Fund and World Bank approved the Economic Recovery Plan. The then new President Ali Hassan Mwinyi permitted luxury goods, such as TVs, to be imported. This enabled the images of Western culture to inundate the Tanzanian market, especially in urban areas, on an unprecedented level (cf. Mangesho 2005).

Since the early 1990s, with the introduction of multi-partyism and economic liberalization, numerous cultural changes have taken place in Tanzania. One of them is the rise of media consumption. Under the pressure of the free market and the privatization of the media, hip-hop – a quintessentially 'oppositional' style - has been channeled through newly established FM radio stations. Before then, there had been only one radio station, the government controlled RTD (Radio Tanzania Dar es Salaam). The rise of independent radio stations since the mid-1990s allowed popular music to potentially become a free medium to engage on air in debating the burning socio-political issues of the day – from state policies to everyday politics.

Although Graebner, using Remmy Ongala's songs as an example of social criticism in the 1980s, has argued that "one is surprised to hear so many [*dansi*] songs on the radio that openly criticize social conditions" (1997, 113), he did not mention that some of Ongala's songs openly met CCM guidelines.[13] Just two examples: *Dodoma*, in which the late prolific composer praised the CCM, and *Narudi Nyumbani* (I am going back home), in which Ongala dealt with rural-urban migrations, urging migrants to go back to the countryside.[14]

Looking at other genres, it is worth noting that in the 1990s the ruling party established a governmental *taarab* band called TOT (Tanzania One Theatre). As Siri Lange has put it:

> [u]p to 1992 there had been no need for CCM to have their own troupe, as all the cultural troupes in the country had been performing *ngoma* songs that supported CCM, its leaders, and the political system in general. The artists fulfilled this role partly because they believed in *ujamaa* in the early years, partly to win the goodwill of the government. This goodwill was needed to get renewals of their permit to perform, to get paid assignments for performing at celebration of various kinds, and if lucky, even tours abroad. With time the political propaganda songs simply became a convention of the nationalized *ngoma* genre. (2002, 170)

The decision to create a new *taarab* band would not have occurred in earlier times. This was not only driven by popular taste, but by "the ruling party's tradition of appropriating popular cultural forms for their own benefit" (Lange 2002, 170).

Notably, besides the birth of new state-owned bands, the economic liberalization period saw the appearance of a new and potentially more independent style known as *Bongo Flava*, a mix of various foreign genres (such as hip-hop, R&B, dancehall and ragamuffin), with a distinctly Tanzanian 'flavour' (all songs and raps are in Swahili).[15] Partly due to the support of radio deejays, this genre has become enormously popular, mostly among people in their teens and twenties. Furthermore, *Bongo Flava* is not played with live instruments, but with a backing-track tune.

New techniques of music recording mean that even Tanzanian youth unable to play a musical instrument or from disadvantaged backgrounds can rather easily use increasingly cheap recording technologies, while many current and former *dansi* musicians cannot afford to buy instruments.[16] As a result, the years after 2000 have seen the appearance of a growing number of *Bongo Flava* artists. One of the underlying reasons is that youths' prospects of finding formal jobs are very limited, and becoming a *Bongo Flava* artist represents a source of revenue.

As far as the social composition of *Bongo Flava* performers is concerned, many are born in Dar es Salaam - often in its shanty-towns - or have moved there to gain access to recording studios and other facilities related to musical production: the possibility of keeping in touch with radio presenters, studio producers, concert organizers and large audiences plays a key role in their artistic careers. *Bongo Flava* artists are mostly men in their early twenties; they have usually completed secondary school.

Regarding the relation between *Bongo Flava* artists, the elders and the state, I will first mention the example of the socio-politically engaged old school rapper, Sugu (literally means: "stubborn"), who has since the 1990s made use of hip-hop to boldly express his political opinions. Although he was never jailed, as Kalikali was, in 2005 he recalled that a few years before, during a concert at the Diamond Jubilee in Dar es Salaam, he was nearly arrested for his openly political attacks. He argued that the police eventually left him in peace because he was wearing a T-shirt with Nyerere's image on it (Sugu 2005).

During my fieldwork I noted that most artists, even those who present themselves as "tough", celebrated the late Nyerere. When, in August 2005 the Ugandan songster, Chameleon visited Dar es Salaam for a show organized by MTV Africa, I saw him displaying a T-shirt bearing the face of Nyerere, while in 2005 in the outskirts of Mwanza I found a painting representing a young unknown rapper with Nyerere at his side (cf. Suriano 2007, 216).

By acknowledging the legacy of Nyerere, these artists may seek to assert that even the youth can be judicious, thus proving that wisdom does not belong only to elders. Stage names such as Professor Jay and Mwana FA (*mwana falsafa*: the philosopher) support this claim.

Similarly, praising Nyerere may also be read as a conscious way to (re)construct bonds between the younger and the older generations, and gain their approval. Some stage names suggest this desire. Emblematic is the case of Daz Baba (born David Celestine Jacob Nyika), previously Daz Mwalimu: both nicknames are inspired by Nyerere's famous epithets *Baba wa Taifa* (Father of the Nation) and *Mwalimu* (Teacher).

As far as topics are concerned, a number of *Bongo Flava* songs and raps, especially those released until the mid-2000s, explore socio-political issues such as HIV/AIDS, corruption and poverty, as well as expectations about family life.

Abdallah Singano has articulated in the magazine *Bang!* that it is precisely due to *Bongo Flava* that some audiences became aware of "the passport sized-bathrooms", and of the precarious living conditions of many Tanzanians; young artists mostly from disadvantaged backgrounds "never forget where they came from and they want us to know about the experiences of other people through their music" (Singano 2004-2005, 26).

Do these modes of communication have broader socio-political effects, or are they just temporary generational outlets without any impact on the Tanzanian society? In my view they can be quite influential. A good example is *Wife*, by Daz Baba. Its chorus says:

> Daz Baba, I have become a grown-up man, now I need a gorgeous woman to live with me, to have children with and to bring them up with, to cope with bad and good times with me. (For the Swahili text, see Suriano 2007, 215)

Here Daz Baba teaches his fellow youth how to deal with marital life in the modern world and promotes the ideal of the nuclear family and an image of marital life in which both husband and wife equally share domestic duties. These lyrics embody the current aspirations of majority of Tanzanian youth. As observed by O'Brien, to get "economic independence, to have enough resources to marry and set up one's own family, is the fundamental aspiration" (1996, 58) of the average African youth.

Furthermore, far from simply aping Western and Christian values, the lyrics above may indirectly challenge ideas about gender relations based on male authority and hierarchy, not necessarily suitable for contemporary youths simply because they are "traditional". Borrowing a statement referring to the progressive role of another popular cultural form, i.e., TV soap operas such as "The Bold and the Beautiful" in a poor Nairobi neighbourhood, it can be argued that *Bongo Flava*, along with "the discursive spaces opened by the media", does not have "the barriers which elsewhere prevent poor people from taking part in debates on key social and moral questions" (Frederiksen 2000, 209).

In 2004, the Kenyan artists Gidi Gidi Maji Maji, whose hit *Unbwogable* had become popular to such an extent that it was appropriated by the opposition before the December 2002 Kenyan elections (cf. Nyairo and Ogude 2005), were appointed "Messengers of Truth" by the United Nations' Agency 'Habitat'. Significantly, Gidi Gidi Maji Maji "were awarded for giving birth to a powerful voice for the disenfranchised urban youth", on the grounds that hip-hop is not "merely a musical genre but a social movement" and "a powerful voice for ... victims of ... poverty and social exclusion" (Mbaria, 2004).

In other words, *Bongo Flava* and related genres such as Kenyan hip-hop, along with new recording technologies, have democratized music making, to some extent enabling young artists to participate in the claiming of the public space. *Bongo Flava*, allowing youth some agency, can be conceptualized as a symbol of the emerging generation in East Africa.

One of the early songs that indicate the relative freedom of opinion acquired after liberalization, and how youths use this freedom to express their political views, is *Ndiyo mzee* (Yes, Sir) by Professor Jay, in which this popular rapper mocked empty promises made by politicians during electoral campaigns. As the journalist Saleh Ally explained to me, even the then President Benjamin Mkapa quoted the slogan *Ndiyo Mzee* in his speeches given a few months after the 2000 elections:

> After the [2000 general] elections this song was listened to many times in the cars of members of Parliament. There came a moment in which ... Mkapa in one of his thanks giving speeches said: "Isn't it like this?" And the crowd ... replied: "Yes Sir!" (Ally 2005)

Although the intention of Saleh Ally was to state that even old people and rural dwellers were aware of *Bongo Flava* music as early as 2000, this comment reveals an attempt by Tanzanian politicians to manipulate the message of a rap originally disparaging them (cf. Nyairo and Ogude 2005, 232). It was not by chance that Professor Jay told me that he wrote the follow up *Kikao cha Dharura. Siyo Mzee* (Emergency Meeting: No, Sir) precisely to distance himself from what he called "fake politicians", proclaiming once and for all the real meaning of his rap (Professor Jay 2005).

In another case, *Ngangari* (Tough) by the crew Gangwe Mobb, was adopted by the opposition. Before the October 2000 general elections, the Civic United Front (CUF, one of the major opposition parties) manipulated the original lyrics. The chorus

> *Gangwe [Mobb] wako vipi?* (x2)
> *Wako ngangari, ngangari kinomaah!*
> What are Gangwe Mobb like?
> They are absolutely the toughest!

was turned into:

*WanaCUF wako vipi?*
*Wako ngangari, ngangari kinomaah!*
What are CUF members like?
They are absolutely the toughest!

The fact that *Bongo Flava* can contribute to the establishment of a democratic public sphere and seems to be "suitable" domain to express "oppositional" identities, does not imply that this genre is necessarily subversive or revolutionary (for contemporary East African popular cultural forms as a "democratic space" see Nyairo and Ogude 2005, 2). Many *Bongo Flava* artists voluntarily put themselves at the service of politicians in both the CCM and the opposition parties, mainly the CUF. In March 2005, a few months before the beginning of the official electoral campaign that led to the presidential election of Jakaya M. Kikwete (CCM), Inspekta Haroun, no longer a member of Gangwe Mobb, released the hit single *Pongezi* (Congratulations) in which he praised the outgoing President Mkapa for peace, unity and union achieved by Tanzania. The chorus goes:

*Hizi Pongezi* (3 times) *kwa Mheshimiwa Raisi Mkapa,*
*Kwa jitihada zake za kujenga nchi...*
*Tulipotoka hata kufika hapa...*
*Nchi ilivyopiga hatua...*
*Umoja, amani na muungano.*

Congratulations, (3 times) His Excellency President Mkapa,
For his efforts in the building of the nation...
From where we have come until our arrival here...
For the steps made by this country...
Unity, peace and union.

It is significant to note that in the last line Mkapa is held responsible for the successful unification of Tanzania, when it is usually Nyerere who is given this acknowledgment.[17] When I asked Inspekta Haroun about the message of this song, he replied: "I did not have any political purpose at all"; and explained that he composed this song just because he dislikes people's attitude of bemoaning everything, therefore he sought to stress the good things done by Mkapa (still President when the interview took place), such as the building of roads, schools and hospitals (Inspekta Haroun 2005; cf. Suriano 2006, 183). A few months later, for the occasion of the official electoral campaign, the President-to-be Kikwete toured the country accompanied on stage by some well-known *Bongo Flava* artists, who invited Tanzanian audiences to vote for him, mainly in the name of the achievements made by Tanzania under previous leaders Nyerere, Mwinyi, and Mkapa. In *Kijani na Njano* (Green and Yellow – the colours of the CCM, and previously of TANU), composed for the campaign, Mwana FA articulates:

> *Rangi ya manjano ndiyo rangi za Kambarage,*
> *Popote alipo Mwalimu namwombea amani kwake*
> *Yeye bado ni baba yetu*
> *Na tubaki watoto wake.*

> Yellow is Kambarage [Nyerere]'s colour,
> Wherever the teacher is, I pray that peace be upon him,
> He is still our father,
> Let us remain his children.

Aside from reiterating the aforesaid bond between the youth and Nyerere, here Mwana FA persuades his audiences to support Kikwete on the basis of the CCM rhetoric that blames the political opposition for betraying the revered Father of the nation.[18]

During the 2005 campaign, Bushoke remade his popular song *Mume Bwege* (The good-for-nothing husband), turning the chorus into CCM *Namba Uani* (CCM Number One). "*Hata wapinzani wanampenda, lakini wanabanwa*" (Even political opponents are fond of him [Kikwete], but they are restrained), he states. It is also worth mentioning the case of Juma Nature and TMK (Temeke) Family from Temeke slum, a pillar of the CUF. At first they were CUF supporters, then during the 2005 electoral campaign they joined CCM and toured with Kikwete (Nganyagwa 2005; cf. Suriano 2007, 212).

Aware that a song can play a more important role than a political speech in encouraging the maintenance of the status quo or in promoting socio-political change, Tanzanian politicians attempt to persuade these *masupastaa* (stars) to perform for them to appeal to new generations and bring them into politics.

The choice of most *Bongo Flava* artists not to condemn the political system is reminiscent of Mbembe's postcolony (1992, 25), with the theme of the ambiguity of people's laughter at the extravagances of power. The ambivalent attitudes of *Bongo Flava* artists towards those in power may reflect more general moral dilemmas in the hybrid postcolonial world, as Jewsiewicki (1989) has written in reference to popular paintings in former Zaire.

African youth have been pessimistically described as a "lost generation" with little to lose, or "a natural opposition"; being "poorly equipped to make their opposition effective", they "are easily manipulated by their elders (O'Brien 1996, 55). This is, however, not the case for *Bongo Flava* artists. If popular music can be an instrument of innovation and self-affirmation, then *Bongo Flava* artists are actively taking part in the re-configuration of public space in Tanzania. Song lyrics and comments made by listeners suggest that for Tanzanian youths *Bongo Flava* has opened up a new space for self-expression. The involvement of some artists in "patron-client relationships" (Gilman, 2001) and the support given by them to (mostly CCM) politicians may be a pragmatic and not necessarily an ideological choice in order to meet their economic inter-ests, since it seems that they get compensated for their performances for making endorsements of the main political parties.

Finally, it is worth emphasizing that more than other genres, *Bongo Flava* allows the youth to express their feelings of disillusionment to the state, shared in the liberalization era by many Tanzanian youths. This is exemplified by the single hit *Kura yangu* (My vote) released in the summer 2005 by Dokta Levi featuring Sugu. This rap explicitly com-plained about politicians (indirectly referring to the ruling party), who had been the same for the last forty years, thus nothing was really going to change with the upcoming elections due to be held four months later.

Despite the increased freedom of speech afforded by *Bongo Flava*, however, a considerable number of artists do not engage with socio-political issues, but instead focus on fun, sex and entertainment.

Are non-engaged lyrics meant to provide momentary escape for audi-ence members? As in the case of *dansi* love songs in the socialist period, this choice may be interpreted as a form of dissent. By ignoring the dic-tates of the former educational cultural policies - still very influential among young artists and audiences (cf. Suriano 2007, 218-9) - youths may be trying to detach themselves from the older generations and assert their autonomy, as well as symbolically contest politicians' unfulfilled promises.

In one of his negative remarks on *Bongo Flava*, *mzee* Ndonho indirectly referred to the dissatisfaction towards the state widespread among young Tanzanians: "Nowadays the problem is that Tanzanian youths are no longer interested in politics" - meaning, by politics, the state and the political parties (*mzee* Ndonho 2005).

## CONCLUSION

In this chapter I have argued that Tanzanian popular music has been a site of everyday production of ideas of the nation. Performances and song lyrics have been historically used to celebrate state policies, and to articulate people's grievances beyond the channels of official politics.

During British colonialism, the cultural production contributed to the achievement of independence and to the shaping of Tanzanian political history. As in the case of *dansi*, between the 1940s and 1950s, music performances were also forms of expression of new identities, and not necessarily a challenge to colonialism.

In independent Tanzania, especially during the socialist period, the state cultural policies shaped both musical production and leisure time. Before the mid-1980s, musicians endorsed the one-party system, or were somehow coerced to respect the will of the ruling party. However, the years prior to 1985 may have been marked by subtle political overtones created by the audiences as a means of expressing political frustrations that were no longer needed in the following period.

After liberalization, *Bongo Flava* music has been a public/democratic space. The *Bongo Flava* phenomenon provides further testimony that popular culture can bring about change; even if this is not necessarily "revolutionary". Rather, popular culture in the "heterodox" postcolony is quintessentially ambiguous: a form of escape and "camouflage" in some cases, and a form of social contestation and consciousness-raising in other cases. As Mbembe has put it,

> the postcolony is made up not of one coherent 'public space' … It is rather a plurality of 'spheres' and arenas, each having its own separate logic yet nonetheless liable to be entangled with other logics when operating in certain specific contexts: hence the postcolonial 'subject' has had to learn to continuously bargain and improvise. Faced with this … the postcolonial 'subject' mobilizes not just a single 'identity', but several fluid identities which, by their very nature, must be constantly 'revised' in order to achieve maximum instrumentality and efficacy as and when required. (1992, 5)

Especially after the mid-2000s, *Bongo Flava* artists have increasingly shown a preference for less socially outspoken lyrics. This disregard for the former educational cultural policies may be a form of escape and a symbolic expression of political dissent.

Lastly, it is difficult to predict where *Bongo Flava* is going. Probably, it will remain a centre of cultural innovation (cf. Burton and Brennan 2007, 14), and an instrument to grasp broader socio-political contemporary dynamics: the nature of *Bongo Flava* as a counterpoint, in music and lyrical terms, means that there will always be a space for Tanzanian musicians to encourage change where it is needed. But this genre may decline, should artists not rise up to the challenge to create new tunes and renew song topics, and should they be reluctant to improve their music skills.[19]

## Notes

1. Cf. Pratt 1976:132; Askew and Kitime 2006. According to them, the "nation-building-period" stretches until 1967 and 1966 respectively.

2. *Mzee* (old) is a term of respect for an elderly man.

3. Ndonho died in 2006.

4. *Binti* literally means: daughter.

5. The culture of politics is a "political practice that is culturally legitimated ... by local knowledge"; besides being "accessible to elites and ordinary people alike", it "may be altered over time through a process of political learning" (Robinson 1994:40, quoted in Geiger 1997:6, footnote 23).

6. All the information on *wigashe* performers in Sukumaland in this and in the following paragraph is based on Songoyi (1998, 2005).

7. Although among Muslims the "Arabized" *taarab* was also perceived as "modern", my interviewees, mainly Muslim men, agree that in late colonialism urban youths saw *dansi* as the "modern" style by definition.

8. CCM (*Chama cha Mapinduzi* - The Party of Revolution) was formed in 1977 in succession of TANU.

9. Similar processes have taken place in other postcolonial contexts in recent times. In 2000 Zimbabwe witnessed a "carefully orchestrated campaign form of African musical nationalism" (Vambe and Vambe 2006:48).

10. Rural socialism (*Ujamaa vijijini*) was implemented between the late 1960s and 1975.

11. According to Salathiel Mwasyeba, in 2005 a Radio Tanzania Dar es Salaam (RTD) long-term employee, both songs were recorded in 1967 (Mwasyeba 2005). However, as "Operation Vijana" celebrated the homonymous operation launched by TANU after 1967, it is likely that this song was released slightly later. Operation Vijana campaigns banned miniskirts, wigs and other western fashions seen as "corrupting" Tanzanian youths, mainly women.

12. Nyerere remained chairman of CCM until 1990.

13. The late Remmy Ongala (born Ramadhani Mtoro Ongala; 1947-2010), was originally from the Kivu Region in Congo (DRC), and moved to Tanzania in 1978.

14. For the lyrics cf. Graebner (1997, 11). It is worth noting that in Tanzania there is a long-standing antipathy of TANU and CCM officials towards urbanization, inherited from the British.

15. The term *bongo* (Swahili slang for "big brain", the augmentative form of *ubongo*, "brain") refers to Tanzania. Although we should differentiate between *Bongo Flava* and "pure" hip-hop (see Suriano 2007), here, for the sake of simplicity, I do not make this distinction. This paragraph on post-socialist music focuses on *Bongo Flava*, partly because my research on contemporary music has concentrated exclusively on this genre, partly because I consider *Bongo Flava* as particularly suitable for the expression of socio-political issues. For more scholarly works on *Bongo Flava*, see bibliography in Suriano 2007. *Taarab* (especially its modern form *mipasho*), *dansi* and *ngoma* are still very popular, though (for *taarab* as "apolitical", cf. Askew 2002). Lastly, it is worth noting that the local elements in Bongo Flava lie in the fact that tunes, lyrics, rhymes, artists' nicknames, and dual rivaries, are often borrowed from Swahili culture (cf. Suriano 2006). Here I do not examine the period after 2005 as I did not witness the 2010 electoral campaign and general elections.

16. This is a common complain among my interviewees who would like to set up new *dansi* bands. Some of them during our interviews in 2009 asked me to sponsor them.

17. Notably, the words "building of the nation" (*kujenga nchi*) resonate with the line: "Oh-oh TANU builds the nation" (*Oh-oh TANU yajenga nchi*), sung by TANU members during the struggle for independence, and then adopted by the CCM.

18. Likewise, the ANC still plays on the rhetoric of its 'glorious' past anti-apartheid political struggle: during the South African electoral campaign in May 2011, the ruling party circulated T-Shirts with the sentence "Don't betray Mandela: vote for Zuma".

19. This opinion has been expressed by the former music journalist Saleh Ally, now focusing exclusively on sport on the grounds that *Bongo Flava* is no longer interesting (Ally 2009).

# Chapter 16

# THE COST AND REWARD OF MANHOOD: THE PRACTICE OF *IMBALU* RITUAL AMONG THE BAGISU

*Dominica Dipio*
*Makerere University, Kampala*

## INTRODUCTION

T his paper focuses on the male ritual circumcision, *imbalu*, among the Bagisu in Uganda, who prefer to be called the Bamasaba, after Masaba their founding father. *Imbalu* that takes place every Even Year is the most important initiation and identity ritual among the Bamasaba. Traditionally, it was mandatory for young men from the age of maturity – eighteen years and above – to undergo the ritual as an initiation into adult life. One of the indicators of maturity was the community's public recognition of their male youth as persons who are strong enough to defend their communities from attacks from neighbouring communities. Another indicator of maturity was marriage and the ability to start one's own family. In the wisdom of the fore-fathers of the Bamasaba, what tests a young man's readiness for these crucial responsibilities was/is *imbalu*. The most important values that the neophyte must demonstrate in the ritual year are courage perseverance and the ability to withstand pain. *Imbalu* is therefore principally an ordeal that prepares one for responsible adult life with all the challenges it presents (Heald 1982, 17). Young men to whom family and community responsibilities are to be passed must display both physical and moral strength and this is seen in their display of masculine supremacy characterised in their courage (ibid., 15).

In this paper, I analyze the characteristics of masculinity promoted in shaping the identity of the Bamasaba that makes it inevitable for emergent masculinities to develop in this context of change. I also pay attention to gender relationships in the context of *imbalu* narratives and performances. The position of Nabarwa, the Pokot woman married to Masaba, from whom circumcision in the community is widely believed to have originated is also of interest. Some of the younger and Western educated generation of Bamasaba tend to be averse to the more traditional version of masculinity endorsed by the ritual. For this category, what it means to be a man is often the alternative courage to stand against the status quo. This makes identity construction, in the words of Ronning and Johannessen, a dialogic one, characterized by border-crossings (2007, vii). Rigid masculinity with its exaggerated manifestations is threatened from within when the members it seeks to recruit turn against it (Nabasuta 2010, 78-94).

Of recent male circumcision has generated interest in scientific circles and it has been hailed as instrumental in reducing the transmission of HIV/AIDS and sexually transmitted disease by up to 60% (Bertran Auvert, et.al. 2005). For circumcising communities like the Bamasaba for whom circumcision is crucial identity marker, this is taken to affirm their traditional wisdom that partly explains the practice on "health" and "cleanliness" grounds, and makes circumcision a convergence point for tradition and science. From one of the origin narratives, the "ill health" of Bamasaba sons and the restoration of their health led to the spread of the ritual. In the "traditional practice,"[1] to symbolize solidarity and create sense of kinship, the *inyembe* (the ritual knife) circumcised several initiates (*bamakoki*) who were bound by the single knife. The knife then becomes a symbol of brotherhood, as significant as blood brotherhood. It is a symbol people swear by. Analysis of the responses of the interviewees show that although health was a key factor in the ritual, the practice has come to assume a much larger position in the world view of the Bamasaba. Indeed their philosophy of life is defined by *imbalu*. In the context of the new threat of HIV infection, the significance of the single knife as a solidarity factor raises questions.[2] On the other hand, the claim that male circumcision reduces sexually transmitted infections, including HIV, is perceived by the Bamasaba as science's endorsement of their ancestral practice. One of the elders I asked about the possibility of transmission of diseases through the single knife used to circumcise many, responded that *imbalu* is stronger than the fear of death. This corresponds with Heald's observation that the initiates face the knife as a warrior does: he must overcome his fear and stand between life and dead as he confronts *imbalu*. For even death must be faced with courage (Heald 1982, 17, 20, 26). Such a mind set does not make it obvious for the Bamasaba to choose to circumcise in the hospital even if it may appear "safer".

My interest in understanding the inner rubrics of *imbalu* as an enduring biennial identity ritual of the Bamasaba took shape from 2008-2010 when I did my investigations synthesized in my documentary film, *Crafting the Bamasaba* (2009). After years of observing the ritual from a distance as an exotic performance, I got interested in interrogating this apparently seamless ritual to understand how it sustains itself amidst cultural flux. With the assistance of a colleague, Wotsuna Khamalwa, I was introduced to Manafwa District where a friendly community willing to share the cultural logic of *imbalu* welcomed my research interests. The main activity of data collection took place in 2008. Participant observation was my principle method: the behaviour, relationships, social interactions, gestures and actions associated with the ritual were particularly important for categorizing and analysing my data. Most of my informants could speak both English and Lumasaba; and translators were handy whenever I needed them. I used film as a method of documentation. This helped me to record actions in real time with their tones and moods; which was useful in the data analysis phase. I interviewed a cross-section of mainly members of the Bamasaba community, and documented the crucial stages of the ritual process. From the multisubjective voices I gathered, I tried to derive coherent meaning of the various actions (Clifford 2002, 52-3). In order to maintain a respectful distance, I refrained from using voice-over in the film. The narratives from the various voices offer a non-linear understanding of *imbalu* that ostensibly presents itself as homogeneous. The fact that this research is about interpretation of culture underscores the multiplicity of meaning that the researcher and informants generate. This only highlights the explosive and inexhaustible nature of symbols.

## KEY MOMENTS IN *IMBALU* RITUAL PERFORMANCE

*Imbalu* has become the quintessence of the Bamasaba identity as it is directly connected to adulthood, responsibility, marriage and continuity. In the Bamasaba calendar, the Odd Year is also called the girl year, and it has a significant relationship to the Even Year. The Even Year (the ritual year) is officially opened in January with the *isonja* dance that begins the ritual process which climaxes in December when the last groups of initiates are circumcised. The Odd Year (girl year) precedes the closing dance, *ineemba*, which takes place in December or January of the Odd Year. This is the dance that flags off the youth who have successfully graduated into Bamasaba masculine identity as 'men'. During this dance girls may identify future husbands from the newly initiated. Interestingly this ritual that celebrates the male and puts masculinity on the social pedestal, is believed to have originated from Nabarwa, a Pokot woman from neighbouring Kenya, whose initial meeting with Masaba ended up in love and marriage. This foreign woman is credited for introducing her husband to a practice that has come to encompass the Bamasaba philosophy of life: no male of a certain age who belongs to the community by birth can escape it in life or in death.[3] What is however intriguing is that although the Bamasaba are surrounded by communities that circumcise women, like the Pokot and the Sabiny, and although Nabarwa herself was circumcised, they do not excise their women.[4]

All key informers see the circumcision of women as unfair because childbirth, which is women's mandate, is itself an ordeal that places them between life and death. Women shed blood just as an initiate does in the courtyard[5] (Heald 1982, 30-1). However, since *imbalu* is the only ritual that equalizes men and opens the door to adult responsibilities and privileges, women are systematically excluded from accessing what is available exclusively to the circumcised. After circumcision, a young man has rights similar to his father (La Fontaine 1967, 254, 256). In omitting the circumcision of women, a woman's difference and inferiority is emphasized. I find convincing the claim that "when the woman [first] cut her daughters, the men saw this made them 'too strong'" in personality (Heald 1982, 30), and thence they limited circumcision to the men alone. In this way, male power subjugates female agency and technically excludes them from competing for public recognition. Circumcision is a significant feature of male and female identity among the Pokot. It prepares both genders for adult life and responsibilities; and the largesse of bride-wealth a woman fetches depends on her stamina and strength of character in withstanding the pain of the razor. This is how the Pokot woman gains the community's esteem (Edgerton 1964, 1295; Mukai, 2006). Circumcision, scarification and body decorations are perceived by the Pokot, both male and female, as the reasonable things to do to enhance one's beauty and suitability for marriage. Bianco's research asserts that circumcision among the Pokot "reconfigures the body and channels its desires into the pursuit of cattle and children, the primary means by which Pokot men and women create intimacy and reconstitute social bonds.... A circumcised woman augments her social stature through marriage and motherhood...." (Bianco 1991, 771). Bianco alludes to the personality strength of the Pokot woman when she says that she "carries her own clan identity with her as she moves from one homestead and patrilineage to another" (1991, 781). This presents a high level of reciprocity between the genders among the Pokot and some degree of independence and equality as both genders pass through the same ordeal.

A number of symbolic actions are involved during the circumcision ritual. I outline Khamalwa's categorization of *imbalu* ritual into seven phases that represent the philosophy of the Bamasaba community (2004, 74-104). This basically corresponds with Heald's three key stages (Heald 1982, 20-2). The first stage is *isonja* dance, which in essence is the initial group dance that brings all the intending candidates together. This phase comprises of dancing and singing with the weight of thigh-bells, that may be up to three or four pairs fastened onto the thighs of each candidate. The purpose here is to gauge the stamina of the candidates to endure challenging situations. One who does not feel strong enough to continue with the dance that progressively gets hectic may pull out at this stage to wait for the next ritual season. Sense of solidarity among the youth of the same age-set (*bamakoki*) begins to build during this dance.

The second phase is *khuwentza* (searching for *imbalu*). This is when the candidate traverses the land to visit far away relatives to announce his readiness to perform the ritual, and to receive their blessings and material gifts. This gift offering follows certain logic: they are either repayments for those gifts given by the candidate's father for a son in this homestead; or they are gifts expected to be reciprocated when the time comes for the giver's son to be circumcised. The logic here is enhancing communitarian spirit of sharing and responsibility. The songs the candidate and the group sing highlight the advice that *imbalu* is not a joking matter, thus the candidate must gauge his resolve before continuing on this road to maturity. Songs like, "*Khekhurongese Khubalya Byamawo*" (Let me escort you to those who ate your mother's bride price) emphasize the importance of the knife and the pain it causes to test a man's bravery. In this song, the initiate is advised, "Be brave so that you are circumcised and begin a new dawn of life". On the other hand, the song, "*Watamba Shisha*" (you were unkind), directly disparages stinginess among the community. Those who cannot offer "even a hen" to support are unkind brothers indeed. The candidate's role at this stage is to dramatize his volition to undergo the ritual; the obligation of the community is to support this process by generous giving (Heald 1982, 22, 30; La Fontaine, 252).

The third phase is *khukhupaka* (thrashing millet). Two weeks before the circumcision day, the initiate candidate begins the long process of beer brewing by thrashing the millet for brewing the ritual beer. His involvement in this process demonstrates his volition and personal initiative to participate in the ritual. The millet that is used for this purpose must be the mature one of the previous year, an indication of his maturing into a man. It is, however, one thing for the candidate to display his volition, and it is another for the elders to assess his fitness for the ritual (Heald 1982, 22; La Fontaine 1977, 253). A good son is the one who abides by the advice of the elders.

The fourth phase is *khukoya* (beer brewing) which takes place two days before the circumcision day. The beer matures on the third day, which is the day that the candidate is circumcised. This is also the day the beer is ready for consumption. Several actions and symbols are embedded in this symbolic phase of transformation. This rite of smearing the candidate with yeast (*khuuakha limela*) is performed by an elder of good conduct who "moulds" the initiate to be a good man. The yeast as unmistakable symbol of change and creative process alludes to the internal shifting going on in the psyche of the boy who is about to become a man. This interpretation agrees with La Fontaine (1977) and Heald (1982, 30-1) who see a link between circumcision as a manifestation of the procreative power of men and beer fermentation as a process change. This solemn rite is performed amidst instructions and admonitions to the candidate to be of good conduct. The initiate is pliant in the hands of the "moulding" elder. The sombreness of the moment and of the performers' dispositions evokes an act of creation. The two days of smearing the candidate and giving solemn instructions culminates into the day of circumcision. Some of the key places the initiate must visit on this ultimate day is the ancestral burial place. The boy is introduced to symbols of ancestral spirit as a way of trusting him with clan secrets. This is also the day of circumcision when the ritual elder slaughters a bull to thank the ancestors for bringing the initiate to the threshold of becoming a man. Body parts of the initiate are smeared with chime and yeast to show the progress he has made. The candidate looks physically disfigured and unpleasant. This is a crucial point in testing the character of the initiate. What he is smeared with looks degrading, but it is a lesson in humility: now he is a thing – a "formless" nobody – wanting to become somebody. His total silence, except in singing songs that express his values, self control and volition to become, is his only way of communicating (Heald 1982, 18).

This is also the tensest of days as the candidate leaves for his final physical journey in the morning, returning at an unspecified time right into the ring to be circumcised. The rest of the community waits for him in tense expectation of how the final moment will turn out to be. On this final day, the initiate visits his maternal clan where a cow is slaughtered in his honour and utterances of blessings are showered upon him. The candidate is then taken to the sacred swamp – *mwitosi* – for the final performance. This is the place of the spirit of *imbalu* symbolized by the frothy, sacred clay that is finally smeared on the candidate who has gone through the processes. At this point, there is no turning back. The eerie and tense atmosphere is intensified by songs like, "*Papa nga Wanganile*" (if father loves me) that expresses the values of every mature Mumasaba. If a father loves his son, he will educate him in the ways of the community, ensures that he gets circumcised and married.

The spirit of *imbalu* is believed to take over as a handful of the people fiercely lead the candidate to the homestead where the surgeon and his assistants are waiting for him. The party approaches from the east, and from a higher ground, symbolizing the Masaba-Nabarwa ancestral mountainous place of origin, for this is also his beginning as a man. The path of the initiate is cleared by the strong group of men that speedily leads him into the ring for the three layered operation to be performed in less than a minute. At this point, "*Khwalera Ikhwalilo*" (we are bringing the penis) is usually sung. To highlight the intensity of emotions at this stage, I quote the song at length:

> We are bringing the penis....
> Mother's child we are bringing the penis ....
> We are taking *imbalu* to court....
> My mother's child we are taking the knife to court
> We are taking the penis to court....
> Aaah....
>
> Father's child we are bringing the penis
> We are bringing the penis
> We are bringing the penis.

The emphasis in this song is the transition of the boy from being "mother's child to "father's" child – a man. "Mother" is repeated four times in the song, while "father" is mentioned once in the last stanza, clearly showing that his successful transition to manhood is still to be tested.

Taking the penis to court has the double meaning of literally taking the boy to the courtyard for the operation; and also emphasizing that this is a moment of judgement for the boy before the community. Only this court(yard) can decide. Only a few observe the details of what happens in the inner ring of the courtyard. The surgeon's whistle informs the mammoth gathering of the successful completion; whereupon the gathering goes wild with jubilation.

The fifth significant stage is *mwikombe* (convalescence). This is the crucial phase of healing: it is long, painful and lonely. There is no display of spectacle here because it takes place in the privacy of the *likombe* – the convalescence hut. It is a delicate phase characterized by inexpressible pain. The neophyte remains in seclusion for three days in the hut. On the third day, relatives, friends and well-wishers come with gifts to visit. The surgeon also comes back on the third day to perform the *khuusaabisa* (purification rite). The surgeon ritualistically purifies him by washing his hands with beer and water, as he goes on to admonish him on what he should, and should not do as an adult Mumasaba. In symbolic actions, he presents to him the ethics of Bamasaba identity, each time cautioning him to choose the good. Implicitly one is free to choose, though the surgeon clearly indicates what leads to the good life. Indeed, the principle of making choices accompanies one throughout life as the values are given in the Manichean binaries of good and evil.

The sixth stage is *khukhwiyalula* (hatching ceremony) where the newly circumcised leaves his convalescence hut and is incorporated into the family after weeks of seclusion. This rite involves burning the banana leaves and mats that the initiate has used as bedding during convalesce period. This is done the night before his incorporation into normal life to show that he has "hatched" into a man.

The seventh and final phase is *ineemba* – commissioning dance. This dance marks the official end of the ritual year. It takes place either in December or in January, during the dry season associated with leisure. The drums as phallic symbols occupy centre stage in this dance that brings together all the newly "hatched" men. This is a moment of display when all those who have gone through *imbalu* are "displayed" to the community through this dance where it is important to be seen and acknowledged. At the end of each dance song, there is an excited din from the young men who point their sticks to the northeast where the ancestors and Nabarwa are believed to have come from. This is also the occasion for the youth to identify prospective wives from the crowd of young women who have come for the three days dance.

The entire phase of the ritual is punctuated with dancing, thematic singing, symbolic actions, storytelling, to evoke the memory of the ancestors and to teach, advice and give admonitions to the initiates. In the words of Joseph Oladejo, ritual gives the candidates a glimpse or taste of myths, legends, and stories of the community that unites them (2008, 207). It also creates the mood to momentarily experience possibilities beyond the initiates' ordinary limitations. This shared knowledge builds emotional bond among the participants who have the same sense of responsibility and obligation towards each other and the community.

## INTERPRETING *NABARWA* AND WOMEN IN *IMBALU* RITUAL

The world view of a people is often enshrined in their myth that influences how they live and relate with the environment. In the context of the Bamasaba, myth occupies a central role in validating the instructions given the initiates to link them with the spirits of the revered places or persons (Khamalwa 2004, 134). The origin myth is learned as a creed; and the valour of community members who have performed *imbalu* before them is evoked as examples to be emulated.

Two related narratives associated with the practice of *imbalu* point to women as the originators of the ritual. In the grand origin narrative of the Bagisu, the founding parents Mundu and Seera emanated from the top of Mount Elgon and the two later had two sons to continue their heritage. One, a herdsman, was Kundu, and the other, a hunter, was Masaba. Kundu is believed to be Kintu whom the Baganda are believed to have originated from. Kundu is said to have brought his cows down from the mountains into the vast plains below. When he saw the vast land with all that his cattle needed, he continued moving south with his animals to where he became the founder of the Baganda, a people who speak intelligible Bantu language. In the Buganda origin narrative, Kintu came from Ggulu (heaven), a place the Bagisu associate with the height of Mount Elgon, also believed to be the abode of God, and where their own founders, Mundu and Seera emerged from. As for Masaba, the hunter son, on one of his hunting expeditions in the mountains, he came upon a beautiful woman – Nabarwa – from a different ethnic group across the mountain. The two fell in love (Khamalwa 2009, 94).[6] She soon came to discover Masaba was not circumcised, and gave him a condition for accepting his marriage proposal: he had to come with her to her brothers so that he could get circumcised. Masaba obliged. His in-laws nursed him to health, and handed him Nabarwa to take to his home as wife. This first narrative appears to be a case of one man in love. His experience did not seem to have been translated into a community practice. In any case, he was circumcised outside his own community.

A much later narrative fore-grounds yet another foreign woman married to Fuuya of the Bumutoto clan[7] as responsible for proposing circumcision as a community practice. This time, the reason for the woman's prescription was the continuous ill health of their male children. She informed her brother Aramunyenye, about the situation. When Aramunyenye visited Fuuya, his brother-in-law, he divined that the boys were suffering from *kumusambwa kwembalu* (the spirit of circumcision), and asked them to be circumcised at once to regain their health. The operation led to the restoration of the children's health. From then, all male children in the community started circumcising. Circumcision became the sacred ritual of *imbalu* that became unquestionable for transmitting the community's core values (Khamalwa 2009, 90-105). In this second narrative, the woman's role is implied as the idea to make circumcision mandatory comes from her diviner brother, Aramunyenye. Thus, in the narratives of the origin of *imbalu*, identity and health discourses combine and go hand in hand. In the documentary film, *Crafting the Bamasaba*, one of the female correspondents mentions that the Bamasaba think of an uncircumcised man as physically unclean because the foreskin is not removed.

The Bamasaba at times refer to Kundu as the son of Masaba who settled south in order to escape the "knife". The Baganda as an ethnic group do not practice ritual circumcision. This piece of information about one of the sons of Masaba having evaded the ritual is itself important in analyzing this ritual that presents itself as cohesive and mandatory. Implicit in this origin narrative is the "freedom" of individuals to break away when they do not feel comfortably accommodated within the value system of the community. The interviews I had with the community explicitly point to the fear of dissent especially from the younger people. This at times leads to frenetic attempt to enforce the practice. The fact that every year, some individuals who are discovered to have evaded the ritual are forcefully circumcised shows that although the official narratives indicate every young man looks forward to the ritual, alternative narratives show that there has always been opposition from some members of the community. My analysis tries to show the changing/unchanging attitude towards community members who carry the practice in a non-"traditional" way.

In *Crafting the Bamasaba*, the informants all agree they honour Nabarwa for prevailing upon her suitor to get circumcised before she married him, thereby emphasizing the original hygiene value.[8] During the circumcision, the participants face east – the direction where Nabarwa is believed to have come from – and all choruses, "circumcision comes from Nabarwa". Her role as a model to Bamasaba women is evoked in order to urge those who marry foreign men, to persuade their suitors to circumcise before their marriage. In this respect, one elder, Abdul Matanda, with a tone that expresses his disappointment, comments that the contemporary Bamasaba women marry "any how", without caring to persuade their "foreign" husbands to circumcise. He applauds the few who still follow Nabarwa's example. To emphasize the different voices on the ritual, another elder contradicts Matanda when he mentioned that they do not demand their daughters to prevail on their suitors to get circumcised; what matters is the love between them. What is evident here is the differing opinion among the community members, and the importance of the physical cut as an identity marker, without necessarily going through the elaborate chain of symbolic actions that have been developed into something of a philosophy of life. For an outsider who wants to marry into the community, the desire of the elders is simply for him to circumcise.

## WOMEN IN *IMBALU* RITUAL

Although *imbalu* is a male ritual, women play some key roles; principal among them is to promote the culture of *imbalu*. During the ritual, especially in the last three days to circumcision, they challenge the boys to be upbeat about "standing" and proving their manhood in the courtyard. The boy's progressive entry into the spirit of *imbalu* is from intermittent to frenetic. In the film the dialectic between seriousness and play is evident: the community stands by and watches the women dare the initiate to enter boldly into the spirit of the ritual (Turner 1982, 35; Heald 1982, 22). The boy progressively warms up to the challenge and begins to dance. The women feature in this slow pace of the start. They confront the boy to demonstrate masculinity and show that he is no longer mother's child but ready to become a man. When the ritual gets into frenzy, it is the men who take the centre stage. Francis Wambete, one of the interviewees, contends that the only reason for women to be present during the ritual is to see how the boy boldly "stood" and bore the pain of the knife; so that they would know "a man is not a person they can play with." In the view of Arnold Wangwe, another informant, the whole point of female presence, especially during the *kadodi* dance is to make the ritual exciting for the initiates, for the more women, the

313

more enjoyable for the participants. Wotsuna Khamalwa adds that the female is responsible for the general welfare of the initiate: they are there to challenge him, but also to take care of his material needs and to spoil him with attention. This corresponds with the community's perception of women as pitiful caretakers (Heald 1989, 57). In terms of gender relation, the ultimate point of the ritual is the celebration of manhood and masculinity as the pillar upon which the community values are hinged. The female presence amounts to "ministering angels to the needs and comforts" (Jones 2001, 113) of the boys who will soon "hatch" into authoritative men.

During the *ineemba* dance, characterised by the phallic symbol of the male drums, the "graduating" young men are allowed to validate their sexuality soon after or even during the three days' dance. This is the dance that celebrates the successful completion of their formation into men ready to begin responsible adult life. Traditionally, young girls are expected to participate in this dance because this is the opportunity for them to identify prospective husbands for marriage in the "girl year". The ambiguity of this space is that while the young man has the license to verify his sexuality, obviously with the woman who has come to celebrate his becoming a man, it is a taboo for him to marry the woman he has verified his manhood with. The woman's usefulness in this space is therefore avowed but at the same time she is despised for playing the litmus for the young man's sexual performance. For some of the initiates, indulging in sex here is a kind of ritual to make a clean break with the indefinite phase of convalescence they have been through. In the film, Khamalwa explains this sexual act in terms of the people's belief that it purges them of all misfortunes and curses they may have incurred in life.[9] The playful cultural logic at the expense of the woman is that, she should have been wiser, and not placed herself dangerously on the road to become an accident victim. Such an adventurous woman is not worth considering for a wife.[10] The community protects young men against such women by establishing a taboo to curtail further relationship with her. If he breaks this official embargo "his family and the lineage would be visited by misfortunes".[11]

Women, nonetheless, do play some significant role during the *imbalu* ritual. One of them is the symbolic shaving of the boy's hair by the paternal aunt before he enters the crucial liminal three days. The fact that it is the paternal aunt who does this is important. I interpret this as the boy's gradual transition from feminine hold to masculine company. This is, therefore, the female's final act of letting go hold of the boy and his connection with womanly, and by allusion, childish things. The woman hands the boy (*umusinde*) to the men to be formed in accordance with the values of the community. In this symbolic transfer of hands, rigid binaries with clear hierarchy of values are established. The feminine is totally denigrated in "crafting" the identity of the Mumasaba[12] (Khamalwa 2004, 127-9). This is the power of ideology and the effective operation of male hegemony where the woman willingly participates in her self-effacement and denigration in the interest of the son's development into a man. In doing this, she sees her interests embodied in that of the community (Gramsci, 1999). The link between woman and the boy is symbolically severed by this act of shaving. The woman's role is in giving birth and feeding the child; but turning him into a man (*busaani*) is the responsibility of fellow men. No woman is involved in the crucial phases of the ritual, some of which are cult-like activities in the sacred groove, where the boy descends into the sacred mud to be immersed into the spirit of the ancestors.

The general opinion of the community is that the surgeon is a special person, who is chosen by the spirit of *imbalu* to perform this sacred role. Nobody can become a surgeon by volition or mere training. Such a person must first be chosen through spirit possession and other signs. The "spirit of circumcision" chooses community members to become surgeons, regardless of their gender. However, the community deems it inappropriate for women to circumcise, and so once a woman is identified to have the potential to become a surgeon, this gift is killed in the bud by a counter rite.[13] The exclusion of women from this category is an area of power play that excludes women from exerting public influence in the community as elders.[14]

Gender discourse is further seen in the physical (temporal and spatial) location of women in relation to men when the initiate is being circumcised. The women, especially the mother, are supposed to be in the house at the crucial moment of the physical cut. As the men make a man out of the boy in the courtyard, the mother, in the company of other women, stays indoors for a number of reasons. She sits silent with legs outstretched, holding the central pillar of the house as if she were giving birth. This mock labour-pain corresponds with what is happening in the courtyard outside as the boy is being "delivered" into a man. This is a moment of severing the metaphorical umbilical cord between mother and child, important for both mother and child. The boy's successful birth into manhood depends on his not crying out to the mother for help. The one who cries for a mother's help even if he is above eighteen years, is disgraceful to be a man. This, now, is a test of personality. In this tense moment, the mother's disposition inside the house is believed to affect the boy's performance in the courtyard. Another reason for keeping women away from the courtyard is the fear that she would fail to control her emotions and thus communicate fear into the boy who is in the delicate "in between" phase. When the women come out, it is to witness the raw flesh and to celebrate with the rest of the community. At this point, the mother who shares in the glory of the son is also congratulated as the bearer of a courageous son.

My argument is that the origin narrative presents a respectful relationship between Nabarwa, a key player in the origin story, and Masaba contrasts the version of masculinity and femininity played by the contemporary Bamasaba (Edgerton, 1964; Bianco, 1991; Mukai, 2006). In the film, Dominic Makwa explains that it is expected for a traditional Mumasaba man to dominate his wife; and indicators of domination include beating her so that she gets to know her place in the house. A Mumasaba also boasts of his sexual prowess as a form of control over his wife and indeed several other women. Although the origin myth does not emphasize the domestic relationship between Masaba and Nabarwa, the fact that two foreign women are associated with the origin of the ritual is indicative of a different form of masculinity that the fore-fathers of the Bamasaba practiced – a form of masculinity that gave adequate space for women to express themselves and have influence on important matters of community.

The Bamasaba women reject frenetic masculinity that emphasizes toughness and disregards gentleness and courtesy as weakness. Although their preference is to marry "real men" who publicly demonstrate their courage, instead of "big boys" – a reference to men from non-circumcising communities, the women are constrained to marry the latter because these men are perceived as more romantic towards their wives. In the film, the regretful tone of Irene Kakai who expresses this sentiment shows that the dominant masculinity performed by the Bamasaba men is inadvertently turning some women away. Matanda who represents the more traditional view also laments that these days their daughters are unlike Nabarwa in persuading their suitors to circumcise. Matanda, however, overlooks the men's hysterical performance of masculinity in the domestic sphere as a possible reason for the women's preference of non-Bamasaba. As far as he is concerned, these women marry such men for money, and he equates them to prostitutes. The different reactions to the same situation show the multiple voices about *imbalu*. Unanimity and cohesion in the appreciation of the ritual is only apparent.

## "TRADITIONAL" AND EMERGING MASCULINITIES

The discussion above indicates change is always happening because we are, to use Bauman's expression, living in times of fluid modernity, where nothing is static. This holds true of the practice of *imbalu* that presents itself as a unifying community ritual. The individual members express their individualities in the way they interpret certain aspects of the ritual (Bauman, 2005). The word "traditional" is therefore used with the awareness that it is a slippery and contested ground (Ringrose 2007, 21-37). Even when the contemporary Bamasaba claims that performing the ritual in the courtyard is the traditional way, compared to going to the hospital, the idea of tradition can only be accepted as relative. The comments made by two of the oldest women interviewed during the research, Ana Maria Musungu and Clementina Nabifo Walulu show that some of the details in the "traditional" performance of the ritual today are not familiar to them.[15] In their view, today the initiates do not know most of the meaning of what they do. The solemn and respect-ful atmosphere that used to characterize the ritual is gone. Musungu who does not identify with the current version of the performance says, "Theirs is *imbalu* of the drums. They dance and feel happy. At our time there were no drums. The things of the past are gone." For Walulu, the obscene songs the participants sing "spoil the world". These comments underline the ongoing change in the practice of *imbalu*. *Crafting the Bamasaba* shows how at the Bumutoto ritual ground the sacred and the profane constantly intermingle. While still maintaining its seriousness, fun, spectacle and commerce have become part of the ritual as many who come to Bumutoto include non-Bamasaba. Wangwe explains that secular business in the ritual ground begins several days prior to the official opening of the *isonja* dance; and these activities that run parallel often contravene some of the values the ritual is meant to inculcate, such as self-control. In the preceding discussion, what repeatedly emerge are the gradually changing faces of *imbalu* performances. One is constantly aware of what has died out in the traditional practice and what persists.

Although the Bamasaba are pragmatically responding to change in many areas, the zeal to construct a more traditional masculinity remains rather unchanged. The value of courage was traditionally prized in the context of the need to form young men who would defend the com-munity from neighbouring ethnic groups with whom conflicts were rampant. Instilling this warrior mentality, a popular motif in traditional masculinity, is still perceived as valid; for courage is not only needed in battles but also in facing all challenges of life (Heald 1982, 17; Rutherford 2007, 81). Courage is still perceived as synonymous with manliness.[16]

Although values of modernity like a book and a pen are now added among the symbols given to the initiates to represent the core values of the community, these are crafted onto "traditional" masculinity. The pen and the book are presented as the contemporary symbols that open up ways for extra progress and upward mobility for the young man in the community. However, the preferred pathway to be fully identified as a Mumasaba is still the *imbalu* ritual performed in the courtyard, even if in its abridged form. It is not uncommon to forcefully circumcise even highly placed members who have tried to evade the ritual. Respondents with university degrees express their willingness to assist in having an evader forcefully circumcised, because "circumcision is an obligation to the Mountain".[17] Such frantic policing, nonetheless, does not take away the disquiet experienced by individual members of the community who may want to construct different identities. As Rutherford contends, defining identity as a past thing is easier than grasping it as something present because identity is unstable by nature (2007, 155). Thus, seeing identity as single is dangerous and explosive for the community. Where there is no room for dialogue, mutual recognition and accommodation of other voices, the precondition for the abuse of justice gets entrenched; and growing individuals are bound to contest such a unilateral identity.

Among the Bamasaba, it is evident that individuals variously show dissent on the traditional mode of the practice. This highlights that a single and coherent way of identity is often contested. As education opens up the community, objection to more public and dramatic display of masculinity is bound to increase. This trend is cogently represented in Timothy Wangusa's novel, *Upon this Mountain* (1989), in which the protagonist, Mwambu, beats the community at its game when his peers who think of forcefully circumcising him as an evader are surprised to discover that he is circumcised in the hospital. Although in the eyes of his peers, he is "less than a man" for not going through it the traditional way, Mwambu feels comfortable about the individual decision he made. He is portrayed as a sensitive, mission educated youth who is attached to the mother. His decision not to "stand" in the courtyard contrasts with the dominant masculinity value of his community. His revulsion to crude masculinity and blood reflects the stories of many young men, in real life, who are reluctant to perform the dominant masculinity demonstration.

In 2008, the year this research was undertaken, Bamasaba young vigilantes forcefully arrested an elderly politician and circumcised him. The *New Vision* newspaper reported that, "sadly, this happens to many men every circumcision year."[18] This incident provoked public reactions condemning the act of the youth in the name of culture. Even if an individual is a member of a community, he/she has rights as an individual, and these have to be respected. Even where the communalistic seems to have supremacy, the independence of the individual cannot be overlooked (Oladejo 2008, 182). Ethical life demands that we live in relation to the other. The healthy relationship between the community and the individual must be dialogic: the community with its values shapes the individual, just as the individual shapes community values (Rutherford 2007, 153).

The demands of rigid masculinity have their flipsides on the community. The younger generation that has been exposed to other cultural values is beginning to question some of the practices in the ritual. This valued position of "standing" during circumcision is contrasted with the circumcision in the hospital where the patient "lies" on his back under anaesthesia. This position associated with effeminateness is perceived as disrespectful for a man. Those who go to hospital often belong to the educated category. Young men who opt for the hospital, in this context, demonstrate alternative courage as those who are not afraid to be associated with the feminine that the dominant value despises. This is a form of courage in its own right. In the film, Peter Wamanga, a Senior Six student, speaks of the option he made to go to hospital when he acknowledged himself to be not strong enough to withstand the pain in the courtyard. He says, "When I go to the village, they seem to discriminate against me...I don't know what is in their heart. But I feel comfortable with what I did." Wamanga represents a new masculine courage that does not follow tradition obsessively.[19] He is one of the few circumcised in the hospital who are willing to share their experiences. He decided he would lose nothing and hurt no one by going to the hospital.[20] He has constructed an identity for himself that he is willing to occupy. It is difficult to speak of a universalised identity even in the context of a unified community, for a cohesive identity naturally excludes other identities (Rutherford 2007, 12). In trying to humanize *imbalu*, Wamanga recommends that the elders give pain relief for the "victims" of the raw knife. He looks at those who perform *imbalu* in the courtyard as victims instead of courageous men. He confesses that when his turn comes to have a son, he will have him circumcised young and in hospital so that it is less painful and the healing process is much faster. Through Wamanga's responses, one sees a range of change overtaking *imbalu* in the near future.

Both Khamalwa and Wambete who strongly ascribe to more traditional forms of the ritual also express fear that *imbalu* as it is practiced is likely to be more openly resisted in the future. In the first place, because of internal and external migrations, those who have lived away from the community may not identify with the details in the ritual practice and may question it. Exposure to new ideas through education is viewed as the clearest avenue to change. Furthermore because of the recent trend that associates circumcision with reduction in infection of sexually transmitted diseases, men, including those from non-circumcising communities, are turning to circumcision for health reasons. This development is bound to reduce Bamasaba sense of prerogative and implied superiority as a circumcising community.[21] For advocates of the traditional ritual like Wambete, the middle ground to avoid future embarrassment with youth who may grow up to contest *imbalu* is to have them circumcised in childhood, before eighteen, the age of volition.[22] Such shifts would change the meaning of the ritual dramatically. It would no longer initiate boys into adulthood as focus would now shift to the physical cut rather than the comprehensive formation of a Mumasaba.

Continuity and discontinuity characterise the current practice of the ritual. 2010 candidates like Brian Kitutu express the desire to be circumcised in the courtyard. This is not so much because he fully understands the meaning of the ritual, but because his father and brothers have been circumcised in the same way. It is a question of *"sheta umwana afwane baba we"* (circumcise the child to resemble his father) – part of the lyric of a popular *imbalu* song. Kitutu, for instance, comments that smearing the candidate with yeast, chime and mud are pointless as these do not reduce pain during the ritual. Yet in the film, one of the interviewees explains the rich symbolic meaning of smearing the candidate with these items which are significant components of the ritual (Heald 1982, 26). Although Kitutu is courageous enough to face the knife, he too is implicitly in favour of reducing pain during *imbalu*. Yet the ability to withstand pain is principle in forming the traditional Bamasaba identity. Besides, most of the youth today are circumcised during school holidays, and they skip a series of instructions that are traditionally given to the candidates in the ritual year. Now they mostly prepare for the physical cut; and the instructions are condensed in the three crucial days of the ritual. What matters is increasingly the physical cut alone.[23] Thus, in this apparently stable and continuous practice of *imbalu*, a close analysis reveals shifting grounds that make it challenging to speak of a single and consistent *imbalu* performance.

## CONCLUSION: *IMBALU* AND CHANGE TRENDS

The principal cultural capital of *imbalu* lies in giving the people what Victor Turner calls the *communitas* experience where their sense of connectedness as Bamasaba is reinforced regardless of social status (1969, 96-7). Courage, generosity and sense of community are cherished values of the community. The ordeal that the young man goes through leads him to the bigger reward of becoming a respectable man in the community and especially sharing the patrimony of the community. The song, "circumcise the child to resemble his father" emphasizes how circumcision equalises all Bamasaba men: no man is superior over the other. The relationship between father and son shifts to that between two equal men. However, the reality of the son being a junior to his father, both in age and in experience cannot be taken away; thus, this may be a ground for conflict between them (La Fontaine, 249). This makes Heald's observation on the connection between *imbalu* and Bamasaba propensity towards violence pertinent. The desired qualities required for *imbalu* cultivated in the young man, such as being daring, fearless, of firm and unyielding in resolve, are the same ones that develop the young man's predisposition towards violence (Heald 1989, 5). This remains a challenge in Bamasaba identity. Since *imbalu* levels all men as equals, hierarchical structure of authority, common to many communities is extraneous to the Bamasaba who are all men (*busaani*) as opposed to the uncircumcised others, referred to as boys (*basinde*). It is *imbalu* that sets them apart with a sense of superiority (Heald 1989, 19-20).

Yet, the values the initiate receives from the surgeon have no affinity to the violence demonstrated in the masculinity that the interviewees talk about in the film. A good Mumasaba is one who is characterised by the extent of his self-control in both word and action (Heald 1989, 73). A number of respondents mention that the need to prove manhood often makes the men obsessive about dominating the other, and this often leads to violence. The admonition the surgeon gives the initiates when he presents the ethics of *imbalu* during *khuusaabisa* rite are excellent human values. It is, however, a challenge for the man who remembers the ordeal in the courtyard to submit even to a fellow man, not to mention anything about women who are perceived as the antithesis of men. By contrast, the woman is expected to be gentle and kind towards others. At the emotional level, men and women are perceived as different: the woman shares the same kind of emotion with the child (Heald 1989, 57-9). The man on the other hand combines superior physical strength and toughness of personality that makes him resolute in resolve. Wambete comments on the difference between the Mumasaba of the past and the contemporary one, and concludes that the present Mugisu is worse in his attitude towards women.[24] This observation corresponds with Rutherford's that although we are living through a time of competing views on what it means to be a man, there appears to be a re-emergence of new forms of chauvinistic attitudes towards women. The omnipotent man who dominates and subjugates the woman has surged back in the popular culture forms and in the media (2007, 87-8, 90).

Bamasaba identity, however, cannot be construed as homogeneous. As discussed above, the attitude of the members of the community vary towards the *imbalu* ritual. When I asked Wangwe what he would like revised in the practice of *imbalu*, he mentioned all things associated with the occult because his identity as a Christian is incompatible with them.[25] Consequently, over the years, the signs of change are visible in the practice of *imbalu*. Religious and sub-cultural identities have become important factors of change (Gallagher, 1999). The only way for the ritual to continue and maintain its vibrancy is, thus to allow the various versions to exist, where individual families may pick or bypass phases of the ritual as they see appropriate to their layers of identities. What is important is to keep the core feature alive. This, in my view, is the reason for the vibrancy of this ritual. On the surface, it appears homogeneous and singular; but when one looks into the rubrics of its practice, there are different versions. The Bamasaba, in spite of external rigidity about *imbalu*, make allowances on how it may be practiced. The community demonstrates awareness of the individuality of its members (Rutherford 2007, 13-4). What they cannot tolerate is when a mature man tries to evade circumcision altogether even after giving him the not-so-prestigious option of doing it in the hospital.

Another factor of change is the economic pressures facing families today which make it too expensive to organise the ritual on a large communitarian scale. Depending on their circumstances, families may invite a surgeon to carry out the operation in the family, with only the immediate members and close relatives in attendance. Even vigilantes who verify an evader's identity check for evidence of the physical cut. Where and how a person was circumcised is not an important issue. People are also progressively getting circumcised at younger ages for the practical reasons of cutting down costs; circumventing the possibility of resistance by sons; and healing faster. Many interviewees, even those in the village, could not often explain why certain actions are performed during the ritual beyond, "It is our culture". This may not be appreciated by younger generation of Bamasaba who may want to practice what they fully understand. Today, a book and a pen are added among the symbols that represent the core values of the community when the surgeon commissions the initiate to be a good Mumasaba. These represent the new values of social success. Circumcision in hospital has become the desirable option for traditionally non-circumcising ethnic groups who also intermarry with the Bamasaba.[26] Such cross fertilization of interactions are bound to continue imprinting change on the practice of *imbalu*. Our times are characterised by a humanity that is sensitive to the individuality of its aggregate members. This sense is a prerequisite for such communal rituals to continue existing without trampling the rights of its members (Owoo 2000, 228 and Rutherford 2007, 154). In the paper, I have also argue that *imbalu* as a symbol of Bamasaba male identity must face up to the challenge of reconfiguring itself by curtailing its excesses of violence and dominant masculinity and become more accommodating of the individuality of its members in order to be relevant in contemporary context.

## Notes

1.  The concept of tradition as static, rigid and pure is only an illusion. Even the so-called traditional way of practicing the ritual is no longer how it was conceived by the fore-fathers. Culture is, after all, lived experience. There are many aspects of the "modern" in the "traditional" practice of the ritual.

2.  There are various voices in my documentary film, *Crafting the Bamasaba* (2009) that comment on the sacredness of the one knife that cuts and binds many in brotherhood; yet the fact he risk of infection cannot be ignored. The advocates of the traditional way argue for the sacredness and cleanliness of the knife; and the claim that the surgeon uses different knives for each candidate. My observation of the circumcision, however, leaves very little room for the surgeon to change knives and at the same time be able to expertly manage the operation within a minute. As for "disinfecting" the knife, it is a remote possibility in such rural settings; except if "disinfection" means sharpening the knife further and applying finely ground powder of kilned bricks on it that is believed to remove germs. The belief in the surgeon as a medium of the ancestral spirit makes what he does unquestionable.

3.  The Bamasaba circumcise even the corpse of a mature man, above 18 years old, who has died without going through the rituals, because they believe burying such a man in their soil brings misfortune to the community. It is the role of the vigilante in the community to hunt down such men because they will ultimately be brought home for burial when they die. These, however, are rare occurrences accompanied by prohibitive penalties; for circumcising a dead body marks the end of the career of a surgeon.

4.  Currently, in the narratives around *imbalu*, Nabarwa does not feature beyond being mentioned as the introducer of the ritual to the Bamasaba. The rest of the narratives are around Masaba, his sons and the values they represent.

5.  See Arnold Wangwe's response in the film, *Crafting the Bamasaba.*

6.  She is believed to have come from the Batwa. Oral narratives also associate Nabarwa with the Pokot of Kenya. The important point here is that she was an outsider.

7.  To date, Omutoto is the sacred ritual ground where the seat of the cultural elders is. It is the official space for the opening and closing of the ritual and other cultural activities. At the crucial moment of the physical cut, the initiates face Mount Elgon – a place synonymous with their origin and what they hold sacred.

8.  In the film, this is particularly mentioned by Abdul Matanda, an elder, and Irene Kakai, a young woman. This, like the reasons for the circumcision of Fuuya's sons, keeps the health and hygiene narrative present along side the cultural identity one.

9.  Dominic Makwa also emphasizes this point when he mentions that during *ineemba*, some of the young men may come to perform this sexual ritual without any sense of responsibility about the women they may have performed it on.

10. When I pressed my interviewees further to explain the logic behind young women's participation in this dance where sexually pleasing the initiates is both encouraged and condemned, Dominic Makwa, Wotsuna Khamalwa and Florence Muthonyi all explain that this was/is the community's way of screening good future housewives from bad ones. This, in my view, is an area that needs further investigation to understand the traditional logic of the community.

11. When I asked my informants whether there are no cases of young men who end up marrying those they verified their masculinity with during the *ineemba* dance, and if so, what hazards they have suffered. Although they acknowledged there are such cases, they could not mention the negative consequences of their decision.

12. This is the singular of the plural word, Bamasaba.

13. This comment from the community is significant in strengthening my earlier argument about the men's systematic exclusion of women in crucial matters of circumcision because this is associated with power relations. The probability that Bamasaba men stopped the tradition of female circumcision early for fear of crafting women with strong personality is high.

14. My interviewees informed me, it is only men who have given birth to at least a son, and have had him circumcised, who qualify to be called elders. This officially means that the father of female children is not considered an elder.

15. The two old women from Manafwa District said very little in response to the questions put to them. What, however, stands out in their response are

their disappointment with the degeneration of the ritual from what they consider was more meaningful at their time.

16. On 25<sup>th</sup> January 2010, when we took the film to the community for the first time, among comments made was the request that our team returns this year to document the ritual performance in a neighboring clan whose show of courage and masculinity is even more dramatic compared to what is documented in the film. The clan considered more courageous is the one that puts its initiates to even greater ordeals.

17. These are the responses of Francis Wambete and Arnold Wangwe, respectively.

18. See *Daily New Vision*, "Forced Circumcision is Unconstitutional", 27 June 2008; "Bagisu Youth Grab UPC man for Circumcision", by Ronnie Kijambu, 25 June 2008; "Forced Circumcision Illegal, Says social affair Minister", by Fortunate Ahimbisibwe, 26 June 2008.

19. Initially, I had made an appointment to interview a mature man of about 40 years, who had been circumcised in the hospital. He became dodgy and I immediately understood the reason for his unwillingness to speak publicly about the circumstance of his circumcision. Wamanga, on the other hand, had no problem with his identity as one circumcised in the hospital.

20. In the film, I was intrigued to note that Wamanga expressed his desire to go to the hospital to his mother, and not the father or uncle. This is understandable in the context of the "feminine" choice he is making. The mother is better placed to appreciate this decision and support it than the father.

21. This sense of superiority, especially in matters sexual, is articulated by various interviewees in the film.

22. The reasons for circumcising the boys in childhood, given by Wamanga, Wambete and Khamalwa are different. The convenience for Wamanga is based on health and for the older people it is the fear of disobedience by their children.

23. Brian Kitutu was a Senior Three student by the time of the interview in 2009. He proudly introduced himself as a candidate for 2010, but the comment he made indicates he knows very little about the symbolic meaning of the ritual actions he is preparing to get involved in. He simply practices it as a tradition.

24. Although Wambete's comment in the film sounds paternalistic, where the woman is not considered a partner but someone inferior to the man, it points to the fact that the condition of women is not getting better. For him, a woman is supposed to do "the simple things like cooking and peeling matoke."

25. In the film, interviewees like Wamanga and Matanda who are Christian and Muslim respectively explain that their religious beliefs determine what they include or exclude in their ritual performance. This is because *imbalu*, practiced in a comprehensive way is a religion in its own right.

26. This trend of wanting to "measure up" to the Bamasaba expectation of men has been clearly articulated by Khamalwa in the film.

# Chapter 17

# (RE)PRODUCING NATIONALISM IN EVERYDAY LIFE: A CRITICAL READING OF OFFICIAL NATIONAL NARRATIVES IN KENYAN RADIO DRAMA

*Dina Ligaga*
*University of the Witwatersrand*

## INTRODUCTION

This chapter argues that one of the most effective ways of reproducing particular notions of nationalism as natural is by circulating them within the realm of the everyday. This chapter critically analyzes the radio play: *Jamhuri Day Special*, aired on 12 December 2004, during Kenya's Independence Day celebrations. This play was produced for the state run Kenya Broadcasting Corporation (KBC), under the umbrella programme *Radio Theatre*. The play represents particular versions of official discourses of nationalism in Kenya that repress or silence others. Using themes drawn from everyday life, those of marriage, love and romance, these official discourses are reproduced and circulated within the radio play as natural and accepted versions of Kenyan nationalism. I argue that by looking at the genre of radio drama and its thematic content, Kenyan nationalism and nationalist ideals can be engaged with and contested in interesting and productive ways. I also hope that the chapter will show ways in which difference is perpetuated through such narratives that are often reflective of the ideologies of the dominant social groups in Kenya.

## BANAL NATIONALISM, ETHNICITY AND POWER

In his seminal book *Banal Nationalism*, Michael Billig (1995) argues that the concept of nation is reproduced within the realm of everyday life through ideological habits such as waving flags, circulating currencies and postage stamps among other aspects. He states that "national identity ought to be seen as a form of life which is daily lived in a world of nation states" (1995, 68), adding that nationalism is often hidden and circulated in forms and habits that are taken for granted. As Michal Skey rightly observes, Billig's work has paved the way for new studies of nationalism which move away from macro-level theorizations and their tendencies to homogenize and collapse disparate nations, to those that focus on issues of representation, circulation, localized meaning-making and contestations (2009, 333). Such studies recognize the extremely fragmented societies that make up the nation and recognize hierarchies of power and differences in gender, sexuality, ethnicity and class. As Umut Ozkirimli stresses, there is need to:

> [R]ectify the elitism of mainstream theories by bringing macro-level and micro-level analyses together, that is by considering the view from below (the 'masses', 'ordinary people') in addition to the view from above (the 'elites', 'intellectuals' or 'state bureaucrats'). (2010, 170)

Such a reading of nationalism challenges Benedict Anderson's argument that "regardless of actual inequality and exploitation that may prevail in each, the nation is always conceived as a deep, horizontal comradeship" (1991, 6-7). Anderson's conceptualization of nation ignores members of society who are marginalized and excluded in nationalist narratives that 'implicitly claim to represent them" (Loomba 1998, 198). Ania Loomba recognizes the danger of such blanket definitions of nationalism and states that "the power of nationalism, its continued appeal, lies precisely in its ability to successfully speak on behalf of all the people" (ibid.). Nations, she states:

> [A]re communities created not simply by forging certain bonds but by fracturing or disallowing others; not merely by invoking and remembering certain versions of the past, but making sure others are forgotten or repressed. (1998, 202)

It is perhaps for this reason that Homi Bhabha disavows the reading of the nation through singular grand narratives. He argues that nations must be understood as products of 'foundational fictions' whose 'origins [in] national traditions' are "as much acts of affiliation and establishment as they are moments of disavowal, displacement, exclusion and cultural contestation" (1990, 5). Bhabha further argues that the nation results from "cultural identifications and discursive address that function in the name of "the people" or "the nation'" constructed through social and literary narratives" (1990, 292). If one applies this idea to a reading of national narratives, it becomes possible to argue that such narratives are metonymic in the sense that they represent only those aspects of the nation that serve specific ideological functions for particular dominant social groups. The manner in which nationalism functions in the post-colony is therefore dictated by ideas of difference and power. Partha Chatterjee, for instance, engages with the manner in which former colo-nizers imagined ideas of nationalism in the former colonies. For him,

> Europe and the Americas, the only true subjects of history, have thought out on our behalf not only the script of colonial enlightenment and exploitation, but also that of our anti-colo-nial resistance and postcolonial misery. Even our imagina-tions must remain forever colonized. (1993, 5)

One of the ways in which this colonization persists is through the prom-inence of ethnicity as a primary index of politics in Africa, a concept of difference that was structured through colonialism. According to Mahmood Mamdani, ethnicity was constructed by the colonial regime to control (African) natives. Native authorities were selected to manage their own affairs but remained tools of the imperialist overlords. This is what leads to what John Lonsdale terms 'political ethnicity', refer-ring to contemporary structures of political rule in African politics in which those who occupy positions of power in the continent use eth-nicity to maintain control of public resources. Lonsdale's theorizing in many ways mirrors those of other theorists of African nationalism who have identified patterns of power structures that revolve around such notions of difference. Frantz Fanon's thesis on independent postcolo-nial nations, for instance, reveals ways in which nationalists embraced ethnic, class and racial interests of the ruling elite that provided them with the power to mobilize those nations' masses in particular ways (1967, 119). Michael Schatzberg equally observes that power in the postcolony resides in the state, and that the class interests of the ruling elite are best served through their ideological manipulations of ethnicity. Such readings become useful starting points for understanding how certain official grammars are constructed within national narratives that are then circulated within the realm of the everyday (Schatzberg 1988, 11). Conversely, these studies show how the so-called masses project their own versions of nationalism that are inherently exclusive of 'others'.

## RADIO DRAMA AND THE 'GENRES OF EVERYDAY LIFE'

One of the distinct characteristics of the genre of radio drama in Africa is its immersion in everyday realities of its imagined listeners (Gunner, 2000; .Gquibtole, 2002; Ligaga, 2005). Rather than focus on explicitly political themes, radio drama has often presented itself as anodyne with an emphasis on moral and educational themes. However, having been produced for the state broadcaster for decades before the liberalization of the media, radio drama in Kenya has, on the one hand, been informed by its politics of production within a state broadcaster, while on the other, has adopted themes drawn from contemporary everyday life, which touch on the perceived realities of those who listen to it. The ensuing tension has called attention to a closer critical analysis of how the genre works. In this chapter, I look at the radio play 'Jamhuri Day Special' aired on 12 December 2004, during Kenya's Independence Day celebrations.

Produced within the umbrella programme, *Radio Theatre*, the chapter shows that the play embraces the institutional ideologies of the state broadcaster, Kenya Broadcasting Corporation (KBC), which are circulated and reproduced through the tropes of love, marriage and romance.[1] Drawing on the theoretical formulations of the functions of nationalism in the realm of the everyday, this chapter seeks to inter-rogate the versions of nationalism that circulated within the 'Jamhuri Day Special' and to argue that such narrow formulations of nationalism knowingly or otherwise exclude other competing national narratives. The play follows the character of Gakuo, a young man whose intentions are to marry Njambi, the woman that he loves. Gakuo intends to have his wedding coincide with *Jamhuri* Day (Independence Day) celebrations because the day represents his unconditional love for both his bride and his country. He visits his grandfather, Mzee Gakuo, to find out about the possibility of holding the ceremony in their family compound, under the sacred Mukuyu tree (a traditional sacred tree), planted on Kenya's Independence Day, on 12 December 1963. However, when Mzee Gakuo learns that Gakuo's fiancée is the granddaughter of a former colonial collaborator, he immediately orders Gakuo to cancel the wedding, as he, a former Mau Mau war veteran, cannot endorse his grandson's marriage to the granddaughter of a traitor. Set mainly in Mzee Gakuo's rural home, the play is a narrative of marriage between Gakuo and Njambi. Both proclaim their undying love for each other throughout the play. The familial focus of the play locates it within a domestic space that is removed from the arena of the public and national. Yet, *Jamhuri Day Special* is an allegory of Kenya's history. The deliberate linkages with specific symbols, images and myths, as well as narratives, not only connect it to popular public narratives of Kenya's history, but also, in many ways perpetuate problematic official grammars of nationalism. It draws attention to a series of narratives about Kenya's history, especially around those who 'fought' for its independence. Such a construction of Kenyan history is often linked to the narrative of the Mau Mau who were among those who fought for the independence of the country. In the past years, this narrative of struggle for liberation has come to occupy a dominant place in Kenyan popular literature and official discourses, and as such, other competing narratives have either been suppressed or forgotten. Thus, the play's opening signals this well circulated narrative through the use the character of an old war veteran whose account of the struggle provide a snapshot summary of the independence narrative that is familiar to the post-liberation Kenyan audience:

> MZEE GAKUO: [...] I remember those days, when we were in the forest... sitting down... telling stories... let me show you how I used to hold the gun, we used to hold it like this [Gakuo laughs]... and we used to wait for the *wabeberu* [colonialists] to come, *ukarathaba tia* [You shoot!].When Kenya became independent, *I kwani mweri cigana*- what was the date?
> GAKUO: 12 December.
> MZEE GAKUO: *Mwaka wa* 63, I remember that year of '63. I remember that. We celebrated in all manner [of ways]. Mmm we had freed ourselves from the yokes of the colonialists. *Mubeberu kwenda* [colonialists, go away]...we said a final goodbye to the white man's oppression. ... We said, *Ciaigana ni ciaigana* – enough is enough!

In the above excerpt, the play uses a memory technique that provides general information about the Independence narrative in which the perceived listener is supposed to create links to other circulating narratives of independence. In other words, Mzee Gakuo's version of the history is sketchy, and delivered in a lighthearted manner, with the assumption that his grandson and by extension the listener, already knows the narrative and have heard it many times. This is why the narrative is extremely condensed, and eludes key aspects of Mau Mau history. The Mau Mau movement in Kenya, which became synonymous with independence struggle in Kenya, was formed in the 1940s, as a militant group, an offshoot of the Kikuyu squatter community that revolted against settlers in the White Highlands in Kenya (Furedi 1990, 105). This is one of the most studied anti-colonial protest movements, perhaps because of its resonance with other struggle movements all over sub-Saharan Africa (Odhiambo and Lonsdale 2003, 3). Nevertheless, it has also created a lot of debate because of the contradictory positions it has occupied in post-independence Kenyan discourses. According to James Ogude, the movement has been "appropriated and negated' throughout Kenya's post-independence history for political gains" depending on the ideology whichever reigning regime has embraced (Ogude 1999, 34). This is a crucial point when one begins to engage with the way that it has been represented in canonical and popular nationalist discourses and the kinds of conflicting spaces it has occupied in these narratives. To quote Ogude further, "the Mau Mau has survived as an ambivalent phenomenon in colonial and postcolonial Kenyan politics... [and has] tended to serve sectarian, conservative and ethnic interests" (ibid.). It is fairly common knowledge, for instance, that Jomo Kenyatta, Kenya's first president, "forcefully denounced Mau Mau" and declared that all Kenyans had fought for Uhuru (Ogot 2003, 19). In other words, he completely nullified the role that the Mau Mau had played in the struggle for independence, and was keen to leave them out of the new national discourse that was being constructed. The Mau Mau became part of what Odhiambo and Lonsdale term 'orderly amnesia', where, in order to construct a new nation, unwanted elements had to be suppressed (Odhiambo and Lonsdale 2003, 4). They represented a 'voice of whole classes of landless' Kenyans, a reality that did not go down well with the new political culture that was being constructed, as "class struggle was [being] excoriated from the vocabulary of politics" (ibid.). The denouncement of the Mau Mau was well captured in Kenyatta's rhetoric of 'Uhuru na Kazi' (Freedom and work) in which he condemned laziness which he associated with robbery and violence leading them to become marginalized at independence (Ogot 2003, 19). Yet, throughout Kenyatta's regime, and during Daniel Arap Moi's regime after him, the Mau Mau was constantly used for various pro-state agendas. Ogude has shown for instance, that at times when Kenyatta faced competition from his political opponent, Oginga Odinga, he "deemed it fit to rally Mau Mau veterans as the custodians of Agikuyu interest, against the perceived threat from Odinga's Luo dominated Kenya People's Union" (1999, 34).

At such points, the Mau Mau were deemed useful for sustaining Kikuyu nationalism, a project that Kenyatta was passionate about. Nevertheless, he kept the idea of the Mau Mau alive in the consciousness of his electorate whenever the need arose, but he never did feel compelled to honor them publicly as part of Kenya's national history even though his political ideology differed from that of the Mau Mau as already explained above. In the same way, Daniel Arap Moi "who was perceived as the lackey of the colonial regime, reaped the spoils of the Mau Mau heroism in order to subvert democracy" (Ogude 1999, 34). For instance, in 2001, Moi made a move to turn important sites in which the Mau Mau battles took place into national monuments[2]. However, this was largely seen as an election ploy to win the support of the large Kikuyu masses, most of who favoured the opposition leadership that eventually saw him toppled out of power in December 2002.

Thus, the inclusion of the Mau Mau narrative in a positive light in this play is not without its contestations. Bearing in mind that the play was produced in 2004, it is interesting to read its production against contemporary politics of the time, during the era of President Mwai Kibaki's regime. This is a significant period because President Kibaki, who took over from Moi, lifted the ban on the Mau Mau in 2003, legitimizing its members for the first time since the colonial era. The Mau Mau had finally been given their place in national history; but this move was seen in some quarters as just another ploy by the government to pacify a majority of its supporters who were sympathizers of the Mau Mau.

Needless to say, the recognition of the Mau Mau has meant that they have become part of the national discourse. The erection of the statue of Dedan Kimathi, one of its leaders and whose narrative is well documented in literary texts such as Ngugi wa Thiongo and Micere Mugo's 'The Trial of Dedan Kimathi' is a case in point. His monument was unveiled in 2007 and is located on Kimathi Street, also named after him. The location, known as Kimathi Triangle is a public reminder of the place of Mau Mau heroes in Kenya today.

However, the play presents nagging tensions created by rifts that exist within this romanticized version of Mau Mau history which I argue is reflective of other unsaid tensions that exist in present day constructions of the Kenyan nation as demonstrated through my analysis of *Jamhuri Day Special*.

In the play, Mzee Gakuo is repulsed by the thought that Gakuo is about to marry the daughter of a former colonial informer. Thus, ironically, even though he celebrates the new nation, he is unable to let go of differences that exists within it. The use of the trope of romance is therefore deliberate to act as a site of tension as well as reconciliation. Indeed, as Ogude argues, in his reading of Ngugi wa Thiong'o's novels, romance is a useful trope for 'testing the reconciliation of ethnicity and nation, tradition and modernity, betrayal and hope and indeed, the possibility of rebirth" (Ogude 1999, 109). The pursuit of reconciliation is problematic precisely because of the tensions that exist within the play's narratives captured in the dialogue below:

> GAKUO: Grandpa, you know what, I want to get married...
> MZEE: [Laughs happily]
> GAKUO: Okay and you know what? I want to tie the knot under this tree...
> MZEE: Oh my grandson, who is my daughter
> GAKUO: Ahhh, she's a girl called Sylvia Njambi
> MZEE: Njambi, ha ha...
> GAKUO: From the famous Tobiko family, yeah
> MZEE: Ati? [What?]
> GAKUO: Yeah, Tobiko-
> MZEE: Tobiko wa Gachania?!
> GAKUO: Ehh
> MZEE: To... To... To...Never! Don't talk beyond that, no, no marriage, no!
> GAKUO: What!!!
> MZEE: Ah ah! We of the Gakuo family shall never ever marry with the Tobikos. *Hapana* [No].
> GAKUO: But...but... grandpa what's wrong with the Tobiko's?
> MZEE: *Ati* Tobiko, the former colonial chief, never!

The immediate reading of this tension shows that Mzee Gakuo and Mzee Tobiko have irreconcilable differences. At this stage, such differences appear absolute and the marriage becomes an impossible feat. Mzee Gakuo's stubborn inability to accept those who were not part of the struggle as family and therefore as citizens of the same nation is in many ways indicative of how differences in Kenyan nationalism are often perceived and treated, yet, as is the intention of the play, such differences are superficial and often based on issues that can in fact be dealt with and resolved. Mzee Gakuo identifies himself as a true hero, a nationalist who belongs to the independent nation, while he considers

Mzee Tobiko as an outsider who should not partake of the 'fruits of independence'. His reaction feeds into existing politics of exclusion that have dominated Kenyan post-independence nationalist discourses.

According to Atieno Odhiambo, the manner in which nationalism has been predominantly defined in Kenyan politics has been around those who 'fought' for independence and those who did not. He states that "over the last 40 years, the question of who is a Kenyan nationalist or not has always been important. In the context in which the term has been used, a nationalist has been one who fought for freedom, *Uhuru*" (2003, 38). In the play, Tobiko is still seen as a traitor several years after independence, and must not partake of *Uhuru*, but remain shunned and ostracized from society. Perhaps even more visible is the fact that it is not him but his grandchild that is being punished, leading to the question that Bethwell Ogot asks elsewhere, "who is a national hero" and who is excluded from being identified as one? (2003, 19). Mzee Gakuo's reaction also forces one to engage with the differences and tensions that existed within and continue to plague the Mau Mau. It is these tensions that draw attention to the fact that it was not as perfect as is usually claimed in various narratives (Odhiambo and Lonsdale 2003, 3-5). In colonial Kenya, the Mau Mau were seen as violent terrorists who disrupted social order, even though their supporters saw them as heroes. In addition, the movement itself was beset with internal strife, and did not consist of a seamless united group fighting for Kenya's freedom, as nationalist discourses want to suggest. John Lonsdale records the rifts that existed within the movement based on varying ideologies among its leaders (2004, 79). Thus, this play enables one to see the national hero as 'imperfect', and also to welcome the possibility of alternative national heroes into the discourses of nationalism.

While 'Jamhuri Day Special' is clearly invested in drawing attention to the narrative of reconciliation and unity through its narrative of marriage, its representation of and interpretation of Kenyan national history remains contested. For instance, in the play, Mzee Gakuo gives a summative account of Kenyan history using a sacred tree, the Mukuyu tree, as a metaphor. Having planted it in 1963 at Independence, Mzee Gakuo traces its growth vis-à-vis Kenya's political history, and attaches specific meanings to its four branches, all of which he sees as representative of specific versions of Kenyan history:

> MZEE GAKUO: You see my child; I had to mark that day in style. I got my eldest son, the late Ndegwa. I told him to plant this tree on Independence Day; and so this tree my grandson is the same age as Independence Day.

335

GAKUO: So … That is to say that this tree is the same age as independent Kenya?

MZEE GAKUO: Mmm *negwo* [that is true]. Eh, how many branches can you see?

GAKUO: I can see four.

MZEE GAKUO: *Negwo.* That is right. They are four. And do you know what the four branches represent, my child?

GAKUO: No…

MZEE GAKUO: No, you don't know. Do you see that place, where you can see the nests?

GAKUO: Over there?

MZEE GAKUO: Yes. Those represent the two decades of the sixties and the seventies, when Kenya enjoyed economic stability. Now, those two other branches on the other side represent the eighties and the nineties, when corruption and mismanagement was at its peak level, bringing our economy to its knees *kabisa* [completely].

The significance of the Mukuyu tree is two-fold. First: it acts as a symbol of Agikuyu culture, and is a sacred symbol of Kikuyu nationalism, a point which I will come back to later in the chapter. The tree and its branches also become symbols of Kenyan independence history, used to measure its political and economic development since independence. Planted by one of Mzee Gakuo's children, the tree is central to the manner in which Mzee Gakuo interprets Kenyan nationalism. It acts, as Michael Billig argues, as a reminder of and marker of his sense of national identity and belonging. As such, he looks at the four branches of the tree as representative of Kenyan politics. According to him, two of the branches represent the era when Kenya was thriving politically and economically, while the latter represents the opposite. The former version draws attention to the Kenya's political leadership, between 1963-1978 when it was under the leadership of Mzee Jomo Kenyatta, and the latter between 1978-2002 when it was under Daniel Toroitich Arap Moi, Kenya's second president. While both regimes are represented, the manner of this representation can be engaged with further. While Kenyatta's political leadership is celebrated as having led to economic development and the creation of a successful nation, Moi's era is interpreted as having led to the destruction of the country.

Mzee Gakuo's Manichean interpretations are however simplified and refuse to engage with the complexities of both Kenyatta and Moi's regimes that contributed to the creation of, and sustenance of ethnic and class differences that persist in Kenya today. His interpretations can be used to shed light on the manner in which contemporary politics have benefited from such simplistic representations of Kenyan nation-alism. For instance, the interpretation of Kenyatta's rule as successful becomes a useful model against which one can understand President Mwai Kibaki's rule in present Kenya. For one, Kibaki adopts the phi-losophy of *uhuru na kazi* underlines notions of hard work and freedom which, which according to Mzee Gakuo, led to economic and politi-cal prosperity. However, what this narrative does not deal with is the continuation of elitist and ethnic politics that defined Kenyatta's regime and which, by implication, are reflected in Kibaki's rule. The play strives rather, to emphasize the narrative of hard work for economic success as is shown in the monologue below:

> GAKUO'S FATHER: I have seen Kenya through years of independence. It has been an experience worth celebrat-ing. And my son's Gakuo's wedding was to be the befitting gift for this. I think Gakuo was right to say that Kenya has offered me enough. I would be rich now. Look at civil ser-vants like Wafula, who invested in sugarcane and maize farming and made it. *Pombe ni kitu ovyo sana* (alcohol is such a useless thing). There's been plenty of opportunities like in farming or even *jua kali* sector; a guy like Mutiso just started with little carvings, now, now he is a major exporter of curios. I shouldn't blame Kenya. For the last 40 years, Kenya has built a fairly good infrastructure which has seen many industries mushrooming. [Music] Our literacy levels are now higher, we have enjoyed reasonable democracy. The other day Kenya proved to be the most peaceful and democratic nation by having a peaceful and smooth transi-tion of power hardly ever seen in the continent.

Gakuo's father's monologue above frames specific ideologies that continue to define contemporary politics in Kenya. The monologue articulates the official narrative of national progress through 'hard work' and 'enterprise' while subtly muting any critique of state power and the state's failure to facilitate economic progress. Going back to the promises made independence, the Jomo Kenyatta regime embraced the rhetoric of 'Freedom and work', to urge the new nation to embrace hard work in order to achieve prosperity. However, this rhetoric of 'hard work', in typical capitalist tradition, masked the reality of inequitable access to state resources and the construction of a political middle class, by passing these off as products of hard work, and in some ways, crimi-nalizing the poor as lazy, while deflecting attention from the klepto-cratic middle class that was slowly crystallizing around the state power, ethnicity and by extension, Kenyatta. Thus, scores of landless Kenyans, including the Mau Mau, were marginalized by the system which had no place for those who could not provide for themselves.[3] Thus, Moi's entry into power in 1978 was seen by most of Kenyatta's allies as a disruption of the construction of this economic power. Moi, during his term, replaced that carefully constructed Kikuyu dominance by creating a powerful Kalenjin economic base in its place (Mueller X, 188). When Kibaki came to power, one of the things he did was to literally delete Moi from the system, replacing Moi's ideologies with those of Kenyatta, along which he modeled the post-2002 Kenyan state. One of the philosophies he adopted was that of '*Kazi iendelee*' [May the work continue], to mark his regime's continuity with Kenyatta's. It is this discourse that the play 'Jamhuri Day Special' embraces by attempting to sanitize both the Kenyatta and Kibaki regimes, by championing them as the basis for Kenya's economic progress, while the Moi regime is literally 'deleted' and dismissed as a failed state.

In this way, the monologue of Gakuo's father can be seen as an extension of Kenyatta's ideologies in which Kenyans are encouraged to compare their wealth with that of others, itself a very capitalist endeavor. What is also interesting in his speech is the way, for the first time in the play members of other ethnic groups are included. However, this is done by stereotypically allocating each member a trade commonly associated with that member's ethnic group. For example, Wafula, a Luhya, is immediately thought of as a sugarcane farmer, given that large sugarcane farms are located in the Western Province of Kenya. Mutiso, a Kamba is associated with stone carving, a trade once again that has been associated with this group in Kenya. This kind of ethnic categorization in itself is problematic as it reduces Kenyans into ethnic enclaves, and suggests that wealth can only be obtained through localized industries. This is a problematic construction because the state controls how resources are allocated, its support of those very local industries is often informed by how the state views members of particular ethnic groups. Only those who support the state are rewarded, thus ensuring a distinctly skewed distribution of economic resources in the country.

Yet, in spite of these obvious divisions, the play strives to present a romantic vision of the nation through the relationship between Gakuo and Mumbi. Through them, for instance, national culture is represented in a way that elicits a sense of national pride and patriotism demonstrated through their dialogue below:

GAKUO: [monologue] I have had fun with Njambi. I remember like last year when the two of us went on a coastal tour. It was fun, it was so much fun.

[Flashback, voice chamber]

NJAMBI: Ahh ... It's so much fun lying on this beach. I see now why people love it here.

GAKUO: You see there's nothing like race here, you see there are whites lying over there.

NJAMBI: It's fun. Look at the beach ... No wonder tourists keep flocking this country. Look at those ships. Are they bringing cargo?

GAKUO: Oh yeah ... yeah.

NJAMBI: Oh God, this is so much fun, I know how they feel when they come here.

GAKUO: Do you know why these people are coming to Kenya?

NJAMBI: Why?

GAKUO: Because Kenya is a land full of plenty.

NJAMBI: Oh yeah.

GAKUO: Africa is so beautiful, this land is so marvelous. I don't think I want to move out.

NJAMBI: You are not supposed to do that, darling.

GAKUO: Sincerely speaking Africa is so beautiful. But not all countries enjoy this kind of fun by the way. This kind of pleasure is only here, because Kenya is a peaceful country.

This romantic presentation of Kenya, although meant to encourage patriotism, also embraces official discourses of tourism that package Kenya as a commodity. Thus, tourism, a staple component of Kenya's economic life, enters into local life. By identifying the significant role that tourism plays in Kenya, one of the ways in which it has been integrated into Kenyan discourse is through centralizing it within both local and international discourses of Kenya. As Grace Musila argues elsewhere, "there has been a sustained marketing of the country as a tourist destination, a process that has coded beaches, wildlife, cultural artifacts and various ethnic groups into the recognizable brand of 'tourist Kenya'" (Musila 2008, 118).

The play encourages a localized consumption of this tourism as a way of encouraging an appreciation of Kenya by its citizens. Couched in official grammar, the play attempts to re-present Kenya to Kenyans through the eyes of fellow citizens and in doing so, deliberately 'others' foreign tourists. This official discourse borrows from an existing archive of tourist descriptions of Kenya;[4] in which the beauty of Kenya is romantically captured in what Musila terms "the colonial archive" in which ideas of Africa as pure, wild and savage are maintained (2008, 117). The recognition of the foreign tourist as the outsider however, diverts attention from tensions and differences that have led to internal differences within Kenya. In the example below, the play gives a hint of such moments of violence, although this is once again constructed as an attack from outsiders rather than conflict from within:

> GAKUO: and then from Mombasa, we visited Malindi, another spectacular city. There we saw the famous Vasco da Gama pillar. God! The tour took us to Lamu, that small coastal tour captivated us with its uniqueness spiced up by the cultural ...these people treated us with. We really enjoyed the traditional mnazi wine...*then there was this bombing in Kitambala. Tourists ran away, all of them! Njambi was in tears! I remember it as if was yesterday* [emphasis mine].

The description of Kenya in this excerpt shows how the tourism industry is disrupted when the stability of the country is threatened. In this case, Njambi's tears become symbolic of the practical reality of the loss of tourism in Kenya. It is also interesting to note how this narrative makes its way into the play to signify the collapse of peace and tranquility of Kenya, when other narratives of internal conflict such as the 1990s ethnic conflict are left out.

Another key element of difference in the radio play is that of a unified Kenyan ethnicity, which is taken for granted throughout the play. The play's setting as well as its adoption of Kikuyu cultures and customs is a case in point. For a play that seeks to narrate Kenya, it has an extremely narrow construction of this nation. This is seen in the use of the Mau Mau narrative as the default narrative of struggle in Kenya. The Mukuyu tree, a sacred tree in Kikuyu culture, is used to symbolize various political moments in Kenya. Lastly, the characters, settings and languages selectively represent the Kikuyu. Overall, the play offers a skewed reading of Kenya's national narrative by zooming in on, and offering only one version of the country's narratives. By emphasizing on only one narrative, the play inadvertently suppresses forty-one other ethnic narratives that form part of the bigger Kenyan national narrative. I argue that the ideological positioning of power is such that it becomes possible to recreate public memories of national narratives along such ethnic lines, to the extent that citizens get into a state of amnesia. Mzee Gakuo habitually slips into speaking Kikuyu and it may seem like a natural position for him to occupy as an old man in the village. However, in many ways, it also signifies the manner in which the play attempts to collapse narratives of national struggle into a Kikuyu 'organic' nationalism. By privileging a single ethnic community as 'the authentic' custodians of the struggle for *Uhuru*, it is possible to argue that the play is suggesting that members of this community are also the legitimate heirs of 'the fruits of independence'. It is perhaps this exercise of valorizing certain narratives when it comes to writing the nation that Atieno Odhiambo (2003) draws our attention to. In acknowledging the centrality of struggle in the narratives of independence in Kenya, he argues that it is impossible to talk about Kenyan nationalism without thinking of who fought for *uhuru*, independence.[5] He argues that, contrary to the history that Kenyans have learned through institutions such as schools and the media, there was no single Kenyan nationalist movement. Thus, the reality is that Kenya is a multi-ethnic nation forces one to rethink the use of a narrative that is representative of one community to represent the nation.

## CONCLUSION

While this paper presents a general critical analysis of the play, 'Jamhuri Day Special' and its reproductions of national narratives within the realm of the everyday, it opens itself to analyses of broader political and social constructions of Kenyan nationalism. Taking the position that existing scholarship tends to ignore specific ways in which nationalism is circulated in the realm of the everyday, this paper engages with different levels of such representations. It looks at a play that selects as its main themes, marriage, love and romance, in order to present a romanticized version of the nation. This is problematic since the play presents these ideas of nation and nationhood as 'accepted' versions of Kenyan nationalism. One of the reasons for this is because such narratives are seen as so commonplace, that the play does not see the need to represent other versions of Kenya's history. Thus, this paper contests that such easy /simplified representations of Kenyans used in the radio play have become part of institutional circulation of the officially sanctioned versions of nationalism in Kenya. The paper hoped to show that such narratives circulated every year, risk the danger of legitimizing specific notions of nationalism, to such an extent that other competing narratives will eventually be deleted from Kenyan history. Therefore, this paper calls for a re-engagement with taken-for-granted notion of Kenyan nationalism.

# *Notes*

1. *Radio Theatre* was first aired in 1982 for Voice of Kenya (VOK). Even though the VOK changed its name to KBC in 1989, it was still the voice of the government, and as such, its programmes were often used to promote national unity and to transmit various government policies. 1982 is the date given by one of *Radio Theatre's* longest serving producers Nzau Kalulu.

2. BBC News, 'Monuments for Mau Mau'.

3. Kenyatta's exchange with Bildad Kaggia, one of the men with whom he was arrested for their involvement with the Mau Mau by the colonial government, is a case in point. Kenyatta is recorded to have told Kaggia, 'look at Kungu Karumba. He has invested in buses and has earned money, but what have you done for yourself since independence?'. See Bayart, *Politics of the belly*. 242.

4. See Blixen, 'Africa', 1937; Ruark, *Uhuru* 1962, and Huxley, 'Flame Trees', 1959.

5. In his chapter, Atieno Odhiambo argues that there are seven theses on nationalism in Kenya. He argues that the manner in which questions of nationalism have always been approached have been by looking at who fought for *uhuru*, thus generating various discourses around it. Various groups have laid claim to Kenyan nationalism, including political leaders of Kenya's first political parties Kenya African Union (KAU), and Kenya African National Union (KANU), particularly those who had been detained; the Mau Mau freedom fighters; members of opposition parties who were 'absent' from the psychodrama of Mau Mau such as Daniel Arap Moi and Charles Njonjo; the ethnic group of the Kikuyu as a whole; the Kenyan intellectual elite; the socialist-leaning opposition parties and the ordinary *mwananchi*, the small man and lastly, the literally scholars who drafted their own nationalisms. See Odhiambo, 'Matunda', 38-44.

# Chapter 18

## ADJUDICATING THE COURT SYSTEM THROUGH DRAMA: AN EXAMINATION OF *VIOJA MAHAKAMANI*'S ROLE ON KENYAN TELEVISION

*Fred Mbogo*
*Moi University*

### BACKGROUND

*Vioja Mahakamani* is the longest running television programme in Kenya. Since its first airing in the late 1970s, it has consistently portrayed the goings-on in a Kenyan court. The programme was developed by popular radio drama actors who shaped their material to work for television. Over time the programme has become instrumental in playing out anxieties that come with the interaction between the rural and urban. These characters are depicted in their daily struggles within a chaotic urban space which is brought into some sense of ordering by the justice system. The phrase *"Vioja Mahakamani"* when translated from Kiswahili to English it loosely means "drama in the Courtroom." This title alludes to the anxiety ridden behavior exhibited by characters who interact with a court so distant in its practices that it altogether ignores customary, popular knowledge and logic and instead relies on a mostly jargon-laden and therefore frequently misunderstood written law instead of administering justice.

Episodes of *Vioja Mahakamani* typically run for between twenty-eight to thirty minutes during which time courtcases are completed. The programme relies heavily on the court as the prime scene of its action. Within the scene a judge presides over a prosecutor's presentation of an offender's crime and the subsequent denials/rebuttals from the accused. The court process in these cases is often simplified to the extent that the accused is unrepresented by a defense lawyer. This deliberate absence of a defense lawyer means that the defendant may not have a chance in the court room to competently defend himself. It also means that the defendant gets to speak for himself and therefore the audience gets an insight into his person in terms of character and position in society. The court case also runs without as much legal jargon as there would have been with the participation of a defense attorney. In Giuseppe Caramazza's (2002) reading of Kenyan media in the text *News reporting and broadcasting* there is strong evidence that a language that employs a terminology linked to a specific profession such as medicine, law or engineering interferes with the audience members outside such professions understanding of the technical speech. In this case, legal representation for the accused in the programme also denies the audience the voice of the accused, who more often than not has been crafted as a character to be identified with. The actors use "street language" (Swahili with first language influences) or *sheng*, "a hybrid of Swahili, English and bastardization of several ethnic vernaculars as opposed to legalese used in courts of law" (Ligaga 2005, 47). It is interesting to note that when a judge, prosecutor and police inspectors are witnesses, they use a more accessible Swahili. The programme is currently aired on Kenya Broadcasting Corporation's channel 1 every Wednesday at 19.30 pm and on Thursdays at 14.00 pm. Though the programme's form has changed over the years as a result of technological shifts such as the move from black and white pictures to full-color, the main actors, including those playing the judge and prosecutors have remained. At the same time, the programme's didactic strategies in matters to do with the law and court operations have been maintained as are interventionist approaches in a variety of issues including the engagement with taboo subjects including Female Genital Mutilation, gender roles and equity, wife inheritance, sexual harassment, among others. *Vioja Mahakamani* is part of a large body of works that have portrayed the nature or processes of courts in Kenya. Others include recordings that are based on individual experiences within courts such as Ngugi Wa Thiong'o's *Detained*; where he elaborately discusses detention orders made towards his confinement in a Kenyan jail; Ojwang and Mugambi's

*The S.M Otieno Case,* where the issues of modernity versus tradition especially on death and burial are brought to the fore in court; Karuga Wandai's *Mayor in Prison,* where the main thrust of the story is an initial unfair incarceration and eventual acquittal of a deputy mayor from a case of fraud; Peter Kimani's *Before the Rooster Crows,* based on a girl's tragic story in which an American soldier is acquitted despite evidence of his having murdered a Mombasa prostitute; John Kiriamiti's series of crime novels including *My life in Crime, My life with a criminal* which give details from different perspectives on John Kiriamiti's meticulously planned robberies and court proceedings that eventually brought him to justice. Lately, there has been a television programme titled *Nairobi Law* whose storylines, as offered by Citizen Television, its producers, are based on non-fictitious stories.[1] Kenya National Television (KTN) is currently running a drama series titled *Be The Judge,* in which court cases based on actual occurrences are discussed with a view to understanding the various perspectives taken into consideration in rulings on such cases.

While these texts give the readers a tour into the practice of law in Kenya, they are based on cases that have had implications on historically known individuals. *Vioja Mahakamani's* storylines on the other hand depend on hypothetical cases where the empathies or sympathies of the audiences may not immediately register. For this reason, *Vioja Mahakamani* becomes a text whose characters are distant and who can therefore be safely mocked. The essence of this distancing it may also be argued, through Brechtian (1968) postulations, is that in defamiliarizing the familiar the audience appreciate the familiar through new perspectives as shed by the programme. The ordinary is presented in an otherwise extraordinary fashion by the programme. *Vioja Mahakamani* is a light hearted drama that seems to follow in the pattern of other works that are created around the professional areas such as medicine, law, education police,, among others. A few good exemplars of these professions are seen in these well –known TV shows such as *Ally Mac Beal, Derrick, Boston Legal, CSI, The Practice, The Monk, House, ER,* and *Girlfriends.* These programmes have been aired and some are still running on various Kenyan television channels.

*Vioja Mahakamani* is shaped in as formulaic manner in which the programmes are built more around the clients of the court. While most of the aforementioned programmes have titles derived from the names of their main characters, these programmes are inclined to present the lives of whichever professionals they are involved with. Instead of focusing on the lives of the protagonists, *Vioja Mahakamani* is more

345

interested in the lives of ordinary seekers of justice within the Kenyan legal system rather than portray the lives of its prosecutors or lawyers. This structure invites the audience to play out/identify their own anxieties with the Kenyan legal system than identify with the absurd lives of the court officials. Court officials as discussed later in this paper are presented as above the problems associated with the ordinary citizens who mostly are unsettled in the urban space. These officials, as is explored further, are presented as being beyond ethnic bias since their language, especially Kiswahili, is punctuated with accents that cannot be easily identified with any one Kenyan ethnic group. It is through this unaccented Kiswahili they present the court as a space that does not condone ethnic stereotyping and court officials as incorruptible since on face value they are 'tribeless'- where they don't speak the implied regional language of any of the accused and cannot be influenced.

## INTRODUCTION

This chapter proceeds with the notion that texts emerge out of everyday activities or rituals that sometimes may be deemed as organized performances. Such "performances", often not deliberately made to entertain but to nuance on emerging issues, like court procedures do, are patterned in ways that easily lend themselves to being aped or copied. *Vioja Mahakamani* is therefore read as a parody or imperfect copy of Kenyan court procedure. Its purpose is to entertain and enlighten its viewers through the intentional use of "distancing" or defamiliarising strategies. Bertolt Brecht's thesis of alienation is employed within the framework of the Bakhtinian idea of heteroglosia that applies the multiplicity of voices within a packaged production that necessarily presents multiple meanings to an audience. Yet in the multiplicity of voices there lies the possibility of distortions and a failure to capture the intended meaning. How the dramas of *Vioja Mahakamani* are directed towards exploring the differences in individual characters be they through class, profession and linguistic competence are discussed as aspects of the parody that not only give the multiplicity of voice its place but also render the drama a viable tool to critically examine issues. Such issues include dichotomies of rural against urban; government verses individual; literate and illiterate; ignorant and informed; and rich verses poor. These contrasts are necessary for the drama of *Vioja Mahakamani* to be experienced by the audiences as an area for the playful misinterpretation of the programme's agenda. The chapter is therefore an examination of the ambivalences/paradoxes when programmes like *Vioja Mahakamani* are employed in discussing "serious" issues as court procedure or the law.

## THE COURT AS A PERFORMANCE SPACE

In an essay by Reddy and Portgieter, titled "Real men stand up for the truth": which explores the Jacob Zuma rape trial the argument is advanced that trials can be treated as 'texts' whose meanings can be read by both players and the public (Reddy and Portgeiter 2006, 511-21). It is on the premise of this idea that Raymond Suttner proceeds in another essay "The Jacob Zuma rape trial: Power and African National Congress (ANC) masculinities" (Sutter 2009, 222-36). Suttner, notes that "a court is a type of theatre", implying that the court is a performance space whose actors range from the Judge, to the accused and their lawyers but also includes those who attend court hearings (ibid).

By virtue of its dramatizing court proceedings, *Vioja Mahakamani* must then be seen as a text that is generated from 'the' text. Here 'the' is used to privilege the court as the original instrument from which *Vioja Mahakamani* is drawn. Yet, while *Vioja Mahakamani* may be seen as a fascimile of court proceedings, it is prudent to note that any reproduction of court proceedings is not necessarily original. Any single court proceeding is a text that borrows from preceding activities of the court even though such borrowings can never repeat the full story exactly. Judges and lawyers behave the way they do following what has been done before in the Kenyan court system. Actors in this text follow the beaten path as Kuloba has opined;

> ...they are guided by previous judgments which are similar, to justify a decision in a present case. Past decisions are kept and referred to in later years; accumulated into historical records for posterity: they are built upon and they are part of a unified and organically-developing social system. (1997, 8)

The difference between an episode of *Vioja Mahakamani* and an ongoing court proceeding is mostly seen in the implications on the accused. While the audiences of *Vioja Mahakamani* know that the court action leads to sentencing they are aware that the accused is merely acting. On the other hand the sentencing of the accused in a 'real' court proceeding is taken seriously as all participants are aware that the implications are not fictitious, they shall experience the full weight of the law if found guilty. Court proceedings take place for the purpose of the dispensation of justice. But they may also educate as observed by Kuloba where they are involved in "...teaching people the right beliefs, the right feelings and the right way to act, molding the moral and legal conceptions and attitudes of a society" (1997, 8). The context of *Vioja Mahakamani's* presentation necessarily makes it a programme that teaches through entertainment. Audiences can appreciate the programme from the comfort of their homes or at other spaces. This lends *Vioja Mahakamani* an accessible face where audiences can watch a court process within a safe environment. While both a court case and an episode of *Vioja Mahakamani* are texts that come from observing goings-on in the Kenyan justice system, they differ distinctly in their manner of portraying previous events. *Vioja Mahakamani's* approach, as opposed to a court procedure's, seemingly distorts the nature of the Kenyan court system. Actors representing the characters of the accused for instance tend to exaggerate their reactions to the sentences proffered by the judge. The language employed by the actors while often being standard Kiswahili, is distorted frequently and a mangled version is preferred. These and many other factors come into play when considering the implications of the proceedings presented in the programme.On the other hand, any court procedure held within the various court houses in Kenya is necessarily lent an air of seriousness, what with such measures as a dress code, language competence, the actors' (players') demeanors among others. In such a court procedure, the judge's ruling, for example, as discussed in Kuloba (ibid.) is guided by previous legal proceedings whose implications were and are taken seriously in the dispensation of justice. Further, the players in this court procedure, unlike the actors in *Vioja Mahakamani*, are trained lawyers. The training given to these lawyers, as shown for example at Moi University's School of Law is more in the direction of how to carry out their work rather than on mere facts.

Students are taken through simulations or moot courts, law clinics and are also placed in other agencies for the purpose of learning how to behave in court. This procedure of training affects the work of such lawyers in a court of law as it acts as a 'rehearsal' for the 'acting' out of the text. Trained lawyers must then behave in a particular manner within the court corridors and in court. Thus, the text that a single court procedure presents to the public is taken seriously as the preparation is thorough, particularly by the court officials. In view of this then, it is possible to conclude that *Vioja Mahakamani* is a text that borrows from another text but creates a new text that may be deemed a distortion of the imitated text. Unlike a specific court case guided by precedence carried on from previous court cases and whose players, the lawyers especially, are specifically trained for the execution of such cases, *Vioja Mahakamani* borrows an outline but chooses to create its own pattern of action. The programme becomes an imperfect replay of court cases and procedures.

## *VIOJA MAHAKAMANI* AS A PARODY

*Vioja Mahakamani* falls within the widely disbursed notion of parody. Margaret Rose's (1993) *Parody: ancient, modern and post-modern* traces the notion of parody to its root Greek word "parodia" or "parodos". Relying more on the theoretical works of Fred W. Householder, she avers that the notion of parodia meant: "a narrative poem of moderate length, in epic meter, using epic vocabulary, and treating a light, satirical, or mock-heroic subject" (1993, 15). On the idea of "parodos" she observes that it defines the "imitating singer" or "singing in imitation" (which Householder suggests was made in contrast to a concept of the original singer). This historical articulation of the notion of parody becomes useful in this chapter as it leads us into the acknowledgment that firstly, parody is necessarily a kind of aping[2] and that secondly, this aping is consciously made with a view of the 'original' in the mind of the imitator. The implication is that *Vioja Mahakamani* as a text cannot be discussed without the consideration of court procedure which is the 'original text' that is imitated. But on a further inspection of parody, Rose notes that theorists, especially of the formalist mould, have defined it as an "imitation of form with a change to content" (1993, 15).

Although fraught with problems, the idea of parody in the context of form and content does point us in the direction of *Vioja Mahakamani's* approach. From a broad perspective the programme is crafted in the image of a court proceeding. The key players in the court proceedings are; the judge, prosecutor, accuser, and witnesses in addition to the accused. These actors are found within a space whose physical presentation, as presented in the set design, is similar in nature to that of a typical courtroom in Kenya. The positioning of the judge behind a huge desk and at a height comparatively more raised than that of the rest of the participants in the court, in addition to the roaming room given to the prosecutor emphasize this lifelikeness. At the same time, the accused is or are paraded behind a barrier with characters in police uniforms keeping guard while the witnesses file into the courtroom from a special room from where they should not have heard the previous witness' accounts. The programme imitates the judge's demeanor in the sense that she presents a seriousness that suggests that the profane or traverse is unwelcome. But all these attempts at recapturing a typical Kenyan court scene are muddled by the interpretation presented through the characters of the accused and witnesses. The physical barriers, for example, are often times crossed when the accused characters express their anger at their opponents. They hope at such moments to express their dissatisfaction with proceedings. The nature of these characters' behavior borders on caricature. They are extra-ordinarily verbose and have names which are deliberately amusing either in their pronouncement or meanings. Consider, for instance, Ondieki Nyuka kwota Oloba Man Gidi, or Tamaa Bin Tamaa Tii Tii (complete with the sound "tii"), and Masanduku Arap Simiti (literally; boxes of Cement!). In that sense *Vioja Mahakamani* seems to successfully imitate the court in physical terms, as evidenced in the set design, but flouts the procedures via the actions and statements of its characters.

## OF MULTIPLE VOICES AND DRAMATIC CONFLICT

For the didactic intent of *Vioja Mahakamani* to be manifest, there has to be a multiplicity of voices. Some will necessarily have to portray ignorance; others will be the 'correctors' who hope to lead the ignorant towards the path of knowledge or right. Still, others will be 'detractors' who experiment on the various ways of filling the gap wrought by ignorance. It is in the confluence of these voices that confusion may arise on the question of whether to take the programme seriously. For in the babble of voices, there is the danger that the preferred voice that should lead the audience to the correct path of knowledge or information about the law and the workings of the Kenyan court system may be drowned out. Instead, the voices of the ignorant or 'detractors' that carry the entertainment value that the programme offers become the more memorable.

Stephen P. Breslow has demonstrated how drama is made from competing ideas, especially in view of its mechanics which celebrate conflict as a source of the drama. He observes:

> Multiple voices form the central fabric of drama. Variable speech patterns and intonations, differing uses of standard, slang and dialectic language created, form a purely textual point of view, the chief differentiating features of dramatic dialogue. (1989, 36-9)

This argument is buttressed by Breslow's reading of Derek Walcott's play titled: *A Branch of The Blue Nile* via the notion of heteroglossia as pursued by Mikhael Bakhtin. Although he acknowledges that Bakhtin's idea of heteroglossia is drawn from readings of the novel as a site in which language becomes an articulator of diverse positions as affected by contexts, Breslow draws from heteroglossia the idea of multiplicity in singleness. He qualifies his reading of Walcott's play via the Bakhtinian heteroglossia by a replay of examples from the *commedia dell'arte*. Indeed, this is best articulated in Bakkhtin's own view of the heteroglotic nature of *commedia dell'arte* where:

> In the *commedia dell'arte* Italian dialects were knit together with the specific types and masks of the comedy. In this respect one might call the *commedia dell'arte* a comedy of dialects. It was an intentional dialectological hybrid. (1989, 36)

Breslow begins a discussion of Walcott's: *A Branch of the Blue Nile* by observing that the playwright's heteroglotic language is brought to a peak as a result of combining his rich African, Patois, French, English, and classical Latin linguistic legacy. Further, the play suggests Breslow, is a continuation of Walcott's "black/white, colonizer/colonized cultural reversals which he played with in his earlier drama, *Pantomime*, by means of his Crusoe/Friday role shifts" (ibid.). Bakhtin's own view of parody gives light to this discussion especially as parody is viewed as a device through which different languages and styles "...actively and mutually illuminate one another" (ibid.). Thus, within a text such as *Vioja Mahakamani* there must be voices pulling in different directions.

The text's capacity to have multiple voices is given a "post-modern" sensibility in Breslow's assessment where it is labeled as "...the text within the text within the text" (ibid.). This argument follows from the Bakhtinian view of the 'parodic' text as bearing languages that degrade. This sense of degradation often happens within the same language so that "the parodying language is not a foreign language but a language belonging to another social group, a different dialect" (ibid.). But in some cases, such as in *commedia dell'arte*, the parodying language is foreign. Therefor there can be bilingual and trilingual comedies. In the case of *Vioja Mahakamani*, the language employed is Kiswahili. Characters express themselves in a variety of versions of Kiswahili. Language use in the programme is framed according to a character's social position within the programme. The judge, prosecutor and police inspectors who are agents of the law speak in standard Kiswahili. When a witness occupies a position in government, for example as a doctor, the language he or she employs is usually standard Kiswahili.

On the other hand, the accused and many of the witnesses speak in a variety of Kiswahili dialects.

Speaking Kiswahili often invites attitude from listeners within East Africa. This is especially in regard to the accent used by the speaker. The reaction from listeners is not uniquely East African, but the world over as people do form opinions about others through the accents that they use in any one language. Miner has argued, using the Ugandan example about how Kiswahili use shapes attitudes when he observes thus:

> One idea about Kiswahili that underpins many of the ascribed (and often contradictory) attributes to its speakers is that it belongs to no one in particular, and so often serves as a kind of linguistic "mask." In this sense, it is associated with transient, uprooted people and the marginal survival strategies in which they engage. (2002, 55)

If it is true that in Uganda that one can 'mask' his identity by their use of Kiswahili, it follows that in Kenya, where *Vioja Mahakamani* is aired, the same can happen. The judge, prosecutor and the police inspectors use this 'mask' to portray a somewhat 'tribeless' face of the law. While it is possible to form an opinion of the judge, or prosecutor's tribe in *Vioja Mahakamani*, through taking a guess after observing their physical features, their use of language is such that they betray no obvious accent associated with particular tribes. This can be contrasted with the heavy accents that the accused and witnesses use even where their main reason for these heavy accenting is to show that they are newly arrived at the urban space from their rural backyard.In tracing Kiswahili accents used in *Vioja Mahakamani* one can note: Ondiek Nyuka Kwota's Luo accent, Alphonce Makokha's Luhya accent, Masanduku Arap Simit's Kalenjin accent, Olexander's Maasai accent, Tamaa Bin Tamaa's Luhya accent, among others. Ondiek Nyokakwota's son is among a generation of the young that speak in *Sheng*. Identifiable accents from other tribes are also occasionally used as depending on new actors brought into the drama. In some cases the programme employs a European character whose Kiswahili accent also betrays his background and sometimes he is forced to speak in English. While the judge personifies the law's authority, she is given a 'mask' so that her Kiswahili is unaffected by an identifiable accent. This allows her to make rulings that might not be construed to be either punitive or lenient to the accused who may be assumed to belong to tribe A or B through their accent. The integrity of the judge therefore remains untainted. She cannot be accused of being tribal as it is difficult to label her tribe. The prosecutor's Kiswahili accent is also played out in a manner that cannot locate it to any one specific tribe. Hence, the prosecutor also portrays an image of the government arm of law enforcement as not aimed at punishing or rewarding any one tribe. The police inspectors also use the same 'unaccented' Kiswahili. As law enforcers, they must be seen as incorruptible. They are above the temptation of the common people. A historical inspection of *Vioja Mahakamani*'s recordings reveals Inspector Wariahe, whose presence in court always caused a stir especially as his Somali accent was quite pronounced in his Kiswahili. His struggles with the language as he described scenes of crime, the details of investigation and nature of arrest always became sources of entertainment. This seems more like a contradiction as police officers in *Vioja Mahakamani* have since been presented in the 'tribeless masks' where their Kiswahili accents are not immediately located within specific tribes. It can be argued that in Inspector Wariahe's time, Somali characters were not presented in the *Vioja Mahakamani*'s court as offenders. They neither were featured as witnesses. In that case, Inspector Wariahe, despite being a policeman, seemed more like a representation of the "other". The distinct physical characteristic of the Somali 'mark' them apart from other Kenyans, especially as regards their hair. This makes it easy for one to tell a Kenyan Somali apart from a Kenyan from another region. It therefore might be suggested that Inspector Wariahe may not be interested in favoring any one specific tribesmen. This is because he is not related to any none-Somalis. Thus, he is incorruptible at that level. But he allows for the police to be laughed at because he allows the viewers of *Vioja Mahakamani* to experience, through him, the weaknesses of the police. In his struggles with language, Inspector Wariahe always turned argumentative and his temper would rise. In many instances the prosecutor had to intervene as a measure of correcting the Inspector's viewpoints or linguistic problems. In such instances Inspector Wariahe's anger would rise to the point that he had to be calmed. At the same time, when compared to the composure of the many of the accused, whose demeanor is relaxed and uncaring, the Inspector's ire seems uncontrollable. Inspector Wariahe's character is an exception in terms of the portrayal of government workers in *Vioja Mahakamani*. The production alludes to the idea that the government is made up of a mosaic of tribes from all over the country with the sole purpose of providing faithful service. But this also implies that these workers have come to terms with the cosmopolitan nature of the government. When compared to many of the accused, who are still finding their way in a multi-cultural and multi-ethnic setting, the government workers are presented as hardworking and law-abiding. The cases in which the characters are involved in include: sale of uninspected milk, storing petrol in a residential house, feeding monkey with tobacco laced bread, running hotels without toilet facilities, illegally participating in hire purchase to regain debts. When these characters are portrayed as victims of crime they are variously duped by some tricksters into taking part in '*karata*' or "*kamari*"- illegal roadside betting, giving money so that it can be doubled after 'prayers', giving in household goods to men sent by the 'owner's' house. These characters come from such estates as Korogocho, Huruma, Matopeni, and Kawangware which essentially are slums. From their Kiswahili accents loaded with their first language influence, the audience is made to place them as people who are attempting to find their space within the urban setting. They seem to be in transition between their rural space and upbringing and the new and necessary urban space in which they hope to make a living. They are jobless, as is the case with Lambert Wekesa and Alphonce Makokha, who in one episode are said to have been brought to 'town' (city) by Omondi Nyuka Kwota. They are also variously, watchmen, cooks, construction, and domestic workers as held in the testimonies of Otoyo Obambla, Mgongo Mture, Maliwasa, Mwala, and Masanduku Arap Simit. Where they are property owners, they are lowly and only manage small properties like food Kiosks, *shambas*, or struggling 'clearing and forwarding' companies as presented in the introductions of Ojwang Mang'ang, Tamaa bin Tamaa, and Ondiek Nyokakwota. The anxieties of the accused and the witnesses who have suffered damage from the offenders are played out in the form of the unsettled language they display. The audience is made to learn of the anguish, and frustrations that these characters undergo in their attempts at settling in these urban spaces. These characters are unmasked to the point that the audience gets to know them well. On the other hand however, the characters of the judge, prosecutor, and court clerk or police inspectors are hardly uncovered. Their emotional sides are not displayed. They seem impervious to the anxieties of urban living. There is a tussle when these two groups of people are placed together in court. The side of the court officials seems high up, untouched and untroubled by the goings-on of the ordinary '*mwananchi*' (citizen). The stories that are told through their body language, especially with the no-nonsense approach of the judge and the almost routine questioning fielded by the prosecutor is that "this is just another day, with another disturbing case." The motivation to succeed displayed by the accused in their own defense and the witnesses, in their attempts at seeing right done, is often in complete contrast with the prosecutor's lack of fervor in court. Kiswahili(s) becomes (a) clear agent(s) through which multiplicity of voices articulate their positions. The different accents of

Kiswahili each presenting the audience with a picture of the social position of the speakers give the programme the multiplicity of voices. Following the Bakhtinian notion of heteroglossia we can conclude that within *Vioja Mahakamani*'s text is a mish-mash of voices each seeking a space for dominance but which, for purposes of presenting a unity of text is deliberately toned down with the ultimate calculation of presenting a specific agenda. But the converse is also true: there are voices in the text which unintentionally become louder or more articulate and often scuttle the agenda of the programme.

## DIGITAL FACILITIES

This emblematic competition of voices is best captured in a *Vioja Mahakamani* episode simply titled "Digital-Facilities". The programme runs on a typical story of a man who, together with his worker moves about in search of the gullible. The trickster in question is Ondiek Nyuka kwota and his worker is Alphonse Makokha. They persuade their victims that on the December 1st of 2009, the Kenya Broadcasting Services is turning digital. Thus all television sets running on the analogue setting will become obsolete. For this reason they are collecting the television sets which use the analogue system at a price of between two and seven hundred shillings only. This they argue is necessary as the sets are not worth any more than that. In any case, they argue, they are out to use the materials from the television sets in the making of utensils and other electronic goods – they therefore are offering a noble service. The case proceeds with the usual line up of witnesses against Ondiek Nyuka Kwota and Alphonce Makokha, who are accused of duping Olexander Josephat into selling them his television set at only five hundred shillings. It is during Olexander's testimony that we learn that he is vulnerable to the con artists. He seems incapable of fending away future con artists as his understanding of issues seems muddled by his inarticulate mastery of language. The prosecutor has to come to his aid on several occasions in order for the court to make sense of what he is trying to say. The Maasai accent in his Kiswahili renders the conversation both comical and absurd. In his narrative, he states that he was leaving his home with his wife in order to attend a wedding committee meeting of a neighbor's son. He cannot pronounce wedding and ends up insisting on "wed ding". He also states that Ondiek Nyuka Kwota and his accomplice took his "tevelison" for television. He talks about how they convinced him about "ten-work", where he means "network". He also mentions "disital" instead of "digital". Ariel becomes "Erio" while "set-piece" comes in for "exhibit"- which is the television in question. He mispronounces "confuse" by using the letter p where it becomes "conpuse".

While these may be English words, his Kiswahili is equally misinforming to the point of being hilarious. He remembers, for example, that some policemen arrested Ondieki Nyuka Kwota and Alphonce Makokha. He refers to them as *"polisi wa kuzurura"* (loitering police) and adds that *"ni kama hawana kazi"* (as though they have no work). When he is informed that they are policemen on patrol, he cannot understand that and insists on what he believes hence the insistence on loitering. When Alphonce Makokha states that he only was a worker following instructions from Ondiek Nyuka Kwota, who is his boss, Olexander easily answers him, but wrongly. Makokha asks: *"naingilia wapi"* (how do I come into the conflict), upon which Olexander smiles, probably thanking his memory, *"kwa nyumba"* (into the house). The literal meaning being that Makokha entered into the house!The whole episode becomes absurd with Olexander stating that once he handed his television set to Ondiek Nyuka Kwota, it stopped working. But the prosecutor asks him whether he tried switching it on, to which Olexander states that he tried to but did not succeed. From the discussion the audience learns that Olexander switched it on without connecting it to a source of power such as electricity. How then can it work? But he is not willing to discuss more on the issue. Nyuka Kwota and Makokha chide him into handing over his television set by stating: *"kwani utakaliwa na bibi?"* (Will you remain oppressed by your wife?). They push him to declare that he is the owner of the television set when his wife seems to wonder why there is a need to hand over the television set. Their persuasion method is meant to attract Olexander's presumed upbringing which frowns on men who have to seek permission from their wives before carrying out a family project or selling a household product.While this character may be presented to the audience in this ignorant nature for comical ends of the programme, he seems incapable of understanding the nature of urban living. While the law redeems him through offering protection from such con artists in this particular case, he is still left vulnerable to future con artists. His understanding of issues in a cosmopolitan space that is constantly inundated with new technology, competing knowledges, rapidly expanding infrastructure, constantly rising costs of living among others are likely to confuse him. At the same time, he does not seem to make any effort to understand what is going on around him, instead he prefers to remain with his interpretation of events as no amount of correcting persuades him to pursue the suggested line.In contrast, the judge sits comfortably behind her huge desk from which she occasionally calls for silence, or orders the accused to ask relevant questions. It is also from this desk that she makes her rulings, from reading a sentence or two from her 'written' notes before launching into a speech about digital and analogue television systems. Her position of power makes her seem all knowing and incapable of being duped. One is therefore tempted to wonder: how can there be such a gulf of knowledge between Olexander the witness and the judge? But there are characters of the mould of Ondiek Nyuka Kwota who know that they can dupe others and consequently they seek opportunities to take advantage of the weakminded/gullible. In his defense, Nyuka Kwota wonders what happened to the principle of 'willing buyer; willing seller.' He argues that he did not coerce Olexander into handing him the television set. As a final plea to the judge he states that he is not well educated. But the judge reserves no sympathy for him, as she goes forth to issue a punitive sentence: a one year jail term with the alternative of a fifty thousand shillings fine. The languages employed in this episode seem to present characters that represent a variety of classes and who are at various stages of 'comfort' with the urban setting. While some are struggling to settle in, as Olexander's character shows, others have elected to fight it out in order to survive- as Nyuka Kwota and Makokha are doing. Still others are unencumbered with the everyday problems and instead display an order that needs to be emulated- these include the judge and urbane prosecutor. The problem with this setting is that there is a temptation for audiences to ignore the preferred agenda being forefronted by the producers and remain enchanted by a character whose performance is endearing in its comedy. The comedy proffered through Olexander's Kiswahili contrasts sharply with the mastery of Kiswahili language that the judge's Kiswahili uses in court to help this victim. Yet to have one standard Kiswahili language used throughout *Vioja Mahakamani* would destroy the programme's essence. In any case, for the intended message to be passed there has to be a depiction of the antithesis of the message. The judge would have nothing to state in terms of the idea of digital and analogue television sets if there wasn't a voice that seems to offer a contrary view.

## CONCLUSION

In this chapter, I have attempted to present the nature of *Vioja Mahakamani*, especially in its dual quest of entertaining while providing pedagogy on legal issues. The approach preferred by the programme, especially through a parody of a typical Kenyan court session, has created a text that prods its audience to re-examine their societal values, the crisis of urban/rural migration, threats from technological advancement, and the continual assault of 'traditional' values by a ruthless economic system. The programme also brings to the audiences' attention the vexing question of ethnic stereotyping; whose negative consequences are a constant source of anxiety within the citizenry through favoritism, prejudice, bias, mismanagement, and their attendant ills. The programme presents characters whose accents are identifiable, in terms of belonging to members of particular ethnic groups or tribes, and may therefore be deemed to be extending the various stereotypes attached to different ethnic groups. This may be deemed as a negative path for the programme to take as it is basically a reinforcement of societal views on the various tribes. Yet, for the programme to capture the anxieties of its main characters, who are ordinary citizens with minimal sophistry in terms of education or wealth, it captures them in their greatest err. This is ironed out by the judge, prosecutor and police inspector who represent the personnel, and in many cases, become the personifiers of the law. Given the multiplicity of meanings that are attributable to the text that is a parody of the court system, it is possible that the programme may as well unintentionally contribute to stereotypes or vices through a glorification of such when *Vioja Mahakamani* star actors play roles of tricksters, or offenders trying to defeat justice. But the audiences seem to be aware that this is just a humourous portrayal that actually uses these stereotypes to show us the ridiculousness of such simple/crude caricatures. In addition, the programme serves to provoke audiences' awareness in court matters besides merely showing possible scenarios within the Kenyan court system.

## Notes

1. Wa Thiong'go, N. *Detained:A Writer's Prison Diary.* Nairobi: EAPL, 1981; Wandai, K. *Mayor in prison.* Nairobi: EAPL, 1993. Kimani, P. *Before the Rooster Crows.* Nairobi: EAPL, 2002; Kiriamiti, J. *My life in Crime.* Nairobi: Spear Books, 1994.

2. Aristotle's notion of art as imitation is explored via the word "ape" where an actor in his work copies the behavior of real life characters: Aristotle. 1970. *Poetics* (Translated with an introduction and notes by Gerald F). AnnArber: University of Michigan Press. Michigan.Et et volore dolor sim quid qui nullandiciam autatum qui consed qui sequamus am haria voluptatem raecum que eveles res maio officiis dipisquam quae non nonsed qui doluptaerum qui con cones comni optat pa di ullibus eosanto tasperum earcit et res maiorro et quas susci a denihitiant quunt.

# Chapter 19

# KENYA'S DIASPORIC CYBER 'PUBLICS' AND THE 'VIRTUAL' NEGOTIATION OF IDENTITIES: EXPLORING THE DISJUNCTURES AND CONJUNCTURES

*George Ogola*
*University of Central Lancashire, United Kingdom*

## INTRODUCTION

There is little doubt that globalisation has accelerated the movement of people around and across the world, the consequences of which have been complex and varied. For many people, this experience of dispersal often leads to both physical and emotional displacement and in many cases a longing for home. Yet home, as conceived in the new surrogate countries by these displaced persons tends to be a place or a space, both real and imagined. To some, home can be historically traced to a physical place while to others it is simply an imagining, a fantastical construct even, to be made and remade. Displacement tends to foster an attachment of migrant populations to specific places, ideas, values and histories. It is this attachment that has led to and indeed sustained Diasporas around the world.

Over the last decade, the Internet has provided a new platform through which Diasporas can now interact, imagine and narrate home, create communities and share their experiences. The Internet has helped create new identities while at the same time shaping and reshaping old identities. Away from the 'homeland' diasporic communities have created new 'homes' online, some unified, many differentiated and fragmented. The development especially of Web 2.0 applications has enabled the ever-growing Diasporas to organise themselves online in even more new ways. The emergence of social networking sites, such as Facebook and weblogs, have enabled attachment to specific geographical spaces even as they allow for the creation of web-based communities, which de-territorialize their identities. For many web users therefore, the Internet now provides a site within which new notions of the self, community and the new forms of sociality are created.

Amongst the largest growing Diasporas in the world has been the African Diaspora(s). Although the movement of Africans from Africa to Western metropolises has a long history, it has particularly intensified in the postcolonial period with the integration of the continent into the global economy and the dynamics of globalisation processes. But accelerating this migratory movement has been the crisis of the African state. Since the 1980s, social, economic and political instability in a number of African countries has induced flight from the African continent.[1] Like other African countries, Kenya has a huge and growing diaspora in the West, primarily based in the United States and Western Europe. Estimates from the World Bank and the Kenya Central Bank indicate that through formal financial remittances back to Kenya, this Diaspora now contributes over US$2 billion annually thus making it the largest single source of external capital into the country.[2] This unremitting attachment by Kenyans abroad to their 'mother' country raises key questions relating to their continued relationship with Kenya and more broadly, with the problematic of 'home' to the Diaspora. Using discussions from the Kenyan blogosphere that took place against the background of the 2007 post-election violence (hereafter referred to as PEV), this chapter seeks to examine the Kenyan blogosphere[3] as a symbolic discursive space in which is demonstrated how, to use the words of Chambers, "contemporary experiences of migrancy disrupts and interrogates the overarching themes of modernity: the nation and its literature; languages and sense of identity; the metropolis; the sense of centre; the sense of psychic and cultural homogeneity" (1994, 23-4). However, precisely because of the big size of this blogosphere, this reading should not be taken necessarily as definitive of the broader Kenyan blogosphere. Instead, it should be seen as providing indicative debates that shed light on both the disjunctures and conjunctures that typically define Diasporas through the virtual spaces in which they now increasingly converge and communicate. The Kenyan blogosphere's significance became especially notable following the Kenya government's banning of live broadcasts in January 2007 at the height of the post-election violence. Although a clear case of state censorship, the government argued that the decision was made in the 'public interest' as live broadcasts would in its view further inflame passions and thus contribute to the conflagration. But its economies of control went beyond such edicts. Soon after, mainstream print media, most notably the *Nation* issued editorial guidelines stopping the use of ethnic references to victims of the violence in newspaper stories. These edicts restricted the debate on the flawed elections, the subsequent violence and indeed one of the central nodes of the conflict, the broader question of identity politics in the country. By refusing to openly debate this question, this media ironically framed the conflict as unambiguously ethnic. Consequently, the Kenyan blogosphere provided a new platform in which different narratives about the conflict however ambiguous, were explored without fear of state censorship.[4] There are a few studies (Goldstein and Rotich, 2008; Makinen and Kuira, 2008) which have attempted to examine the role this blogosphere played as an 'alternative' to the mainstream media during this period. These studies however seem to fall victim to the populist narration of cyberspace as *ipso facto* 'open' and 'democratic' without exploring the nuances of 'popular' participation, even if they do acknowledge the problem of access. 'Popular' participation can sometimes be more symbolic than real. While this chapter acknowledges the occasional overlaps between the two, it does not suggest they are mean the same thing. The task here therefore is to challenge but also set out an agenda for a more rigorous study of Kenya's online communities. Among other things, the chapter seeks to do the following: to interrogate how the PEV framed the debates on the Kenyan blogosphere. I am particularly interested in the textual narratives within the blog discussions - what do they tell us about the Kenyan Diaspora particularly with regard to their presumed homogeneity? More broadly, I am also interested in how, to paraphrase Cohen (1999), diasporic displacement encourages blog participants to question the prevailing notions of national culture, national identity, ethnic solidarity and de-territorialized new hybrid personal and collective identities. The chapter also aims to assess the 'openness' of the blogs. I am especially interested in the power relations between the blog authors and the contributors. Are there some invisible economies of control that make the much-vaunted 'openness' both problematic and ambiguous?

## UNDERSTANDING DIASPORA

The diverse nature and experiences of migrant populations has meant that the concept of Diaspora is widely contested. The term has therefore been variously defined. For instance, Lavie and Swedenburg argue that Diaspora refers to "the troubled relationship or dual loyalty that migrants, exiles, and refugees have to places- their connections to the space they currently occupy and their continuing involvement with 'back home'" (1996, 14). In addition, citing Rouse (1996), they note that "diasporic populations frequently occupy no singular cultural space but are enmeshed in circuits of social, economic and cultural ties encompassing both the mother country and the country of settlement" (ibid.). On the other hand, Manger and Assal provide a more conceptual argument, noting that the notion of Diaspora "opens up avenues for understanding processes in the post-modern world, a world of transnationalism, of travelling, of cross-culture borrowing and of mixed hybrid cultures" (2006, 7). Further, they suggest that it helps us understand the "tension between globalisation and identity, between homogenising trends and reinforced cultural heterogeneity, between flow and closure, flux and fix" (ibid.).

A similar conceptual approach is used by Clifford who conceives of the term Diaspora as: "a signifier, not simply of transnationality and movement, but of political struggles to define the local and distinctive community, in historical contexts of displacement" (1994, 321).

William Safran writing in Manger and Assal's (2006) volume takes a different approach, instead discussing the features that constitute Diaspora. Safran explains that Diaspora is constituted by "expatriate minority communities defined by a history of dispersal, myths and memories of the homeland, alienation in host country, desire for eventual return, ongoing support for homeland, collective identity importantly defined by this relationship" (2006, 12-3). It is arguable that central to the understanding of Diaspora is the problematic of what is meant by 'home' or 'homeland'. Home implies both location and space. Indeed, Manger and Assal observe that homeland in Diaspora "is not only defined by its ancestral roots nor is the desire for return necessarily physical or even restoration in the sense of creating a nation-state - homeland may remain part of an imagining" (ibid.). Cohen (1997) provides a similar definition but also talks about the "collective trauma experienced by the expatriate minority, a troubled relationship with the majority and a sense of community transcending national frontiers" (ibid.).

Significantly, most of these definitions tend to figure Diasporas as homogenous groups, collectively aggrieved, uniformly alienated and sharing in common values. This assumption can be misleading. Precisely because of the different reasons for migration and the varied experiences within the old and surrogate host countries by migrant communities, some scholars now suggest an approach that acknowledges Diasporas as internally incoherent and fragmented. To this end, Cohen thus talks about "a victims diaspora, imperial diaspora, trade diaspora, labour diaspora" (cited in Manger and Assal 2006, 13). This differentiation is useful as an entry point into understanding the Kenyan diaspora.

## THE GROWTH OF THE KENYAN DIASPORA

The beginnings and growth of the Kenyan Diaspora in Western metropolises has historically been closely linked to the pursuit of higher education (Okoth, 2003). In the years preceding the country's independence, many Kenyans travelled abroad for further education, some later returning home to join the struggle movement. Among them was Kenya's first President Jomo Kenyatta who studied in Moscow and London before returning to Kenya to play a leading role in the country's independence movement. On attaining independence in 1964, Kenyatta's government sent hundreds of young Kenyans abroad on education scholarships. While some returned to work in government and big business others stayed abroad. However, this period (1964-1978) also coincided with the Cold War struggle between the United States and the USSR. Africa had also become an ideological battleground for the East-West rivalry with both Washington and Moscow aggressively courting Kenyan students with various educational scholarships. The United States education exchange programmes especially saw hundreds of Kenyans leave for the US to pursue university education. A particularly popular programme was the famous 'Kennedy student airlifts'[5] of the 1960s, which enabled hundreds of young Kenyans to migrate to the US. There were also similar airlifts to the East with Moscow being a particularly popular destination for some Kenyan students. These airlifts began a familiar migratory pattern, one that has since seen thousands of Kenyans migrate to and settle in North America and Europe.

During the 1980s through the 1990s a new migratory flight occurred. This period coincided with the rule of former president Daniel arap Moi. In a bid to consolidate his presidency after an attempted coup to topple him in 1982, Moi waged a ruthless war on his political opponents. Many politicians, scholars and journalists opposed to his regime were thus forced into exile, most fleeing to Norway, Sweden, Britain, Canada and the United States to escape torture, incarceration or assassination. Without detailing the politics of the Moi state, it is now widely documented that from 1982, Moi presided over a state in serious disarray both politically and economically.[6] Political repression and economic mismanagement which resulted into low-level clandestine ethnic violence, the privatization of the state, a flagging economy and therefore lack of job opportunities for many Kenyans, created conditions that made migration abroad particularly attractive to many people. As a result, many Kenyans dispersed to Europe, the United States, Canada and Southern Africa.

This brief reference to the Moi state is important for it had implications on the constitution and character of the Kenyan Diaspora. The *a priori* conception of Kenya as home by the Kenyan Diaspora may therefore be problematic precisely because of the varied reasons for these Kenyans' migration abroad. More broadly, it reminds us of the need to conceive of relationships between migrants and their 'mother countries' as both varied and specific. We should not necessarily ascribe the latter with the characteristics of 'home' particularly against the context of a migration occasioned either by repression or conflict.

## THE MAKING OF NEW 'HOMES' ONLINE: DE-TERRITORIALIZATION AND RE-TERRITORIALIZATION OF IDENTITIES ONLINE

As the Kenyan Diaspora has continued to grow, so has its presence online. Kenya's online community is organised around numerous blogs, discussion forums, news sites and social networking groups created by and for Kenyans living outside the country. These provide lively platforms and spaces in which various debates on and about the country are conducted. As noted above, there is no universally agreed conception of Diaspora. Similarly, studies on the manner in which diasporic identities are formed is just as varied. While some (Manger and Assal, 2006) emphasise that diasporic conditions lead to identities that are not necessarily territorially inscribed, others are more cautious, instead noting how this de-territorialization functions. Cheran (2003), for example, argues that this de-territorialization becomes a (re)source of new imagination for diasporic nations. He observes that the concept of the nation has long been linked to a singular state and territory and that Diasporas challenge the mono-dimensional and territorially bound ideas of the nation. Elsewhere (Cheran, 2002) in his study of Sri-Lanka's

Tamil diaspora, he also notes that it is landscapes not territory that have played a central role in the formation of Tamil identities. Yet it is also the case that alienation in the new surrogate countries acts as a powerful force for the recuperation of the familiar, hence the many ethnic cultural enclaves in most Western metropolises. For example, 'China towns' are found in London, Paris and New York as are African markets, festivals, Churches, bars and eating houses. Significantly then, while de-territorialization takes place among Diasporas, a corresponding re-territorialization also occurs hence the existence, and indeed, vibrancy of the 'ethnic enclaves' in the Western metropoles. The Kenyan blogosphere provides good example of the process of de-territorilization and re-territorialization that take place within migrant communities. Within this 'open' blogosphere, broadly conceived as a transnational community are articulated practices that both de-teritorrialize and re-territorialize simultaneously. As with globalization where the drive towards the homogenization of cultures tends to do the very opposite, the Internet as a transnational social space tends to both transcend but also reinforce parochial identities. An interesting feature of the Kenyan blogosphere is the existence of blogs that take their names from Kenya's ethnic groups. Examples include: www.kikuyunationalism.com; www.Jaluo.com; www.Kisii.com; www.Kalenjin.net and many others. The taglines of these blogs are often expressive of their intent. For example, www.Kisii.com, describes itself as 'home of the Abagusii people', www.Jaluo.com says *'kama jaluo rade gi joluo wete gi'* (trans: Where Luos meet other Luos), while www.Kikuyunationalism.com (Now www.muigwithania 2.0) talks of 'anchoring the atomized citizen within the rhetoric of the collective'. These blogs were particularly active during the PEV. This chapter argues that such ethnic markers are used primarily as a mechanism for attracting users around ethnicity as well as very specific interests. They were intended to exclude the 'ethnic Other' thus participating in Kenya's political crisis by validating difference primarily on the basis of tribe. But the reasons for this exclusion are much more complicated. The ambivalent relationship individuals or sometimes whole communities have with the nation-state is often a function of the state's denial of the latter's interests and rights. The existence of these blogs as well as the discussions that took place in them seemed to demonstrate not only this ambivalent relationship with the nation-state but also how various ethnic groups and individuals related differently to the nation-state. These blogs became sites for channelling pent-up frustrations against the state. Broadly, the blogs revealed various resistance cultures, which as Lowe is wont to say, articulate cultural forms that are in most cases materially and aesthetically at odds with the resolution of the citizen of the nation (1996, 30). But the reasons for such resistance are often varied. In an email correspondence with the founder of Kikuyunationalism.com Joseph Ndungu, the blogger claimed he started the blog, "first as an avenue for venting anger at what was happening in Kenya, then as a means of promoting positive ethnicity, cross cultural understanding, political awareness, justice and peace"[7] He claimed that during the election crisis, Kenya was "undergoing a resurgence of ethnic nationalism particularly amongst young people who realize that identifying with *the masses* (emphasis mine: *note the conflation of the ethnic with the masses*) offers some form of protection. Before PEV, one could excuse themselves as not having a tribe and not speaking the language but the violence in Kenya showed that a last name on your ID was enough to get you in trouble. I think the shock of these events has made some feel that they cannot run away from their *true identity*" (emphasis mine). The blog opens with an interesting commentary in which the blogger affirms the legitimacy of the tribe. Part of the commentary reads:

> I am not yet willing to give up on the concept of tribe. I am unwilling to grant that Kenyan liberals are right in their claims that tribe is a limited concept that has no place in the modern world. I am unwilling to accept their definitions that my history and heritage are small and uninteresting, lacking in depth and complexity, beauty and joy.
>
> I am not yet willing to give up on the concept of tribe.
>
> Tribe lets my friend say, "my name means one born at night," and my other friend to say, "I belong to the people who shape metal," and yet another friend to say, "I bring rain in the dry seasons." Tribe marks the changing of generations, Maina to Irungu, Kamau to Peter.
>
> Tribe celebrates how we have lived, how we have loved, how we have suffered, how we have mourned. We are the descendants of Gatego, the generation riddled with syphilis and Ngige, the generation decimated by locusts. To say these names is to claim that our stories are not yet done. We are not yet done. We are here.
>
> I am unwilling to relinquish tribe…

> I am often seduced by the invitation to identify myself as national, international, or cosmopolitan. I am tempted by the idea that I can and should transcend tribe. I am compelled by the idea that I would be a better person if my allegiances were less local, less idiosyncratic, less wedded to the nine clans that face Mount Kenya. But I believe in this love.
>
> I believe in its potential. I want to see where it leads.

This entry was the subject of an interesting discussion by a number of contributors one of who commented thus:

> As an African in the diaspora ... I hope there are enough like you who will help us to understand and appreciate the rich history and culture of the African people. I, like yourself, believe that embracing our heritage is the key to our future. I would encourage all the peoples of Africa to explore and share this most valuable treasure while the possibility still exists.

Another contributor, specifically referring to Kenya's post-election conflict however disagreed, indeed, arguing for the 'tribe' to be disinvested with agency as a form of identity. He writes:

> This is why when you mention that you are a Kenyan in some parts of the world today the first thing they ask you is 'what tribe are you?' It happened to me a lot especially after the post election chaos and for this reason alone I'm not proud to be part of a Kenyan tribe. I'm sorry mate but yes the colonizers were in fact right- tribe has no place in this world but you are wrong in going on to claim that they define history as 'small and uninteresting, lacking in depth and complexity, beauty and joy'- they don't!'
>
> For in fact this has nothing to do with tribes. My argument is... yes each tribe in Kenya forms a unique description of its people, their practices and in fact their unique beauty. I however believe we can still keep this uniqueness and depth as Kenyans not as Kikuyu or Kalenjins or whatever. If we do in fact hope to compete on the world stage we have to look past tribes and work together.

He continues:

I agree when you say tribe helps to recognize diversity. But wouldn't you rather just have a country made up of different regions; 'men from that hill are bowlegged. Children from that place run like the wind..........' rather than a country split by tribes; 'the Kikuyu love their money, the Luos are proud, the Kalenjins run like the wind...' I pray that when the next generation produces its offspring, our beloved country will have forgotten who is from what tribe and just live like we should as Kenyans.

The limitations of which you speak are only here because our parents and grandparents insisted like you in keeping tribe as part of their kids growing up. When we move to the cities we look for our tribes for favours. Don't forget the folklore but when you do, teach the new generation this; remember 2008 and think twice about the kind of Kenyans you want you kids to grow up as.

Another contributor blamed Europeans for 'Africa's identity crisis', suggesting that "they have set the world on a path of self-destruction". He argued that Africa is like:

The human body and different tribes as different parts of that body. Each part of the body has a role to play and I believe we can all agree that no part is so small as to be insignificant.

Like the parts of the body the different tribes evolved over time to serve an organic purpose. Large parts like arms and legs are obvious but would be useless if the nervous system is not working. What if something like the thyroid or pituitary gland is not functioning. Take away a hand or a foot and the body loses mobility, take the eyes or the ears and what will be the consequences.

I believe I have made my point. Each tribe is important and must be recognized and nurtured as we would each part of our own body.

If this happens in the right way not only Africa but the whole world will benefit because Europeans have set the world on a path of destruction and it's going to take the basic wisdom and ancient knowledge of the tribes of the remaining indigenous peoples of the world to put it right.

Although Ndung'u's blog post seems to contest the repudiation of the tribe as a legitimate identity marker, it also seems to validate difference on the basis of the same. But there is also a specific context within which this blog must be read. It needs to be remembered that the international news narrative on the PEV that was circulated and legitimized by a number of Western media organizations and indeed sections of the local press was that the Kikuyu, Kenya's most dominant tribe, were being 'persecuted' by other ethnic groups, mainly the Luo and the Kalenjin. The tragic case of a Church in Eldoret set on fire with hundreds of Kikuyus sheltered in it provided a powerful image of this 'persecution'. This provided an unequivocal endorsement of the narrative about the Kikuyu being the 'victims' of the PEV. Alternative narratives were therefore to be contested. Almost deleted from discussions of the PEV was the fact that hundreds of Luos were murdered in reprisal attacks in Naivasha and indeed that overall, more Luos were killed during the violence than any other ethnic group. In this blog the writer makes the point that Kikuyu nationalism has to be reasserted. The affirmation of the tribe within this blog thus silently validated that mainstream narrative of Kikuyu persecution and in part re-enacted the very differences that were central to the raging political conflict.

This cultural and political re-territorialization was also to be seen in another blog: www.Bankelele.com, authored by a 'Nairobi banker'. Although originally constituted as a financial blog (note the Bank in the title) with stock listings, share prices and local bank profiles, this blog became one of the most engaging political blogs in the Kenyan blogosphere following the flawed elections. Most of the postings however focused on the impact of the election violence on the country's economy. One of the most popular subjects on the blog was the impact of the political crisis on the government's much-vaunted Vision 2030 programme, an economic masterplan, which seeks to make Kenya an industrialised nation over the next two decades. In one example "Elections derail Kenya" (3 Jan 2008), the blogger responded to the crisis mainly with a call to unity, deliberately avoiding any discussions of the ethnic dimension to the conflict. The blogger mainly expressed his concerns and fears about the impact this crisis was going to have on the economy and the government's 2030 vision. Responding to the posting, 'Anon,' a contributor, criticised the posting, arguing that it read

> Like the middle of the road milk toast editorials in the Kenyan papers. Everybody loses, everybody wins and please let us not point fingers because people are dying. If Kibaki had let the people have their way at the polls we could not be here. Full-

> stop... Now that the fire is at Kibaki's door all of a sudden we are ALL Kenyans, before then unless you were GEMA[8] you were a 'pumbavu'(trans: stupid). waKenya wengine [trans: some Kenyans] are fed up. There will be no peace until justice is meted out.

This contributor invokes Kenya's popular political history as a guiding text to the discussion of the crisis in what has recently been described by the head of Kenya's National Cohesion and Integration Commission (NCIC) Mzalendo Kibunja, as Kenya's 'crisis of exclusion', after an 'ethnic' audit revealed that 40 per cent of civil service jobs were occupied by members of the tribes whose leaders have had the presidency since independence.[9] With the state broadly seen as a resource to be protected by whole ethnic groups, the relationship between ethnicity and the state becomes a major site of political discussion both offline and online. In the example above, the mention of a familiar abusive word 'pumbavu' routinely used by President Mwai Kibaki juxtaposed with the Gema community, a grouping of ethnic communities with close cultural and political associations and geographically located around the Mt. Kenya region, presences the silences the Bankelele blog author seems to ignore. By arguing that "waKenya wengine are fed up[trans: other Kenyans are fed up]" an interesting play on a language which forms part of the discourse of political marginalisation in the country, the contributor is in fact underlining the disillusionment with the status quo. There is also an implied assertion of Gema culpability and a suggestion that they have been privileged at the expense of other communities who have just as much right to the privileges of citizenship. In another example 'Kenya is Burning, Stop the Fighting' (4 Jan 2008), a contributor 'Shook_1' metaphorically talks of how several Kenyans have now been excluded from the state by an ethno-political class alluding to a common phrase that "this country has its owners."

He then quotes George Carlin's famous phrase: "It's one big party, and you ain't in it!" The existence of these ethnic blogs calls for a rethink on the populist validation of the Kenyan blogosphere and Diaspora as being post-ethnic. The discussions on the PEV revealed tensions over belonging and citizenship, the collective memory of the homeland and what visions to create of and for it, what to presence and what to silence, what to remember and what to forget, all subject in part on the perceived proximity of the discussant to the political centre. That centre was defended or pilloried depending on whether it was seen to provide access to or deny one the privileges of state citizenship.

# BLOGGING AND THE PRIVATIZING
# OF THE PUBLIC SPHERE

Cheran (2003) has argued that the epistemological categories for analyzing diasporas must be extended to include roles played by such variables as class, gender, race and sexuality. He calls for the need to examine how these intersect with the more widely recognised identity formations such as nationality and ethnicity. It is an argument whose relevance is especially germane in the analysis of Kenyan blogosphere during the PEV. While it is true that anyone with access to the internet can author a blog or set up a website, most of the popular blogs are often created by a relatively small privileged 'techno-elite.' It is important to recognize therefore that the Kenyan blogosphere, as indeed many such diasporic blogospheres, is dominated by this elite. It is they who shape and direct the debates therein. As a consequence, this 'techno-elite' becomes particularly influential in authorizing very specific narratives about the issues being debated. In the Kenyan blogosphere, blogs such as Bankelele, Kenyanpundit, tHiNkErsroom [10] among others seemed to authorize the interpretation of the violence within a very specific framework with their discourse drawn predominantly from a patently neoliberal cultural, economic and political archive. As a consequence, it was an economistic, if reductionist interpretation of the crisis that was validated across most of the blogs with discussions mainly revolving around the implications of the PEV on the national economy. What was especially notable was the manner in which the blog authors usurped the voices of contributors in the discussions by covertly setting the tone and parameters of 'popular' engagement. A number of the blog authors strategically adopted the use of the plural pronoun 'we' in their postings to frame their perspectives as inclusive and mainstream, while alternative viewpoints were positioned as partisan, non-mainstream and therefore illegitimate. In addition, the adoption of the plural pronoun 'we' was strategic as it enabled two critical issues. Firstly, it allowed the bloggers to position themselves as part of the publics they were addressing by appearing to speak with them and not at them. Secondly, they used the pronoun to covertly authorize their individual positions on the subject as normative.

It is also worth noting that unlike the blogs which took their names from Kenya's ethnic groups and which exhibited a rather ambivalent relationship with the state, this latter category seemed to invest a lot of agency in the nation-state. Most of the topics revolved around fears over the disintegration of the country, the need for constitutional reform and the need for political stability. In one of these discussions, the author of Bankelele in his post 'Elections derail Kenya' (3 Jan 2008) argued that between the two presidential candidates, he would "make money with a Kibaki win" but cautioned that "to redress the country's economic imbalances, Kenya needs Raila Odinga."[11] It was a very modernist interpretation of the crisis, with individual self-interest being privileged. A contributor going by the name 'Kenyanstraydog' described the contributors to the post as "the petty black bourgeoisie." He urged them to "listen to 'real' Kenyans and its quite simple, Kibaki rigged the elections. No deep philosophy here, just basic primal power grab, a primal response followed." Another contributor 'Marshatall' noted that the post-election violence had been an eye-opener "as far as ethnicity and politics are intertwined in Kenya." The contributor argued that it was "hard to understand how professionals can retreat into their tribal cocoons and unleash propaganda not based on ideology." He then claimed to have grown up with *"Wambuas, Otienos, Chepchumbas"*, a heritage he was proud of. He expressed his amazement that people were not talking about "Kibaki's economic record," arguing that economic prosperity under Kibaki had given Kenyans "a chance to participate in politics because their basic needs had been met." The former president, Moi he argued, "managed political discontent by keeping people poor!"'Ssesbonge', another contributor, wrote that there was a lot of expectation built into the elections and urged readers to realise that country's economic recovery would be based on political stability. He writes: "I can't tell you how frustrating it is for some of us who have always wanted to come back *home* and build our country." These discussions mainly reflected class anxieties with fears expressed about the negative impact of the violence on the country's economy. Development/progress was primarily seen in economic terms. Equally notable were the silences within the narratives proposed by the authors and validated through the discussions. For instance, not much is made of the fact that Kibaki's 'good' economic record was only 'good' because of the terrible state in which the Moi administration had left the economy, nor the fact that Kibaki had in fact been Moi's finance minister and Vice-President for several years. Such silences were to be found in most of the discussions. In the blog *tHiNkErsroom*, one of the main posts was the piece 'Kenya is Burning, Stop the fighting!' In trying to explain the crisis, the blogger largely blamed the political elite for failing the country. The post also explained the conflict as a function of class tensions in the country. A related blog entry 'Tribalism and the Youth' (14 Jan 2008) had the blog's author accuse his generation of failing the country *a la* the old guard. Clearly finding the contemporaneity of 'the tribe' problematic, even inconsistent with 'nationhood', he accused some youth of embracing a political culture which legitimized exclusion from the political centre on the basis of ethnic stereotyping. He writes:

> Without a doubt one of the most uttered sentences in Kenya today is along the following lines ...
> 'Me? A tribalist? No! I am no such thing!
> A more refined version goes as follows.
> I am not a tribalist! In fact I have friends who are Kikuyu/ Luo/Kamba etc.

A contributor Patrick Gathara, also a blogger,[12] while agreeing that tribalism in the country is a problem that needs to be tackled, argued that the blogger "is in danger of confusing it with tribe". He writes:

> It is surely not a problem that we have 42 or so ethnic communities. It is surely the problem that one's ethnicity is an element in a political equation. The way you put it, we are to fear the notion of tribe. I do not think that shows like *Vioja Mahakamani*[13] should be trashed simply because they make fun of our stereotypes. Neither should the topic be out of bounds to our humorists. Humour is indeed one way of disarming the power of the tribal notion. One, though, does need to be careful".

But the blogger responds thus:

> What I take considerable issue with is the instant that very notion of tribe is used to give those of your tribe favours or to deny others anything, I draw the line right there. Completely unacceptable... As for humour, that is indeed a complex beast. Many things can be hidden in that vehicle. Have you watched any blackface performances?

These examples illustrate the limited scope of debates or narratives that were allowed to circulate within this 'open' social space. More importantly, they demonstrate the imbalance of power relations between the contributors and the blog authors online. Authorship by a small 'techno-elite' tended to validate the hegemony of a limited ideological spectrum, despite claims to 'openness'.

# THE 'MESTIZA CONSCIOUSNESS' AND RELIGION AS A (NEW) SOCIALITY

The dislocation that results from migration often forces migrants to negotiate the ambivalence of living between two or more cultures. It is a negotiation that forces them into a cultural state of being 'in-between' (Morales 2002). Explaining the plight of the Hispanics in the United States, an experience codified in the 'Spanglish' phenomenon, Morales describes it as: "a displacement from one place, home, to another place, home in which one feels at home in both places, yet at home in neither place, it is a kind of banging-one's head against the wall state, and the only choice you have is to embrace the transitory (read transnational) state of being in-between" (2002, 7). Such 'crisis' of belonging or lack of, can result into what Gloria Anzaldua (1999) has described as the 'mestiza consciousness', a consciousness of borderlands where new identities are configured as a result of the multiple cultural encounters. The 'mestiza consciousness' is often reflected in the use of hyphenated names and identities by disaporic communities. But it also results in the construction of either new or more transnational forms of social- ity. Religion particularly becomes or provides tropes and or narratives around which the 'in-betweeners' congregate. There was a notable use of hyphenated identities and the appropriation of religious narratives in a number of the Kenyan blog discussions. For example, a contributor in a discussion in *Bankelele* (3 Jan 2008) calls her son 'Kenyan-American-Kikuyu.' The hyphenated name points to how various heritages are implicated in the making of being and in the negotiation of a new iden- tity. Claiming to be writing from the United States, the contributor goes on to say that:

> We are praying along with his birth family here for the safety
> of his family who remain in Nairobi. This moment is not the
> Kenya we are so proud of and that I want my son to come to
> when he is a man. Thank you for keeping us informed – you
> are doing God's work.

Christianity seemed to provide some of the contributors with a habitat of meaning to draw upon in their discussions. One sees similarities with what Benitez observes of the experiences of the Salvadoran Diaspora in the United States, where he talks of "a theological re-interpretation of the experience of migration and a re-transcription of religious nar- ratives to explain their plight" (2005, 332). He borrows Vasquez's argument about a "hermaneutics of movement whereby migrants transform their travels across national borders into moral journeys, theodicies of religions conversion, rebirth and edification" (2001, 30). Biblically-grounded narratives are often routinely appropriated to explain diasporic experiences of migration. Benitez further argues that religion also tends to provide extended social networks and social capital for the migrants. In the post 'Elections derail Kenya' in *Bankelele*, a contributor going by the name Imani, for instance, wondered how "godless the country has become." She writes:

> Presidents come and go but one day we all will stand before God. Let's do what we can to restore sanity in our country, seek to love your neighbour even though he may be from the 'wrong tribe'. We are all made in God's image and in him there is no Kikuyu or Luo". She then implores readers to "please stop and pray for 'our' country.

The Kenyan blog discussions appropriated a number of biblical narratives and religious imagery to authorize a specific kind of morality with regard to the interpretation of the conflict. Christianity, in particular, helped provide not only the means of interpretation but also the social capital required in the imagination of a new collective to help individuals address the experience.

## IDENTITIES AS 'FRAGILE SUBJECTIVITIES'

This chapter argues that for these Kenyan diasporic publics to be constituted online, users must first acknowledge some relationship with Kenya either as 'home' or as a symbolic imaginary representing some notion of 'home' however ambiguous that construct might be. Furthermore, Kenya is addressed both as a private and public space and an imagining representing certain shared but also specific values. Kenya thus becomes, to use the words of Goergiou, a "synonym to familiarity, intimacy, security and identity against the unknown, the distant and large" (2006, 85). The concerns raised in these blog discussions were precisely because of the perceived threats to the notion of 'home'. But as Georgiou (2006) notes, 'home' in the diaspora remains "ambiguous and incomplete" (ibid.) hence the contradictions in the narratives mediated. The discussions on the Kenyan blogosphere disrupt our assumptions about three key issues: firstly, that there is a uniform conception of Kenya as home, secondly, that the Kenyan Diaspora is homogeneous and thirdly, that they are necessarily indisposed to be 'post-ethnic' particularly online. The varied readings of home in the discussions as well as the different categories of the blogs reflect the heterogeneity of this Diaspora. We have noted that there was a deliberate construction of specific ethnic spaces through which offline ethnic rivalries were extended. These blogs became sites for the articulation of predominantly ethnic interests. Indeed, as noted earlier in the discussion, the use of ethnic names on the blogs was a way of congregating specific ethnic constituencies. It was a validation of difference on the basis of tribe despite arguments by some blog authors such as Ndung'u of *Kikuyunationalism* that they were simply repudiating the idea that the tribe as a form of identity was redundant within national and transnational environments.

The point here is not to essentialize ethnicity as being retrograde or primordial. Instead, as discussed elsewhere in the chapter, it is to be noted that these ethnic blogs became spaces for articulating certain group fears as well as disillusionment with the exclusionary tendencies of the nation-state. Through them national citizenship was depicted as an abstraction especially by communities who felt they were alienated from the political centre and thereby denied the privileges of citizenship. These blogs thus became spaces utilized by ethnic groups to contest their homogenization into a national culture and into a nation in which they were only bit players. It is however also true that there were those to whom the tribe, broadly conceived, was considered a part of being, a subjectivity that is not inconsistent with other forms of identities. Following the government's banning of live broadcasts and the introduction of various editorial controls in the coverage of the PEV by local media, much was made of the Kenyan blogosphere becoming the alternative space within which open discussions on the PEV migrated. This chapter regards this assumption to be problematic. We especially note the rather uneven power relations between the blog authors and contributors. We have argued that most of these blogs were authored by a 'techno-elite' who often determined what was discussed and how it was discussed. They selectively validated specific narratives about the violence. Alternative viewpoints were often invalidated through the narrative voices adopted by the blog authors. Meanwhile, we have also argued that a rather Western cosmopolitan cultural lifestyle and a neo liberal reading of democracy were passed on as unequivocal and normal. The chapter also argues that the epistemologies for the analysis of Diasporas need to extend to include variables, particularly class consciousness, which is often not given adequate agency. Class anxieties were very prominent in the discussions that took place in blogs such as *Bankelele*, *Kenyanpundit* and *tHiNkErsroom*, with the terms for the discussions covertly set by the blog authors. It is therefore important that we begin to look at how other social-organizing principles such class and even gender intersect with those identities often regarded as generic and normal. The discussion also reveals that diasporic displacement, as indeed noted by Lavie and Swedenburg, "is not experienced in precisely the same way across time and space, and does not unfold in a uniform fashion. Rather, there is a range of positionings of Others in relation to the forces of domination and *vis-a-vis* other Others" (1996, 4). The manner in which migrants integrate in their surrogate countries is varied and so is their relationship with the Other. As a consequence, the discussions reflect how diasporic identities are in fact shaped by shifting variables, often temporal, spatial and experiential. One, for instance, noticed transnational, national but also sub-national narratives attending the debates on the violence as well as defining the contributors' definition of self and the collective they imagine they belong to. This explains the varied agency given to religion, the nation-state, the ethnic group, and to social class. For some, religion provides a new transcendent sociality and therefore identity, replacing the nation-state as the primary reference of belonging. There is a tendency to invoke biblical narratives in the quest to understand and explain the crisis.

But one also notes a more general diasporic experience define these identities. Some of the discussions revealed the ambivalent relationship between this Diaspora and their surrogate countries, especially the United States and the UK. For some, this diaspora's relationship with the UK, for example, seemed to be encumbered by the history of the colonial relationship between Britain and Kenya. Here, popular memory becomes crucial in the construction of identity. Their identity is thus strongly shaped by the reconstructed experiences of Kenya's colonial history. A throwback to some of the elements of the 1960s pan-Africanism was used to structure some debates.

For some of the contributors, there was a subconscious conflation of ethnicity and race and of ethnic identity and African identity. The diasporic experience is also a racial experience, which explains the said conflation. Migrant communities on the social and political margins in Western metropolises often explain their plight in large part to the racialized politics of exclusion, hence the (re-)creation of solidarities/communities around race, considered perhaps to be more relevant within the context of these surrogate countries. The African identity therefore became to some, naturalized as the pre-eminent identity with which to define the self in relation to the rest. So that in some of the blogs, being Kenyan is also sometimes conflated with being African and being black- often used interchangeably. It is therefore arguable that the Kenyan diaspora's reflections on the PEV were also shaped by these metropolitan racial and cultural encounters.

## CONCLUSION

As the Internet becomes even more widely available and Kenyan online communities expand, the platform will become an important site for both cultural and political organization with direct impacts offline. Technology in general and ICTs in particular are becoming major instruments in the country's cultural, social and political organization and transformation. Populist readings of their positive impacts will no doubt be seductive to many researchers. But as the chapter demonstrates, it is important that we examine the Internet as a complicated social space replete with contradictions, disjunctures and conjunctures. Research on Kenyan online communities must therefore subject totalizing and populist assumptions about the internet to rigorous critical scrutiny.

## *Notes*

1. Okoth (2003) notes, for example, that the number of documented Kenyan citizens in Germany was only 576 in 1980, but had doubled to 1,222 by 1990 and ballooned to more than 5,200 by the end of 2001.
2. See http://allafrica.com/stories/201008060043.html. Accessed 16/3/11
3. A sample list of Kenyan blogs can be found in the blog aggregator www. Kenyaunlimited.com. Kenya is now said to have the third largest number of bloggers in Africa based in and outside the country, after South Africa and Nigeria according to an African blog aggregator, Agrigator. See http://www.businessdailyafrica.com/Kenya+has+third+highest+number+of+blogs. Accessed 16/03/11
4. It is to be noted however that in various blogs and websites, postings were sometimes subject to moderation by the blog authors or webmasters. Indeed, heated debate over the violence even led to a temporary shut-down of one of the most popular Kenyan discussion forums www.Mashada.com
5. The so-called 'Kennedy airlifts' was a scholarships programme funded by a grant from the J.F Kennedy family foundation but organised by Thomas Joseph Mboya, a popular Kenyan labour leader. President Richard Nixon however later won state department funding for the famous 'airlifts'.

6. For a detailed reading of this period see for example, Haugerud 1995; Atieno- Odhiambo, 2002, Young 2003, Shatzberg 2001.

7. Email correspondence with the author (28 August 2008)

8. Gema is an acronym for Gikuyu Embu Meru Association. Founded in 1971, it is a loose politico-cultural grouping of the Gikuyu, Embu and the Meru, who were brought together through a combination of factors ranging from shared political, economic and cultural interests. The group was banned by the Moi administration in 1980 having been associated with attempts to change the constitution when Moi ascended to power, a move that that was intended to sabotage the his presidency.

9. See http://m.standardmedia.co.ke/headlines.php?id=2000032707 (Accessed 13 April 2011)

10. This blog is authored by one of Africa's most recognised bloggers Ory Okolloh. A Harvard graduate, she also set up Ushahidi.Com, an open sources site that was used to 'crowd source' information on the PEV from witnesses. The software was later used in other crisis situations including the earthquakes in Haiti and Chile in 2010.

11. The two presidential candidates Mwai Kibaki and Raila Odinga stressed different skills during their campaigns. Kibaki, for example, promoted his economic credentials while Raila mainly campaigned on an agenda of political reform. Kenya, the latter argued, was in need of urgent political reform without which the country would still stagnate economically.

12. Gathara blogs at www.gathara.blogspot.com under the name 'Gathara's world'.

13. This is a long running TV comedy show famed for playing on local ethnic stereotypes to discuss wide ranging social, economic and political issues in the country. Before the deregulation of the airwaves in the 1990s, it was by far the most popular show on Kenyan television.

# Bibliography

Abdulaziz, Mohammed and Ken Osinde. 1997. "Sheng and English: Development of Mixed Codes Among the Urban Youths in Kenya." *International Journal of the Sociology of Language* 125. 1: 43-64. Accessed 18, March, 2011. doi: 10.1515/ijsl.

Achebe, Chinua. 1983. *The Trouble with Nigeria.* Nairobi: Heinemann Educational Books.

Akama, John. 1991. "The Evolution of Tourism in Kenya". *Journal of Sustainable Tourism* 7.1:6-25.

_____. 1999. "Marginalisation of the Maasai in Kenya". *Annals of Tourism Research* 26.3: 716-718.

Allen, Morgan. 2010. "Dr Gichora Mwangi, Leading Kenyan Theatre Artist and Mentor of New Work, Dead at 38." October 5, 2004. Accessed February 10, 2010. http://www.playbill.com/news/article/88807.

Amateshe, Andrew ed. 1988. *An Anthology of East African Poetry.* London: Longman.

Amoko, Apollo. 1999. "The Missionary Gene in the Kenyan Polity: Representations of Contemporary Kenya in the British Media." *Callaloo* 22.1: 223-239

_____. 2001. "The Problem with English Literature: Canonicity, Citizenship, and the Idea of Africa." *Research in African Literatures* 32. 4: 19-43.

_____. 2011. "The Resemblance of Colonial Mimicry: A Revisionary Reading of Ngugi wa Thiong'o's "*The River Between*". *Research in African Literatures* 36. 1:34-50, http://www.jstor.org/stable/3821318, accessed 29/03/2011.

Amuka, Peter. 1992. "The Play of Deconstruction in the Speech of Africa: The Role of Pakruok and Ngero in Telling Culture in Dholuo." *Reflections on Theories and Methods in Oral Literature*, edited by Okombo, Okoth and Jane Nandwa, 66-87. Nairobi: Kenya Oral Literature Association.

Amuta, Chidi. 1989. *The theory of African Literature.* London: Zed Books.

Amutabi, Maurice. 2007. "Intellectuals and the Democratisation Process in Kenya." *Kenya: the Struggle for Democracy,* edited by Murunga, Godwin and Shadrack W Nasiong'o, 197-226. London: Zed Books.

Anderson, B. 1991. *Imagined Communities: Reflections on the Origin and Spread of Nationalism.* London: Verso.

Anderson, Rachel. 1974. *The Purple Heart Throbs*. London: Hodder and Stoughton.

Anzaldua, G. E. 1999. *Borderlands/La Frontera : The New Mestiza*. San Franciso : Aunt Lute Books.

Appadurai, Arjun. 2005 [1996]. *Modernity at Large: Cultural Dimensions of Globalization*. Minneapolis and London: University of Minnesota Press.

Appiah, Kwame Anthony. 1991. "Is the Post- in Postmodernism the Post- in Postcolonial?" *Critical Inquiry* 17. 2: 336-57.

_____. 1992. *In My Father's House: Africa in the Philosophy of Culture*. New York. Oxford University Press.

Aristotle. 1970. *Poetics*. Translated by F. Gerald. Ann Arbor: University of Michigan Press.

Armah, A. K. 1985. "Masks and Marx: The Marxist Ethos vis-a vis African Revolutionary Theory and Praxis." *Presence Africaine* 131:35-65.

Ashcroft, Bill. 2001. *Post-colonial Transformations*. London: Routledge.

Askew, Kelly M. 2002. *Performing the Nation: Swahili Music and Cultural Politics in Tanzania*. Chicago: University of Chicago Press.

_____. 2003. "As Plato Duly Warned: Music, Politics and Social Change in Coastal East Africa." *Anthropological Quaterly* 76.4: 609-636. Accessed 28 March, 2011. doi: 10.1353/anq.2003.0049.

Askew, Kelly and John F. Kitime. 2006. "Popular Music Censorship in Tanzania." *Popular Music Censorship in Africa*, edited by Michael Drewett and Martin Cloonan, 137-56. Burlington, VT: Ashgate.

Auvert, B, Taljaard, Sobrigwi-Tambekou Lagarde and Puren Sitta. 2005. "Randomized, Controlled Intervention Trial of Male Circumcision for Reduction of HIV Infection Risks: the ANRS 1265 Trial." *PLOS Medicine* 2: 1112-1122.

Bâ, Mariama. 1981. *So Long a Letter*. London. Heinemann.

Bahador, Khan. 1968. *Essays on the Life of Muhammad*. Lahore: Premier Press.

Bakthin, Mikhail. 1982. *The Dialogic Imagination: Four Essays*. Austin, Texas: University of Texas Press.

Barber, Karin. 1987. "Popular Arts in Africa." *African Studies Review* 30. 3: 1-78.

_____ ed. 1997. *Readings in African Popular Culture*. Oxford: James Currey; Bloomington and Indianapolis: Indiana University Press.

_____. 1997. "Introduction." *Readings in African Popular Culture*, edited by Karin Barber, 1-15. Oxford: James Currey.

Barber, Karin, John Collins and Alain Ricard. 1997. *West African Popular Theatre*. Oxford: James Currey.

_____. 2007. *The Anthropology of Texts, Persons and Publics*. Cambridge: Cambridge University Press.

_____. and P. F. de Moraes Farias. 1989. *Discourse and its Disguises: The Interpretation of African Oral Texts*. Birmingham: Centre of West African Studies, University of Birmingham.

Bardolph, J. 1977. "Abdulrazak Gurnah's *Paradise and Admiring Silence*: History, Stories and the Figure of the Uncle." *Contemporary African Fiction*, edited by Derek Wright, 77-89. Bayreuth. Bayreuth African Studies Series.

Barungi, Violet. 1998. "The Last One to Know." *A Woman's Voice: An Anthology of Short Stories Written by Ugandan Women*, edited by Mary Okurut, 54-66. Kampala: Femrite Publications Ltd.

Barz, Gregory. 2004. *Music in East Africa: Experiencing Music and Expressive Culture*. New York: Oxford University Press.

Bauman, Zygmunt. 2005. *Liquid Modernity*. Polity.

Bauman, Lisa. 1990. "Power and Image: Della Rovere Patronage Late Quattrocento Rome." Ph. D. diss., Northwestern University.

Bayart, Jean-François. 1981. "*La politique par le bas en Afrique Noire*: Questions de Methode." *Politique Africane* 1:53-82.

Bekou-Betts, Josephine. 2005. "Western Perceptions of African Women in the 19th and 20th Centuries." *Readings in Gender in Africa*, edited by Andrea Cornwall, 20-24. Bloomington & Indianapolis: Indiana University Press.

Bellah, Robert N., and Richard Madsen et al. 1996. *Habits of the Heart: Individualism and Commitment in American Life. 1985.* Berkeley, LA and London: University of California Press.

Benge, Okot. and Alex Bangirana eds. 2000. *Uganda Poetry Anthology*. Kampala: Fountain Publishers.

Benitez, J. L. 2005. "Communication and Collective Identities in the Transnational Social Space: A Media Ethnography of the Salvadoran Immigrant Community in the Washington DC Area." PhD. Diss., University of Ohio.

Benjamin, Walter.1968. *Illuminations*. New York: Schocken Book.

Benjamin, Walter. 1968. "The Story Teller: Reflections on the Works of Nikolai Leskov." *Illuminations: Essays and Reflections*, 83-109. Trans. Harry Zohn, New York: Schocken.

Benson, Peter. 1986. *Black Orpheus, Transition and Modern Cultural Awakening in Africa*. Berkeley: University of California Press.

Berman, Marshall. 1983. *All that is Solid Melts into Air: The Experience of Modernity*. New York: Simon and Schuster. London and New York: Verso.

Bernault, Florence. ed. 2003. *A History of Prison and Confinement in Africa*. Trans. Janet L. Roitman Portsmouth, NH: Heinemann.

Bhabha, Homi. 1983. "The Other Question: The Stereotype and Colonial Discourse." *Screen* 24.6:18-36.

_____. 1990. "Introduction: Narrating the Nation." *Nation and Narration*, edited by Homi Bhabha, 1-7. Oxon: Routledge.

_____ 1990. "Dissemination: Time, narrative, and the Margins of the Modern Nation." *Nation and Narration*, edited by Homi Bhabha. 291-323. Oxon: Routledge.

_____. 1994. *The Location of Culture*. New York and London: Routledge.

383

Bhambra, G. K. 2007. *Rethinking Modernity: Postcolonialism and the Sociological Imagination*. Basingstoke: Palgrave Macmillan.

Bianco, A. B. 1991. "Women and Things: Pokot Motherhood as Political Destiny." *Journal of American Ethnologist* 18:770-785.

Biersteker, Ann. 1996. *Kujibizana: Questions of Language and Power in Nineteenth- and Twentieth-Century Poetry in Kiswahili*. East Lansing, Michigan: Michigan State University Press.

Billig, Michael. 1995. *Banal Nationalism*. London: Sage.

Biko, Steve. 1978. *I Write What I Like: Selected Writings of Steve Biko*. London: Heinemann.

Blishen, E. 1971. "Introduction." *Song of Prisoner* Okot p' Bitek, 1-40. New York: Third Press.

Blixen, Karen. 1937. *Out of Africa*. London: Putnam.

Blommaert, Jan. 1999. *Language Ideological Debates*. Berlin: Walter de Gruyter.

Boehmer, Elleke. 1991. "Stories of Women and Mothers: Gender and Nationalism in the Early Fiction of Flora Nwapa." *Motherlands: Black Women's Writing from Africa, the Caribbean and South Asia*, edited by Susheila Nasta, 3-23. London: The Women's Press.

_____. 1992. "Motherlands, Mothers and Nationalist Sons: Representations of Nationalism and Women in African Literature." *From Commonwealth to Post-Colonial*, edited by Anne Rutherford, 229-245. Sydney: Dangaroo.

Bose, S. 2006. *A Hundred Horizons: The Indian Ocean in the Age of Global Empire*. Cambridge, Mass. Harvard University Press.

Brecht, B. 1968. "The Street Scene." *The Theory of the Modern Stage*, edited by E Bentley. Middlesex: Penguin. 85-96.

Brennan, James, Andrew Burton and Yusuf Lawi eds. 2007. *Dar es Salaam. Histories from an Emerging African Metropolis*. Dar es Salaam: Mkuki na Nyota.

Breslow, Stephen. 1989. "Trinidadian Heteroglosia: A Bakhtinian View of Derek Walcott's Play *A Branch in the Blue Nile*." *World Literature Today* 63.1:36-39.

Bryce, Jane. 1997. "Women and Modern African Popular fiction." *Readings in African Popular Culture*, edited by Karin Barber, 118-124. Oxford: James Currey.

Bryce- Okunlola, Jane. 1997. "Popular Writing in Africa." *Writing and Africa*, edited by Mpalive Msiska and Paul Hyland . London: Longman.

Buckley, Nick. ed.1998. *Gentle Nature*. Sussex: The Born Free Foundation.

Bukaayi, Lillian. 2009. "Gender power relations in Soga Marriage Songs." *Performing Change*, edited by Dominica Dipio, Lene Johannessen and Stuart Sillars, 143-159. Oslo: Novus Press.

Burckhardt, Jacob. 1945. *The Civilization of the Renaissance in Italy, 1860*. Trans. S.G.C. Middlemore. Oxford and London: Phaidon Press Ltd.

BBC News. 2010. "Monuments for Mau Mau" http://news.bbc.co.uk/2/hi/africa/1236807.stm. Date of access, 17 February, 2010.

Cabral, Amilcar. 1973. "National Liberation and Culture." *Return to the Source: Selected Speeches*, 39-56. New York: Monthly Review Press.

Callahan, D. 2000. "Exchange, Bullies and Abuse in Abdulrazak Gurnah's *Paradise*." *World Literature Written in English* 38. 2: 55 - 69.

Callinicos, Alex. 2011. "Whither Marxism?" *Economic and Political Weekly* 31. 4. PE9-PE17 http//:www.jstor.org/stable/4403713 Accessed March 30, 2011.

Cannadine, David. 2001. *Ornamentalism: How the British Saw their Empire*. Oxford: Oxford University Press.

Caramazza, Giuseppe. 2002. *News Reporting and Broadcasting*. Nairobi: New People.

Chakava, Henry. 1996. *Publishing in Africa: One Man's Perspective*. Nairobi: East African Educational Publishers.

Chakrabarty, D. 2000. *Provincializing Europe: Postcolonial Thought and Historical Difference*. Princeton. Princeton University Press.

Challen, Edward. 2006. *Love your Muslim Neighbour*. London: Day One Publications.

Cham, Mbye B. 1987. "Contemporary Society and the Female Imagination: A Study of the Novels of Mariama Bâ." *Women in African Literature Today*, edited by Eldred Durosimi Jones, 89-101. London: James Currey.

Chambers, I. 1994. "The Broken World: Whose Centre, Whose Periphery?" *Migrancy, Culture and Identity*, 67-92. London: Routledge.

Chatterjee, Partha. 1993. *The Nation and its Fragments: Colonial and Postcolonial Histories*. Princeton: Princeton University Press.

Chebii, J and Lugulu. 2007. "Pedagogical Methods in Law: The Moi University Experience." *Moi University Law Journal* 1. 2: 196.

Chege, Michael. 1998. "Africans of European Descent." *Transition* 73. 7: 74-86.

Cheran, R. 2003. *Diaspora, Circulation and Transnationalism as Agents for Change in Post-Conflict Zones of Sri Lanka*. Berlin, Germany: Berghof Foundation for Conflict Studies.

Cheran, R. 2002. *The Sixth Genre: Memory, History and the Tamil Diaspora Imagination*. Colombo: Marga Institute.

Chimerah, Rocha. 1998. *Kiswahili: Past, Present and Future Horizons*. Nairobi: Nairobi University Press.

Chimombo, Steve. 1994. *Napolo and the Python: Selected Poems*. Portsmouth: Heinemann Educational Publishers.

Clifford, J. 1994. "Diasporas." *Cultural Anthropology* 9.3: 302-338.

_____. 2002. *The Predicament of Culture: Twentieth-Century Ethnography, Literature, and Art*. London: Harvard University Press.

Cloete, Elsie. 2002. "Re-Telling Kenya: Wambui Waiyaki Otieno and Mau Mau's Daughter." PhD. Diss., University of the Witwatersrand, Johannesburg.

Cohen, R.1997. *Global Diasporas: An Introduction*. London: UCL Press.

Cohen, R. 1999. "Diasporas and the Nation-State: From Victims to Challengers." *Migration, Diasporas and Transnationalism*, edited by S. Vertovec and R. Cohen, 266-279. Cheltenham: Edward Elgar Publishing.

Cruise O'Brien and Donald B. 1996. "A Lost Generation? Youth Identity and State Decay in West Africa." *Postcolonial Identities in Africa*, edited by Richard Werbner and Terence Ranger, 55-74. London and New Jersey: Zed Books.

Childs, Peter and Patrick Williams. 1997. *An Introduction to Post-Colonial Theory*. Edinburgh: Pearson Education.

Comaroff, Jean and John Comaroff eds. 2006. *Law and Order in the Postcolony*. Chicago and London: University of Chicago Press.

Crehan, S. 1995. "The Politics of the Signifier: Ngugi wa Thiong'o's *Petals of Blood*". *Postcolonial Literatures: Achebe, Ngugi, Desai, Walcott*, edited by Parker, M. and Starkey. London: Macmillan Press.

Conrad, J. [1899] 2007. *Heart of Darkness*. London: Penguin.

Cooper, B. 2008. "Returning the Jinns to the Jar: Material Culture, Stories and Migration in Abdulrazak Gurnah's *By the Sea*." *Kunapipi* 30. 1: 79 - 96.

Calder, Angus, Jack Mapanje and Cosmo Pieterse eds. 1983. *Summer Fires: New Poetry of Africa*. London: Heinemann.

Chimerah, Rocha. 1989. *Kiswahili: Past, Present and Future Horizons*. Nairobi: Nairobi University Press.

Cook, D and M Okenimkpe. 1997. *Ngugi wa Thiong'o: An Exploration of his Writings*. Oxford: James Currey Ltd.

Davidson, Basil. 1983. *Modern Africa*. London and New York: Longman.

Davies, Boyce Carol. 1990. "Introduction" to *Ngambika: Studies of Women in African Literature*, edited by Carol Boyce Davies and Anne Adams Graves, 1-24. Eritrea: Africa World Press.

Dako, Kari and Bryce, Jane. 1999. "Textual Deviancy and Cultural Syncretism: Romantic Fiction as a subversive Strain in Africana Women's Writing." *Arms Akimbo: Africana Women in Contemporary Literature*, edited by Janice Lee Liddell and Yakini B Kemp, 219-229. Orlando: University of Florida.

De Certeau, Michel. 1984. *The Practice of Every Day Life*. Translated by Stephen Rendall. Berkeley: University of California Press.

De Lombard, Jeannine. 1995. "Mzee's New Clothes: Neocolonial Detention as the Spectacle of Invisibility." *Ngugi wa Thiong'o Texts and Contexts*, edited by Charles Cantalupo, 49-60. Trenton, NJ: African World Press.

Duder, C.J.D. 1991. "Love and the Lions: The Image of White Settlement in Kenya in Popular Fiction 1919-1939." *African Affairs* 90.16: 427 - 438. Accessed January 21, 2008. www.jstor.org <http://www.jstor.org/>

Dyer, Richard. 1997. *White*. London: Routledge.

Ebila, Florence. 2002. "Ugandan Women Watering the Literary Desert." *The Women's Movement in Uganda: History, Challenges, and Prospects*, edited by Aili Mari Tripp and Joy Constance Kwesiga, 162-173. Kampala: Fountain Publishers.

_____. 2003. "The Dilemma of Being a Feminist." *Wordwrite* (3).

Edgerton, B. R. 1964. "Pokot Intersexuality: An East African Example of the Resolution of Sexual Incongruity." *American Anthropologist* 66: 1288-1299.

Ellis, Stephen. 1989. "Tuning in to Pavement Radio." *African Affairs* 88. 352:321-30.

Fabian, Johannes. 1978. "Popular Culture in Africa: Findings and Conjectures." *Africa* 48. 4: 315-34.

_____. 1990. *Power and Performance: Ethnographic Explorations through Proverbial Wisdom and Theatre in Shaba, Zaire*. Madison: University of Wisconsin Press.

Fair, Laura. 2001. *Pastimes and Politics: Culture, Community and Identity in Post-abolition Urban Zanzibar, 1890-1945*. Athens: Ohio University Press.

Falk, E. 2007. *Subject and History in Selected Works by Abdulrazak Gurnah, Yvonne Vera and David Dabydeen*. Karlstad: Karlstad University Studies.

Faniran, O. J. 2008. *Foundations of African Communication*. Abuja: Spectrum Book.

Fanon, Frantz. [1963] 2004. *The Wretched of the Earth*. Trans. Richard Philcox. New York: Grove Press.

Fanon, Frantz. 1967. "Pitfalls of National Consciousness." *The Wretched of the Earth*. London: Penguin books.

Farah, Nuruddin. 1992. *Close Sesame*. Saint Paul, MN: Graywolf P.

_____. 2003. *From a Crooked Rib*. London: Penguin.

_____. 1992. *Gifts*. London: Serif Publishers.

_____. 2007. Knots. New York: Riverhead - Penguin.

_____. 2003. *Links*. Cape Town: Kwela Books.

_____. 2005. *Links*. London: Gerald Duckworth & Co. Ltd.

_____. 2000. *Maps*. London: Penguin.

_____. 1976. *A Naked Needle*. London: Heinemann.

_____. 1982. *Sardines*. London: Heinemann.

_____. 1998. *Secrets*. Cape Town: David Philip.

_____. 1992. *Sweet and Sour Milk*. Saint Paul, MN: Graywolf P.

Finnegan, Ruth. 1970. *Oral Literature in Africa*. Nairobi: Oxford University Press.

Foss, M. 1971. *The Age of Patronage: The Arts in Society 1660-1750*. London: Hamish Hamilton.

Foucault, Michel. 1972. *The Archaeology of Knowledge*. Trans.lated by A.M. Sheridan Smith. New York: Pantheon Books.

_____. 1991. *Discipline and Punish: The Birth of the Prison*. Translated by Alan Sheridan. Harmondsworth: Penguin.

_____. 2001. "Theory, Literature and Moral Considerations." *Research in African Literatures* 32. 4: 1-18.

Frank, Marion. 1995. *AIDS-Education through Theatre*. Bayreuth: Bayreuth African Studies.

Frankenberg, Ruth. 1993. *White Women, Race Matters: The Social Construction of Whiteness*. London: Routledge.

Frederiksen, Bodil F. 2000. "Popular Culture, Gender Relations and the Democratization of Everyday Life in Kenya." *Journal of Southern African Studies* 26. 2: 209-22.

Freund, Bill. 1984. *The Making of Contemporary Africa: The Development of African Society since 1800*. London: MacMillan Press.

Friedan, B. 2001. *The Feminine Mystique*. New York: Norton and Company.

Frye, Northrop. 1971 [1957]. *Anatomy of Criticism: Four Essays*. Princeton: Princeton UP.

Furedi, Frank. 1990. *The Mau Mau War in Perspective*. Nairobi: Heinemann Kenya.

Gallagher, P. M. 1999. *Clashing Symbols*. London: Darton.

Gardner, Viv. 2005. "Contested Terrains: A Personal Journey through Image, (National) Identity and Ethics." *Research in Drama Education* 10. 2: 189-199.

Garuba, Harry. 2008. "No-man's Land: Nuruddin Farah's Links and the Space of Postcolonial Alienation." *Literary Landscapes: From Modernism to Postcolonialism*, edited by Attie de Lange et al, 180-197. Basingstoke: Palgrave Macmillan.

Garuba, Harry. 2008. "Race in Africa: Four Epigraphs and a Commentary." *PMLA: The Changing Profession 1643-1648*.

Gavron, Jeremy. 1994. *Darkness in Eden: The Murder of Julie Ward*. London, Harper Collins.

Geiger, Susan. 1997. *TANU Women. Gender and Culture in the Making of Tanganyikan Nationalism, 1955-1965*. Portsmouth: Heinemann.

Georgiou, M. 2006. *Diaspora, Identity and the Media: Diasporic Transnationalism and Mediated Spacialities*. Cresskill, NJ: Hampton Press.

George, R. Marangoly. 1996. *The Politics of Home: Postcolonial Relocations and Twentieth Century Fiction*. Cambridge: Cambridge University Press.

Gerard, Albert. 1981. *African Languages Literature: An Introduction to the Literary History of Sub-Saharan Africa*. London: Longman.

Ghai, Dharam and Yash Pal Ghai eds. 1970. *Portrait of a Minority: The Asians in East Africa*. Nairobi: Oxford University Press.

Ghosh, D. and Davidson, L. S. 2009. "Ocean of Stories: An Introduction." *Transforming Cultures eJournal* 4. 2: i - iv.

Ghosh, D. and Muecke, S. 2007. "Natural Logic of the Indian Ocean." *Cultures of Trade: Indian Ocean Exchanges,* edited by Devleena Ghosh and Stephen Muecke, 150 - 163. Newcastle: Cambridge Scholars Publishing.

Gilman, Lisa. 2001. "Purchasing Praise: Women, Dancing, and Patronage in Malawi Party Politics." *Africa Today* 48. 4 :43-64.

Gikandi, Simon. "African Literature and the Social Science Program." Paper commissioned by the Social Science research Council, New York. Unpub. Ms.

_____. 1987. *Reading the African Novel.* Nairobi: Heinemann Kenya; London: James Currey; Portsmouth, NH: Heinemann Educational Books.

_____. 2000. *Ngugi wa Thiong'o.* Cambridge: Cambridge University Press.

_____. 2011. "Review: Travelling Theory: Ngugi's return to English." *Research in African Literatures* 31. 2:194-209, http://www.jstor.org/stable/3821053. Accessed May 20, 2011.

_____ Gikandi, Simon and Evan Mwangi. eds. 2007. *The Cambridge Guide to East African Literature in English Since 1945.* Cambridge: Cambridge University Press.

Gilmore, Leigh. 1994. *Autobiographies: A Feminist Theory of Women's Self Representation.* Ithaca, New York: Cornell University Press.

Gilroy, P. 1993. *The Black Atlantic. Modernity and Double Consciousness.* London: Verso.

Githiora, Chege. 2002. "Sheng: Peer Language, Swahili dialect or emerging Creole?" *Journal of African Cultural Studies* 15. 22: 159-181.

Givanni, J. ed. 2000. *Symbolic Narratives/African Cinema: Audiences, Theory and the Moving Image.* London: British Film Institute, Oxford: Blackwell Publishers.

Godwin, Ken. 1982. *Understanding African Poetry: A Study of Ten Poets.* London: Heinemann.

Goldstein, J and Rotich. 2008. *Digitally Networked Technology in Kenya's 2007-8 Post-Election Crisis.* Berkman: Berkman Centre for Internet and Society.

Goldsworthy, David. 1982. *Tom Mboya: The Man Kenya Wanted to Forget.* London and Nairobi: Heinemann Educational Books.

Gombrich, Ernst H. 1966. "The Early Medici as Patrons of Art." *Norm and Form,* 35-57. London: Phaidon.

Gorlier, C. 2011. "Post-Marxism in an African Context: The Usability of Antonio Gramsci." *Research in African Literatures* 33. 3:97-103, http://www.jstor.org/stable/3820684 Accessed March 28, 2011.

Graebner, Werner. 1997. "Whose Music? The Songs of Remmy Ongala and Orchestra Super Matimila." *Readings in African Popular Culture,* edited by Karin Barber, 110-17. Bloomington: Indiana University Press.

Gramsci, A. 1999. "Hegemony." *Literary Theory: An Anthology,* edited by Julie Rivkin and Michael Ryan, 673. Oxford: Blackwell Publishers.

Green, Michael. 1997. *Novel Histories: Past, Present and Future in South African Fiction.* Johannesburg: Witwatersrand University Press.

Gregson, Ian. 1996. *Contemporary Poetry and Postmodernism: Dialogue and Estrangement*. Basingstoke: Macmillan.

Griffiths, Gareth. 2000. *African Literatures in English: East and West*. Harlow: Pearson Education.

Gunner, Liz. 2000. "Wrestling with the Present, Beckoning to the Past: Contemporary Zulu Radio drama." *Journal of Southern African Studies* 26. 2: 223-237.

Gurnah, A. 1994. *Paradise*. London: Bloomsbury.

_____. 1997. *Admiring Silence*. Harmondsworth: Penguin.

_____. 2001. *By the Sea*. London: Bloomsbury.

_____. 2005. *Desertion*. London: Bloomsbury.

Gyekye, Kwame. 1987. *An Essay on African Philosophical Thought: The Akan Conceptual Scheme*. Cambridge: Cambridge University Press.

Habermas, Jürgen. 1989 [1962]. *The Structural Transformation of the Public Sphere: An Inquiry into a Category of Bourgeois Society*. Translated by Thomas Burger and Frederick Lawrence. Cambridge: Polity Press.

Habwe, John. 1998. "A Discourse Analysis of Swahili Political Speeches." PhD diss., University of Nairobi.

Hale, Thomas A. 1990. "Artist and Audience: The Problem of Africanism in African Literature of Western Expression." *Artist and Audience: African Literature as a Shared experience*, edited by Richard Priebe and Thomas Hale. Washington DC: Three Continents Press.

_____. 1990. *Scribe, Groit, and Novelist: Narrative interpreters of the Songhay Empire*. Gainesville: University of Florida Press.

Hall, Stuart. 1995. "Negotiating Caribbean Identities." *New Left Review* 209: 3-14.

Hammer, Joshua. 2006. "The Kenyan Cowboy". *Outside Magazine*. Accessed March 26, 2008. http://outside.away.com/outside/destinations/200612/kenya-thomas-cholmondeley-7.html.

Hancock, Graham. 2007. *Lords of Poverty*. London: Camerapix.

Harraway, Donna. 1992. "The Promises of Monsters: A Regenerative Politics for Inappropriate/d Others" *Cultural Studies*, edited by Lawrence Grossberg, Cary Nelson and Paula A. Treichler, 295-337. New York: Routledge.

Haugerud, Angelique. 1995. *The Culture of Politics in Modern Kenya*. Cambridge: Cambridge University Press.

Heald S. 1982. "The Making of Men: The Relevance of Vernacular Psychology of the Interpretation of a Gisu Ritual." *Africa: Journal of the International African Institute* 52:15-36.

_____. 1989. *Controlling Anger: The Sociology of Gisu Violence*. London: Manchester University Press.

Heron, G.A. 1972. "Introduction", *Song of Lawino/ Song of Ocol* by Okot p' Bitek, 1-33 London: Heinemann.

_____. 1976. *The Poetry of Okot p' Bitek*. London: Heinemann.

Herzig, Pascale. 2006. *South Asians in Kenya: Gender, Generation and Changing Identities in Diaspora*. Munster: LIT Verlag.

Hick, John. 2010. *Philosophy of Religion*. New Jersey: Prentice Hall.

Hill, Christopher. 1980. "Robinson Crusoe." *History Workshop* 10.1: 6-24.

Hiltzik, Michael. 1991. *A Death in Kenya: The Murder of Julie Ward*. New York: Delacorte Press.

Hirschman, Albert O. 1970. *Exit, Voice, and Loyalty: Responses to Decline in Firms, Organizations, and States*. Cambridge: Harvard University Press.

Hofmeyr, I. 1994. *We Spend Our Years as a Tale That Is Told: Oral Historical Narrative in a South African Chiefdom*. London: James Currey.

_____. 2007. "The Black Atlantic Meets the Indian Ocean: Forging New Paradigms of Transnationalism for the Global South - Literary and Cultural Perspectives." *Social Dynamics* 33. 2: 3 - 32.

Holden A. and J. Lene eds. 2007. *Reading of the Particular: The Postcolonial in the Postnational*. Amsterdam: Rodopi.

Hollingsworth, Mary. 1994. *Patronage in Renaissance Italy: From 1400 to the Early Sixteenth Century*. Baltimore: John Murray.

_____. 1996. *Patronage in Sixteenth Century Italy*. London: John Murray.

Howe, Russell Warren. 2000. "Men of the Century." *Transition* 86: 36-50.

hooks, Bell. 1994. *Outlaw Culture: Resisting Representations*. New York: Routledge.

Huggan, Graham. 1994. "The Postcolonial Exotic: Salman Rushdie and the Booker of Bookers." *Transition* 64: 22-29.

Hughes, Langston. 1959. *Selected Poems of Langston Hughes*. New York: Vintage Books.

Hutcheon, L. 1985. *A Theory of Parody: The Teachings of Twelve Century Art Forms*. New York: Methuen.

Huxley, Elspeth. 1983 [1959]. *The Flame Trees of Thika: Memoirs of an African Childhood*. Leicester: Ulverscroft.

_____. 1980 [1935]. *White Man's Country: Biography of Lord Delamere*. London: Chatto and Windus.

Imbo, S. O. 2002. *Oral Traditions as Philosophy: Okot p'Bitek's Legacy for African Philosophy*. Lanham, MD: Rowman and Littlefield.

Jackson, Robert. 1992. "Juridical Statehood in Sub-Saharan Africa." *Journal of International Affairs* 46: 1.

Jameson, Fredric. 1975. "Magical Narratives: Romance as Genre." *New Literary History* 7. 1: 135-163.

_____. 1988. "Modernism and its Repressed; or, Robbe-Grillet as Anti-Colonialist." *The Ideology of Theory Essays, 1971 – 1986: Situations of Theory* 1: 167-180.

Jewsiewicki, Bogumil. 1988. «*Présentation: Le Langage Politique et les Arts Plastiques en Afrique.*» *The Canadian Journal of African Studies* 22.1:1-9.

_____ and Henri Moniot eds. 1988. *Dialoguer avec le Léopard? Pratiques, Savoirs et Actes du Peuple Face au Politique en Afrique Noire Contemporaine.* Québec: Edition Safi.

Joseph, Christopher Odhiambo. 2005. «Theatre for Development in Kenya: Interrogating Ethics of Practice.» *Research in Drama Education* 10.2: 189-199.

Joseph, May. 1999. *Nomadic Identities: The Performance of Citizenship.* Minneapolis: U of Minnesota.

Julien, Eileen. 1992. *African Novels and the Question of Orality.* Indianapolis: Indiana University Press.

Juma, Matthews Anyumba. 2007. Note in the inside sleeve of the CD album Dorina by Okatch Biggy (EHS 2702). New Jersey: Equator Heritage Sounds.

Kaarsholm, Preben. 1999. "*Si ye Pambili* - Which Way Forward? Urban Development, Culture and Politics in Bulawayo." *Sites of Struggle. Essays in Zimbabwe's Urban History*, edited by Brian Raftopoulos and Tsuneo Yoshikuni, 227-256. Harare: Weaver Press.

_____ and Deborah James. 2000. "Popular Culture and Democracy in Some Southern Contexts : An Introduction." *Journal of Southern African Studies* 26. 2: 189-208.

Kabira, Wanjiku, Muthoni Karega and Elizabeth Nzioki eds. 1991. *Our Secret Lives: An Anthology of Poems and Short Stories.* Nairobi: Phoenix.

Kalliney, P. 2008. "East African Literature and the Politics of Global Reading." *Research in African Literatures* 39. 1: 1 - 23.

_____. 2009. "East African Fiction and Globalization." *Teaching the African Novel*, edited by Gaurav Desai, 259-273. New York: The Modern Language Association of America.

Kantai, Parselelo. 2007. "In the Grip of the Vampire State: Maasai Land Struggles in Kenyan Politics." *Journal of Eastern African Studies* 1.1:107 - 122.

Kapur-Dromson, Neera. 2007. *From Jhelum to Tana.* New Delhi: Penguin.

Kariuki, John. 2000. "Why Benga is the True National Music." Sunday Nation, March 26. Accessed May 28, 2006. http://www.nationaudio.com/News/DailyNation/26032000/Features/LS3.html.

Kearney, J.A. 2006. "Abdulrazak Gurnah and the Disabling Complexities of Parochial Realities." *English in Africa* 33.1: 47-58.

Kearney, M. 2004. *The Indian Ocean in World History.* New York and London: Routledge.

Kellman, Steven G. 1976. "The Fiction of Self-Begetting." *MLN* 91.6: 1243-56.

Kennedy, Dane Keith. 1987. *Islands of White: Settler Society and Culture in Kenya and Southern Rhodesia, 1890-1939.* Durham: Duke University Press.

Kenyatta, Jomo. 1968. *Suffering without Bitterness.* Nairobi: EAEP.

Kercher, Leonard. C. 1981. *The Kenyan Penal System: Past, Present and Pros-pect.* Washington: University Press of America.

Kerr, David. 1991."Participatory Popular Theatre: The Highest Stage of Cultural Under-Development?" *Research in African Literatures* 22. 3: 55-79.

_____. 1995. *African Popular Theatre.* London: James Currey Ltd

Keshubi, Hope. 1998. "Joanitta's Nightmare." *A Woman's Voice: An Anthology of Short Stories written by Ugandan Women,* edited by Mary Okurut, 28-41. Kampala: FEMRITE Publications Ltd.

Khamalwa, W. 2009. "Myth and Core Values." *Performing Change,* edited by Dominic Dipio, Lene Johannessen and John Sillars Stuart, 90-105. Oslo: Novus Press.

Khamalwa, W. 2004. *Identity, Power, and Culture.* Bayreuth: Bayreuth African Studies Series.

Kiguli, Susan. 2007. "FEMRITE and the Woman Writer's Position in Uganda: Personal Reflections." *Words and Worlds: African Writing, Theatre and Society,* edited by Susan Ardnt and Katrin Berndt, 169- 184. Eritrea. Africa World Press.

Kimani, Peter. 2002. *Before the Rooster Crows.* Nairobi: East African Educa-tional Publishers.

Kitogo, Shani A. 2002. "The Poets' Contribution to Political Development. A Case Study of Saadani Abdu Kandoro." PhD diss., University of Dar es Salaam.

Kiriamiti, John. 1994. *My Life in Crime.* Nairobi: Spear Books.

_____. 1989. *My Life with a Criminal.* Nairobi: Spear Books.

Kiyimba, Abasi. 2008. "Male Identity and Female Space in the Fiction of Ugandan Women Writers." *Journal of International Women's Studies* 9.3: 193-222.

Knappert, Jan. 1961. " The Figure of the Prophet Muhammad according to the Popular Literature of the Islamic people." *Journal of the East African Swahili Committee* 31: 24-31.

_____. 1967. *Traditional Swahili Poetry: An Investigation into the Concept of East African Islam as Reflected in the Utenzi Literature.* Leiden: E.J. Brill.

Kuloba, R. 1997. *Courts of Justice in Kenya.* Nairobi: Oxford.

Kunene, Mazizi. 1982. *Ancestor and the Sacred Mountain.* London: Heine-mann.

Kurtz, John. 2002. "Crossing Over: Identity and Change in Marjorie Oludhe Macgoye's *Song of Nyarloka." Research in African Literatures* 33. 2: 100-118.

Kwani Trust. 2003. *Kwani?* 1. Nairobi: Kwani Trust.

_____. 2003. *Kwani?* 2. Nairobi: Kwani Trust.

_____. 2007. *Kwani?* 3. Nairobi: Kwani Trust.

_____. 2007. *Kwani?* 4. Nairobi: Kwani Trust.

_____. 2008a. *Kwani?* 5 part 1. Nairobi: Kwani Trust.

_____. 2008b. *Kwani?* 5 part 2. Nairobi: Kwani Trust.

_____. 2010. *Kwani?* 6. Nairobi: Kwani Trust.

Kyomuhendo, Bantebya Grace and McIntosh, Keniston Marjorie. 2006. *Women. Work and Domestic Virtue in Uganda 1900-2003.* Oxford: James Currey.

Kyomuhendo, Goretti. 2002. "What is the future of Ugandan writers?" *Wordwrite* 1.

La Fontaine, J.S. 1977. "The Power of Rights." *Man* 12: 421-437.

Kyomuhendo, Goretti. 2007. "To be an African Woman Writer: Joys and Challenges." *Words and Worlds: African Writing, Theatre and Society*, edited by Susan Ardnt and Katrin Berndt, 185-192. Eritrea: Africa World Press.

La Fontaine, J.S. 1967. "Parricide in Bugisu: A Study in Inter-Generational Conflict." *Man* 2: 249-259.

Lange, Siri. 2000. "Muungano and TOT: Rivals on the Urban Cultural Scene." *Mashindano! Competitive Music Performance in East Africa*, edited by Frank Gunderson and Gregory F. Barz, 67-85. Dar es Salaam: Mkuki na Nyota.

Larraine, Jorge. 1994. *Ideology and Cultural Identity: Modernity and the Third world Presence.* Cambridge: Polity Press.

Lavie, S. and T Swedenburg eds. 1996. *Displacement, Diaspora and Geographies of Identity.* Durham: Duke University Press.

Lasch, Christopher. 1991 [1979]. *The Culture of Narcissism: American Life in an Age of Diminishing Expectations.* New York and London: W.W. Norton and Company.

Law Society of Kenya. 2007. "Countering the Culture of Short Memory in Combating Human Rights Violation in Kenya." *Law Society of Kenya Human Rights Report 2005/2006.*

Lea, John. 1999. "Positioning of Host Populations in the Tourist-Host Relationship." *Journal for Sustainable Tourism* 7.1. Accessed March 24, 2007. http://www.codesria.org/Links/Publications/asr4_2full/ajulu.pdf <http://www.codesria.org/Links/Publications/asr4_2full/ajulu.pdf>

Leman, P. 2009. "Singing the Law: Okot p'Bitek's Legal Imagination and the Poetics of Traditional Justice." *Research in African Literatures* 40. 3: 109-128.

Levenson, Michael. 1991. *Modernism and the Fate of Individuality: Character and Novelistic Form from Conrad to Woolf.* New York: Cambridge UP.

Lewis, R.W.B. 2002. *Dante: A Life.* London: Phoenix.

Lewis, S. 1999. "Impossible Domestic Situations: Questions of Identity and Nationalism in the Novels of Abdulrazak Gurnah and M. G. Vassanji." *Thamyris* 6: 215-229.

Ligaga, Dina. 2005. "Narrativising Development in Radio Drama: Tradition and Realism in the Kenyan Radio Play *Ushikwapo Shikamana*." *Social Identities* 11. 2: 131-145.

_____. 2005. "*Kwani?* Exploring New Literary Spaces in Kenya." *Africa Insight* 35.2:46-52.

Lindfors, Bernth. 1991. *Popular Literatures in Africa*. Africa World Press, Inc.

_____. 1993. "Okot p'Bitek." *Dictionary of Literary Biography*, edited by Lindfors, Bernth and Reinhard Sander. Detroit: Gale Research Inc.

Lo Liyong, Taban. 1965. "Can we Correct Literary Barrenness in East Africa?" *East Africa Journal* 2. 8: 5-13.

Loomba, Ania. 1998. *Colonialism/Postcolonialism*. London: Routledge.

Lonsdale, John. 2004. "Moral and Political Argument in Kenya." *Ethnicity and Democracy in Africa*, edited by Bruce Berman, Dickson Eyoh and Will Kymlicka, 73-95. Oxford: James Currey.

Lopez, Alfred ed. 2005. *Postcolonial Whiteness: A Critical Reader on Race and Empire*. Albany: State University of New York Press.

Lowe, L. 1996. "Heterogeneity, Hybridity, Multiplicity: Asian American Differences." *Immigrant Acts: On Asian American Cultural Politics*, edited by Lisa Lowe, 132-155. Durham and London: Duke University Press.

Lubwa p'Chong, 1986. "A Biographical Sketch." *Artist, the Ruler*, by Okot p' Bitek, 1-12, Nairobi: Heinemann.

Luce, Louise Fiber. 1991. "Neocolonialism and *Présence Africaine*." *African Studies Review* 29:1: 5-11.

Luvai, Arthur ed. 1988. *Boundless Voices: Poems from Kenya*. Nairobi: EAEP.

Mabala, Richard ed. 1980. *Summons: Poems from Tanzania*. Dar el Salaam: DUP.

Macgoye, Marjorie. 1998. *Make it Sing and Other Poems*. Nairobi: EAEP.

Makinen, M. and Kuira M. 2008. "Social Media and Postelection Crisis in Kenya." *International Journal of Press/ Politics* 13.3:328-335.

Marx, Karl. 1970. "The Eighteenth Brumaire of Louis Bonaparte." *Selected Works in One Volume*. London: Lawrence and Wishart.

Maughan-Brown, David. 1979. "Black Literature Debate: Human Beings Behind the Work." *Contrast* 48.

Mda, Zakes. 1993. *When People Play People: Development Communication Through Theatre*. Johannesburg: Witwatersrand University Press.

Mamdani, Mahmood. 1996. *Citizen and Subject: Contemporary Africa and the Legacy of Late Colonialism*. Kampala: Fountain Publishers.

_____. 2004. "Race and Ethnicity as Political Identities in the African Context." *Keywords: Identity*, edited by Nazia Tazi, 4-8. Cape Town: Double, Storey Books.

_____. 2006.*Citizen and Subject: Contemporary Africa and the Legacy of Late Colonialism*. Princeton: Princeton University Press.

Manger, L. and M Assal, eds. 2006. *Diasporas Within and Without Africa: Dynamism, Heterogeneity, Variation*. Uppsala: Nordic Africa Institute.

Mangesho, Peter. 2003. "Global Cultural Trends: the Case of Hip-Hop Music in Dar es Salaam." MA diss., University of Dar es Salaam.

Mangua, Charles. 1971. *Son of Woman*. Nairobi: East African Educational Publishers.

Mangwanda, Marcel Khombe. 2009. "Subverting the Dominant Gender Discourse in Congolese Popular music: Mbilia Bel's 'Eswi yo Wapi' and Mpongo Love's 'Monama Elima.'" *Muziki: Journal of Music Research in Africa* 6.1: 120-130.

Martin, Denis-Constant, ed. 2002. *Sur la piste des OPNI (Objets politiques non identifiés)*. Paris: Karthala.

Masilela, Ntongela. 1996. "The `Black Atlantic' and African Modernity in South Africa." *Research in African Literatures* 27. 4: 88-96.

Masilela, Ntongela. 2011. "Black South African Literature from the 'Sophiatown Renaissance' to 'Black Mamba Rising': Transformations and Variations from the 1950s to the 1980s. Lecture presented on April 30, 1990 at University of California at Santa Barbara. Accessed September 1, 2011. http://pzacad.pitzer.edu/NAM/general/essays/nxumalo.htm.

Mason, Mary. 1998. "The Other Voice: Autobiographies of Women Writers." *Women, Autobiography, Theory - A Reader*, edited by Smith Sidonie and Julia Watson, 321 - 331. Madison: University of Wisconsin Press.

Mazrui, Ali. 1973. "Aesthetic Dualism and Creative Literature in East Africa." *Black Aesthetics in East Africa*, edited by Zirimu, Pio and Andrew Gurr, 30-40. Nairobi: Eat African Literature Bureau.

_____. 2007. *Swahili Beyond the Boundaries: Literature, Language and Identity*. Athens, OH: Ohio University Press.

Mazrui, Alamin and Ali Mazrui. 1993. "Dominant Languages in a Plural Society: English and Kiswahili in Post-Colonial East Africa." *International Political Science Review* 14. 3: 275-292.

Mbaria, John. 2004. "'Unbwogable' Duo Named Messengers of Truth by UN-Habitat." East African, September 20 - 26.

Mbeki, Moeletsi. 2009. *Architects of Poverty: Why African Capitalism Needs Changing*. Johannesburg: Picador.

Mbembe, Achille. 1992. "Provisional Notes on the Postcolony." *Africa* 62.1: 3-37.

Mbowa, Rose. 1999. "Luganda Theatre and its Audience." *Uganda: The Cultural Landscape*, edited by Eckhard Breitinger, 227-246. Bayreuth African Studies. Kampala: Fountain Publishers.

Mboya, Ker Paul. 1997 [1938]. *Luo Kitgi gi Timbegi: A Handbook of Luo Customs*. Kisumu: Anyange Press.

Mboya, T. Michael. 2009. "'My Voice is Nowadays Known' - Okatch Biggy, Benga and Luo Identity in the 1990s." *Muziki: Journal of Music Research in Africa* 6.1:14-25.

Mboya, Tom. 1963. *Freedom and After*. London: Andre Deutsch.

Mbughuni, L. A. and Gabriel Ruhumbika. 1974. "TANU and National Culture." *Towards Ujamaa. Twenty Years of TANU Leadership*, edited by Gabriel Ruhumbika, 275-87. Kampala; Nairobi; Dar es Salaam: East African Literature Bureau.

McClintock, Anne. 1985. *Imperial Leather: Race Gender and Sexuality in the Colonial Contest*. New York: Routledge.

McKeon, Michael. 1987. *The Origins of the English Novel 1600-1740*. Baltimore: The Johns Hopkins UP.

Menocal, Maria Rosa. 1994. *Shards of Love: Exile and the Origins of the Lyric*. Durham: Duke UP.

Mlama, Penina Muhando. 1991. *Culture and Development: The Popular Theatre Approach in Africa*. Uppsala: Nordiska Afrikainstitutet

Miner, E. 2002. "Discursive Constructions of Kiswahili Speakers in Ugandan Popular Media." *Political Independence with Linguistic Servitude: The Politics About Language in the Developing World*, edited by S. Obeng and B Hartford, 185-207. New York: Nova Science Publishers.

Morales, E. 2002. *Living in Spanglish: Searching for Latino Identity in America*. New York: St.Martin's Press.

Mortimer, Mildred. 1990. *Journeys Through the French West African Novel*. London: James Currey Ltd.

Mudimbe, V. Y. 1988. *The Invention of Africa*. Madison: University of Wisconsin press

_____. 1994. *The Idea of Africa*. Bloomington: Indiana UP.

Mueller, Susanne D. 2008. "The Political Economy of Kenya's Crisis." *Journal of Eastern African Studies* 2. 2: 185-210.

Muga, Wycliffe. 2009. "Why Moi Lost his grip on Rift Valley." *The National Star* August 20.

Mugambi, N. H. 2010. "Masculinity on Trial: Gender anxiety in African Song Performances." *Masculinities in African Literary and Cultural Texts*, edited by Helen N. Mugambi and Allan Tuzyline, 78-94. Oxfordshire: Ayebia Clarke Publishing.

Mukai, C. 2006. "In Pokot, FGM still goes on Unabetted." *New Vision Newspaper*, April 11.

Musila, Grace. 2008. "Between the Wildebeest, Noble Savages and Moi's Kenya: Deceit and Cultural Illiteracies in the Search for Julie Ward's Killer(s)." *The Journal of Commonwealth Literature* 43: 115-133.

Mustapha, Sophia. 2009. *The Tanganyika Way*. TSAR Publications.

Mutua, Makau. 2008. *Kenya's Quest for Democracy Taming Leviathan*. Colorado: Lynne Rienner Publishers.

Mwangi, Evan. 2007. "Hybridity in Emergent East African Poetry: A Reading of Susan Kiguli and Her Contemporaries." *Africa Today* 53. 3: 41-62.

Mwaura, Bantu. 2007. "Orature of Combat: Cultural Aesthetics of Song as Political Action in the Performance of the Mau Mau Songs." *Songs and Politics in Eastern Africa*, edited by Kimani Njogu and Hervé Maupeu, 201-40. Mkuki na Nyota: Dar es Salaam; IFRA: Nairobi.

_____. ed. 2006. *Jahazi* 1. 1. Nairobi: Twaweza Communications.

Nabasuta, H. M. and Jita, T.A. Eds. 2010. *Masculinities in African Literary and Cultural Text*. Oxfordshire: Ayebia Clarke.

Nabweru, Philo. 1998. "Where is She?" *A Woman's Voice: An Anthology of Short Stories written by Ugandan Women*, edited by Mary Okurut, 67-73. Kampala: FEMRITE Publications Ltd.

Nagar, Richa and Helger Leiner. 1998. "Contesting Social Relations in Communal Places: Identity Politics among Asian Communities in Dar es Salaam." *Cities of Difference*, edited by Ruth Fincher and Jane M. Jacobs, 226 - 251. New York: Gilford Press.

Nannyonga-Tamusuza, Sylvia. 2002. "Gender, Ethnicity and Politics in Kadongo-Kamu Music of Uganda. Analysing the Song Kayanda." *Playing with Identities in Contemporary Music in Africa*, edited by Mai Palmberg and Annemette Kirkegaard, 134-48. Uppsala: Nordiska Afrikainstitutet.

Nasta, S., ed. 2004. *Writing across Worlds: Contemporary Writers Talk*. London: Routledge.

Nasta, S. 2005. "Abdulrazak Gurnah's *Paradise*." *The Popular and the Canonical: Debating Twentieth-Century Literature 1940-2000*, edited by David Johnson, 294-343. London: Routledge and Open University P.

Ndege, George. 2008. "Benga: Kenya's International Music in Waiting." Accessed March 18, 2010. http://kilimanjaroentertainment.com/2008/?p=700.

Neke, Stephene. 2003. "English in Tanzania: An Anatomy of Hegemony." PhD. diss., University of Gent.

Neuberger, Ralph. B. 1986. *National Self-determination in Postcolonial Africa*. Boulder, co.: Rienner.

Newell, Stephanie. 1997. Writing *African Women Gender, Popular Culture and Literature in West Africa*. London: Zed Books.

Nfah-Abbenyi, Juliana Makuchi. 1997. *Gender in African Women's Writing: Identity, Sexuality and Difference*. Bloomington and Indiana: Indian University Press.

Njogu, Kimani. 2004. *Reading Poetry as Dialogue*. Nairobi: Jomo Kenyatta Foundation.

Njubi, Francis. 2009. "Remapping Kiswahili: A Political Geography of Language, Identity and Africanity." *African Studies in Geography from Below*, edited by Michel Arrous and Lazare Ki-Zerbo, 105-131. Michigan: African Books Collective.

Nnaemeka, Obioma. 1997. "Urban Spaces, women's places: polygamy as sign in Mariama Bâ's   novels." *The Politics of (M)othering: Womanhood, Identity and Resistance in African Literature*, edited by Obioma Nnaemeka, 147-161. New York:Routledge.

Nuttal, Sarah. 2001. "Subjectivities of Whiteness." *African Studies Review* 44.2:115-140.

Nyairo, Joyce and James Ogude. 2005. "Popular Music, Popular Politics: Unbwogable and the Idioms of Freedom in Kenyan Popular Music." *African Affairs* 104.415: 225-49.

_____. 2005. "East African Popular Culture and Literature." *Africa Insight* 35.2: 2-3.

Nyamweru, Celia. 2001. "Letting the Side Down: Personal Reflections on Colonial and Independent Kenya". *Global Multiculturalism: Comparative Perspectives on Ethnicity, Race and Nation*, edited by Grant H. Cornwell and Eve Walsh Stoddard, 69-192. Oxford: Rowman & Littlefield Publishers Inc.

Obama, Barack. 2008. *Dreams from My Father: A Story of Race and Inheritance*. Edinburgh: Canongate Books.

Ochieng', W. R. 1989. "Independent Kenya, 1963-1986." *A Modern History of Kenya 1895-1980*, edited by W.R. Ochieng, 202-218. London, Nairobi, Ibadan: Evans Brothers.

Odanga, Eric. 1999. "The Pioneers of Benga." Sunday Nation, February 28. Accessed May 2, 2008. http://www.nationaudio.com/News/DailyNation/280299/Features/SE3.html.

Odhiambo, E. S. Atieno. "Kula Raha: Gendered Discourses and Contours of Leisure in Nairobi, 1946-63" (unpublished paper).

_____. 2002. "Hegemonic Enterprises and Instrumentalities of Survival: Ethnicity and Democracy in Kenya." *African Studies* 61.2: 224-249.

_____. 2003. "Matunda ya Uhuru, Fruits of Independence: Seven Theses on Nationalism in Kenya." *Mau Mau and Nationhood: Arms, Authority and Narration*, edited by Odhiambo, Atieno and John Lonsdale, 8-36. Oxford: James Currey.

_____ and John Lonsdale. eds. 2003. *Mau Mau and Nationhood: Arms, Authority and Narration.* Oxford: James Currey.

_____. 2004. "Ethnic Cleansing and Civil Society in Kenya 1963-1992." *Journal of Contemporary African Studies* 22.1: 29-42.

_____. 2007. "From the English Country Garden to 'Mikambo Mibale': Popular Culture in Kenya in the Mid Nineteen Sixties." *Urban Legends, Colonial Myths: Popular Culture in East Africa*, edited by Ogude, James and Nyairo, Nyairo, 155-172. Trenton, NJ: Africa World Press.

Odhiambo, Christopher Joseph. 2008. *Theatre for Development in Kenya: In Search of Effective Procedure and Methodology.* Bayreuth: Bayreuth African Studies.

Odhiambo, Tom. 2005. "The City as a Marker of Modernity in Postcolonial Kenyan Popular Fiction." *Scrutiny* 10.2:46-56

_____. 2007. "Sexual Anxieties and Rampant Masculinities in Postcolonial Kenyan Literature." *Social Identities* 13. 5: 651-663.

Ofuani, O. A., Okot p'Bitek. 1985. "A Checklist of works and Criticism." *Research in African Literatures* 16. 3:370-383.

Ogbaa, Kalu. 2003. *A Century of Nigerian Literature: A Select Bibliography.* Trenton: Africa World Press.

Ogolla, Lenin.1997. *Towards Behaviour Change: Participatory Theatre in Education and Development.* Nairobi: PETAD.

Ogot, Bethwell. 2003. "Mau Mau and Nationhood: The untold story." *Mau Mau and Nationhood: Arms, Authority and Narration,* edited by Odhiambo, Atieno and John Lonsdale, 8-36. Oxford: James Currey.

Ogude J. 1999. *Ngugi's Novels and African History: Narrating the Nation.* London: Pluto.

_____. 2011. "Ngugi's Concept of History and the Post-Colonial Discourses in Kenya." *Canadian Journal of African Studies? Revue Canaddiene des Etudes Africaines* 31.1:86-112. accessed:31/03/2011. http://www.jstor.org/stable/485326 <http://www.jstor.org/stable/485326>

_____. 2001. "The Vernacular Press and the articulation of Luo ethnic citizenship: The case of Achieng Oneko's Ramgogi." *Current Writing* 13. 2: 41-54.

_____. 2007. "'The Cat that Ended Up Eating the Homestead Chicken': Murder, Memory and Fabulization in D. O. Misiani's Dissident Music." *Urban Legends, Colonial Myths: Popular Culture and Literature in East Africa,* edited by Ogude, James and Joyce Nyairo 173-202. Trenton NJ: Africa World Press.

_____. 2009. "The State as a Site of Eating: Literary Representation and the Dialectics of Ethnicity, Class and the Nation State in Kenya." *Africa Insight* 39.1: 5-21.

Ogundipe-Leslie, Molara. 1987. "The Female Writer and Her Commitment." *Women in African Literature Today,* edited by Eldred Durosimi Jones. Trenton: Africa World Press.

Ojaide, Tanure. 1986. "Poetic Viewpoint: Okot p'Bitek and his personae." *Callaloo* 27. 2: 371-383.

_____. 1996. *Poetic Imagination in Black Africa.* Durham NC: Academic Press.

Ojwang, Dan. 2004. "Writing Migrancy and Ethnicity: The Politics of Identity in East African Indian Literature." PhD. Diss., University of the Witwatersrand, Johannesburg.

_____. 2009. "Kenyan Intellectuals and the Political Realm: Responsibilities and Complicities." *Africa Insight* 39. 1: 22-38.

Ojwang, J and K. Mugambi eds. 1989. *The S.M. Otieno Case: Death and Burial in Modern Kenya.* Nairobi: Nairobi University Press.

Okola, Donald and Joyce Colijn. 1995. "The Sigoti Teachers Group: A Grassroots Approach to Educational Theatre." *Communication in Development:*

*Experiences in Western Kenya*, edited by Mumma Opiyo and Loukie Levert, 88-98. Nairobi: KDEA.

Okoth, K. 2003. *Kenya: What Role for Diaspora in Development?* Migration Policy Institute.

Okumu, Caleb Chrispo. 2005. "A World View of Benga: Truths and Lies about the Region's Popular Music." Paper presented at the Lake Victoria Festival of Arts, Kisumu, May 26 - June 1.

Olali, Tom. 2004. "The Veneration of the Prophet: The Role of Kasida ya Hamziyah During the Maulidi Festival of the Lamu Archipelago, Kenya." PhD. diss., School of Oriental and African Studies, University of London.

_____. 2008. *An English Rendition of a Classical Swahili Poem*. South Bend: Sahel Publishing.

_____. 2008. *Performance of a Swahili Poem During the Lamu Maulidi Festival*. South Bend: Sahel Publishing.

Oloo, Adams. 2007. "Song and Politics: The Case of D. Owino Misiani." *Songs and Politics in Eastern Africa*, edited by Kimani Njogu and Herve Maupeu, 177-198. Dar es Salaam: Mkuki na Nyota Publishers.

Olaniyan T and A Quayson eds. 2009. *African Literature: An Anthology of Criticism and Theory*. Oxford: Blackwell Publishing Ltd.

Olaussen, M. 2009. "Refusing to Speak as a Victim: Agency and the arrivant in Abdulrazak Gurnah's novel By the Sea." *Africa Writing Europe: Opposition, Juxtaposition, Entanglement*, edited by Maria Olaussen and Christina Angelfors, 219-246. Amsterdam: Rodopi.

Oluoch-Olunya, G. 2000. "Contextualising Post-Independence African Writing: Ngugi wa Thiong'o and Ayi Kwei Armah Compared." Ph.D. diss., University of Glasgow.

Omolo, K. 2002. "Political Ethnicity in the Democratisation Process in Kenya." *African Studies* 61.2: 210-221.

Omondi, Washington. 1973. "Evolution and Change in Style of Thum, the Luo Lyre." Paper presented to the Institute of African Studies, University of Nairobi.

Ondigo, Yahya. 2006. *God's Blessings to Humanity*. Nairobi: Signal Press.

Onyango-Ogutu, B. and Roscoe, A. A. 1974. *Keep my Words: Luo Oral Literature*. Nairobi: EAPH.

Orwell, George. 1950. *Shooting an Elephant and Other Essays*. New York: Harcourt, Brace and World.

Owoo, N. K. 2000. "Audiences and Critical Appreciation". *Symbolic Narratives/African Cinema: Audience, Theory and the Moving Image*, edited by Givanni June, 228-231. London: BFI.

Oywa, John. 1997. "Okatch Biggy is the Star to Watch." *Sunday Nation*, June 8.

Owuor, Y. A. 2009. "Contemporary Projections: Africa in the Literature of Atrocity (Aftrocity)." *Writers, Writing on Conflicts and Wars in Africa*, edited by Okey Ndibe and Chenjerai Hove, 17-26. Uppsala: the Nordic Africa Institute.

Ozkirimli, Umut. 2010. 2nd ed. *Theories of Nationalism: A Critical Introduction*. Basingstoke, Hampshire (England); New York: Palgrave Macmillan.

Partington, Stephen, D. 2008. "Poetry and Pride: An Encomium for Aimé Césaire." *Jahazi* 3: 64-66.

Pearson, M. N. 1998. *Port Cities and Intruders: The Swahili Coast, India, and Portugal in the Early Modern Era*. Baltimore: The Johns Hopkins University Press.

P' Bitek, Okot. 1972. *Song of Lawino*. Nairobi: East African Educational Publishers.

_____. 1971. *Two Songs: Song of Prisoner and Song of Malaya*. Nairobi: East African Educational Publishers.

_____. 1968. *Theatre Education in Uganda, Educational Theatre Journal* 20. 2: 308.

_____. 1973. *Africa's Cultural Revolution*. Nairobi: East African Educational Publishers.

_____. 1974. *Horn of my Love*. Nairobi: East African Educational Publishers.

_____. 1986. *Artist the Ruler: Essays on Art, Culture and Values*. Nairobi: East African Educational Publishers.

Pierce, Steven and Anupama Rao eds. 2006. *Discipline and the Other Body: Correction, Corporeality, Colonialism*. Durham and London: Duke University Press.

Pike, Charles. 1986. "History and Imagination: Swahili Literature and Resistance to German Language Imperialism in Tanzania, 1885-1910." *The International Journal of African Historical Studies* 19. 2: 201-233.

Piroli, Marta. 2006. "Finding Voices: Italian American Female Autobiography." M.A. Diss., Miami University, Ohio.

Pratt, Cranford. 1976. *The Critical Phase in Tanzania, 1945-1968, Nyerere and the Emergence of a Socialist Strategy*. Cambridge: Cambridge University Press.

Pratt, Mary. 1991. "Arts of the Contact Zone." *Modern Language Association* 33-40.

_____. 1992. *Imperial Eyes: Travel Writing and Transculturation*. London: Routledge.

Prentki, Tim. 1998. "Must the Show go on? The Case for Theatre for Development." *Development in Practice* 8. 4.419-429.

Prestholdt, J. 2009. "Mirroring Modernity: On Consumerism in Cosmopolitan Zanzibar." *Transforming Cultures eJournal* 4. 2: 165 - 204.

Rabine, Leslie. 1985. "Romance in the Age of the Electronic Harlequin Enterprises." *Feminist Criticism and Social Change*, edited by Judith Lowder Newton and Deborah Silverton Rosenfelt. New York: Methuen.

Radway, Janice. 1984. *Reading the Romance Women, Patriarchy and Popular Literature*. Chapel Hill: The University of North Carolina Press.

Rao, Vyjayanthi. 2009. "In conversation with Filip de Boeck and Abdou Maliq Simone Urbanism beyond Architecture: African Cities as Infrastructure." *African Cities Reader*, edited by Edgar Pieterse and Ntone Edjabe. Cape Town. African Center Cities and Chimurenga.

_____. 2011. "Conversation with Ngugi wa Thiong'o." *Research in African Literatures* 30.1:162-168, http://www.jstor.org/stable/38220479, accessed 28/03/2011..

Ranger, Terence. 1975. *Dance and Society in Eastern Africa, 1890-1970: The Beni Ngoma*. London: Heinemann.

Reddy, V. and Portgeiter, C. 2006. "Real Men Stand up for the Truth: Discursive Meanings in the Jacob Zuma Rape Trial." *Southern African Linguistics and Applied Language Studies* 24.4: 511-521.

Ribeiro, F. R. 2010. "Destined to Disappear Without a Trace: Gender and the Languages of Creaolisation in the Indian Ocean, Africa, Brazil, and the Caribbean." *Indian Ocean Studies: Cultural, Social, and Political Perspectives*, edited by Shanty Moorthy and Ashraf Jamal. London: Routledge.

Rodrigues, A. L. 2004. "Beyond Nativism: An Interview with Ngugi wa Thiong'o." *Research in African Literatures* 35.3:161-67, http://www.jstor.org/stable/3821300.

Ronning, H. A. and L Johannessen eds. 2007. *Reading of the Particular: The Postcolonial in the Postcolonial*. New York: Rodopi.

Rose, Margaret. 1993. *Parody: Ancient, Modern and Post-Modern*. Cambridge: Cambridge University Press.

Ruark, Robert. 1962. *Uhuru*. London: Hamish Hamilton.

Ruganda, John. 1980. *The Floods*. Nairobi: EAPH.

Rushing, Andrea B. 1979. "Images of Black Women in Modern African Poetry: An Overview." *Sturdy Black Bridges: Visions of Black Women in Literature*, edited by Roseann P.Bell, Bettye J. Parker and Beverly Guy-Sheftall, 18-24. New York: Anchor Books.

Rutherford, J. 2007. *After Identity*. London: Lawrence and Wishart.

Safran, William. 1991. "Diaspora in Modern Societies: Myths of Homeland and Return." *Diaspora* 1.1: 83-93.

Said, Edward. 1979. *Orientalism*. New York: Pantheon Books, 1978; reprinted ed., New York: Vintage Books.

_____. 1983. *The World, the Text, and the Critic*. Cambridge: Harvard University Press.

_____. 1994. *Culture and Imperialism*. London: Vintage, 1994.

_____ and Sayer, Geoff. 1998. *Kenya: The Promised Land?* Oxford: Oxfam.

Samatar, Ahmed ed. 1994. *The Somali Challenge: From Catastrophe to Renewal?* Boulder, CO: Lynne Rienner, 1994.

Samuelson, Meg. 2007. *Remembering the Nation, Dismembering Women? Stories of the South African Transition.* Pietermaritzburg. University of Kwazulu-Natal Press.

Sass, Louis A. 1987. "Introspection, Schizophrenia, and the Fragmentation of Self." *Representations* 19: 1-34.

Schatzberg, M. 2001. *Political Legitimacy in Middle Africa: Father, Family, Food.* Bloomington and Indianapolis: Indiana University Press.

Schild, Ulla. 1980. "Words of Deception: Popular Literature in Kenya." *The East African Experience: Essays on English and Swahili Literature,* edited by Ulla Schild, 25-33. Berlin: Dietrich Reimer Verlag.

Schimmel, Annemarie. 1985. *And Muhammad is His Messenger: The Veneration of the Prophet in Islamic Piety.* Chapel Hill: The University of North California Press.

Schwerdt, D. 2001. "Monstering the Interior: Internal Journeys Over External Landscapes." *Re-Imagining Africa: New Critical Perspectives,* edited by Sue Kossew and Dianne Schwerdt, 27-41. Huntington: Nova Science Publishers.

Scott, James.1990. *Domination and the Arts of Resistance.* New Haven and London: Yale University Press.

Selwin, Tom. ed. 1996. *The Tourist Image: Myths and Mythmaking in Tourism.* New York: John Wiley.

Serumaga, Robert. 1971. *The Elephants.* Nairobi: Oxford UP.

Shaw, Carolyn Martin. 1995. *Colonial Inscriptions: Race, Sex and Class in Kenya.* Minneapolis: University of Minnesota Press.

Shariff, Ibrahim. 1988. *Tungo Zetu.* Trenton N. J.: Red Sea Press.

_____ and Jan Feidel. 1986. "Kibabina's "Message about Zanzibar": The Art of Swahili Poetry." *Research in African Literatures* 17. 3: 496-524.

Shule, Vicensia. 2008. "Tanzanians and Donors: Opposing Audiences in Public Theatre." *CODESRIA 12th General Assembly Governing the African Public Sphere Yaoundé,* Cameroun 07-11/12/2008.

Sicherman, C.M. 1989. *Ngugi wa Thiong'o: A Bibliography of Primary and Secondary Sources, 1957-1987.* London: Hans Zell.

_____. 1989. "Ngugi wa Thiong'o and the Writing of Kenyan History", *Research in African Literatures* 20. 3:347-370.

_____. 1998. "Revolutionizing the Literature Curriculum at the University of East Africa: Literature and the Soul of a Nation." *Research in African Literatures* 29. 3: 129-47.

Siddiqi, Jameela. 2002. *The Feast of the Nine Virgins.* London: Bogle L'Overture.

Sidonie, Smith and Julia Watson eds. 1998. *Women, Autobiography, Theory - A Reader.* Madison: University of Wisconsin Press.

Simatei, T. P. 2001. *The Novel and the Politics of Nation Building in East Africa.* Bayreuth: Bayreuth African Studies.

_____. 2010. "Kalenjin Popular Music and the Contestation of National Space in Kenya." *Journal of Eastern African Studies* 4.3: 425-434.

Singano, Abdallah. 2005. "Hip hop as a Culture for the Youth." *Bang!* 3. December 2004 - February 2005

Siundu, Godwin. 2005. "Multiple Consciousness and Reconstruction of Home in the Novels of Yusuf Dawood and Moyez Vassanji." PhD. Diss., University of the Witwatersrand, Johannesburg.

Skey, Michael. 2009. "The National in Everyday Life: a Critical Engagement with Michael Billig's Thesis of Banal Nationalism." *The sociological Review* 57. 2: 331-346.

Slater, Montagu. 1959. *The Trial of Jomo Kenyatta* 2nd ed., rev. London: Secker & Warburg.

Slaughter, Joseph. 2004. "Master Plans: Designing (National) Allegories of Urban Space and Metropolitan Subjects for Postcolonial Kenya." *Research in African Literatures* 35.1: 30 - 51.

_____. 2006. "Enabling Fictions and Novel Subjects: The Bildungsroman and International Human Rights Law." *PMLA* 121.5: 1405-1423.

Smith, A. 1989. *East African Writing in English*. Basingstoke and London: Macmillan Publishers.

Ssewakiryanga, Richard, and Joel Isabirye. 2006. "'From War Cacophonies to Rhythms of Peace': Popular Cultural Music in Post-1986 Uganda." *Current Writing* 18. 2:53-73.

Steinhart, Edward. 2006. *Black Poachers, White Hunters: A Social History of Hunting in Colonial Kenya*. London: James Currey, Nairobi: EAEP, Ohio University Press: Athens.

Steiner, T. 2009. *Translated People, Translated Texts: Language and Migration in Contemporary African Literature*. Manchester: St Jerome Publishing.

Steyn, Melissa. 2001. *Whiteness just isn't what it Used to be: White Identity in a Changing South Africa*. Albany: State University of New York Press.

Stratton, Florence. 1994. *Contemporary African Literature and the Politics of Gender*. Routledge: London.

Songoyi, Elias M. 1988. "The Artist and the State in Tanzania. A Study of Two Singers: Kalikali and Mwinamila." MA diss., University of Dar es Salaam.

_____. 2005. "The Form and Content of Wigashe Dance Songs of the Sukuma." PhD. Diss., University of Dar es Salaam.

Soyinka, Wole. 1976. *Myth, Literature and African World*. Cambridge: Cambridge University Press.

Stapleton, Chris and Chris May. 1990. *African Rock: The Music of a Continent*. Dutton Books: New York.

Suriano, Maria. 2006. "'Utajiju! Bongo Flavour 'In Da Houze'. The Music of a New Generation: Youth Culture and Globalisation". *Proceedings of the Institute of Kiswahili Research Jubilee Symposium-2005*, edited by J. S. Madumulla and S.S. Sewangi, 173-93, vol. 2. Dar es Salaam: Institute of Kiswahili Research.

_____. 2007. "'Mimi ni msanii, kioo cha jamii': Urban Youth Culture in Tanzania as Seen through Bongo Fleva and Hip-Hop." *Swahili Forum* 14: 207-23.

Suttner, R. 2009. "The Jacob Zuma Rape Trial: Power and the Africa national Congress (ANC) Masculinities." *Nordic Journal of Feminist and Gender Research* 17. 3:222-236.

Takem, Tiku John. 2005. *Theatre and Environment Education in Cameroon.* Bayreuth: Bayreuth African Studies 76.

Taylor, Clyder R. 1998. *The Mask of Art: Breaking the Aesthetic Contract - Film and Literature.* Bloomington: Indiana UP.

Taylor, Charles. 2004. *Modern Social Imaginaries.* Durham: Duke University Press.

_____. 1998. *Sources of the Self: The Making of the Modern Identity.* Cambridge: Cambridge UP.

Theroux, Paul. 1996. "Rajat Neogy Remembered." *Transition* 75/76, Anniversary Issue: Selections from Transition 1961-76, 69: 4-7.

Tibatemwa-Ekirikubinza, Lillian. 1999. *Women's Violent Crime in Uganda: More Sinned Against than Sinning.* Kampala: Fountain Publishers.

Tindyebwa, Lillian. 1998. "Looking for My Mother." *A Woman's Voice: An Anthology of Short Stories written by Ugandan Women,* edited by Mary Okurut, 1-15. Kampala: FEMRITE Publications Ltd.

Topan, Farouk. 2006. "Why Does a Swahili Writer Write? Euphoria, Pain, and Popular Aspirations in Swahili Literature." *Research in African Literatures* 37. 3: 103-119.

Toulabor, Comi. 1991. *"La derision politique en liberté au Mali."* *Politique Africaine* 43: 36-41.

Tsuruta, Tadasu. 2003. "Popular Music, Sports, and Politics: A Development of Urban Cultural Movements in Dar es Salaam, 1930s-1960s." *African Study Monographs* 24.3:195-222.

Turner, V. 1969. *The Ritual Process: Structure and Anti-structure.* London: Routledge and Kegan Paul.

_____. 1982. *From Ritual to Theatre: The Human Seriousness of Play.* New York: PAJ Publications.

Ugah, Ada. 1982. *Naked Hearts; Preceded By Anatomy Of Nigerian Poetics.* Braunton: Merlin Books.

Vail, Leroy, and Landeg White. 1983. "Forms of Resistance: Songs and Perceptions of Power in Colonial Mozambique." *American Historical Review* 88. 4: 883-919.

Vambe, Maurice T. and Vambe, Beauty. 2006. "Musical Rhetoric and the Limits of Official Censorship in Zimbabwe." *Muziki* 3.1: 48-78.

Van Erven, Eugene. 2001. *Community Theatre: Global Perspectives.* London and New York: Routledge.

Vansina, Jan. 1985. *Oral Tradition as History.* London: James Currey.

Varsquez, M and Marquadt, M. 2003. *Globalizing the Sacred: Religion across Americas*. New Brunswick: Rutgers University Press.

Vassanji, M. G. 1994. *The Book of Secrets*. London: Picador.

Vasquez, Michael, C. 2000. "Hearts in Exile: A Conversation with Moses Isegawa and Mahmood Mamdani." *Transition* 86: 126-150.

Verschoor, Jenni. 2009. "Patronage, Business and the Value of Art: The Corporate Arts Sponsorship of Absa Bank and Hollard Insurance." M.A. Diss., University of the Witwatersrand, Johannesburg.

Waliaula, W. K. 2010. "Staging Masculinity in the East African Epic." *Masculinities in African Literary and Cultural Texts*, edited by Helen N. Mugambi and Allan Tuzyline, 13-24. Oxfordshire: Ayebia Clarke Publishing.

Wa Mungai, Mbugua. 2008. "'Made in Riverwood': (Dis)locating Identities and Power through Kenyan Pop Music." *Journal of African Cultural Studies* 20. 1: 57-70.

Wandai, K.1983. *Mayor in Prison*. Nairobi: East African Educational Publishers.

Wangusa, T. 1989. *Upon this Mountain*. London: Heinemann.

Ward, John. 1991. *The Animals are Innocent: The Search for Julie's Killers*. London: Headline.

Ware, Vron. 1992. "Memories of Danger: Race, Gender and Memories of Empire." *History and Theory* 31.4: 116-137.

Warah, Rasna. 1998. *Triple Heritage: A Journey to Self Discovery*. Nairobi: Rasna Warah.

Wa Thiong'o, Ngugi. 1964. *Weep Not Child*. London: Heinemann.

_____. 1965. *The River Between*. Nairobi: East African Educational Publishers.

_____. 1967. *A Grain of Wheat*. London: Heinemann.

_____. 1972. *Homecoming: Essays on African and Caribbean Literature, Culture and Politics*. London: Heinemann.

_____ and Micere Mugo. 1977. *The Trial of Dedan Kimathi*. London: Heinemann.

_____. 1981. *Detained: A Writer's Prison Diary*. Nairobi: East African Educational Publishers.

_____. 1982. *Devil on the Cross*. London: Heinemann.

_____. 1986. *Decolonising the Mind: The Politics of Language in African Literature* Oxford: James Currey; Portsmouth, NH: Heinemann Educational Books

_____. 1993. *Moving the Centre: The Struggle for Cultural Freedoms*. London: James Currey.

_____. 1997. *Writers in Politics: A Re-engagement with Issues of Literature and Society*. Oxford: James Currey; Portsmouth, NH: Heinemann Educational Books.

_____. 1998. *Penpoints, Gunpoints and Dreams: The Performance of Literature and Power in Post-Colonial Africa.* Oxford University Press.

_____. 2000. "Europhonism, Universities, and the Magic Fountain: The Future of African Literature and Scholarship." *Research in African Literatures* 31. 1: 1-11.

_____. 2009. "The Myth of Tribe in Africa." *Transition* 101: 16-23.

Watt, Ian. 1963. *The Rise of the Novel: Studies in Defoe, Richardson and Fielding, 1957.* Harmondsworth: Penguin.

_____. 1997. *Myths of Modern Individualism: Faust, Don Quixote, Don Juan, Robinson Crusoe.* Cambridge: Cambridge University Press.

Whitlock, Gillian. 2000. *The Intimate Empire: Reading Women's Autobiography.* New York and London: Casell.

Wilford, Hugh. 2008. *The Mighty Wurlitzer: How the CIA Played America.* Cambridge, Massachusetts: Harvard University Press.

Williams, Kevin. 2003. *Understanding Media Theory.* London: Arnold.

Williams, P. 1999. *Ngugi wa Thiong'o.* Manchester: Manchester University Press.

Wilson, J. 2010. "General Introduction." *Rerouting the Postcolonial: New Directions for the New Millennium,* edited by Janet Wilson, 17-21. London: Routledge.

Wrong, Michela. 2001. *In the Footsteps of Mr. Kurtz: Living on the Brink of Disaster in the Congo.* London: Harper Collins.

Wrong, Michela. 2009. *It's Our Turn to Eat: The Story of a Kenyan Whistleblower.* London: Fourth Estate.

Young, T. ed. 2003. *Readings in African Politics.* Bloomington & Indianapolis: Indiana University Press.

Quayson, A. 1997. *Strategic Transformations in Nigerian Writing: Orality and History in the Work of Rev. Samuel Johnson, Amos Tutuola, Wole Soyinka and Ben Okri.* Oxord: James Currey.

Zirimu, Pio. 1973. "An Approach to Black Aesthetics." *Black Aesthetics in East Africa,* edited by Zirimu, Pio and Andrew Gurr, 55-62. Nairobi: East African Literature Bureau.

## CINEMATOGRAPHY/DISCOGRAPHY

al-Tirmidhi, Ahmed. Kitab Shama'il al-Mustafa. With Commentary by Ibrahim al-Bajuri. Dar al-taba'a al-'amira, Bulaq.1276 AH/1859-60 A.D

Bob Nyanja: Malooned. Nairobi: Cinematic Solution Production.

Bushoke. "CCM Namba 1". In Nyimbo za CCM, Kampeni 2005. Dar es Salaam, 2005 (pirated CD).

Daz Baba. "Wife." In Elimu Dunia. Dar es Salaam: GMC Wasanii Promoters, 2005 (CD).

Dokta Levi, featuring Sugu. Kura Yangu, 2005 (videoclip, East African TV).

Dipio, D. 2009. Crafting the Bamasaba. Kampala: MAK-NUFU Production.

Inspekta Haroun. "Pongezi", 2005 (played on Clouds FM).

Mangwea. "Mtoto wa Jakaya." In Nyimbo za CCM, Kampeni 2005. Dar es Salaam (pirated CD).

Mubarak, Zakee. Al-Mada'ih an-nabawiyyah fi'l-adab al-'arabi. Cairo: Matba 'at Mustaf a al-ba abi al-hubalabi wa aul aduhu,1943.

Mwana FA. "Kijani na Njano." In Nyimbo za CCM, Kampeni 2005. Dar es Salaam, 2005 (pirated CD).

Nyadundo, Tony. "Obama" 2008.

Okatch Biggy & Orch. Super Heka Heka: "Rose Nyar Yala" in Helena Wang'e Dongo. (BIGGY 003) Nairobi: Biggy Sounds Productions.

Okatch Biggy & Orch. Super Heka Heka: "Caleb Doctor" in Helena Wang'e Dongo. (BIGGY 003) Nairobi: Biggy Sounds Productions.

Okatch Biggy & Orch. Super Heka Heka: "Agutu Nyowila" in Okello Jabondo. (HEKAC04) Nairobi: Biggy Sounds Productions.

Okatch Biggy & Orch. Super Heka Heka: "Okello Jabondo" in Okello Jabondo. (HEKA C04) Nairobi: Biggy Sounds Productions.

Okatch Biggy & Orch. Super Heka Heka: "Nyathi Nyakach" in Nyathi Nyakach. (BIGGY 00/04) Nairobi: Biggy Sounds Productions.

Okatch Biggy & Orch. Super Heka Heka: "Isaiah Ogwe" in Nyathi Nyakach. (BIGGY 00/04) Nairobi: Biggy Sounds Productions.

Okatch Biggy & Orch. Super Heka Heka: "Adhiambo Nyakobura" in Adhiambo Nyakobura. (BIGGY C05) Nairobi: Biggy Sounds Productions.

Okatch Biggy Live (Video) Nairobi: Alwan Communications Ltd, 1996.

Osusa et al. Retracing the Benga Rhythm: Narrative, Music CD and Documentary DVD. Nairobi: Ketebul, 2008.

Poxy Presha: "Otonglo Tyme" in Vita Kwaliti. (MWK 027) Nairobi: Music World (K) Ltd.

Professor Jay. Mapinduzi Halisi. Dar es Salaam: GMC Wasanii Promoters, 2003 (CD).

_____. J.o.s.e.p.h. Dar es Salaam: GMC Wasanii Promoters, 2005 (CD).

Remmy Ongala and Orchestre Super Matimila. «Narudi Nyumbani.» Ahadi/ Nairobi, 1987 (cassette).

_____. «Dodoma.» In Mambo. Realworld/Virgin America, 1992 (CD).

Sargent, Joseph. Ivory Hunters. 1989 (VCR)

Super Vea. "Pongezi kwa Rais Nyerere." 1967 (recorded, cassette, RTD archives).

_____. "Operation Vijana." 1967. (recorded, cassette, RTD archives).

wa Mutiso, Kineene. "Archetypal Motifs in Swahili Islamic Poetry: Kasida ya Burudai ".phD diss., University of Nairobi, 1996.

# WEBSITES AND WEBPAGES

www.Bankelele.blogspot.com

www.Kenyaunlimited.com

www.Kikuyunationalism.wordpress.com

www.thinkersroom.com/blog/

www.jaluo.com

www.kisii.com

www.kalenjin.net

www.gathara.blogspot.com

http://bankelele.blogspot.com/2008/01/elections-derail-kenyas-vision.html
<http://bankelele.blogspot.com/2008/01/elections-derail-kenyas-vision.
html> . Accessed May 22, 2011.

http://muigwithania.com/2008/03/27/not-willing-to-give-up-on-tribe/#
comments. Accessed May 23, 2011.

http://www. tHiNkErsroom.com/blog/2008/01/. Accessed March 23, 2011.

http://www.businessdailyafrica.com/Kenya+has+third+highest+number+of+
blogs
<http://www.businessdailyafrica.com/Kenya+has+third+highest+number+of
+blogs> . Accessed March 16, 2011.

http://allafrica.com/stories/201008060043.html . Accessed March 16, 2011.

http://m.standardmedia.co.ke/headlines.php?id=2000032707. Accessed April
13, 2011.

# INTERVIEWS AND INFORMAL CONVERSATIONS

Ally, (mzee) Mustafa. Interview with author. September 7, 2005, Mtakuja
Street, Mwanza, Tanzania.

_____. Interview with author. April 8, 2005, Sinza, Dar es Salaam, Tanzania.

_____. Informal conversation with author. February 2009, Survey, Dar es
Salaam.

Azizi, (binti) Ali (born Mwasaburi Ali). Interview with Author. November 20,
2000, Ilala, Dar es Salaam, Tanzania.

Inspekta Haroun (born Haroun Kahena). Interview with author. April 10, 2005,
Kijitonyama, Dar es Salaam, Tanzania.

Kabwela (mzee) (born Ismael Juma Mlima). Interview with author. September
14, 2005, Ilemela Mwanza, Tanzania.

Kamba, (binti) Hadija. Interview with author. September 8, 2000, Buguruni,
Dar es Salaam, Tanzania.

Mama Elisa (born Sabina Petro). Interview with author. September 5, 2000,
Buguruni, Dar es Salaam, Tanzania.

Masunga, (mzee) Erasto. Interview with author. October 3, 2005, Busweru, Mwanza, Tanzania.

Mwasyeba, Salathiel. Interview with author. April 2, 2005, RTD, Dar es Salaam, Tanzania.

Ndonho, (mzee) Hezeroni. Interview with author. October 5, 2005, Isamilo, Mwanza Tanzania.

Nganyagwa, Innocent. Interview with author. November 5, 2005, Msasani, Dar es Salaam, Tanzania.

Ngoffilo, (mzee) Masalu. Interview with author. October 7, 2005, Mbugani, Mwanza, Tanzania.

Professor Jay, (born Joseph Haule). Informal conversation with author. October 2005, Mwanza.

Sigda, (mzee) Shaban (born Shabani Hassani Selemani). Interview with author. October 7, 2005, Uhuru Street, Mwanza, Tanzania

Sugu, (born Joseph Mbilinyi). Interview with author. March 22, 2005, Sinza, Dar es Salaam, Tanzania.

Ministry of Education, Science and Technology. 2001. Kenya Schools and Colleges Drama Festival Official Programme. /

# Contributors

**Dominic Dipio** teaches theatre and film at Makerere University, Uganda. She is also a film producer and critic. Her films include *Crafting the Bamasaba: beyond the physical cut* (2009) and *A Meal to Forget* (2009).

**Susan N. Kiguli** is a Ugandan poet and academic. She holds a PhD in English from the University of Leeds sponsored by the prestigious Commonwealth Scholarship Scheme. Her research interests fall mainly in the area of Oral Poetry, Popular Song and Performance Theory. She is a Senior Lecturer in the Department of Literature, Makerere University, Uganda, and has served as the chairperson of FEMRITE (Uganda Women Writers' Association).

**Dina Ligaga** is a Lecturer in Media Studies, University of the Witwatersrand, South Africa. Her research interests include popular culture and representation, broadcast and new media cultures and postcolonial literature. She has published journal articles in these areas. She is also co-editor of the book, *Radio in Africa: Publics, Cultures, Communities* (2011).

**Fred Mbogo** is a lecturer at Moi University's Department of Literature, Theatre and Film Studies where he is also in the process of completing his PHD studies. He holds a Master of Arts Degree in Dramatic Arts from the University of The Witwatersrand. He writes and directs plays in Kenya and has contributed articles to *The East African Drum Magazine*, artmatters.info, Young Eagles Magazine, among others.

**T. Michael Mboya** teaches in the Department of Literature, Theatre and Film Studies, Moi University, Kenya. He specializes in the popular culture of the Luo of Kenya, and in East African literature in English.

**F. Fiona Moolla** teaches in the English Department at the University of the Western Cape. She is the author of the forthcoming book to be published by UCT Press and Lynne Rienner, "Being At Home Everywhere": The Individual in the Novels of Nuruddin Farah, as well as the following journal articles: "When Orature Becomes Literature: Somali Oral Poetry and Folk Tales in Somali Novels" which will appear in Comparative Literature Studies, "The Body Unbound: Ritual Scarification and Autobiographical forms in Wole Soyinka"s *Aké: The Years of Childhood*" in *The Journal of Commonwealth Literature* and "Border Crossings in the African Travel Narratives of Ibn Battuta, Richard Burton and Paul Theroux" in *The Journal of Postcolonial Writing*. Dr. Moolla is also the author of short fiction and children's books on literary topics.

**Edwin Mosoti** is a PhD candidate at the Department of African Literature, University of the Witwatersrand. He received an MA in film and literature from Maseno University. His current research interests revolve around literary traditions how they inform and feed contemporary African poetry written in English in East and West Africa.

**Grace A. Musila** is a Senior Lecturer in the English Department at Stellenbosch University. Her research interests include Gender Studies, Eastern and Southern African literatures, African popular culture, African intellectual archives and postcolonial whiteness in Africa.

**Isaac Ndlovu** is a postdoctoral fellow at the CAS, UCT. His publications include: "Coded Narratives of Nongoloza, Doggy Dog: Narrating the Self and Nation in Jonny Steinberg's *The Number*". *Current Writing*. (2010) 22.2:119-130 and "Gender, the subaltern and the 'silent interlocutor' in M.G. Vassanji's *The Gunny Sack* and *The Book of Secrets*", forthcoming in *Emerging Perspectives on M. G. Vassanji* (2012) (ed.) Da Silva, T. S and Makokha, J. K. S.

**Christopher Joseph Odhiambo** is an associate professor at the Department of Literature, Theatre and Film Studies, Moi University. He teaches and researches on Post colonial Literatures and intervention drama forms.

**Tom Odhiambo** is a Senior Lecturer in the Department of Literature at the University of Nairobi. He was awarded a PhD in African Literature at the University of the Witwatersrand, Johannesburg, in 2004. He was a Researcher at the Witwatersrand Institute for Social and Economic Research between 2003 and 2007.

**George Ogola** is a Senior Lecturer in Journalism, School of Journalism, Media and Communication, University of Central Lancashire. He has published widely in the areas of African media and popular culture.

**James Ogude** is Professor of African Literature in the School of Literature and Language Studies at the University of the Witwatersrand, South Africa. His research interests include the African novel and the Postcolony, Popular Culture in East Africa and Black intellectual traditions. He is the author of *Ngugi's Novels and African History: Narrating the Nation* (1999). He has also co-edited, *Urban Legends, Colonial Myths: Popular Culture and Literature in East Africa* (2007), among other edited works.

**Tom Olali** holds a PhD in African Studies from the School of Oriental and African Studies(SOAS),University of London and a n MA in Swahili Studies from the University of Nairobi. His field of interest is in Swahili Islamic Civilization. He is a full time faculty member in the department of Linguistics and Languages at the University of Nairobi. He has published widely on Islamic Civilization. Among his works is *An English Rendition of a Classical Swahili Poetry* (2008), *The Performance of a Swahili Poem during the Maulidi Festival* (2008). His Swahili novel *Mafamba* won the 2010 Wahome Mutahi Literary Award. He has also written *Mwongozo wa Utengano* among other publications.

**Maria Olaussen** is Professor of English at Linnaeus University in Sweden. This essay is part of a larger study on literary representations of the Indian Ocean World and the research is carried out in the interdisciplinary project Concurrences: Conflicting and Simultaneous Voices in Postcolonial Spaces. Olaussen's latest book is the edited collection *Africa Writing Europe: Opposition, Juxtaposition, Entanglement* (2009). She has published on African literature, postcolonial theory and feminist studies.

**Garnette Oluoch-Olunya** (PhD) is an independent researcher and consultant in Literature and Culture. She is guest editor of *Jahazi* 3&4, a journal of Performance, Arts & Culture published in Nairobi, Kenya.

**Godwin Siundu** is a Senior Lecturer in the department of Literature, University of Nairobi. He researches in the area of East African Asian writing.

**Lynda Gichanda Spencer** a Lecturer in the Department of English at Stellenbosch University, South Africa, also taught in the field of English Studies at the University of South Africa and Vista University. Her research interests include Contemporary women's writing, Popular Culture in Africa, African women's writing, East African fiction and African Studies. She is currently working on her PhD.

**Maria Suriano** is a Lecturer in African History at the University of the Witwatersrand, Johannesburg. Her research interests include leisure, popular culture and identity in colonial and postcolonial urban Tanzania, East African intellectual and cultural history, and East Africa and its cultural connections with, and 'within' the Western Indian Ocean region.

# Index